ICAL-MILITARY SYSTEMS:

Comparative Perspectives

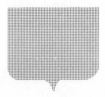

SAGE RESEARCH PROGRESS S[

WAR, REVOLUTION, AND P[

SERIES EDITORS: Charles C. M[
and Sam C. Sarkesian

Sponsored by the Inter-University
on Armed Forces and Society

Chairman: MORRIS JANOWITZ
Associate Chairman: CHARLES C. MOSKOS
Associate Chairman: SAM C. SARKESIAN
Executive Secretary: JAMES A. LINGER
Secretary: DAVID S. CRIDER
Executive Council:

Albert Biderman   Peter Karsten
Henry Bienen   Catherine Kelle[
Martin Blumenson   Seymour Melma[
James Buck   Laurence Radwa[
Vincent Davis   Bruce M. Russett
Alexander George   Claude E. Welch, Jr
Samuel P. Huntington   T. Alden Williams
A. A. Jordan   Adam Yarmolinsky

Membership Committee:

David C. Eaton—Secretary
Thomas Blau
C. I. Eugene Kim

Counsel: Maury Jacobs

POLITICAL-MILITARY

SYSTEMS

Comparative Perspectives

Edited by CATHERINE McARDLE KELLEHER

SAGE RESEARCH PROGRESS SERIES ON
WAR, REVOLUTION, AND PEACEKEEPING

Volume IV (1974)

 SAGE PUBLICATIONS   *Beverly Hills   /   London*

For information address:

SAGE PUBLICATIONS, INC.
275 South Beverly Drive
Beverly Hills, California 90212

SAGE PUBLICATIONS LTD
St George's House / 44 Hatton Garden
London EC1N 8ER

Printed in the United States of America

International Standard Book Number 0-8039-0414-2(c)
0-8039-0415-0(p)

Library of Congress Catalog Card No. 74-77094

FIRST PRINTING

CONTENTS

INTRODUCTION

Catherine M. Kelleher

The current critical, if not intellectual, fashion is to dismiss symposia as an outdated form—a medium of professional communication more in tune with an age of unhurried scholarship and intermittent publication of research. In almost every professional review, one finds cries to heaven regarding the lack of a common analytic framework in this collection, or aggressive critical point-scoring about the unevenness of the contributions in that volume, or even deprecating remarks (sotto voce to be sure) about the validity of the cross-case comparisons left to the discerning reader of a third set of essays. The hapless editor is alternately the subject of castigation and commiseration—for yielding the editorial whip too gently or too objectively or perhaps not even at all.

Undeniably, there is usually a core of truth in these criticisms—and quite apart from the advantages of taking the offensive first, any editor would be ill-advised to ignore them. But there would seem advantages of at least equal value to be gained in a broader-gauged approach to symposium presentations. The intellectual process of comparison simply does not only involve categorization—the filling of similar boxes across time and space, boxes which have been painstakingly constructed in parallel and specific, if confining, fashion. Kuhn's fanciful exploration of the emergence of scientific paradigms notwithstanding, comparison at a minimum also involves the conscious consideration of exclusionary criteria and differentiation across levels of analysis as well. Without a scope which encompasses or allows for the play of these analytic functions, any area of knowledge or theory cannot continue to expand or, over the long run, to survive. Carried to the extreme, the risks of decay through taxonomic rigidity, mindless self-fulfilling replication, and eventually of conceptual reification are just too great. Alternatively (and given the present state of disarray among all the social sciences, more realistically put) it is not at all clear that a scientific comparison of the types of pins involved is of any greater long-run intellectual or disciplinary profit than an idiosyncratic belief about the number of angels atop them.

Moreover, the present degree of regional specialization and narrow disciplinary orientation makes the need for a broadly-cast framework all the more urgent. By design, a symposium report or research annual should at least encourage the broadening of individual research perspectives. But these also can allow greater opportunity for the happy (and sometimes decisive) intervention of the serendipity factor—the chance juxtaposition which allows unparalleled occasion for analysis in sharp relief, or for the development of conceptual insight amidst a welter of detailed case study material, or the weighing of cross-level similarities against differences. Efficiency and organization, after all, yield some place to the scholarly values of richness and analytic subtlety.

This collection of essays represents a modest attempt to find an interesting middle ground between a volume encased in an organizational straitjacket and one exemplifying the "hundred flowers" approach. All of the essays stem from the biennial conference of the Inter-University Seminar on Armed Forces and Society, held in Chicago on October 12, 13 and 14th, 1973. Organized under the general guidance of Morris Janowitz and the Executive Council of the IUS, the conference had as its theme "The Comparative Analysis of Political-Military Systems: Perspectives into the 1980s" and was chaired by Catherine M. Kelleher. Each of the articles was commissioned within this thematic framework, tested through public presentation or subsequent circulation, reviewed and revised, and then set in place within this volume by the editor. The intended result was a broadly-defined, richly detailed collective view into the present state of political-military systems in the less-developed countries and in the socialist states.

On the simplest level, this volume represents a cross-national collection of considerable substantive originality and broad analytic scope. The range of national experiences analyzed, the rich insights into civil-military relations at the various levels of political and economic development, usually obscured by the general labels of "less developed" or "socialist," are noteworthy in themselves. And the opportunity to include the perspectives of distinguished national scholars as well as the work of a number of talented younger American researchers is one which the IUS and the editor welcome.

More important, however, is the degree of thematic convergence which at least one careful reading of the essays reveals. A concern which cuts across almost all the essays is the need to review and recast the analytic categories used in assessing military intervention in the political arena. To paraphrase this theme broadly: it has now been more than a decade since the seminal works on political role of the military, especially in the "new nations"—a decade which has seen considerable, if not always cumulative, empirical work on national and regional patterns. It is, therefore, time to assess what has been learned and what changes must be made in future research orientations and strategies. The specific concerns of the authors can seemingly be principally divided among three broad categories: a focus on

1. military organization and its significance for social and political roles

2. the military as a political actor appropriately analyzed in terms of comparison with other actors

3. the military as reflective and often responsive to broader societal cleavages, especially ethnic tensions and conflicts.

The first theme is perhaps most explicitly developed in the essays by Khuri and Obermeyer, and by Welch. Khuri and Obermeyer argue that, for the Middle Eastern nations at least, the military must be assessed in terms of a threefold function: as a profession, a model (and engine) of development, and as a microcosm of the state—to paraphrase their title somewhat. The significance of the military, therefore, cannot be accurately depicted in terms of the environmental circumstances surrounding a particular coup or a particular short-run pattern of military intervention/withdrawal. Rather the analyst must examine the historic evolutionary experience of the military—the changes in its structure, its relation to the social context, and its comparative position vis-à-vis other coexisting organizations. The six eras Khuri and Obermeyer depict, their richly-detailed discussion of the patterns revealed provide a valuable stimulus for further cross-regional comparison.

Claude Welch's essay on African armies echoes this analytic theme. On the basis of an analysis of military coups in Africa since 1967, Welch concludes that organizational variables are far better predictors of success than are socio-political or "environmental" variables. He describes three types of military regimes defined by this organizational analysis: regimes which are "personalist," "corporatist" or defined by "interventionary professionalization." Finally, Welch projects from this base the continued, increasingly "usual" political participation and inter-vention of all African militaries into the 1980s.

Several of the authors concerned with the military in the socialist states touch on similar perspectives. Jorge Dominguez's seminal essay on the military in Castro's Cuba serves as a provocative bridge—an examination of a revolutionary military organization fusing roles defined in traditional and ideological terms as "civilian" and "military." Dominguez finds through detailed examination of political conflict patterns, that the ideal of the "civic soldier" has penetrated all levels and issue-areas of Cuban political life and now encompasses the behavior of about two-thirds of those holding elite positions in all sectors. This, in turn, has facilitated organizationally adaptive behavior by the military and has legiti-mized new demands for resource allocation or shifts in broader military objectives and missions both internally and vis-à-vis the entire elite.

Jerzy J. Wiatr's essay on public perceptions of the Polish military provides a more traditional and contrasting perspective on the significance of these themes in the socialist experience. Surveying media images as well as public opinion results, Wiatr finds the military in Poland to be viewed largely in terms of its historic legacy, one in which both successes and heroic failures appear to be equally valued. The military's present organizational characteristics, its approaches to socialization and training, its assumption of new or adapted objectives are perceived as of secondary importance, if at all. The prospects that in the future the military will receive or achieve greater prestige vis-à-vis the party or other state institutions seem very problematical.

In his stimulating review essay on the recent study of Chinese military politics, Jonathan Pollack adds yet a third socialist perspective. He provides not only summarizing judgements but also original insights into the critical lines of organizational cleavage; the conflict between commander and commissar; the tensions between functional sectors, and across command levels; and the differ-ences among generations, and personal friendship nets, reflected in field army affiliations. Pollack argues persuasively that these are key factors in the explica-tion of the nature and extent of the role of military leaders and cadres in the political arena—at this point and in the crisis of succession which will surely follow Mao's death. Moreover, these findings emphasize the need for detailed systemic comparison of the experience of all socialist states with these issues, most especially of the Soviet Union.

A second cross-cutting concern is the need to consider the military primarily as political actors—an elite allied with and indeed best compared to other competing elite political groups. Henry Bienen and David Morell take perhaps the strongest position on this question in their essay "Transition from Military Rule: Thailand." These authors explicitly reject the categorical dichotomization of military and civilian rule and suggest rather that a mixed system always exists—one which, even in the extreme, involves some degree of on-going relations between military and civilian elites, between military and civilian institutions. Using the often-neglected process of transition from military rule as their analytic focus, Bienen and Morell argue the critical variables for adequate contextual description as well as the prediction of eventual outcomes are (1) the extent of popular participation in the existing, military-dominant system, (2) the nature of military penetration of the society, and (3) the degree of institutionalization within the armed forces themselves. Their substantive cast—the Thai experience where since 1932 the military have not only been dominant but also operated more like a political machine than an ideal-type distinct "professional" entity—provides both supporting evidence and a clear base point for their future comparative efforts concerning Nigeria and elsewhere.

The essays by Mazrui on Uganda and Lowenthal on Peru advance the argument for a political approach in other contexts. Although very different in scope and in analytic mode, both argue that the rhetoric and activity of particular military regimes are at best only secondarily related to organizational factors, socialization patterns or professional norms peculiar to the military, whether in the less-developed states or in general. Far greater explanatory power can be gained by relating the behavior of military rulers to political context—to past tradition, and to the prevailing attitudes and preferences of competing or concurrent elite groups.

Mazrui's approach is the more unconventional—the analysis of the present military regime in Uganda as a continuation (in social policy at least) of the apostolic puritanical tradition established during the missionary-dominated colonial period. Clearly, the idiosyncratic political style and personal religious convictions of a General Amin play a considerable role. But, as Mazrui persuasively argues, Amin's preferences and the fact of military rule itself only result in particular prominence for values long embedded in the societal hierarchy—the pursuit of piety, decency, and propriety as defined from a puritanical or "anti-native" perspective. He concludes with an interesting cross-national validation of his thesis—the relatively similar practises of the supposedly antithetical socialist, secular regime of Julius Nyerere in Tanzania.

Lowenthal begins with a rather more familiar question set: why are the policies and practises of one military regime (present Peru) seemingly so different from those in the same region (say, for example, present Brazil) or even from those which might be predicted from established conceptual categories about the generally conservative thrust and political instabilities inherent in military rule?

During the past five years, Peru's "Revolutionary Government of the Armed Forces" has unquestionably brought about major shifts in both substance and structure in areas of domestic and foreign policy—all seemingly with relative ease and success. Lowenthal finds the critical explanatory factors to be the interplay between (1) basic shifts within the military institutions themselves, (2) the economic and social transformation in Peruvian society which had for so long outpaced changes in the political system, and (3) the significant shifts in civilian approaches to Peru's long-apparent problems. Indeed he concludes that, given the cumulative impact of background and context, it is remarkable that the goals and means promoted by the military regime since 1968 have taken so long to become governmental policy.

Highlighted in Nugroho Notosusanto's insightful essay on the Indonesian armed forces is another topic most amenable to political analysis, the problem of generational succession and the routinization of military legitimacy. Like many post-independence military forces, the TNI faces a dual political paradox. On the one hand, it is committed legally and operationally to perform two co-equal functions—the securing of national defense and internal security, and the provision of socio-political leadership. On the other, it faces the inevitable problems, even under a military regime, of adaptation to a more professional ethic—with the requisite changes in career patterns, education, and organizational structure, and the necessarily reduced involvement in non-military affairs. Key to the resolution (or even the future shape) of the paradox is the process by which the "Generation of 1945"—the military elite who emerged during national liberation and pacification—relinquishes power and legitimizes the adoption of new standards and traditions. Notosusanto concludes that at least there has been a self-conscious, stable beginning to what must be a long-term redefinition and restructuring.

A third theme—the nature and role of the military as a reflection of and a response to broader societal cleavages—is highlighted by the "ethnic" focus in the essays by Guyot, Lemarchand, Remington and Prifti. Although starting from very different initial concerns, each author eventually confronts the paradoxical social position of the military—the symbol and sometimes the instrument of national unity and yet also, a crucial element in the achievement and maintenance of political dominance by particular social, especially ethnic, groups. Given the prevalence of ethnic divisions as a source of social conflict, especially in the developing world, the result must be a military which is perceived neither as neutral in internal pacification functions nor as reliable in achieving inter-ethnic tolerance, or fundamental national unity.

In his essay on Burma and Malaysia, James Guyot describes perhaps the classic situation in less developed areas: domination of the numerous and "political" army by the ruling ethnic group, with skilled minorities fulfilling controlled technological functions, and more primitive ethnic groups relegated to the lower ranks. Guyot finds this pattern despite (1) the quite different ethnic distribution in each case (Malays constituting only about one-half the population while Burmans constitute at least seventy percent) and (2) the divergent patterns of military origin and post-independence political intervention by the military. Perhaps of even greater significance for future research, Guyot concludes that the appropriate comparative standard must be the allocation of roles along ethnic lines in other "modern" state institutions—a standard which will help predict to the stability of present patterns.

René Lemarchand's article suggests that the proportions of ethnic distribution may, at the extremes, become critical to longer-run military missions. In his analysis of the military's role within former Belgian African colonies, Lemarchand finds ethnic identification a primary criterion for elite recruitment in the highly-stratified Rwanda and Burundi. Zaire, on the other hand exhibits a pattern of broader, and less politically relevant ethnic distribution. Of particular significance for future conflicts and military intervention, therefore, is the high potential for explosive, ethnically-related spill-over across national boundaries.

Remington's richly-detailed essay on Yugoslavia echoes this latter theme but uses a somewhat different approach. She finds that especially since 1968 and the enunciation of "general peoples' defense," the deliberate design of the Yugoslav military force has been to establish a stable mosaic. The attempt has been to bridge the disintegrative forces inherent in the five non-state nations and numerous smaller minority groups—by combining regular and irregular units within a general defense framework, by establishing legal equality between locally-based territorial defense units and the centrally-directed regular forces, by energetic recruitment of non-Serbians into command positions. Yet success has been limited and Remington believes, promises to remain so, given the long traditions of ethnic hatred, the heroic resistance heritage and the impending succession crisis after Tito's death. Whatever the resulting chaos, therefore, the army will be neither permitted nor capable of acting as an autonomous force for national unity.

Prifti's essay on Albania thus well fulfills its avowed purpose of contrast with the Remington work. Given the absence of significant ethnic tensions, the Albanian military faces the more classic problems of a socialist system—the intermittent struggle against excessive domination by the party. In contrast to the Yugoslavian experience, (and of course, Wiatr's Polish analysis) the existence of personal loyalty network encompassing the military and political elites and the common partisan tradition have provided the preferred basis for dampening or resolving a broad range of "national security" disputes.

This, of course, represents only one interpretation of the many points of convergence and useful comparison across the collected essays. It is also more than likely that the several authors will hardly recognize the wisdom drawn from their own efforts. But all this represents only one more argument for the value of a collection, deliberately constructed to maximize broad substantive coverage, and wide-ranging analytic perspectives. The amount of courage required seems a worthwhile investment.

Not surprisingly, this effort has not been made alone. An editor's first thanks must be to the contributing authors, those who wrote and rewrote for the volume and submitted to constant rushing and revision with charm and aplomb. A deep debt is owed to Morris Janowitz who provided the original impetus for convoking the Chicago conference and for arranging this volume, and provided generous, patient guidance throughout.

Last but not least, thanks to the working crew: to David Stauffer, for editorial work; to Jacqueline Gereaert, Susan Fake Stewart, Robert Schwartz and Sue Stauffer for conference arrangements; to Bob Beattie and Peter Levine, to Donna Gotts and Lorel Janiszewski, and especially to James A. Linger and David S. Crider for all manner of assistance above and beyond the call of duty.

−Catherine M. Kelleher
Ann Arbor, Michigan

I.

POLITICAL-MILITARY SYSTEMS

The Third World

TRANSITION FROM MILITARY RULE: THAILAND'S EXPERIENCE

Henry Bienen and David Morell

A major gap in the literature on the military and political development, which this essay only begins to fill, concerns the process of
transition away from military rule to a mixed civil-military system.
Such a system may or may not involve large degrees of popular participation in governance. Its principal characteristic, however, is the entry
of significant civilian elements (both individual and institutional) into
a political process previously dominated by the armed forces. Much
more attention has been paid in the last decade to military intervention[1]
and to the military as a putative modernizer[2] than to the way that
individual and institutional civilian elements enter or reenter a political
process that has been dominated, at least ostensibly, by the military.
Recently there have been a number of attempts to synthesize positions
which stressed the importance of the organizational and sociological
characteristics of militaries per se and those which stressed wider
societal factors such as weak institutionalization or levels of participa-
ation or ethnic relationships.[3] There seems to be a growing agreement
that we must explain connections among variables. Our analyses must
link general characteristics which pertain to militaries, and unique
features of individual armed forces organizations, to wider societal
factors.

Analysts seem increasingly willing to discuss military-civilian
relationships—clearly a step in the right direction. It is a mistake to
dichotomize regimes as "military" or "civilian" if, by this labeling
process, we neglect the on-going relationships which exist between
armed forces personnel and civilians both in regimes which are headed
by uniformed personnel and those which are not. The significance of
whether or not a regime is headed by a military man or men involves
the question "matters for what"? We are concerned with participation
by elites and non elites, with the ways that decisions are made and
implemented, with the ability to obtain compliance for decisions
made, with degrees of centralization of authority, with the emphasis
certain decision-makers give to growth or redistribution policies. But
we cannot assume that knowing whether a regime is a military one or
not provides a good grasp on the answers to these questions. We can,
of course, hypothesize that military regimes have certain character-

3

istics which lead to certain regime outcomes; however, cross national studies have not established particular hypotheses for most of the concerns listed above.

Indeed, as empirical work is done on armed forces organizations we begin to demystify the term "the military." While the special organizational features of a particular military can be hypothesized to set it apart from other groups in society, only empirical work can show whether there are distinctive norms attached to an armed force and whether or not socialization processes are such that the military operates as a distinct entity. We must subject the military to the same search for internal factions, ethnic splits, generational gaps, functionally based divisions, and hierarchically based conflicts as have been characteristic in the treatment of parties and civil services.

The taxonomic dichotomy between military and civilian regimes will not stand. There are political systems in which civilian supremacy is clear, where the military operates under civilians whose own power does not depend on the armed forces but in which armed forces have a great deal to say about domestic and foreign policy formulation, even implementation, and in which the military controls important shares of the society's resources. The USA and the USSR are examples. There are societies in which the regime is a military regime in name but in which all government is highly limited in its scope and where central government has very little impact on political life outside of a capital city and a few towns, e.g. as in Togo. There are civilian regimes that seem to depend increasingly on the military or a part of it for continuation in power, e.g. China during the Cultural Revolution. The alliance may be between traditional elite and army or between party and army. The lines between the latter two may be very blurred, as, for example, when the army and party were forged out of the same experience in China during the 1920s and 1930s. There may be a narrow civilian leadership operating on top of a basically military regime, e.g. Pakistan. Or there may be a military regime of sorts operating on top of a civil service regime. This would describe many African countries. And within the last type, there are many gradations and a good deal of flux in the determination of power between military, police, civil service, and civilian politicians.

Some of these hybrid systems may be quite vulnerable to interest group pressures. The level of political participation and the kinds of existing civilian organizations are important factors in judging the nature of military-civilian relations. Nigeria and Ghana, as military governments, have strong civil service components which both "make" and implement policy. In other military regimes civilian organizations can exert pressures and political groupings are near the surface. Argentina has been an example of a country where military rule has been lengthy and at times pervasive but where political participation has been high even under military rule with political parties, trade union organizations, and mass movements of continuing importance through periods of military rule.

In some military systems, the rule of law as expressed by a free or relatively free judiciary and due process continues to be a factor for those who contend for present or future power. There are military regimes in which people can speak their minds, e.g. Nigeria. And there are no lack of regimes where systematic torture and arrest without redress occur, e.g. Greece, and Brazil. There are of course regimes which are arbitrary but which through their own lack of organization and cohesion are not systematic about repression, e.g. Uganda. There are military regimes where at various times military personnel have tried to fill many roles in society, for example, when Burmese officers were appointed to run factories or when Nigerian officers were appointed to public corporations and boards with military and police Governors operating on top of civil service administrative structures. Some militaries—both "in" and "out" of power—have tried to carry out non-military functions in a wide range of social and economic fields. Indonesia and the Philippines both have civic action programs; in Latin America civic action efforts often have been seen explicitly as counter insurgency programs. In Africa, militaries often have been highly resistant to civic action programs.

All this has been by way of saying what is obvious. Military-civilian relations range across a wide spectrum of relative power positions. There is variability with regard to military functions in both military and civilian regimes as conventionally denoted. There are many reasons for military intervention and military performance in power relates to intervention, to civilian institutions and to groups' power to aid or impede the military, and to the military's own composition.

If we are concerned with the transition away from military rule we must bear all this in mind. Since many of the so-called civilian and many of the so-called military regimes are mixed systems, a transition from military rule is likely to be a transition to a mixed system although the nature of the mix may be altered in the process. There are different kinds of transition. The military in power may itself set a deadline by which it says it would like to see civilian rule restored. This means arriving at some new formula by which the Head of State becomes chief executive by virtue of some process other than achieving leadership of the armed forces. It may mean holding new elections for a Parliament, as in Ghana before the second coup or it may mean calling some kind of consultative assembly or constitutional convention. It may be that the military seems to set the rules of the game for this kind of transition, as in Nigeria today. A military regime might suddenly collapse from its own lack of will and capacity and from outside pressures, as the Sudanese regime collapsed under Abboud. Or the military may be split over its continuance in office, accompanied by strong civilian pressures, with some civilians trying to get the military to transfer power and others urging it to stay in to protect them against social and political change, e.g. Argentina. Again outside powers can sometimes prop up or bring down a military regime.

Military regimes will also try to transform themselves. For example a modest transformation occurred when the Thai military allowed a Parliament to operate between February 1969 and November 1971. But power was clearly maintained by the military during this period and it was able and willing to abrogate the experiment. However, the transformation may be a more radical one, as in the Ataturk model. Ataturk had insisted that Turkish officers who wanted to have a political role resign their commissions and enter into civilian politics by forming new parties. The South Korean military for a time seemed to be moving in this direction, only to revert to a rather "pure" military rule. Nasser never had much success in building a mass political organization; yet the UAR is an odd hybrid of a regime. In a sense the UAR is headed by civilianized military personnel whose base of power remains their close connection to elements in the armed forces.

In Spain, the Leader is a victorious general from the civil war and many high officials have military backgrounds. The Falangist party has been allowed to atrophy. The regime is a mixture of personal autocracy, military rule, very limited parliament, an important civil service base, and it has now introduced a dose of monarchial legitimacy for good measure. Zaire is a variation on the theme of a leader with a military background whose power rested on both his military command and on his dominance of a powerful political clique, who tried to create a civilian base of power while holding on to his military one.

In Turkey itself the Ataturk period of military rule was followed by a long period of civilian rule in which many former officers were important. But independent parties ruled until the military reintervened in 1960-61 when the army withdrew some distance, though making it clear that party politics would be allowed to operate only within certain limits. It reintervened in 1971, yet it continues not only to allow but also to insist on the maintenance of party coalition in a National Assembly.

We could proliferate examples of mixed types and transitions away from regimes heavily dominated by officers. We can also be more systematic. Transitions from military rule may involve large amounts of popular participation or limited amounts. They may be characterized by a phased reentry of civilians into the political process. We want to sketch out those elements which we think are crucial to different kinds of transition from military rule and point out those factors which constrain the possibilities of any transition being undertaken at all, presenting material from Thailand by way of illustration.

One may usefully first return to the matter of military intervention. The study of military interventions ought to be linked to the study of prospects for the military as a modernizing institution. When we understand the reasons for specific military interventions, exploring the links between the military and other political institutions and groups, we can better assess the future evolution of armed forces in society and we can better judge the military's capacities to deal with specific problems. The factors that explain military intervention also reveal the limits of the military's political capacities and the constraints on transition from military rule. Even if we have no general theory to explain military intervention, a dissection of the specific components of an intervention may reveal the potentialities for the kind of rule that the intervening military will exert. At this point, we cannot say that large scale armed forces intervene more than small scale ones, or that presence or absence of "mass" parties before military intervention is a distinguishing variable.[4] Algeria, Argentina, Mali, and Ghana had supposedly strong parties. They always appear weak after we see the military intervene. Similarly, we can argue that civilian elites who give way to the military suffered from loss of legitimacy. But if legitimacy, or strength of party, are to be distinguishing criteria, they must be measured independently of the fact of military intervention. Also we cannot say that professional armies don't intervene but accept civilian supremacy while armies with weak professional ethos do intervene. There must be independent measures for professionalization in armed forces apart from any reluctance to intervene.

We can also agree with Zolberg that it is difficult to sort out the relationship between military motives for making a coup and military intentions about rule.[5] Indeed, both may change during the coup process. Nonetheless, it is relevant whether the military has a specific program for rule, whether it reacts out of fear for its own prerogatives, or whether it makes demands for more resources.

We can think of military intervention in terms of three rough phases which are defined perhaps more by the different political contexts in which the military operates than by factors peculiar to the military's own organization. Indeed, although military factionalism is one internal factor critical in the different phases, military factionalism must itself be seen as an outcome of the interactions between military and civilian politicians and bureaucrats and more broadly as an outcome of the military's interactions with social and ethnic groups.

There is an initial stage during which the military may for the first time make overtly threatening demands on the government of a new nation; it may settle conflicts between civilian contenders or may itself take over the government. Tropical Africa presents us with many examples of this phase. The next phase can be considered one in which there is a struggle for stability after the seizure of power. The criteria for inclusion in this category are: (1) a regime dominated by the armed forces, (2) a military leadership that has a great deal of continuity with the original leaders of the coup, and (3) a situation that has not been characterized by a number of coups and counter-coups. Thus we are still dealing here with a first generation of military leaders, although some change in the top leadership may take place. The third rough category is that of institutionalized intervention with Latin America presenting several examples. Here the military cannot bring about political stability nor give up aspirations to rule. Military coup may become the accepted method for achieving political change for groups within the armed forces, for certain civilian leaders, and for citizens who remain bystanders to coups.

In each of the three phases, the military has different immediate political problems. In the first it must pick up the political pieces left by civilian regimes or by its own coup and must find allies and support from political groups. In the second it must build support by reaching down into society and maintain military cohesion. In the third phase the military is split, by definition, and must maintain some autonomy from civilian groups and keep military disputes within bounds.[6]

Of course, these phases are analytical ones. In reality, situations may be blurred. After one intervention an armed force may move quickly into a relationship with its society of institutionalized intervention. Dahomey already seems a candidate; with others in the wings. The process of institutionalized intervention is especially interesting for thinking about problems of transition from military rule; it is a situation either where one coup faction succeeds another or where periods of military rule and civilian rule alternate. During the military periods there are strong pressures for return to civilian rule, while during the civilian periods everyone keeps looking over his shoulder to see if the men in green or khaki are heading for the radio station, post and telegraph, and presidential or prime ministerial residences.

In these cases of institutionalized intervention—which can be seen in Argentina, almost as the defining case,[7] but also in Peru, Bolivia, Brazil and Turkey—the following features appear. Social forces in a country can be characterized as what Huntington calls "massive"; that is, levels of political participation are high and political strife between class or regional groups is very intense in periods of military and civilian rule. Indeed, military intervention can be understood as an attempt to choke off political participation. In Africa, class conflict is rarely so well defined but ethnicity provides a substitute massive social force. And military intervention has sometimes taken place in the name of confining ethnic tension, although military intervention and rule exacerbated it in Nigeria in 1966 and in Uganda today.[8]

In situations of institutionalized intervention, the military is typically split over the very question of continued military rule. Some elements feel that the goals of the coup have been attained when a specific regime is brought down, e.g. the Goulart regime in Brazil, the Nkrumah regime in Ghana, the second Margai regime in Sierra Leone. Others feel that the military must undertake a sweeping reconstruction of social, economic and political life. Or some may feel that it is too dangerous to abdicate again to civilians either because dominant civilian forces will once again come to the fore or because the military elements fear that their own privileges cannot be maintained under a civilian regime. However, the military's role and benefits can be determined through bargaining between military and civilians. Possibly more critical is the military's fear that old scores will be settled if certain civilians regain control. Needler reports one Dominican colonel's reaction after the coup of 1963, when he was asked his attitude toward a return of Juan Bosch: "If Bosch ever comes back, he will throw me into jail so deep I will never find my way out."[9] Where the military has engaged in violence against civilian opponents, the fear of this settling of accounts is intensified. Where the military has engaged in a great deal of internal violence, those elements who have emerged on top will be extremely reluctant to give up the direct levers of physical control.

We are suggesting in sum that—where violence has occurred during the coup process, during the period of military rule, or within the military itself—the transition back to civilian rule is unlikely to be voluntarily undertaken by those elements who have been on top in the military. Could one envision it in Uganda now? We are also suggesting that, where there have been high levels of mass participation in politics which provide the base for civilians (as for Arevalo in Guatemala, Peron in Argentina, or Menderes in Turkey) the military is not likely to be reconciled to a return to civil government, unless they can engineer a shift in popular opinion away from a particular party and leader or unless the party itself changes.[10] Both these conditions appear to have been met in Ghana between 1966-69. And the popular base of the Nkrumah regime was not felt to be wide by military leaders in any case.

We are focusing on participation, the nature of military penetration of society, and institutionalization of armed forces as critical variables in the transition process.

We are carrying out two case studies in order to look at problems of transition from military rule. Field work has been completed in both Nigeria and Thailand. Thailand is an example of an aborted move to increase civilian political participation through an elected parliament. By the late 1960s, a combination of political stability and economic growth had given rise to new social forces in Thailand and new voices demanding participation in the political process. A new Constitution was promulgated in June, 1968; the Thai national elections in February 1969, the country's first in eleven years, introduced a group of politicians dependent on electoral constituencies for their political support. The November 1971 coup ended this; martial law was enforced, political parties dissolved, the 1968 Constitution revoked and the House of Representatives and Senate dispensed with. Between 1969 and 1971, MPs had acted as tribunes and brokers and as checks on the bureaucracy. A number of elected representatives were engaged in political education and politicization of the rural populace,[11] but the November 1971 coup choked off rural political participation.

In Nigeria, a military coup in January 1966 and a second coup in July 1966 decimated the top officer corps. A bloody civil war followed on the heels of military rule. The military Government successfully maintained the territorial integrity of Nigeria, split up the Nigerian Federation of four regions into a twelve state system, and in 1967 introduced civilian commissioners into the Federal and State Governments. These Governments were headed by military or police officers but they functioned after the introduction of civilian commissioners as Cabinet governments with many former major politicians in the governments. Moreover, the Nigerian military Government publically maintained its commitment to a return to civilian rule during 1976. This public resolve to get out of power is not believed by wide segments of the political elite, while the military is itself clearly split over the issue of withdrawal from formal ruling roles.[12]

The following pages focus on the Thai case during the 1969-71 period, in which limited transition mechanisms were in evidence. Work is continuing on the Nigerian example, providing additional insights into problems of transition from military rule.

Thailand's 1969-71 Transition

The armed forces, and especially the Royal Thai Army, have maintained their hegemony since 1932. They continued to dominate the political process during the 1968-1971 constitutional era, using both traditional mechanisms of control and the government's Saha Pracha Thai (SPT) Party. For the past 15 years Thailand has been ruled by a single group of men: the military officers who rose to power in the Sarit coup of September 1957.

The Army officers in the ruling group share certain viewpoints based on their long history of working together in the Bangkok garrisons, their common Army Academy schooling, and their mutual participation in the 1957 coup. Nevertheless, friction exists, based on the personal rivalries and competing ambitions that mark leadership groups everywhere in the world.

The Army's pervasive influence throughout the political system is exercised through placement of senior military officers in key leadership positions in civilian agencies, injection of the armed forces into non-military institutional roles, and co-optation of non-military elites under the general policy guidance of the military hierarchy. As contrasted with other developing countries in which the military intervenes in politics, the dynamics of the Thai political process require that the military be analyzed as a political machine, with many senior military officers functioning as "military/politicos."

Political Resources Available to the Thai Military

Power available to the military can be disaggregated in terms of six political resources: legitimacy, authority, status, wealth, coercion and information.

LEGITIMACY

The Thai military is endowed with the generally accepted right to lead and rule the nation. People accept the concept that might makes right, and evidence a continuing desire for strong, decisive (martial) leadership. Further legitimacy comes to the armed forces from the monarchy.

The armed forces as an institution have been the pre-eminent political force ever since the overthrow of the absolute monarchy. Except for the brief 1944-47 period when they were in disfavor owing to wartime collaboration with the Japanese, the military's continued control over the political process has been threatened only by internal fragmentation and factionalism, not by the emergence of other powerful groups. Thus the Thai political system has become well accustomed to seeing its top leadership in uniform. Although many intellectuals and some royalists would prefer otherwise, the remainder of Thai society considers military rule, or at least long-term military tutelage, legitimate and reasonable.

AUTHORITY

The Thai military has great authority, used to the utmost in achieving and maintaining control over the political process. The many Cabinet and bureaucratic positions held by senior military leaders permit access to budgets, personnel, and other sinews of bureaucratic power; "double hatting" further increases access to authority positions.

The Thai Army is able to intervene so often and so successfully in the Thai political process not so much because it has the tanks and guns, but because its leaders have the will to intervene, and because it is the best organized, and disciplined institution in Thai society. Military leaders' potential opponents are disorganized and fragmented; they are also timid, *greng jai,* afraid of causing bloodshed. The Army, too, would prefer to avoid bloodshed, but it is willing to risk this if necessary in pursuit of personal, institutional and national goals.

A Monopoly of Organized Political Capability. No competing institutions or organized interest groups have emerged in Thailand to challenge military dominance of the political process. To some extent, the armed forces have actively prohibited such groups from emerging; but far more important is their effective co-optation of potential competitors through tacit or explicit alliances.

Rather than challenging the military's authority, the monarchy has reached a tacit agreement with the military regarding political equilibrium. The Army is satisfied to see the Chakri Dynasty retain the throne under a constitutional monarchy with the King as Chief of State, no republic, and performance of religious and cultural activities by the royal institution. In return, the monarchy agrees (tacitly) to refrain from explicit political activities, leaving unchallenged the Army's monopolistic control over authoritative rule making.

Though Thailand has been called a "bureaucratic polity,"[13] the civil bureaucracy is fragmented and relatively unorganized; it does not pose a serious threat to the military's power. Thailand's rapid economic progress during the past 15 years—under military rule—has been characterized by a high degree of cooperation between soldiers and civil bureaucrats. The military has been especially successful in co-opting civilian specialists to implement and manage the national development effort.

The economic, commercial and business community in Thailand remains dominated by Chinese (Sino-Thai) enterprises. The Thai military elite has participated actively in these organizations over the past two decades, preempting unilateral growth of politically-relevant economic power by Chinese businessmen. Actions taken by military leaders in the economic sphere provide another example of their ability to co-opt potential competitors into a mutually beneficial arrangement. Labor unions have remained a negligible force.

The student community (and young, post-graduate intellectuals has also been co-opted into at least tacit support of the military regime. Thai cultural traditions, such as respect for elders, patience, and rectitude preclude major student demonstrations against the regime. More important, however, most Thai students continue to believe that the most desirable careers lie in the bureaucracy.

The Buddhist hierarchy and the Sangha, by virtue of their numbers and the respect accorded them by the rest of society, represent a potentially powerful political force. But because the Thai branch of Theravada Buddhism is more pacifist, contemplative and apolitical than the Mahayana branch found in Vietnam—or even other Theravada branches—the church has not intervened in Thai politics. Religious ceremonies are granted for many military occasions, such as the blessing of Thai troops leaving for combat in Vietnam. Monks and ex-monks play an important role in village-level political activity in Thailand,[14] but this does not negate the conclusion that there is no Buddhist political challenge to the military at the national level.

Historically, the police have been a principal organized competitor to the military. Police/military rivalry was particularly intense in the mid-1950s, when Field Marshal Phibun retained control by balancing General Sarit's Army against General Phao's police. Sarit's 1957 coup brought this era to an abrupt end, and ever since the military has controlled police manpower, budgets, deployment and equipment.

Finally, to date the military's monopoly of political power has not been challenged by the rural sector. The villagers generally remain content to rely on governmental paternalism and on the natural plenitude of the Thai agricultural environment to meet their aspirations and needs. There are signs that this situation has begun to change, with villager demands becoming an increasingly potent element in the Thai political equation. "Civic incorporation" seems likely to be one of the major issues of the 1970s, along with the related problem of rural insurgency; but over the past four decades the village populace has certainly not challenged the military's monopoly of political power.

In summary, since the usual sources of political organization— a politicized public, a politically influential business community, large trade unions, activist students, a powerful press, a concerned religious institution, an aroused monarchy, an independent civil bureaucracy or effective political parties—were either non-existent or very weak, the Thai military has continued as the only organized segment of the society able and willing to occupy chief positions of authority.

Internal Cohesion of the Military Elite. Despite the factionalism described by Riggs, Wilson[15] and others, one of the operative characteristics of the Thai military hierarchy is its institutional cohesion. Factions have spheres of influence and hegemony in which they operate unfettered; individual leaders are permitted to take action on their own, without close scrutiny from the Cabinet; membership in particular factions or groupings shifts and changes with the flow of events. In fact, the tensions inherent in these conflicts produce, in the manner of a multiple dialectic, strong pressures for political and bureaucratic performance and innovation. Nevertheless, on major issues—continued military rule, for example—the group evidences great cohesion.

On a day-to-day basis, military cohesion is seen in the "old boy

ties" between graduates of the same class at the Military Academy
or the National War College, close links between men involved in a
particular event (the 1932 coup promoters, the 1947 coup initiators,
officers in the Thai unit which fought in Korea, and the 1957 inner
military clique), inter-marriage between leading families (Thanom's
son is married to Praphat's daughter), and membership on the same
corporate boards or joint participation in business operations.

Widespread participation in and tolerance of corruption play a
crucial role in maintaining military cohesion, cutting across factional
or personal cleavages to produce common requirements for mutual
protection. Factional competitors on governmental issues may sit
on the same corporate boards or participate jointly in the spoils
from a particular contract. If no one at the top is "clean," no one
can betray his fellows.

STATUS

In Thai political culture, the soldier ranks fairly high in terms of
social prestige, although the Army and other military branches still
depend on transfers of this vital political resource from the monarchy.

Sarit cultivated an image of strength, efficiency and close ties
to the palace; Thanom and Praphat, since 1963, have been less successful in maintaining such an image. Many of the present military leaders
come from middle class backgrounds. In contrast to their 1932 pred-
ecessors, and in contrast to their counterparts in the bureaucracy
today, most have not had extensive foreign education. In sum, status
available to the armed forces on their own is moderate, supplemented
by transfers of this resource from the monarchy and by the fact that
the generals do, after all, control the nation politically and economically.

WEALTH

The military group's access to economic resources is a source of
future political power, as well as a principal mechanism for using
political power to achieve national and personal objectives. Thai
military/politicos function as a group much like an American urban
political machine; they use spoils, patronage and pressure. Civilian and
technocrat elements are co-opted through judicious use of funds and
bureaucratic position; students are co-opted through the promise of
future access to status and wealth. A military leader's personal faction
is created and expanded by giving his supporters a share of the take.

In a systematic manner, commercial enterprises and banks (with military leaders on the boards of directors), state enterprises, quasi-legal business ventures and the other means of raising capital are related to and combined with contracting procedures, opportunities for kickbacks, and control over bureaucratic assignments to constitute the military's base of economic power. Access to these economic resources provides the military with the grease which lubricates the entire Thai political system and keeps it moving forward.

COERCION

As would be expected, the military ranks very high in terms of access to and use of this potent political resource. Most threats are implicit, though political prisoners were arrested and jailed without trial under the provisions of Sarit's interim constitution (and much later, in 1972). In the period before the re-opening of the political system in 1968, martial law was in force throughout the country, communists and all "leftists" were suppressed, the press was censored, students were tightly controlled, and strong controls were maintained over all other aspects of politics. This serves to describe the situation during the post-coup period as well.

Over the past 40 years, the Thai military establishment and elements thereof have shown that they are willing to employ force in pursuit of domestic political objectives. Troop deployments and budget allocations reflect a continuing preoccupation with "coup and counter-coup." Although most of these events have been intra-military squabbles, the military did intervene in November 1947 to dismiss the strongest, most promising non-military government Thailand has had in its constitutional era; the Sarit coup of 1957 ended a two-year period of Phibun-style electoral politics; and three years of legislative politics were ended by military coercion in 1971.

Thus, there is never any question in the minds of politically-conscious Thais that the Army is prepared to employ its battalions of infantry, batteries of artillery and armored units whenever this is deemed necessary in order to uphold the Army's political interests.

INFORMATION

The military collects and uses vast amounts of information on the activities and potential power of factional competitors within the armed forces and the bureaucracy. Many intelligence agencies exist to spy on one another. They have far less information on economic, social and political problems of the rural populace, and they showed in the 1968-71 period that they were not particularly interested in increasing their access to this political resource.

Availability of timely, reliable, relevant information is an important source of the Army's continuing political power. Although the primary purpose of military intelligence units seems to be collection of information on rivals within the armed forces, they all produce extra-military intelligence as well. These agencies include: (1) the Intelligence Directorate of Supreme Command Headquarters, (2) the Armed Forces Intelligence and Operations Center, (3) the Intelligence Section of the Army Operations Center, (4) the Intelligence Directorates of the Army, Navy, Air Force and Marine Headquarters, (5) the Intelligence Sections of the 1st, 2nd, and 3rd Army Headquarters, and other lower echelon military units.

Other intelligence agencies within the civilian branches of government add to the flow of political information reaching military leaders. Pre-eminent sources of political information within the civil area are: (1) the Thai National Police Department, especially the Special Branch of the Criminal Investigation Bureau, (2) the Department of Central Intelligence within the Prime Minister's office, (3) the Intelligence Section of the Communist Suppression Operations Directorate, and (4) information available to the Department of Local Administration within the Ministry of Interior.

With the return of political parties to the political scene in 1968, a new source of political information became available to military leaders. Through contact with elected MPs, through SPT Party branch offices, and through visits to provincial areas, the military leadership was provided with new kinds of information. The government political party provided a significant forum for the provision of such inputs to the leadership, although contact with independent MPs was also important. But most such information was simply rejected by the military as irrelevant to their principal political concerns.

TWO ADDITIONAL SOURCES OF STRENGTH

Two additional sources of political power available to the Thai military lie outside the resource analysis framework. One is the skills of individual military/politicos. The Thai military structure over the past several decades has been remarkably successful in producing officers with a high degree of political skill. In fact, it is fairly certain that their capabilities in bargaining, negotiation, patronage, factional maneuvering, and related political activities far exceed their purely military effectiveness. The Thai military system rewards the politically astute officer with rapid promotions and early access to the economic assets which allow him to develop his own set of followers (his personal political machine). In response to these incentives, skilled politicians like Thanom, Praphat, Krit, Prasert and others have progressed to the top levels of the political hierarchy.

Second, the Thai armed forces provide opportunity for upward mobility and career achievement. The military system has been highly achievement-oriented, in contrast to the royal ascriptive pattern which it supplanted in 1932. Young men of middle-class and lower-middle-class backgrounds have been able, by attending the Military Academy, to enter a career system which placed no limits on their upward mobility. Their own skills and diligence permitted them to attain the most powerful positions in their country. Though the civil bureaucracy has also provided opportunity for high achievers to advance rapidly,[16] for the past four decades the armed forces have been the paramount institution for upward mobility.

Dynamics of Military Rule:
Mechanisms for Control and Co-optation

Using the sources of power outlined above, military/politicos over the past two decades have concentrated on several mutually-related policy objectives: continued independence from foreign control, economic development, maintenance of internal security, political stability, and a minimum of violence, and, throughout, continued military supremacy.

The process by which military leaders retain control over the political process may be analyzed in five facets: (1) the Cabinet and civil bureaucracy, (2) the legislature and political parties, (3) the business and financial sectors, (4) foreign policy, and (5) internal security affairs. We will discuss only the first and second here.

MECHANISM 1: Bureaucratic Control

The bureaucracy has been controlled by assignment of military officers to crucial positions of authority over civilians and by the continual process of co-opting bureaucrats to work amiably and effectively for the military regime.

One of the intriguing features of the Thai bureaucratic polity is the assignment of individuals to several high-level positions at the same time, thus achieving control and coordination at the top of the government. In addition, the military controls the bureaucracy through the assignment of supporters or relatives to important subordinate positions, through periodic rotation of potential civilian competitors, and through fragmentation of power and responsibility among various civil agencies,[17] through insistence on traditional modes of committee decision making, and through central control over budget allocations.

Although all these techniques for influencing the civil bureaucracy contributed to their success, of even greater importance in explaining continued military control over the Thai bureaucracy is the phenomenal success of the policy of co-opting civil servants to work for them. Analysts of the role of the military in developing countries note that a military institution is unable to produce, in sufficient numbers, the men needed to effectively and efficiently run the government: economic planners, engineers, statisticians, irrigation specialists, community development officers. The conclusion is therefore often drawn that military leadership, even when it enjoys monopoly over the use of force and internal cohesion, cannot by itself rule a nation; it thus must turn either to a political party or to the bureaucracy. The further implication is that, by so doing, the military loses much of its influence to civilian bureaucrats or political party agents.

In Thailand, the military has for 40 years used civilians to administer the country for them. Except for the post-war interregnum (1944-47), they have never divested themselves of ultimate control over government policies and programs. Partly, this remarkable performance reflects traditional Thai characteristics of pragmatism and fatalism—the ability to live with a sub-optimal situation (in Thai, *plong tok*). More significantly, however, it demonstrates the degree to which Thai military leaders do *not* exhibit military socialization patterns of the type frequently discussed in the literature on the military and political development.[18] Rather, Thai military leaders have acted as politicians skilled in bargaining, negotiation, compromise and patronage.

Thai military rule has been characterized by decentralization. Army officers permit civil bureaucrats a wide range of freedom to execute economic development programs, budget, fiscal or foreign exchange reforms, and even counter-insurgency programs, without day-to-day direction from military chieftains. Thus at least the most senior technocrats are given strong incentives to remain within the system, since in many respects they are able to carry out the programs they themselves feel are best for the country. Yet these incentives are contingent on their continued tolerance of overall military leadership. These contingent incentives toward co-optation are reinforced by the traditional view of the bureaucrat as working "in the service of the King."

MECHANISM 2: Legislative and Party Control

The constitution promulgated in mid-1968 was the first to be set forth by a leadership group which had been in power for several years, in contrast to the other seven constitutions, all promulgated subsequent to a military coup (and which have been termed "faction constitutions" because they legitimized the power base of the particular faction which prevailed).

To contest the February 1969 national elections, several political parties re-emerged. The military, by controlling the government party and actively supporting independent candidates as well, demonstrated their ability to participate effectively in electoral politics.

The Saha Pracha Thai Party was established by the military in preparation for the 1969 National Assembly elections. The party's elected component, however, was composed primarily of ex-MPs, ex-Governors and businessmen. Thus there was a major gap (and resultant tensions) between elected SPT members and the party's leadership core of eight men—seven of whom were military or police officers.

Military control over the legislative process rested on (1) dominance over the SPT Party, and (2) representation in the appointed Senate, in which military and police officers comprised 75 per cent of the membership. Despite these control mechanisms, on several occasions the parliament failed to carry out the expressed wishes of the country's leaders.

While the military was in control, younger officers pressured to do away with the trappings of democracy in 1971 in order to protect their own political power base. Legislators were perceived as a threat to bureaucratic privilege. Originally tagged as a "rubber stamp" for decisions made by the military leadership, Thailand's National Assembly surprised critics by its willingness to question executive decisions on several important and controversial issues. The legislature played an important role in national fiscal and budgetary decisions. Due to opposition from the Assembly, reflecting widespread discontent amongst the general public, the executive

agreed to rescind certain tax increases. The Assembly as an institution and the MPs as individuals also began to fulfill important
functions in Thailand's economic development and modernization
process. They influenced the allocation of provincial development
funds and inter-acted with bureaucratic decision-makers in the National Economic Development Board, Ministry of National Development, Office of Accelerated Rural Development and similar development agencies.

The Thai legislators between 1969-71 began to articulate the
aspirations and grievances of their constituents and to represent their
interests to specific government agencies. The country's military
leaders, particularly through the SPT party framework, were now
faced with a far wider range of articulated demands from the lower
echelons of the Thai polity than were being presented to them in
the pre-1968 era.

In sum, the very existence of an elected legislature and political
parties in Thailand, reappearing after a gap of nearly a decade, began
to permit a re-allocation of power at the top of the political system
and to suggest the creation of greater opportunities for participation
at the bottom.

The military in Thailand has clearly been the major source of
political power in the country. Still, many officers did not feel that
their own interests could be secured in a transitional period. They
believed that their vital institutional and personal interests were
threatened by new institutions and civilian decision makers and
they reintervened or, more accurately, carried out a coup inside a
regime already dominated by the military. Yet the legislature was
not a powerful body. Indeed, it had only residual powers permitted
to it by the military. By 1971, the legislature had not created its own
base of power independent of the executive; thus it was vulnerable to
the action of even a small group within the military.

If Thailand was and is likely to be an example of a polity dominated by the military, any "transition" from military rule means
taking into account the continued dominance of the military while
devising a gradual expansion of the political roles of extra-bureaucratic institutions.

A viable government political party seems especially crucial in
this regard. This is particularly important where the military has
been long and powerfully entrenched. In this case, there is clear
utility for a one-party dominant system, in which the military's
own interests can be represented. A good example is the Democratic
Republican Party which emerged in South Korea after the 1961

military coup; another is the government party which emerged in
Turkey under Ataturk. To be successful, a government party must
take an active role in establishing rural branches, selecting good
candidates, and providing the forum for two-way interaction between
bureaucratic leaders and elected politicians. Thailand's Saha Pracha
Thai Party in 1968-71 performed adequately only the last function.

Thai politics are characterized by excessive factional competiton
between bureaucratically-based cliques, a situation not likely to
change in the near future. It is naive to expect that this competition
can be excised from the workings of a government political party.
It is essential to the development of incipient extra-bureaucratic
institutions that competition between military and bureaucratic
factions—patrons and clients—be steadily transferred to the electoral
and legislative arenas. To some degree, this process was underway in
1969, 1970 and 1971, but it was overwhelmed by other factors. To
the degree that generals and ministers who today hold all the power
perceive it in their own interest to compete with one another in
extra-bureaucratic politics, expanding their own bases of power with
the citizenry and the elected representatives, the political system
will develop.

This transfer of bureaucratic factionalism into a broader political arena is potentially de-stabilizing. The best that can be done is
to devise a system in which factions have a reasonable chance to
participate in electoral politics, relying on candidate restrictions,
some appointed members of the House, gradually increasing the
status of the elected institution, and the growth of participant attitudes among the people at large to keep such competition within
bounds. Since the 1957 Sarit coup, the Thai bureaucratic polity
has been remarkably adept at limiting intensive factional competition, in the interests of all its leading participants. It does not seem
theoretically impossible for such agreement on limits and "rules
of the game" to be applied as well to competition within a government political party.

There is no reason why a dominant one-party system should
not have an active, vocal opposition; and Thai political history indicates that this could be the case again. But the fundamental issues
of politics during a transition from military rule concern gradual
change within a framework of stability and order, slow accrual of
extra-bureaucratic power, and effective curbs on bureaucratic
excesses while also curbing excesses of legislative intervention. It is
all a question of timing; a "responsible" government political
party and a "loyal" opposition both have vital roles to play.

In many developing polities, including Thailand, transition from military rule requires that steps be taken to de-centralize decision-making to lower echelons of the bureaucracy and de-concentrate power from the capital city to provinces, districts and villages. Such alterations in bureaucratic structure can be accomplished by re-organization of the bureaucracy and by local elections.

Part of the long-term answer to the transition problem lies in de-centralization of decision-making authority, followed by effective de-concentration of political power. This requires changes in the organization of the national bureaucracy and the tax structure, and provision for local control over bureaucratic performance. In the Thai case, one of the long-term objectives might be development of a modernized version of the old *monthon* concept, regional centers for administrative decision-making and program implementation.

De-concentration of power away from the metropolitan center to the periphery will take even longer, but it too remains an important long-term objective. Local government institutions could be given increased power to collect and allocate tax revenues. Eventually, District Officers and Governors could be made subject to periodic popular election, perhaps with the slate of candidates having their eligibility certified by the Ministry of Interior in Bangkok. Police and other now-independent agencies could be placed under the control of these elected officials, ensuring far greater responsiveness to popular wishes and providing mechanisms for curbing local excesses.

These steps, however, are not pre-requisites for the initial phases of transition from military rule. The gradual creation of viable extra-bureaucratic institutions at the national level, linked in a multitude of ways to the bottom of the political system is equally feasible, and is not dependent on the latter for its success. De-centralization of authority and de-concentration of power are threatening to the existing bureaucratic and military oligarchy, and success of the transition attempt can easily be jeopardized if these long-term goals are pressed too early. As with so much of the transition process, timing of demands for structural modifications is all important.

CONCLUDING REMARKS: The Events of October 1973

Thailand's transition ended abruptly on November 17, 1971, when the Army reasserted total dominance over the political system. However, this coup contained within itself the next transition phase

in Thai politics, the overt inception of which was seen in the bloody
events of October 1973. Students, angered by the military's continued recalcitrance in refusing to promulgate a new constitution
and re-open opportunities for political participation and grievance
resolution, took matters into their own hands. The arrest of a few
student activists precipitated a week of increasingly powerful demonstrations. When the crowd of some 400,000 refused to disperse,
Army and police components opened fire, and two days of total
confrontation produced some 69 dead and 875 wounded demon-
strators (official statistics). It also produced an end to the military
regime, as the Prime Minister (Field Marshal Thanom Kittikachorn),
Deputy Prime Minister (Field Marshal Praphat Charusathien) and
powerful young military leader Colonel Narong Kittikachorn
(Thanom's son and Praphat's son-in-law) were forced to flee the
country. The King appointed as Prime Minister a respected civilian,
Dr. Sanya Thammasak, Rector of Thammasat University, a former
Chief Justice of the Supreme Court, and a member of the Privy
Council. The new government promised to devise a new constitu-
tion, allow political participation through elections, and reconstitute another transition from military rule.

   These cataclysmic events must be viewed in the context of
emerging political aspirations demolished in the 1971 coup. Although
the 1969-71 transition period evidenced many broadly-perceived
imperfections, the opportunity did exist for political participation
and grievance resolution. The November 1971 coup and subsequent
return to repression turned the nation's political clock back 10 or
perhaps even 20 years.[19] The following months witnessed new
activity by a "loyal opposition", who in the face of military repression wrote and spoke against the coup and its leaders, demanding
a return to open government. This new political opposition, centered
among certain intellectuals—epitomized perhaps by Dr. Puey Ung-
phakorn who wrote from his self-imposed exile in London—found
an increasingly responsive student majority ready to exchange
political passivity for activism.[20]

   The explosion of October 1973 produced major shifts in two
political resources critical to continued military rule: legitimacy and
coercion. The King finally decided that his nation's continued stability required a transfer of legitimacy from the military coup group
to respected civilian leaders like Sanya (and, by implication, to the
students). His unwillingness to support continued military repression
and bloodshed undercut the military's legitimacy as rulers. Thanom,
Praphat and Narong were ordered to leave; seeing that the legitimacy

transfer had been effected, they complied rather than continue a futile effort. The new Army strong man General Krit Sivara ordered his troops to refrain from entering the fray, and the revolution was consummated. Although Praphat in particular retained access to many coercive resources, without royal legitimacy he could not employ them.

Whether the post-October 1973 transition from military rule in Thailand will be lasting or again emphemeral remains to be seen. Principal issues revolve around the King's continued perceptions regarding use of his overwhelming resources of legitimacy and status, the ability of civilian "royalists" and "progressives" to forge a cooperative alliance to replace the mutual animosity of previous periods of non-military rule, the ability of the new government to manage the economy and gradually mobilize the rural peasantry into political participation, the implications of the Thanom-Praphat-Narong precipitous departure for patron-client networks in the bureaucracy, military and business sector, and continuing decisions made by today's top military leaders faced with a totally new situation. One thing is certain: the subject of transition from military rule remains a most worthy issue for study in the Thai context.

Notes

1. For discussion of military intervention see, among others, Finer (1962), Lieuwen (1964), Bienen (1968), Welch (1970), Van Doorn (1972), and Janowitz (1954).

2. See, among others, Johnson, J. (1964), Pye (1966), Bienen (1970), and Schmitter (1973).

3. For example, Stepan (1971), Luckham (1971), Perlmutter (1970).

4. For a discussion of the absence of parsimonious theory to explain military intervention in Africa, see Zolberg (1973).

5. Zolberg (1973: 311-312).

6. For a fuller discussion of these phases see Bienen (1968).

7. See Springer (1968), also De Imaz (1970).

8. Morrison, Mitchell, Paden, and Stevenson (1972) ranks countries for communal instability from independence to 1969. Countries with a high value on communal instability are Sudan (38), Ethiopia (30), Zaire (27) Nigeria (27) Chad (17), Rwanda (15), Kenya (14), and Uganda (12). Half have military regimes. We would argue that Zambia which has a low score also has severe communal instability. Dahomey, the most coup-ridden African country has a low score (1) but has had ethnic conflict over leadership composition. Of the countries with zero scores, Botswana, Central African Republic, Gabon, Gambia, Guinea, Lesotho, Liberia, Malawi, Niger, Senegal, Tanzania, Togo, and Upper Volta—only the last two and the CAR have had military regimes. While there is not a perfect correlation between communal instability and military intervention, there is a positive relationship which is clear. See Morrison, Mitchel, Paden, and Stevenson (1972, 122-131).

9. Needler (1968).

10. Needler (1968).

11. The material on Thailand presented below is part of a larger work by David Morell based on four years of field work in Thailand in which interviews were carried out with Thai MPs, civil servants, and military personnel.

12. The Nigerian case study will be part of a larger work carried out by Henry Bienen and Martin Fitton on politicians and politics in a military regime.

13. See Riggs (1966).

14. See Soontornpasuch (1968) and (1969).

15. Wilson (1962).

16. Recent evidence suggests that opportunities for social mobility in the civil bureaucracy may be coming to an end, with new elite recruitment restricted to holders of foreign degrees, most of whom are the children of the bureaucratic elite. See Dieter-Evers and T. H. Silcock (1967).

17. For example, responsibility for agricultural development was fragmented among *five* different ministries: Agriculture, National Development, Interior, Finance and the Prime Minister's Office. A similar situation existed with regard to education, with responsibility divided among the Ministry of Education, Ministry of Interior, Prime Minister's Office, and National Education Council.

18. Janowitz (1964).

19. See Morell (1972).

20. Political opposition to the military leaders during 1972 is documented in Morell (1973).

ETHNIC SEGMENTATION IN MILITARY ORGANIZATIONS: BURMA AND MALAYSIA

James F. Guyot

Burma and Malaysia are markedly plural societies, societies in which the allocation of organizational roles among ethnic segments is an important characteristic of the military as well as of other major modern institutions such as the civil bureaucracy, political parties, and economic organizations.[1] Consequently we need to know something about the plural structure of these societies if we are to gain a firm understanding of how the military relates to the rest of society now and what potentials there are for change. I will first set out the pattern of ethnic pluralism in these two countries in relation to two broad imperatives, the political and the technological. Then I will note how the tensions between these two imperatives have been reflected across the face of both the civil bureaucracy and the armed forces in the course of the divergent movements these two nations have made from colonial dependence toward autonomous development in a moderniz-ing world. What is particularly striking in this analysis is the persis-tence of the same general form of ethnic segmentation across the independence threshold and its seeming potential to endure through the near future.

The Burmese and Malaysian cases form an appropriate base for examining the general how and why of the persistence of ethnic segmentation within military organizations. The primary rationale for their pairing is the very differences in their recent military experience despite a common colonial heritage. In one country the military has intervened decisively in the political life while in the other, the con-stabulary role has been maintained. This places our two cases at opposite ends of one of the main axes along which the comparative analysis of political and military systems has been so extensively developed in recent years.

Other signal differences between the two might even justify consideration of this pair as a small sample of the diverse experiences of the developing countries in the postwar world. Burma's overall strategy for political and economic development following indepen-dence has been an increasingly "inward-looking" one while Malaysia is an outstanding "outward-looking" example. In per capita GNP Burma is probably one of the ten poorest nations of the world while

Malaysia stands just behind Japan and the island city-state of Singapore as one of the richer nations of Asia. The population range of the pair—from 10 million to 25 million—spans third world nations with an aggregate population of over one-quarter of a billion (Taylor & Hudson, 1972: 306-11; 295-8).

A consideration of their similarities—both descendants of the British imperial tradition in Asia—does suggest the limitations inherent in viewing such a two-case sample as representative of a larger population. Still, some structured generalizations from this sample to other countries in the developing world may well be ventured. Even a cursory glance reveals related patterns of modified but persistent ethnic segmentation in countries other than mother India, the modern source of both the institution of "class companies" and the rationale for recruitment from "martial races " (Cohen, 1971: 45ff.; 180-194). The patterning of military roles on ethnic elements may also be found in non-British areas of Asia, such as the Philippines and Indonesia (Gregory, 1974), and as well in Africa (Enloe, 1973) and in the ex-Commonwealth Caribbean.

The pattern of ethnic pluralism common to both Burma and Malaysia today is one in which a dominant majority (the Burman and the Malay segments) stands counterpoised between (1) a set of more modern, urban minorities and (2) a set of less modern, peripheral minorities.[2] Though similar in form, these two societies differ greatly in population proportions. The Burman majority encompasses about 75-80 percent of the population of Burma while the Malay "majority" fluctuates around the 50 percent mark, depending on the definition used and the territory included.

The modern, city-based minorities are largely creatures of the colonial connection—a demographic consequence of the free trade in factors of production and the inability of the local population to adapt rapidly to the staffing needs of the expanding economy and the colonial bureaucracy. They have been the intermediaries between the colonial power and the colonized country. At the same time some members of these urban minorities have also been collaborators with the ethnic majority in the independence struggle. Regardless of the areas of mutual interest and shared history, one political imperative of the independence movement and its aftermath has been the displacement or control of these formerly favored groups by the major ethnic segment.

The peripheral minorities were typically wards of the metropolitan power, brought into the colonial orbit as buffer areas against neighboring empires and treasured by their guardians for their natural charm and their need for protection. With the coming of independence for the territory that was once a colony, hill tribes or outer islanders presented a major political problem. How could the new nation keep them in against the centrifugal appeal of independence on their own and the irredentist urges of neighbors? Often the answer involved peripheral minority groups in military events—both as members of special units and as their opponents in the field.

In Malaysia the Chinese are the most important of the urban minorities, with lesser political roles taken by Indians, Ceylonese and Eurasians. The Chinese comprise some 35 percent of the total population and about 60 percent of the urban population.[3] Their relative modernity is of a piece with their greater command of the English language and modern higher education. Chinese hold a disproportionate share of the wealth and economic power of the nation, both historically and as successors to the British in the board room and on the rubber plantation. During the postwar years average annual income for Chinese males ran at about twice the average for Malay males. Even though Malays made up over sixty percent of the agricultural labor force they are primarily in the traditional, rice growing sector, owning as late as 1970 less than forty percent of the land devoted to rubber. Moreover, Malay ownership in 1970 of share capital in companies operating within West Malaysia stood at 1.5 percent compared to 24 percent for non-Malays and the remainder for foreign interests (Silcock, 1963; Second Malaysia Plan, 1971-1975: 39-40).

The size of the Chinese segment and the gradualism of the process by which Malaysia gained independence have guaranteed the Chinese a continuing partnership role in running the government Fundamental to the political system, however, is the Malay need to maintain hegemony, symbolic and real, over *Tanah Melayu* (the land of the Malays), a need that is expressed in periodic recalibrations of the balance of who gets what and why. One such recalibration was the constitutional crisis of 1969, when a section of the Chinese community overreached themselves as a result of electoral victories, Malay riots followed, and an emergency government entrenched Malay rights in the constitution and launched a New Economic Policy boldly calculated to "reduce and eventually eliminate the identification of race with economic function."[4]

The peripheral minorities are principally the Dyaks and Kadazans of East Malaysia. The former Borneo territories were a point of conflict in Indonesia's confrontation with Malaysia, and indeed a low grade insurrection has continued from the mid-1960s to the present.

But the prime political significance of these groups has been to serve as balance against the urban minorities.

In colonial Burma, Indians along with Eurasians, Chinese and Sino-Burmans composed the urban minorities. They gave to Rangoon the aura of an Indian town and occupied a majority of the seats at the university even though these groups in total never exceeded ten percent of the population of the country at large. The most politically important group were the Indians, whose number was halved by wartime emigration and whose power was further reduced by the economic nationalism of independent Burma, especially that of the military government that took over in 1962. What leadership roles remained for urban minorities were taken up by the Chinese and Sino-Burmans, ethnic categories less clearly differentiated from the Burmans than the Chinese of Malaysia are from the Malays. The over-arching political problem cast in ethnic form has been the relation of the river basin Burman majority with the hill tribes—the Shan, Karen, Kachin, Chin, and other less well-defined groups. The collection of insurrections that have been running during the last quarter century began with several varieties of communist movements. While the communist elements have continued with varying strength, the insurrection at large quickly took on an ethnic hue, with between three and four ethnic armies in the field at any one time (Trager 1966: 95-139).

The political imperative at work on the road to and through independence reflects the need for a developing polity to shape a national identity which both distinguishes the new nation from its colonial past and integrates the various sub-groups into one nation.[5] Burma and Malaysia have followed different strategies for creating their national identities. Burma cut the colonial connection decisively and looked for its model more in the past glories of a Burman empire, while Malaysia lingered longer in the colonial cocoon and adopted a more accommodating stance toward cultural diversity. Yet the overall outcomes in the allocation of organizational roles among ethnic segments were similar in form in both cases. Members of the majority ethnic group, more so than those of the urban minorities, moved in to displace the British in the politically important roles and into economic roles as well to the extent that they were defined as politically important. Members of the peripheral minority groups came to occupy politically important roles largely as a token presence.

The technological imperative active within the plural society framework reflects the need for a modernizing nation to make efficient use of those talents and motivations available in the resident population which are appropriate to the operation of such modern complex organizations as an oil refinery, a psychiatric hospital, an airline or air force, a rubber research institute, a small arms factory, the local branch of a multinational enterprise, or a telecommunications system. The most concentrated readily exploitable reservoir of those human resources is the more modern, urban minorities. But the political imperative is to reduce or restrain the power of these groups. Thus, the needs of political development and of overall modernization come into conflict. This conflict is readily resolved to the extent that organizational roles can be defined as primarily technical or primarily political and rarely both. Such a cognitive map was devised by the British in the distinction drawn between generalists and specialists; the map was made real in the flowering of discrete generalist and specialist services both at home and abroad.[6] It follows that after independence in the colonies members of the urban minorities will be more readily tolerated in the specialist rather than the generalist services.[7] The peripheral minorities are caught up in the tension between political and technical allocative forces only to the extent that they possess specialized competences, e.g., as "martial races."

Let us now take a look at the trend over time in the distribution of ethnic group members across organizational roles where it can be seen most clearly, in the civil bureaucracy. In the British scheme of colonial governance the political element was the generalist elite cadre, the Indian Civil Service (ICS) and its successor and cousin services, the Burma Civil Service (BCS) and the Malayan Civil Service (MCS). In Malaysia, in line with the political imperative, the locals who began to move into the politically significant generalist service were Malays rather than Chinese or Indians. When non-Malays were permitted to enter the MCS as part of the constitutional compromise that launched the new nation, they came in under a quota.[8] Meanwhile, on the specialist side, in conformance with the technological imperative, non-Malays formed the bulk of the local recruits to the education, public works, medical and other specialized services. The persistence of these proportions is particularly impressive. In Table I five Class I services are arrayed in descending order of the political significance of their functions. The almost perfect decline in the percentage of local officers who are Malay as we go from the top to the bottom of each column demonstrates the clear correlation of race with organizational role at independence in 1957 and as well ten years later.

This persistence is based largely on the ethnic sorting process that goes on within the educational system, with Malays tending to

TABLE 1
Malays as a Percentage of Local Officers in Each Class I Service

	MCS	Police	Education	Public Works	Medical
1957	91%	51%	12%	21%	13%
1968	86%	45%	35%	19%	8%

Source: Adapted from David S. Gibbons and Zakaria Haji Ahmad, "Politics and Selection for the Higher Civil Service in New States: The Malaysian Example" Journal of Comparative Administration, 3.3, November, 1971, Figures 3-7.

follow the arts stream up through university level, while non-Malays predominate in the sciences. Following independence, the government undertook to increase the enrollment of Malays in the science faculties at the university, raising the Malay proportion of those entering science faculties from less than one-tenth to almost one-quarter. At the same time, the general push to get more Malays into higher education raised the overall Malay portion of the entering class from a little over one-fifth to almost half. Since the Malays strongly preferred arts, this left the correlation of Malay enrollments with arts and non-Malay enrollments with science standing at +.27 in the 1969/70 school year, not a significant decline from the +.30 correlation for the 1960/61 school year (Table II).

TABLE II
Malays as a Proportion of First Year Enrollments at the University of Malaya*

	Malays in Arts[1]	Malays in Science[2]	Malays in the University	Correlation of Malays with Arts and non-Malays with Science
1960/61	32.0%	7.2%	21.2%	+ .30
1965/66	45.0%	11.5%	31.4%	+ .35
1969/70	53.0%	23.3%	44.6%	+ .27

*Adapted with minor corrections from the White Paper, TOWARDS NATIONAL HARMONY, January 23, 1971

1. Faculty of Arts and Faculty of Economics & Administration.
2. Science, Agriculture, Engineering, Premedical, Medicine.

Colonial Burma showed much the same pattern of development in ethnic apportionment between generalist and specialist services. As

the British moved out of the ICS and BCS posts, their replacements
were overwhelmingly Burman, drawn up from the large pool of Extra
Assistant Commissioners in the Provincial Civil Service or BCS, Class
II. Burmans also held the great majority of the lower grades in the
Police. But the Class I level remained almost totally British and
Eurasian until independence. Engineering and the Medical Service
were practically Indian preserves, while the Indians shared Post &
Telecommunications and the Railroad with the Eurasians.

   With independence, the Indian contribution to the civil service
contracted drastically, yet a general correlation of urban minorities
with technological organizational roles remained. By the 1960's,
however, the Revolutionary (Army) Government sought to get to the
root of the ethnic imbalance in technical fields by requiring Burmans
at the university to enroll in sciences while leaving the arts to the
ethnic minorities. Recently there has also been an attempt to advance
members of the peripheral minorities by a system of preferences in
education.

   How does our ethnic analysis of organizational roles hold for
the armed forces? Information is less available here, but what evidence
does exist confirms the expectations that follow from what we have
found on the civil side. First, let us be clear about dividing up the
armed forces into those with a more technological function and those
with a more political flavor. It seems obvious that where little sophisticated weaponry is involved the army would be less responsive to
technological requirements than the navy and the air force. Within
the army such specialized units as Signals or Engineers would be
more technologically concerned.

   The technological concerns of the navy and air force complement
their political irrelevance. In a military establishment devoted primarily to internal security they are too small a chunk of the armed manpower of the nation to be a force of political significance. Even with
the reduction in the role of Commonwealth forces in Malaysia during
the late 1960's and the introduction of more technically sophisticated
equipment, the Malaysian military has maintained a balance among
the services that kept the navy and air force together at about one-
seventh of the men regularly under arms, as shown in Table III. In
Burma, where the armed forces have been more seriously engaged
in internal security undertakings and in managing the economic and
political affairs of the country, the size of the navy and air force are
proportionately smaller, totalling some 12,500 to 13,500 compared to
the army's estimated 130,000.[9]

   The Malay martial tradition had been incorporated almost whole

TABLE III

Service Distribution of Malaysian Armed Forces

Year	Army	Navy	Air Force
1964-65*	19,000	2,100	?
1965-66*	25,000	2,100	1,500
1966-67	26,000	2,100	2,000
1967-68	27,600	3,000	3,600
1968-69	28,000	2,800	3,000
1969-70	38,750	3,000	3,000
1971-72	43,000	3,000	4,000

*Including Singapore

Source: The Institute for Strategic Studies, THE MILITARY BALANCE (London, 1964-69; 1971).

into the armed forces of British Malaya with the formation in 1932 of the Malay Regiment, a totally Malay unit. Non-Malay local forces were not introduced until some twenty years later during the Malayan Emergency, an insurrection in which the insurgents were drawn almost entirely from the Chinese segment of the nation, even though the cause was a class revolutionary one. At that time the government made a move toward ethnic balance in the armed forces by establishing a multi-racial Federation Regiment. It was to have 50 percent Chinese and 25 percent Indian and Eurasian troops, but enlistments from the non-Malay side were slow in coming. Today non-Malays are most heavily represented in the navy and the air force, with Chinese contributing over half the officer corps in the air arm because, it is said, of the lack of technically qualified Malays (Department of the Army [1972], Area Handbook for Malaysia and Singapore). The peripheral minorities are represented in the Sarawak Rangers from East Malaysia, a group recruited for what might be considered technological reasons—the need for good jungle trackers. Their use has not been confined to the jungles or to Borneo. In the total armed forces Malays accounted for 65.4 percent of the officer corps in 1969, according to official figures.[10] Some non-Malays are said to have reached high rank, but none of them hold line commands.

In colonial Burma, there were almost no Burmans in the Burma army (Furnivall 1948: 178-184); Von der Mehden 1970). This resulted more from a lack of interest and acceptability than from a lack of talent; prior to the final triumph of the British forces, the kingdom of Burma had maintained a fairly effective military force and several Burman units were indeed organized during World War I. The armed force deployed by the British was made up not only of Englishmen and Indians but also of Karens, Kachins, Chins, Shans and Arakanese—all organized on a "class company" basis. This recruitment of hill people for internal security forces was viewed by Burmese nationalists as politically motivated, the application of the "divide and rule" principle. The British rationale was more technological, the carry-over from India of the habit of recruiting the martial races from highland areas. In the late 1930s the government became aware of the need to recruit Burman troops, but by then it was too late. By August 1939, the Burma Defense Force included among its locally-recruited troops some 472 Burmans, less than one-eighth the total (Furnivall 1948: 183-4). The overwhelming Burman element in the postwar army came as successor to the Burma Independence Army, a totally Burman group and a highly-politicized one, that quite literally shot its way in.[11]

As in Malaysia, the subordinate, more technically oriented branches were the natural abode of most of those members of the urban minority groups who entered the armed forces. From its prewar inception the Burma Navy had a large input from the urban minorities, primarily because of high educational requirements.[12] Even after independence the air force was commanded in succession by a Karen, a Burman Christian, and an Anglo-Burman. In the course of the twenty-five years of multi-colored insurrection, there was a winnowing out of the urban minorities, particularly the Karens. In 1949 whole Karen battalions had gone underground and the Commander-in-Chief, Lieutenant-General Smith-Dun, himself a Karen, was retired from command. The army in independent Burma continues to draw heavily on Shans, Kachins, and other hill peoples, with the Chins playing a particularly loyal role (Chin forces were brought into Rangoon for the 1962 coup). But the main contribution of the peripheral minorities has been in the lower ranks. It is said that the overall proportion of non-Burmans in the armed forces has been in secular decline since 1962.

Thus, in two Southeast Asian countries, of the same colonial parentage, yet following different political and economic development strategies, there is a common pattern of ethnic segmentation in organizational roles within the military. This is particularly noteworthy since the political functions performed by military institutions in the two countries have been so different. The nucleus of today's Burma army was established in a political movement and since independence the military has twice intervened in politics, once as a caretaker regime and then as a revolutionary government which rules today. The Malaysian armed forces, however, are institutional successors to the British forces of pre- and post-independence days. When Malaysia had her major post-independence constitutional crisis it was the civil service rather than the military that intervened. This common pattern—in which the army draws its membership dispro-portionately from the majority ethnic group, while urban minorities are confined primarily to staff and specialist units within the army or to the navy and air force, with peripheral minorities occupying the lower levels of command in the army—developed as the ethnic major-ity displaced the British in the central, more politically important roles.

The pattern bids fair to continue for two reasons. One is that the political imperative—that the ethnic majority must control major political institutions—is linked so closely to the problem of national identity and the very survival of the nation. The other is that the technological imperative has considerable force but limited scope in these two countries. It is true that the channeling of ethnic segments into the arts or science streams of the educational-occupational system will persist, grounded as it is not only in surviving institutional structures but also quite significantly, in cultural differences in inter-ests, in values, and to some extent in aptitude patterns. The scope of the technological imperative will probably remain limited, however, since the likelihood of a significant magnification of the importance of technology and consequent shifting of service roles is very small within such internally preoccupied armed forces.

The twin terms, political imperative and technological impera-tive, have been used here as empirically derived concepts, convenient linguistic repositories for particular constellations of interacting social forces observed in our two cases. They will need much further refine-ment if they are to be used as tools for analysis in other social settings, of the dialectical influences shaping the linkage between ethnic seg-ments and military structures. A first step toward such refinement is to note the relationship of these concepts to others now current in social analysis. While there is no one-to-one correspondence, there are significant points of similarity between what I have called a technological imperative and what Daniel Bell (1973) refers to as the "economizing mode" in policymaking, and between my political im-perative and his "sociologizing mode." A further rough parallel would seem Mao's dynamic of "red" and "expert" orientations. The broad provenance of these conceptual referents—from post-industrial United States to contemporary China—suggests that there may be a wide variety of situations in which one could fruitfully analyze the tensions between optimum utilization of human resources and the politically-defined needs for particular rates (and types) of ethnic participation. In military institutions as in other public organizations in less developed countries, the outcome is reflected in the pattern of ethnic segmentation of organizational roles.

Notes

Acknowledgements: In revising this paper for publication, I am indebted for critical comments to Ann Gregory and Frank N. Trager.

1. The concept of a plural society originated in Southeast Asia where John S. Furnivall used it to explain social relations in a colonial setting in Furnivall, J.S. (1948: 303-312). The concept was refined and developed in a form applicable to both dependent and independent countries and linked more closely to political process in Smith, M.G. (1960) and Despres, L.A. (1967).

2. An excellent overall view of Burma's plural society is of course, Furnivall, J.S. (1948). This is applied to the post-independence period as well in Guyot, J.F. (1966) and Lissak, M. (1970). The more important urban minority is documented in Chakravarti, N.R. (1971) while the general situation of the peripheral minorities is analyzed in Connor, W. (1969) and in Leach, E.R. (1960).

For Malaysia, the general picture can be found in Freedman, M. (1960) with more recent developments noted in Guyot, J.F. (1969); Esman, M.J. (1972); Means, G.P. (1972); and Rabushka, A. (1973).

3. From the 1970 population and housing census figures on community groups as adapted by Rabushka, A. (1973: 21, 24).

4. From Second Malaysia Plan 1971-1975 (1971: 1).

5. Guyot, J.F. (1971: 67-84).

6. For an excellent general analysis of the generalist v. specialist argument in colonial and post-colonial administration see Braibanti, R. (1959: 258-304).

7. Interesting parallels to this line of reasoning might be found in the occupational survival rates of middle class engineers or doctors compared to lawyers following class-based revolutions. Hybrid solutions to the problem of political versus technical imperatives are the Soviet system of dual leadership in managing factories immediately after the revolution by means of a red manager in tandem with a bourgeois engineer, and the Chinese alternation over time between commands to be red and to be expert.

8. For the most extensive treatment see Tilman, R. (1964).

9. Institute of Strategic Studies (1969; 1971).

10. The National Operations Council (1969: 23)

11. Guyot, D. (1966: 55-65).

12. Tinker, H. (1967: 312-336).

INDONESIA: ARMED FORCES AND SOCIETY INTO THE 1980s

Nugroho Notosusanto

It has been a decade since the publication of Morris Janowitz's classic The Military in the Political Development of New Nations: An Essay in Comparative Analysis. *In his preface the author stated that "one of the purposes of comparative analysis is precisely to analyze societal change in such a fashion that the conclusions and hypothesis can in fact be assessed by unfolding events" (Janowitz, 1964). This paper hopes to assess Janowitz's generalizations by the unfolding events in Indonesia.*

Historical Background of the Indonesian Armed Forces

When the Dutch consolidated their colonial power in Indonesia at the beginning of the twentieth century after three hundred years of intermittent war, they all but destroyed the indigenous military institutions of the various Indonesian peoples. But they did, however, use Indonesians in their colonial forces, both as individual troops and in small auxiliary formations which were restricted to certain trusted units (such as the Legion of Mangkunegoro). The Dutch colonial army (the *Koninklijk Nederlands-Indische Leger—KNIL*) had Indonesian soldiers but only few Indonesian officers whose highest rank before World War II was major. They were trained at the Officers School of Meester Cornelis (now Jatinegara), a suburb of Jakarta, and at the Royal Military Academy in Breda, the Netherlands. After the German occupation of the Netherlands in May, 1940, the Dutch opened the Royal Military Academy of Bandung (Indonesia) and the Training Corps for Reserve Officers (*Corps Opleiding Reserve Officieren— CORO*), also in Bandung. These schools trained a handful of second generation Dutch-educated Indonesian officers who were to play an important role in the Indonesian Armed Forces. Among them were flight officers who later served in the air branch of the Dutch Army. A handful of Indonesian naval officers were also trained before German occupation at the Royal Institute of the Navy at Den Helder (the Netherlands). After the first year of their occupation during World War II, the Japanese gave basic military training to almost all young and not-so-young Indonesians. They also recruited soldier *auxiliaries* (*heiho*) who, in certain parts of the country, could reach the rank of subaltern officer, established the Volunteer Army for the Defense of the Fatherland (*Tentara Sukarela Pembela Tanah Air—Peta*) in Java and the Volunteer Army (*Bo-ei Giyugun*) in Sumatra. These volunteer armies were wholly officered by Indonesians, although with Japanese supervisors at their side. The Indonesian officers were ranked as battalion commanders, company commanders and platoon commanders and underwent a minimal training for two months, four months and six months, respectively.[1] It is obvious that Dutch military training was professionally more complete than that given by the Japanese, but it seems that the latter gave more in terms of combat leadership with a stress on "spirit" rather than materiel.

Two days after the Japanese surrender to the Allies, the Indonesians proclaimed their independence—on August 17, 1945. The demoralized Japanese troops were unable to prevent the Indonesians from taking over government offices in various parts of the country. But they did succeed in surprising the *Peta*-battalions and other armed units by disarming and disbanding them before they realized what was happening. Only police units were not disarmed, perhaps because the Japanese adhered to the Western principle of a non-combatant police force, which should remain intact even if the army surrenders or withdraws from occupied territories. But the Indonesian police evidently were not loyal to that principle and used their arms to support the struggle to maintain independence.

The government of the newly established Republic of Indonesia decided to adopt a low posture in order to avoid in any way offending the Allied troops, which were about to land. They did so even to the extent of not immediately forming a national army. Instead they formed local militia units called the People's Security Body (*Badan Keamanan Rakyat—BKR*)—to maintain law and order. This policy was not popular among the youth, who were caught by a revolutionary fervour and were burning for a show of force to establish the sovereignty of the Republic vis-a-vis the Japanese, then acting as agents of the Allies charged with maintaining the *status quo* (i.e. no Indonesian independence).

A large segment of the youth—most of them ex-members of the *Peta*, *heiho* and para-military organizations during the Japanese occupation—entered the local *BKR*'s and made the best of it by using it as a "vehicle for the Struggle." Their leaders were well educated and certainly highly motivated. They wrested arms from the Japanese, often with appalling losses, and proceeded to seize official buildings and centres of communications in order to establish the authority of the Republic. Very loosely organized, with no central headquarters and no military ranks and hierarchy, they acted largely on their own, without orders from the Central Government. (In fact, the Central Government was not consolidated as yet and was not in the position to give specific orders). The *BKR*'s were coordinated by the local National Committees, comprising the local socio-political forces, which included themselves. Soon they developed a freedom fighters ethos, considering themselves vanguards of the Revolution and guardians of the Republic.

Other young people were not happy with the *BKR*'s considering them too "stuffy," and formed "struggle organizations," a cross between political clubs and armed bands. It should not be surprising that the members of these organizations also considered themselves freedom fighters.

After six weeks of independence, the Government realized it was impossible to be independent with no apparatus of power, especially when threatened by outside forces. So, on October 5th, 1945, the Government created an official army called the People's Security Army. Barely a week earlier the Government appointed a Chief of the National Police, thereby uniting the various police units into one organization.

The man entrusted with the task of organizing the Army was an Indonesian retired major of the *KNIL*, Oerip Soemohardjo, who was assisted by the group of younger generation, Dutch educated officers (graduates of the Royal Military Academy and *CORO* of Bandung) in forming the General Headquarters of the Army. In fact, however, the Army was formed from below rather than from above. The local *BKR*'s were pronounced the local units of the Army and thus commanders and members assumed military ranks. Until then command experience among Indonesians had never been higher than battalion level; afterward the most respected among the local Army leaders formed regiments and even divisions. Realizing that Army Headquarters would never function effectively without the support of the local commanders, Oerip Soemohardjo and his colleagues called an all-Army Conference to elect a commander-in-chief and a chief of staff. Colonel Soedirman, an ex-*Peta* battalion commander who organized a regiment in his region and soon thereafter became divisional commander, was elected Commander-in-Chief of the Military Forces of the Republic, while Oerip Soemohardjo was re-elected Chief of Staff. Both then received official appointments and were duly sworn in by the President. Soedirman's prestige was due to his negotiating and organizational skill and his tactical talent. He succeeded in obtaining arms from the local Japanese in return for a guarantee of their personal safety. He distributed the arms among the ex-*Peta* units and put them under his command. Later he achieved fame by pushing back the British forces in the Battle of Ambarawa.

Officers and men of the Army whether ex-*Peta*, ex-*heiho*, ex-*KNIL* or fresh from school were all young men, most of them in their early twenties or late teens. So the Army became representative of an entire age-group, later known as the *Generation of 45*. The Police officers were also mostly younger men, recruited during the Japanese occupation. They too considered themselves freedom-fighters. It has already been noted that the young police had used their arms not to maintain the *pax nipponica* on orders of the Allies, but to establish the authority of the new Republic of Indonesia against the Japanese military administration's attempt to maintain the *status quo*.

Using Janowitz's classification of armed forces in new nations, it is clear that the Indonesian Armed Forces belong to the armed forces established during the struggle for national liberation.[2] It is exactly this origin which has become the basis of the "ideology" of the Indonesian Armed Forces. The Armed Forces consider themselves the "embodiment of the armed fighting People"[3] and hence "a people's army, a national army and an army of freedom fighters."

Meanwhile the "struggle organizations" were still operating, creating a troublesome dualism between them and the (regular) Army of the Republic. After two years of difficulties, the struggle organizations were fused into the regular army which, for psychological reasons, changed its name to the Indonesian National Army (*Tentara Nasional Indonesia—TNI*). Since that moment in June, 1947, the *TNI* has been considered the "vehicle of armed struggle" of the Generation of 45. From time to time, however, desintegrative tendencies were evident within the Armed Forces when former members of the struggle organizations joined their associates in certain political parties in a rebellion against the Government, as, for example, in the Communist Rebellion of 1948 at Madiun and the extremist Moslem Rebellion of 1949.

The Internal Organization
of the Indonesian Armed Forces

The Indonesian Armed Forces consist of the Military Forces (also known by its historical name *Tentara Nasional Indonesia,* abbreviated *TNI*), comprising ground force, navy and air force on the one hand and the National Police on thè other. The Military Forces, or *TNI*, are organized into main commands, consisting of two kinds of command—territorial and operational.[4]

Indonesian territory is divided into four defense area commands: the 1st Defense Area Command comprises Sumatra and West Kalimantan (West Borneo); the 2nd Defense Area Command comprises Java, Bali and Nusatenggara (Lesser Sundas); the 3rd Defense Area Command comprises Sulawesi (Celebes) and East and South Kalimantan (East and South Borneo); the 4th Defense Area Command comprises the Moluccas and Irian Java. Each defense area command consists of several military regional commands, naval regional commands and air force regional commands. The army regional commands are further divided into military zone commands which are sub-divided into military district commands and these into military sub-district commands, down to the village level, where non-commissioned officers in charge of territorial affairs advise the village heads on local security problems.

The main operational commands are the National Strategic Command, which is in peace time a skeleton organization, and the National Air Defense Command. In time of war, the National Strategic Command can be activated fully to handle the armed forces' striking force consisting of the infantry, cavalry and paratroop brigades of the Army Strategic Reserve as well as certain units of the Navy and Air Force.

The main commands of the Armed Forces use the personnel and materiel managed by the services. The services themselves no longer have operational responsibilities other than for the Police. The National Police have several police regions in every province, divided into police zones, which in their turn are divided into police districts, and further into police sub-districts, and finally into police sectors.

Army troops are divided into mobile battalions—organized into the brigades of the Army Strategic Reserve but managed by the several big regional commands in peace time—and the territorial battalions, which are distributed among the regional and zone commands. Usually the older enlisted men are put in the territorial battalions where their duties are physically less exacting than in the mobile battalions but where their experience in social intercourse with the people is more needed in the framework of "territorial management."

The Minister of Defense and Security is also Commander of the Armed Forces and the highest authority on military as well as sociopolitical activities of all services. Directly under him are the service chiefs of staff (Army, Navy and Air Force) and the Chief of the National Police. Also under him are the commanders of the four defense area commands and the other main commands. The Minister is assisted by the Staff of Defense and Security coordinated by the Deputy Commander of the Armed Forces. The Staff is divided into three branches: the Operational Staff, the Administrative Staff and the Staff for Functional Affairs; each is headed by a chief of staff. The Staff for Functional Affairs is uniquely Indonesian and is specifically set up to assist the Minister in managing the socio-political part of the Dual Function of the Indonesian Armed Forces. Every member of the Armed Forces serving outside the Defense and Security establishment is coordinated and managed by this Staff. Each defense area command has a Council for Functional Affairs chaired by the Commander himself. This Council coordinates and manages the members of the Armed Forces serving in a non-military capacity within the boundaries of the particular defense area command. In this way inter-service rivalry is no longer possible, in the center as well as in the various regions.

Analyzing the skill structure of the Indonesian military, we can say that the categories of heroic leader and military manager[5] are applicable. The type military technologist, however, has not developed enough to be a separate class. It should be stated here that military managers are the products of the 23 years since the end of the War of Independence. During this period the elite nucleus of each service consists of people having the qualifications of both the heroic leader and the military manager. But many serving outside the defense and security establishment only have the qualifications of military managers. Examples include secretary generals, director generals, directors at the various non-military departments of government, as well as military serving in the field of industry or banking.

It should be borne in mind, however, that the present elite cadre and elite nucleus of the Indonesian Armed Forces still consist of the Generation of 45, who fought in the revolutionary War of Independence of 1945-1949, although in recent years members of the younger generation have begun to enter the elite cadre, especially in the Air Force. Though too young to have taken part in the War of Independence, they still had the opportunity to participate in the dozen or so internal security operations conducted by the Armed Forces against the various rebellions in the country. This generation could be called the "interim generation," because they are between the Generation of 45 and the truly new generation assuming officer commands after the country had been generally pacified.

The Generation of 45 could be divided into three *sub-generations* based on their previous career or military educational background. The first sub-generation are those who, like Oerip Soemohardjo and the older Police leaders, had already had a long career in the colonial forces. To this sub-generation also belong those who had a career during the Dutch pre-World War II Colonial Period and who were recruited into the *Peta* Army as battalion commanders. (They were selected by the Japanese because of their pre-War standing in Society, as government officials or as leaders of the Nationalist Movement.) Most of these people were in their late thirties or in their forties. Because of their experience in "normal" circumstances and their age, they were on the whole less well-adjusted to the requirements of the turbulent, revolutionary times in comparison with the second sub-generation, which became the nucleus of the Generation of 45. The second sub-generation consists of graduates or ex-cadets of the Royal Dutch Military Academy, or the *CORO*, who had, if any, only a very short career in the *KNIL*. To this second sub-generation also belong the platoon commanders of the *Peta* and part of the company commanders. They were still at school or had very brief careers as civil servants at the end of the Dutch period and the beginning of the Japanese occupation, and were trained at the *Peta* officers training corps in Bogor. We should also include those who as young men were trained by the Dutch in their Naval Officer School or who had a training as volunteer pilots of the Military Air Service; and further, those trained by the Japanese at the several nautical schools and academies. Professionally the least equipped of the three sub-generations, they became mentally the best adapted to lead the armed struggle of the Indonesian revolution and are at present at the very top of the hierarchy in the Armed Forces and as in the Republic. To the third sub-generation belong graduates of the Indonesian national military academies or officers' schools, opened after the birth of the Indonesian Military Forces during the War of Independence.

Today the entire first sub-generation has retired. The elite nucleus consists of the second sub-generation, with some members of the third sub-generation entering. In the Air Force an officer from the third sub-generation has already become service chief of staff.

Considering the "total careers" of Indonesian officers of the Generation of 45 (i.e. their careers including the period before they became officers of the Armed Forces of the Republic of Indonesia), we would conclude that they don't fit neatly into the two types of military careers, namely, the prescribed versus the adaptive careers.[6] Their total career seems to be very adaptive indeed. Perhaps we could start using the two categories with the third sub-generation, but we might need more time to discern the pattern. The "additional and unusual experiences"[7] which make up the adaptive career of Indonesian officers would be a posting or a course abroad or a position in a delegation meeting foreign parties, as well as missions in representative bodies. It is also known that many officers who had been members of the teaching staff of the Army Staff and Command School in Bandung during its formative years (the 1960s) acquired a certain insight in socio-political affairs.

In trying to discern the *social profile* of the Indonesian military elite, we have to remember the differences in background of the military generations and sub-generations. The members of the Generation of 45, especially those of the leading second sub-generation certainly have one thing in common, that is their motivation in entering the Armed Forces. Theirs was not a "careerist" motivation but rather an "ideological" one. Their main drive was to participate actively in the physical struggle to defend Independence, to establish and uphold the authority of the Republic of Indonesia, especially against foreign encroachments. They realized that in order to succeed they have to organize themselves. At first they had two kinds of organization, an official one (the *BKR* and later the Army) and the "struggle organizations." Later the two organizations fused into the *TNI.*

The American categories of upper, middle and lower classes might well be used within an Indonesian context, but the terms should be defined more specifically in order to avoid misconceptions. We can use the term "upper class" to denote direct descendants of the indigenous Indonesian rulers, the sultans and susuhunans, and other princes. The term "middle class" can be used to designate the stratum which in the largest part of the nation is called *priyayi*, i.e. the bureaucratic group and the business group at the end of the Dutch colonial period and during the Japanese occupation. The "lower class" includes peasants, street and market vendors, and manual laborers. A temporary survey undertaken by the Center for Armed Forces History in 1973 revealed that the elite nucleus of the Indonesian Armed Forces since 1945 has tended to come from the middle class, particularly from the lower middle class (the petty *priyayi* and their equals). They are sons of district heads, clerks (government as well as sugar factory), elementary school teachers, small shop (*warung*) owners, etc. This survey still pertains only to the Generation of 1945.

Contrary to Janowitz's conclusion that army officers in the new nations have to strive to establish the image of the heroic fighter and of honor in combat,[8] Indonesian officers have to strive to establish the image of a military manager to get into the highest positions or to reach the rank of general officer. This is because the officers of the Generation of 45 generally already have the image of a heroic fighter.

The term "professional" and "political ideology" should be used with a certain reserve in connection with the Indonesian Armed Forces in its present stage of development. There are two reasons. First, as an army of national liberation 28 years old, the Indonesian Armed Forces have not extensively developed professionalism and a professional tradition. And many of its present members did not plan to pursue a professional military career when they joined the Army. Second, even today it is the deliberate policy of the Armed Forces leadership to avoid becoming a professional armed forces in the Western sense. The professed ideal is that of a "people's army, national army and freedom fighters' army." That is why the official term "values" is more useful than the term "ideology."

The official manual on the values of the Indonesian Armed Forces *Dharma Pusaka 45* issued in November, 1972, stresses the identity of the *TNI* as an army of freedom fighters (*tentara pejuang*). The essence of being a freedom fighters' army is "identify itself with the nation and the state and saving it in times of crisis." The professed position of the Indonesian Armed Forces is to be an integrating force in society by taking steps and promoting policies which are in the interest of the whole people and not only in the interest of one group, including the Armed Forces. The position of an integrating force is being expressed by the dual stabilizing and "dynamizing" role. Stabilizing and "dynamizing" is seen in the background of the efforts to strengthen national integration by preventing instability and social conflict caused by inter-ethnic, inter-religious or inter-regional strife, as well as by pushing the necessary reforms or breaking through impasses.[9]

Politically, a centrist position is taken: promoting democracy based on the Pancasila goes against Western type "liberalism" as well as against communism. Operations conducted against extremist rebellions are cited as an illustration, namely: against the extremist Darul Islam, against the separatist movements of the *APRA* (Military Forces of the Just King), against the "Republic of the South Moluccas," the movement of the ex-members of the Dutch Colonial Army in South Sulawesi, the great rebellion of Sumatra and Sulawesi, as well as the two communist uprisings.

The 28-year history of the Indonesian Armed Forces can be viewed as a lengthy struggle for integration. The internal cleavages within and between the services are caused by two different factors, the objective factors inherent in the process of formation of the Armed Forces and the subjective factors originating from outside the military. The objective factors lay in the very origins of the Armed Forces which were a result of more or less spontaneous action of individuals or groups of individuals. Differences in background, between Dutch military educated, Japanese military educated and non military educated, were not serious causes for cleavage. Differences in regional, religious and ethnic backgrounds have never been a serious problem. From the beginning Christians could occupy top positions in the Armed Forces, notwithstanding the fact that 90 percent of all Indonesians are Muslims. It is hardly noticed that the second Chief of Staff of the Armed Forces and the present Minister of Defense/Commander of the Armed Forces are both Christians. More serious were the differences in outlook between the ex-*BKR* people and the ex-struggle organization people, and among the ex-struggle organization people themselves. (Ex-members of the *Pesindo* or Socialist Youth were very hostile against the *Hizbullah* or Moslem Youth, for instance.)

This condition was intensified by the subjective factors residing in the various political parties, political groups or politicians who attempted to have and increase their backing within the Armed Forces. They were continuously trying to promote their "faction" within the *TNI* by setting up the services against each other as well as by trying to use individuals of the services. Where formerly all three services (Army, Navy and Air Force) were under the C-in-C of the Military Forces, or *TNI*; in the period after the War of Independence (1945-1949), the politicans were able to abolish the position of C-in-C and Chief of Staff of the Military Forces. Each service then had its own Chief of Staff, a post which was later changed into a service commander.

For the next fifteen years the battle was fought between the "integrationists" within the Armed Forces and the politicians trying to apply a policy of "divide and rule" within and between the services. In 1963 the Police was officially proclaimed the fourth service of the Armed Forces, but it also had a Commander of the Police Force. In 1962 a Staff of the Armed Forces was established under a Chief of Staff of the Armed Forces, but with very limited administrative responsibilities. Each service commander reported directly to the then President Sukarno in his capacity as Supreme Commander of the Armed Forces, who used his position to strengthen his personal control within the Armed Forces.

It was only after the abortive *coup* of the Indonesian Communist Party in October, 1965, that the Indonesian Armed Forces were able to affect a real integration. These attempts at politicising the Armed Forces, which started very early during the War of Independence and continued under the efforts of the special bureau of the Communist Party of Indonesia to recruit cadres and activists from among the military in the fifties and sixties, were the main cause for the cleavages within the military. As soon as the subjective factors ceased working, the efforts to achieve integration met with more success. The cohesion within the Armed Forces was never stronger than it is today.

In addition to the absence now of strong external efforts to politicize the Armed Forces, the causes for cohesion are: (1) success in performing the Dual Function (continuous success in military operations and leading role in national life); (2) improved management (orderly career management [tour of duty, tour of area, promotions,] and integrated education [armed forces academy, armed forces staff and command School]); and (3) unified organizational structure.

Armed Forces and Society

The role of the Indonesian Armed Forces in society is officially formulated under the name of the *Dual Function.* As we have seen in its historical background, the Armed Forces had its origins in the youthful freedom fighters of 1945, both in the *BKR* and in the struggle organizations. Out of the ethos of being a freedom fighter first and a (professional) soldier second has come the concept of the Dual Function, namely, the function of freedom fighter, later broadened into the function of socio-political force, and the function of (professional) soldier, later broadened into the defense and security function or military function. The Indonesia military's foremost interest is to increase national resilience and the way to accomplish this is through national development or modernization. National resilience is the condition necessary to achieve the National Aim as formulated in the Preamble of the 1945 Constitution: ". . . to improve general welfare, to promote intellectuality in national life and to participate in the efforts to realize a world order based on independence, eternal peace and social justice."

The socio-political function of the Armed Forces is directed towards intensifying the acceleration of national development with its objectives in the ideological, economic, spiritual/religious and socio-cultural fields.[10] The socio-political functions is performed through *karyawan* (functionals or trustees, i.e. members of the Armed Forces serving outside the Department of Defense and Security, including the Armed Forces). The "functionals" or trustees are put in legislative as well as executive bodies as the need arises. The Armed Forces do not participate in elections (because that would certainly cause dissension within its ranks), but get a certain number of seats in the representative bodies. "Functionals" also serve in executive agencies as ministers, provincial governors, managers of state firms and banks, etc. Contrary to previous practice, the "functionals" are now chosen carefully according to their abilities. Generally as well as particular policy is formulated at all levels throughout the various commands. In practice, discussions about policy are being conducted continuously in the various councils and staffs, while policy can be proposed from above as well as from below. But the ultimate decision is made by the Minister of Defense/Commander of the Armed Forces for the whole, and by the various commanders for each echelon.

The means to perform the socio-political function, especially to perform "social mobilization" to support the goals of national development, is a grouping of all functional groups called the *golongan karya* (meaning "functional groups"). The *golongan karya* or *golkar* achieved an enormous victory. There was some controversy in the international press about campaigning, but there was a general impression that the elections themselves were held according to the principles of a universal, free and secret ballot.

The close partners of the military in the present *New Order* government under president Suharto are the technocrats. They are all members of the same generation as the military elite and have the same commitment to national development and modernization. Of the 18 ministers in the present cabinet, 13 are civilians (9 university professors), 3 military and 2 party leaders.

Not all members of the intelligentsia are associated with the *golkar,* however, many of them remain outside and feel free to express their opinion and frequently their dissatisfaction or criticism through petitions or demonstrations or through the press. The press is free to criticise the government, including the Armed Forces. Since the latest election of 1971 there have been no shutdowns of newspapers nor has there been press censorship. The only actions taken have been against certain newspapers or magazines and were connected with libel and obscenity, subsequently coming before the courts.

The military are particularly wary of interreligious and inter-regional strife and of ethnic tensions (including hostility towards the Chinese minority). But the motto is "persuasion, not coercion." Only in cases of open violence will force be used as it is elsewhere in the world. In fact, the style of government and life nowadays can be called more relaxed than in most neighboring countries. Contrary to the policy of the previous government under President Sukarno, foreign relations are motivated by the desire to make as many friends as possible rather than undertake "confrontations." Relations with the Soviet Bloc are relatively good; only with the People's Republic of China are relations still frozen—since the abortive coup attempt of the Communist Party in October, 1965. Only when stability is threatened does the military take a tough stand, because it is their conviction that stability is the only key to success in national development for the sake of national prosperity and social justice.

In terms of Janowitz's categories of civil-military relations in new countries, the Indonesian case belongs to the fourth category— civil-military coalition. The military serves as an active political bloc in its support of civilian parties and other bureaucratic power groups.[11] But the pattern is not exactly equivalent to those existing in other countries where the civil-military coalition model prevails, for example in Jordan, Iran, (both are kingdoms) or Turkey. This is due primarily to differences in historical background.

Perspectives into the 1980s

For the past three or four years the leadership of the Indonesian Armed Forces has been preoccupied with the problem of succession of generations. They calculated that in the 1980s the leadership of the Armed Forces would be in the hands of the younger generation, while the "Generation of 45" would by then be retired. They have been pondering the problem of how to ensure a continuity in policy based on the continuity of the Dual Function after the younger generation has taken over. They know, of course, that changing conditions and changing situations would necessarily change both outlook and policies, but they hope that at least the basic ideas they have stood for would continue to be cherished by the younger generation.

In an attempt to ascertain what has been conceived as a transfer of values, the Third Army Seminar was held in early 1972 at the Army Staff and Command School in Bandung. The initiative was taken by the School because the staff realized that more than half the class of 1972 consisted of officers of the younger generation, that is officers who had attended the newly reopened Military Academy in 1957 and after. (The Military Academy was discontinued following the capture of the revolutionary capital of Yogyakarta in 1948 and remained closed for the next nine years.) And the staff sensed that differences in perception and attitude between the older and the younger generations were becoming pronounced; they therefore concluded that the time had come for an open dialogue between the generations about what values should be transferred. The plan was approved by the Army leadership and was even taken over by the Minister of Defense and Security, although the conduct of the Seminar remained in the hands of the School.

The Seminar became a much discussed and much publicized event and was attended by almost everybody in the Armed Forces elite from President Suharto (then Minister of Defense and Security) down to the Military regional commanders. The main papers were prepared by the staff, with the assistance of university professors, who traditionally have taught at the school. Quite a few talks and additional papers were given by members of the elite, including President Suharto. Many technocrat ministers of the Cabinet—formerly university professors lecturing at the School—were also present, addressing the Seminar on the Socio-political Function of the Armed Forces in connection with their particular field.

After three days (and nights) of intensive discussions, during which the officers of the new generation (mostly majors) participated wholeheartedly and fully, a final formulation was reached which reflected not only what the older generation wanted to transfer as an "inheritance" but also what the younger generation was prepared to accept as an inheritance. Several items were deleted and others reworded, but a consensus was reached. It was then clear to old and young within the Armed Forces what paths should be followed in the coming years and which values were considered sufficiently desirable to be transferred and continued.

At the end of the year The Minister of Defense and Security ratified the document as an Armed Forces manual called *Dharma Pusaka 45* (The heritage of good deeds of 1945). The manual not only presents what values are to be transferred but also the way in which it should be done. It is the task of the present generation to transfer the *values of 45* and the *TNI values of 45* through correct examples, through education and through communication. Therefore, deliberate steps have been taken by the present leadership of the Armed Forces to maintain maximum continuity in the years to come, beginning in the 1980s. The management of these efforts has been entrusted to the Chairman of J-3 (Personnel) with the assistance of two staff organs of the Armed Forces at the Department of Defense and Security, specifically, the Centre for Mental Direction and the Centre for Armed Forces History.

The present well-integrated organizational structure of the Armed Forces will be maintained and improved, and it is to be expected that the infant diseases of the Armed Forces have been completely overcome. The cleavages of the older generation have been reduced to a negligible minimum, while the younger generation has a more common background in education, professional training and experience and a well-defined doctrine. There are no longer outside forces in a position to create dissension and disunity within the services. With the well-integrated mission-type organization now in existence, no inter-service rivalry can be brought to the fore.

The only factor which could create problems for the Armed Forces would be a setback in the economic field caused by a too rapid population increase, creating serious unemployment and perhaps unforeseen circumstances which would cause social unrest endangering the stability of the country. Such unrest would compel the Armed Forces to use force, which in turn would create "civil-military frictions." But if the present positive trend in economic development continues, the Armed Forces can relinquish more and more of its involvement in non-military affairs and need only guard the really strategic points in the administration of the country. However, it is clear that the Armed Forces will never completely abandon what they perceive to be their responsibility towards the People, namely, to be active in the total life of Indonesian society as an integrating, stabilizing and dynamizing force, ensuring that the National Aim will be realized in the near future.

Notes

1. Notosusanto (1971).
2. Notosusanto (1971: 13).
3. Indonesia, Staf Pertahanan-Keamanan (1967:17).
4. The latest structure is based on Presidential Decision Number 79 of 1969.
5. Janowitz (1964: 41).
6. Janowitz (1964: 45).

7. Janowitz (1964: 46).
8. Janowitz (1964: 56).
9. Indonesia, Departemen Pertahanan-Keamanan (1972: 11-12).
10. Indonesia, Departemen Pertahanan-Keamanan (1967: 99-114).
11. Indonesia, Departemen Pertahanan-Keamanan (1967: 5-7).

THE SOCIAL BASES FOR MILITARY
INTERVENTION IN THE MIDDLE EAST

Fuad I. Khuri and Gerald Obermeyer

"Long live the army, long live the people, long live fulān" (i.e. the officer in power) is a slogan that often punctuates military take-over in the Arab World.[1] The chanting crowds may not all be partisans, but they all hope and expect the military experience to be transferred to other institutions and organizations in the society. These hopes and expectations find expression in a variety of actions, measures and policies, which are intended to either establish legitimacy for military rule or build up the image of the military as a model of development. The military in the Middle East is not only a profession, but also a model of development and a microcosm of the state.[2] This triple character of the military, symbolically summed up by phrases such as "the people's army," "the army for and of the people," "the lasting unity between the army and the people," "the army is the people," and other similar expressions—results not so much from historical or cultural experiences as from the strategy of social change.[3]

The ascent of the military to power is not a uniform experience—it changes with time and social circumstances. Therefore, any comprehensive understanding of the role of the military in politics requires an account of the changing structure of the military, the social bases for recruitment, and a comparative analysis of the military vis-a-vis civilian organizations in society. The focus of analysis should be upon the military as a social process rather than upon the simple power politics of individual coups, attempted coups or counter coups. Individual coups may or may not alter the historic character of military intervention.

The Changing Structure of the Military:
A Historical Sketch

It is not the intention here to discuss the effects of new technology on military tactics and the organizational aspects of war that result therefrom. Instead, we shall concentrate on the social links that tie the military to society and the changing character of these links as the military and society change. We mean by military that segment of society which is organized for war, even though it may perform other peacetime activities. From a structural point of view the military history in the Arab World can be divided into six periods: (1) the classical period which began with the rise of Islam and ended with the downfall of the 'Umayyad dynasty; (2) the florescent period, which continued on until the rise of the Mamlūk and later the Ottoman empires; (3) the imperial period, which extended into the middle of the nineteenth century and was characterized by the bureaucratization of the military; (4) the reformational period, which began with the Ottoman reforms (al-tanzimāt) of the nineteenth century and ended with the downfall of the Empire at the end of First World War; (5) the formative period under the colonial administration which continued in one form or another through the Second World War; and (6) the developmental period, which began after the achievement of national independence and has continued until the present day.

These periods are not chronologically rigid; they overlap, intervene, and interpenetrate. In this evolutionary attempt, we shall necessarily forsake the details of history and concentrate instead on the structural qualities of the military organization, irrespective of the ethnic identity of the ruling regimes. The imperial era, for example, included peoples of various ethnic backgrounds (Byzantines, Mamlūks and Ottomans) but is lumped in one category because the military organization of these conquest groups was based more or less on the same unity—the garrison. The focus is upon the processes and structural regularities of the military organization in history, rather than the sequence of events in history. This structural analysis of history is meant to demonstrate a point and by no means claims to be a complete explanation.

A major political achievement of Islam was the unity it brought to the otherwise quarreling tribal factions in Arabia. Islam is a combination of faith and derived law; its effects on organization, military or otherwise, stem as much from the structure of the society itself as from its direct teachings. In a society split by tribal factions deriving legitimacy from various and separate myths of origin of descent, monotheistic religion—which derives legitimacy from a singular faith—tends to cut across tribal affiliations and ideologies without necessarily destroying tribal allegiances (Hurewitz 1969: 232). In fact, the early Muslims took advantage of the military-like structural characteristics of the Arabian tribes in order to disseminate the teachings of Islam and expand its conquests. The expansion of Islamic conquests into Syria, Iraq, Persia and North Africa, during the reigns of the Orthodox Caliphs and the 'Umayyads, was carried out largely by tribally organized military action. The Arab Muslim troops were divided into corps consisting of several tribes or sections of tribes (Hell, n.d.). Combat units were not uniform in size; they were composed of sections of tribes under a prince agreed upon by the tribesmen (Hindi, 1964: 13-14). The maneuvers of combat units in battle were coordinated by a general commander (qā'id) delegated by the Caliph. Military camps in the occupied land were composed of various tribes. Basra (a city in Southern Iraq) region, for example, was divided between the 'Azed, Tamīm, Bakir, 'abd-Qaīs, and al-Aīiyya tribes.

These "garrison towns" ('amṣār), in fact, were sedentarized models of the tribal segmentary system; quarters of the city were allotted to tribal segments in both Kufa and Basra. The Caliphate was by no means a center of war operations—this was left to the discretion of individual commanders in the battlefield. The Caliphate had two main functions: coordination of war activities and the redistribution of the booty. The first was accomplished by developing a very intricate system of communication between the commanders in the battlefield and the Caliph in power; the second by requesting victorious troops to share the loot with others, or by imposing a poll-tax (jizya) on the conquered peoples who chose to remain faithful to their non-Islamic beliefs. The wealth which found its way to the Caliph's treasury was reallocated through various channels to the "believers" in order to support war operations or to keep order between tribes.[4] Recruitment to combat units was carried out by individual tribes or sections of tribes according to local custom. All men capable of carrying arms were expected to take part in war. There were no legal procedures that forced them to do so; war was a moral duty enforced by tribal ethics (Hindi, 1964: 192-193; ᶜAmmāsh, 1967: 32-33). Discipline was enforced by making each tribal segment responsible for the conduct of its members. The diwan (the council presided over by the Caliph) was a tribal as well as a pay roll roster.

The role of Arabian tribes in military action began to dwindle sharply at the downfall of the 'Umayyad dynasty of Damascus around the middle of the eighth century (ᶜAmmāsh, 1967: 33-34). New political forces began to emerge. The settlement of tribes in the occupied territories, the expansion of Arab conquests to include peoples of various ethnic origins, the growing complexities of government, the continuous struggle for power between Arab claimants to the Caliphate, and the gradual bureaucratization of government—

these factors all contributed to change the structure of the military. With the beginning of the Abbasid dynasty in Iraq around the middle of the eighth century, non-Arab Muslims, mostly Persians and Turks—but later on Tartars and Kurds—came gradually to assume control of the government machine including military operations. The Caliphate changed from a compromise institution militarily reliant upon independent Arabian tribes (CAmmāsh, 1967: 32-34) to a moral office in the name of which conquests were undertaken by peoples of non-Arab origin. The chief governmental powers were concentrated in the hands of the vizier or the sultan of Persian, Turkish, Tartar, or Kurdish origin who had the authority to appoint or depose other officials including military officers and sometimes the Caliph himself.[5] The person invested with the vizierate or *sultānate* would naturally tend to bestow offices on partisans belonging to the same ethnic origin as the vizier or *sultān* himself.

This florescent period witnessed the rise and fall of many dynasties of different ethnic backgrounds: the Abbāsids of Iraq and the Fatimids of Egypt (909-1171) who were Arab; the Persian Buwayhids (945-1055); the Saljūqs (1055-1258) who were Turkish; the Tartar Mongols (1055-1258); and the 'Ayyūbids (1169-1250) who were Kurdish. The period is also characterized by the intermittent rise and fall of several independent states of Persian, Turkish or Arab origins.[6] Thus, the most notable feature of the military organization of this period was its ethnic and structural complexity. Three types of organization can be distinguished: the clan-based military organization of the Saljūqs and the Mongols; the dual structure of the military, which included professionals (Caskar) and volunteers (*jund*) and was most pronounced during the early part of the CAbbāsid, Fāṭimid and the 'Ayyūbid dynasties; and the fief system of military power and organization that spread with the decline of the authority of the capital city, particularly during the latter part of the CAbbāsid dynasty.

From a structural point of view, the uniqueness of the military organization during this period is not to be found in the clan-based military organization of the Saljūqs or the Mongols or in the rise of the military fiefs established around a ruling house or chief, but rather in the dualistic character of the army made up of professionals and volunteers. The professional soldiers were kept on a permanent footing and paid out of the state treasury (*bait al-mal*), but the volunteers were not entered on the register (*diwan*) and received no fixed pay. Throughout the florescent period professional soldiers were recruited from non-partisan groups (non-partisan to the

Caliphate) who were Muslims of non-Arab origin. They were responsible for the defense of the Empire, the expansion of its territories,
and the maintenance of the regime in power. The local Arab communities, who were partisans to one claimant or another, were
excluded from permanent military service. In general, the wars these
Muslim, non-Arab professional soldiers fought against other Muslims
outnumbered by far the wars they fought against the infidels. The
wars fought against the infidels, who in those days were the Crusaders
and the Byzantines, were considered to be *jihad* (holy wars) and
therefore had a greater appeal to the common man in the Muslim
world. In *jihad,* the professional soldiers acted as the spearhead of
the army, assisted and backed up by volunteers drawn from the
neighboring areas of the battlefield. For example, the army of
Ṣalāḥ al-Dīn al-Ayyūbī (who is known in Arab history as the main
defender of the Muslim faith against the Crusaders), was composed
of a professional core (*ᶜaskar*) and volunteers (*jund*). The professional core in his permanent service was composed basically of
three groups: the Nurīya, the 'Assadīya, and the Ṣalāḥiya. Nevertheless, every war al-Ayyūbī fought against the Crusaders drew to
his army "multitudes of volunteers" who took part in the battle
and retreated to their villages afterwards (Saᶜdāwī, 1965: 13-14).

This dualistic character of the military, *ᶜaskar* and *jund* was
gradually replaced by the garrison as the basic unit of military
organization in the imperial period. The garrison which came to
symbolize the authority of the imperial power was best developed
under the Ottomans particularly between the early part of the sixteenth and the nineteenth century. It evolved from Byzantine
(which included Crusader) and Mamlūk prototypes and was not
exclusively Ottoman. The garrison represents an early attempt at
military socialization. In the garrison troops were trained, disciplined, indoctrinated, and taught the arts of war, politics, rebellion
and intrigue. Unlike the tribally-based army of the classical
period or that of the semi-bureaucratized professional core and the
non-bureaucratized volunteers of the florescent period, the garrison
was an integral part of a formal bureaucracy controlled by the
Sulṭānate, the highest focus of authority in the Empire. Enlisted
soldiers received regular pay; loot and booty were not regular
rewards for military success.[7]

In the Arab territories, the Ottoman garrison struck no social
links with the communities in which it operated since it was composed of Turkish officers and soldiers (Zein, 1968: 35) and assigned
to the Ottoman *wāli* who was appointed by the Sulṭān in Istanbul.

The Janissaries who, up until the seventeenth century, were recruited
from the Christian communities of the Empire were, as a rule, stationed outside the ethnic communities to which they belonged.
The politicization of the Janissaries into the Ottoman military system
was so severe they were completely and deliberately cut off from
the ethnic communities of their origin as well as from their immediate families.

This type of military organization based on the garrison continued until the early part of the nineteenth century when structural
reforms (*tanzimat*) were introduced. Under these reforms, military
academies, were opened in the capital city of the Empire with
French and Prussian instructors to train and reorganize the army
according to advanced European standards. For the first time in
the history of the Ottoman empire, Sunni Muslims from the major
cities and towns of the Arab World were admitted to the military
academy in Istanbul. This was one method the Ottomans used in order
to Turkicize the Empire. Arab soldiers recruited into the army were
stationed outside the communities of their origin. North African
Arabs were stationed in Syria and Iraq; Syrians and Iraqis were stationed in Ḥijāz and Yemen. Military service outside the local community was so unpopular that Arab leaders towards the end of the
nineteenth century demanded that soldiers from a particular
willāya remained in their home soil during peaceful time (Zein,
1968: 102, 155-156). The attempt to Turkicize the Empire, while
it generated and enhanced Turkish nationalism which later crystal-
lized in nationalistic movements such as the Young Turks, simultaneously created a counter movement, Arab nationalism (Zein,
1968), formulated by officers trained in Turkish military academies.

To many Arabs, the Ottomans were brethren; they (the
Ottomans) confessed Islam and implemented Islamic law in the
courts of the Empire. However, the military bureaucracy was organized to deal with an empire made up of various ethnic communities
and consequently failed to establish roots in any particular group
outside Turkey. Serving in the Ottoman army was considered by the
ordinary Arab to be a "suicidal journey to nowhere."[8] The fact
that soldiers served outside the ethnic community of their origin
and had to serve interests that did not relate directly to the needs
of their own communities helped to widen the gap between the
military and society.

The colonial period differs in this respect from the preceeding
one. The military recruitment policy of the colonial administration
favored minority groups (Hurewitz, 1969: 152-153) in order "to

fashion what they believed to be a reliable organization" (Janowitz, 1964: 52).[9] In spite of this policy, the colonial experience narrowed the gap between the military and society and provided the initial foundations for the dualistic character of the military as a profession and a model of development. It is for this reason that we consider the colonial experience a formative period. It is a period which began in the Arab countries east of the Mediterranean after World War I and in North Africa even earlier. It is marked by the creation of independent states once only small provinces under Ottoman rule. The policy of "divide and rule" may have prolonged colonial control; but it also invited greater participation in government, thus increasing political awareness on behalf of the ethnic communities that constituted the state. Some ethnic communities were favored over others, but this apparently did not interfere with the establishment of administrative, military, and political institutions. These institutions defined the rights and obligations of participation without necessarily controlling the degree of participation.

In Egypt, the first to join the army were the young men of wealthy families who had an appreciation for horsemanship, polo-playing, and similar sports, and were attracted by officers' commissions in the cavalry regiments (Vatikiotis, 1961: 232). In Syria and Iraq, the young men of land-owning families joined the officer corps (Abu-'Uras, 1969: 31; Torrey, 1963: 54). Emphasis here must be placed upon national background: Egyptian, Syrian, Iraqi. Those officers who came from wealthy, land-holding families became models of upward mobility for other young men, irrespective of social standing in society. By the same token, soldiers recruited from minority groups, particularly in Syria, Iraq and Lebanon, presented themselves as imitative models for peasants regardless of ethnic origin. Peasants—as well as tribesmen living at subsistence level—came to regard the soldier with a fixed salary, along with a pension and retirement plan, as having accomplished the elementary requirements for social mobility (Khuri, 1969: 29-44; Kishk, 1969: 26; al-Razzaz, 1967: 38). In brief, the army in its entire structure came to serve as a channel of upward mobility for all classes and ethnic groups.

However, the military during the colonial period failed to reach all groups in society. They came to represent only a segment of society and not the entire society. After independence, the military began to open recruitment to the officer corps in favor of new, emerging groups—sons of civil servants or bureaucrats, educated young men of peasant background who graduated from high school, university graduates, and the like (Kirk, 1963: 73-74; Torrey, 1963: 55). Two related factors account for this shift: a broader recruiting policy based on less stringent criteria for selection making the army less attractive to the young men of wealthy, landed families who had used it previously as a channel to accumulate status symbols; and secondly, the fact that these young men were gradually drawn to the growing national market economy based upon industry, commerce and agriculture. The shift to broader recruitment while altering the class composition of the officer corps did not necessarily change its ethnic composition.[10]

It was only after independence that the military organization came to assume the triple character of a profession, a model of development and a microcosm of the state with tentacles reaching, through compulsory military service, to all groups in society. After achieving independence, many Arab countries had to contend directly or indirectly with internal and external wars of great importance. The most significant of these wars have been the Kurdish war of northern Iraq, the French-Algerian war, and the series of wars and confrontations with Israel. Whether or not military defeats and frustrations have given rise to military take-over of governments as is commonly held by some observers of the military in the Middle East (Rustow, 1963: 4, 9-10; Berger, 1964: 363; Khadduri, 1963: 42; Halpern, 1963: 256; Qardāwī, 1971: 8) is debatable. Nasser's words in this respect are very telling:

> I have always been a staunch believer in military life, and military life knows a single duty: to be ready to die in defending the borders of the country. If so, why is it then that our army found it necessary to operate in the Capital (Cairo) and not on the borders?
>
> Let me declare emphatically that what promoted us to take action was not the defeat in Palestine, the bad weapons, or the crisis of the Officers' Club—these were not the real sources from which the course of the revolution began to flow, these were factors that helped to accelerate the flow—but, as I stated earlier, these never were the origin and the foundation of the revolution (Nasser, n.d.: 19).

Rather, it is the national effort invested in the army at the expense of other state organizations that makes it an obvious instrument of intervention. In other words, the military interferes in politics after it in fact exercises power.

In Syria and Egypt, a good part of the national budget, sometimes reaching between 60 and 70 percent of the total budget, has been allocated to the military. The military is the first sector to employ modern, but imported technology—the word "imported" is very significant for it suggests that the military develops techno- logically much earlier than industry or agriculture. Weaponry is relatively simple to import and operate compared to industrial and agricultural machinery which require the development of a whole complex of manpower. This technological gap between the military and industry turns the former into what Mūrād (1966: 46) calls "the technical college of society." Literacy, security of employment, and standardized patterns of work; insurance against death, sickness and accidents; family benefits and allowances; indemnity, pension or retirement policies; an elaborate system of rewards, increments, promotion or demotion—all these are applied to the military before they are generalized to other organizations in the private or the public sectors. "The best occupational heaven," the expression that Vatikiotis (1967: 139) uses to describe military careers in Jordan, is applicable in varying degrees to all countries of the Middle East. Not only does the military grow to become the first modernized organization, if not a modernizing one, but it is the first to become a welfare institution in the sense that food, clothes and shelter are provided on a collective basis, thus reinforcing the image of the military as an instrument of social development (Zahr al-Dīn, 1966: 252).

The modernizing effect of the army upon society is question- able. There can be no doubt that the potential of the military for transforming society is indeed great in view of its relatively superior organization and its capacity to resort to force. However, the re- lationship between the military and other political and social insti- tutions limits its capacity to modernize. Given certain historical conditions the army can serve as a rational mechanism of change, but it is by no means a magic tool independent of social realities. "Reality," here, simply refers to the social and technological develop- ment extant at any one time and place. Because the economic base of society is too simple to provide for the technological trained soldier, the modernizing role of the soldier becomes limited. Most soldiers upon release from active service tend to become shop- keepers or taxi drivers in urban Lebanon, or return to the simple tribal life of the Western Desert in the case of the Bedouin of Egypt.[11] Vatikiotis (1967: 87) notes that two-thirds of the Bedouin in Jordan who left a regiment after a five-year enlistment returned to their tribes.

Especially after independence, the military is the first organi- zation to boast a nation-wide process of selection, embodying

the ideology of the state. Recruitment to specific military units is
often carried out according to the ideology of the state rather than
combat performance. Following the policy of the state in Lebanon,
for example, military units are deliberately arranged to include
soldiers and officers of various sects that constitute the country. In
Syria, where the military is believed to serve as a "national mold,"
(al-ṣahr al-qawmī), units bring together the ruralite and the urbanite,
the literate and the illiterate, the Sunni and the Alawi, the Christian
and the Muslim, the Kurd and the Arab, the tribesman and the peasant. Similarly, in Jordan soldiers from the north are stationed in the
south and those from the south in the north. The army comes to be
thought of as a national organization, reflecting the structure of
society (al-Jundī, n.d.: 45; ᶜUmrāh, n.d.: 193), and not necessarily
a "nationalistic" one (Berger, 1964: 263). Nationalism is not the
most explicit characteristic of the military organization; some
political parties, voluntary associations or secret societies express
nationalistic sentiments more so than the military. The army seems
to serve as a generalizing symbol which is sometimes transferred
to the wider Arab community as well. Like the segmentary system,
the army is so expandable and manipulable that it may serve as a
communication process. ᶜAmmāsh (1967), Ḥassan Muṣṭafa (1964)
and Khaṭṭāb (1969) insist that Arab unity could be maintained
only by military unity first.

The image of the military as an instrument of development and
national integration needs not and does not always conform to the
practice. Since there is a relation between thought and action, this
image does enhance the probability of military intervention without
necessarily determining its directions. Many a coup begins on one side
of the political spectrum and shifts to the other depending upon
prevailing domestic political conditions. It is sometimes jokingly re-
marked of a military coup in Syria to have instructed its followers
"to signal to the left but drive to the right" (al-Jundī, n.d.: 39).
Whether or not the military intervenes decisively and the outcome
of its performance will depend upon the social context in which it
operates and the structure of other political institutions that compete
with it.

The Social Basis of Intervention

The data from the Middle East show clearly that military intervention has taken place in peasant-oriented societies such as Syria,

Egypt, Algeria, Sudan, and Iraq and less so in tribally organized ones
such as Jordan, Saudi Arabia, or the Gulf emirates. When the military
intervenes and takes over government in a tribally-based society,
such as Libya for instance, its performance takes on an entirely different direction, often coupled with the attempt to found a new religious
order. Peasantry in the Middle East, as elsewhere, is a part society in
the sense that authority and control lie beyond the immediate group
or community. The structure of peasant communities accommodates
for both external demands and local needs; peasant systems react to
change in the outside world while at the same time operate relatively
independently.

The rise of independent states in the Middle East and the development of national bureaucracy brought the peasantry into the
mainstream of national politics. Because they constitute the greater
part of the population and because they are a part social system,
peasants were transformed into "the masses" (al-jamāhīr)—the raw
material from which the new nation is forged. National policies,
whether in education, economics or politics, find greater support
among peasants than the more autonomous tribesmen. Nationalistic
movements of various shades and colors spread more easily among
peasants than among other segments of society, tribesmen or townsmen alike.[12] Peasants are more prone to change, more receptive to
new forms of law and government, more responsive to policies of
national integration than are the wary and aloof tribesmen. Socialism, practiced or confessed, has become the dogma of those
military regimes which operate in peasant-based countries with a
clear history of feudalism (e.g. Egypt, Syria, Iraq) and economic
deprivation.

These characteristics of peasantry influence to a marked degree
the composition and performance of the military. A peasant as a
soldier or an officer, however incomplete his socialization into the
military profession may be,[13] is influenced by the values of its
organization. True, he is not entirely freed from his previous commitments and community-based ties which he tends to superimpose
upon the military experience; nevertheless, he uses these ties to
affect structural change in society. The performances of the military
regimes in Syria and Iraq lend support to this view. The ruling
military regimes in Iraq, many of whom are from the town of
Tīkrit,[14] and in Syria since the breakup of the United Arab Republic
in 1961, seem to have drawn support from ties of friendship, family,
sect or community. The Syrian officers responsible for ending the
unity with Egypt came originally from Damascus and were linked by

descent and affinal ties as well as commercial interests.[15] The series of other coups, which began in 1963 and were engineered by various factions of the military affiliated with the Ba^cth party, were shaped by various communal ties.[16] Factionalism within the army came to produce "the wings of the party" which was in reality a locus of coalitions derived from community based ties (al-Jundī, 1969b: 160-161).

However, it must not be understood from this that a ruling junta which is linked together by a variety of community-based ties is incapable of affecting structural changes in society. It is in fact these juntas that have executed reformative and socialistic measures of all kinds, enforced land reforms and various policies of nationalization including formal education. This is a clear instance of an "informal group" (Wolf, 1966: 2) generating processive change in the formal organization of society, which suggests that one way to understand complex ideologies is to trace them back to elementary social relationships.

Where the military serves a dual function as a profession and a model of development, the socialization process into the profession is never a complete one, nor is it intended to be. The principle that the army should restrict its activities to war operations, as is generally held by civilian regimes that come to power through democratic or semi-democratic means (al-Quwaltī, 1970: 224, 379), is immediately dismissed as a bourgeois or petit bourgeois attitude.[17] The partial socialization of the soldier has implications for the role of the army in social development and that of the civilian (al-sha^cb or "the people") in war. Instead of a professional army, emphasis is placed upon "the ideologized army," a slogan used by the military regimes affiliated to the Ba^cth party in Syria to cleanse the military organization of non-party affiliates (al-Jundī, 1969b: 154). In principle, if not in practice, an "ideologized army" is not built primarily for war but for transformational purposes to induce lasting structural changes in the total society. Implicit in the idea of an "ideologized army" is the assumption that combat performance in war depends on the revolutionary setting of the individual soldier. Many who hold this view cite "the lack of revolutionary experience" among soldiers to account for the Arabs having lost the wars to Israel.[18] Combat performance, they claim, can be reduced to the psychological experiences of individual soliders: bitterness (marāra), pain ('alam), and spiritual shock (hazza ruḥiyya).[19]

If an army is built primarily for transforming society, the success of its task is not or should not be measured by its accomplishments on the battlefield. The Egyptian claim to victory in the 1956 and 1967 wars (the first lost to the British, French and Israeli combined forces and the second to Israel) and the Syrian claim to victory in the 1967 war, must be understood in this context (Abd al-Hamīd, n.d.: 40, 42, 197; ᶜAwdah, 1969: Mustafa, 1969: 213). The fact that these wars did not distract the military from its trans-formational policies is, in itself, taken as a measure of victory. It is not simply a question of the morale of the troops or a cultural dictum (such as the saying, with a tinge of cynicism, that "the Arabs never lost a war in history") that prompted these two regimes to claim victory to a lost war; it is rather the perceived logic of social change and the role of the army in bringing about this change that forces them to interpret it in this way.

The other side of the argument relates to the role of "the people" (al-shaᶜb) in war. The same ideological principle that holds the army responsible for structural change in society likewise dele-gates to "the people" the responsibility for war activities. It is on the basis of this principle that victory or loss in war, particularly with Israel, is believed to depend upon the degree of political con-sciousness and mobilization of the people. It is held that military victory with Israel can be attained only by "a war of liberation"[20] or by "militarizing society" (Bitār, 1970: 293). Unsure of their power base, the military regimes, particularly in Syria and Iraq, have sporadically followed two formulae in their attempt to militarize the people: rationing tea, sugar, gasoline, rice, and bread in times of peace as well as in war and distributing arms though mainly on a partisan basis.

However, this kind of military ideology is not equally meaning-ful to all segments of a society. Unlike peasantry, a tribal system is a total social entity in that autonomy and the ultimate source of authority reside within the unit itself.[21] The effect of this differ-ence between tribal and peasant structures on the military organi-zation should be clear. A peasant is more apt to adopt the military model whereas the tribesman is more likely to adapt military life to the tribal model. In Jordan soldiers belonging to a particular tribe are reluctant to serve under officers of different tribal origin and do so only with a "scornfulness" (Vatikiotis, 1967: 92). The division of labor in the Jordanian army—with the bedouin tribes controlling the ground and armoured car regiments while the towns-men and Palestinians control the technical services—is seen by a Palestinian Commando organization to be deliberately engineered by King Hussain to retain his supremacy over the army.[22] However, such a military division can also be traced back to its sociological roots. The King was confronted with a specific social cleavage, tribes versus peasantry and townsmen, and has simply institutionalized the conflict.

In other tribal-based societies such as Saudi Arabia, North Yemen, Libya and the Gulf area, the standing military power is composed of two distinct but related arrangements, a regular army and a national guard or militia. The efforts to establish a regular army came as a result of a modernization process given impetus by the discovery of oil in Saudi Arabia, Libya and the Gulf and by a "republican" regime with outside support in Yemen.[23] The organizational differences between a regular army and the national guard are striking and hold important implications for the understanding of the military in tribal societies of the Middle East. The regular army, which sometimes includes a small air force and a token navy, is recruited from settled tribes, townsmen or foreign mercenaries. In the case of Saudi Arabia the army is recruited mainly from Hijazi people (Hurewitz, 1969: 251). In the Yemen the Shafi^{c}i peasants of the south were only brought into the regular army in the context of modernization. Tribal soldiers are usually in favor of a status quo situation. This is the reason that Glubb did not initially favor the recruitment of Palestinian peasants and townsmen into the Jordanian army. The situation in Libya is not yet clear; King Idris' efforts to regularize the Cyrenaican Bedouin troops as a core of a regular standing army were unsuccessful (Hurewitz, 1969: 233-273) and little is known yet of the Qadhdhāfī reign. The regular army in the Gulf, which until recently was known as the Trucial Oman Scouts, is composed mainly of Dhofaris, Baluchis and the Bani-Kaab in addition to Adenis, Persians, Indians and Pakistanis; only one of which can claim local tribal roots (Barrat, 1973: 47-49).

By contrast, the national guard is built upon the tribal structure of each individual country. Recruitment to the national guard often takes the form of levies drawn from loyal tribes (Hurewitz, 1969: 236, 252, 257). Unlike the regular army, the national guard retains in various degrees the authority of the tribe over its individual recruits. It is organized mainly for domestic purposes, to defend the standing regime, and therefore, it is bound to expand substantially in time of crises by calling up untrained tribal reserves. In North Yemen, for instance, a tribesman is carried on militia roster with only the obligation to mobilize at the command of his tribal shaikh. For this irregular duty he receives 3 YR per month. Strictly speaking, the national guard is more of a political arrangement than a military one. Excepting perhaps knowledge of equipment, professional socialization into the guard hardly surpasses the type of manly training a tribesman receives in the group of his origin. The regular army, which requires a greater measure of training, discipline and absence from kinsmen has generally been unpopular with tribesmen. For this reason, recruitment then depends upon either the settled tribes who subsist on cultivation, townsmen and foreign mercenaries, or upon combination of these.[24]

Jordan is perhaps the one country where a regular army has been rather successfully organized with a tribal base—a fact that makes the Jordanian experience a model for other tribally organized societies, particularly in the Gulf.[25] Even in Jordan, however, the regular army is built upon an intricate system of balance between tribes vis-a-vis peasants and townsmen. Compared to other monolithic bureaucracies, the Jordanian situation poses a curious puzzle. It is the only bureaucracy that brings together diverse tribal factions under a compromise institution, the Kingship, without formally manipulating religion as a common element of unity.[26] The *Wahhābiya* movement in Saudi Arabia, the *Sanūsiyya* in Libya, the *Zaydiyya* in Yemen, and other such movements, have historically united under a religious banner what would otherwise have been quarrelling tribal factions. Even "the cultural revolution" of Qadhdhāfī of Libya today, which is encapsulated in the Islamic *sharīᶜa,* can be fit into the same pattern. In the future, the *Sanūsiyya* of Cyrenaica may have to cope with a sister movement, the "Qadhdhāfiyya," that appeals to non-tribal segments of society— the urban masses and peasants of Fezzan and Tripolitania.

Bureaucracies, kingships or religious movements, separately or together, coordinate the interests of tribal factions through an intricate system of redistribution based on tribal loyalties. This is so because a tribal arrangement is a total social system which retains its identity within any complex organization be it the state or the military. Power in a tribal-based society is a product of the balance of interests between the distinct tribal groups constituting the state. This means that any military intervention to take over government represents a threat to the political balance and accordingly to the very existence of the state which includes the military organization itself. A tribal arrangement that subsumes military life under the dictates of its own organization (such as the national guard) can not equate this military model with the tribal system and still keep its structure intact. Hence, military attempts to take over government in tribally organized societies have always come

from non-tribesmen—namely, from officers of peasant or urban backgrounds, as it has in fact been the case in Jordan (Vatikiotis, 1967:
131). The mutiny that took place in Jordan in February, 1974, and
which was engineered by enlisted tribesmen, was essentially a protest
against low salaries and high cost of living, not a challenge to the
legitimate authority of the state.

The Military as a Political Institution

Generally, the military intervenes when it grows at a rapid rate
and overshadows other organizations in society, particularly established political groups and civil bureaucracy.[27] Whether a profession,
a model of development or both, the military is essentially a political
institution—it is the sole instrument of force in the country (Campbell, 1963: 105) and a crucible in which community leaders and
national heroes are molded. The military competes with other political groupings for the control of the decision-making process. Whether
it succeeds or not depends upon the structure of political allignment
extant at the time.[28] It is not simply a question of cultural values
that promotes a military take-over of government; rather it is the
degree of military development vis-a-vis other institutions which
determines whether or not the army will assume political power.

In those countries of the Middle East where the military has
succeeded in taking over government, political groupings could be
divided into two types: moralistic political parties, and constellations (ḥizbiyyāt) of power composed of dynamic coalition between
community leaders. Generally, the phenomenon of a political party
with an explicit platform incorporating various interests and cutting
across ethnic or social groups has been entirely absent. Political
parties such as the Baᶜth Party, the Syrian Nationalist Party, and
a series of other groupings that have recently sprung from Nasserite
or the socialistic-communistic movements,[29] come closer in content
and organization to a mission rather than an effective political party.
Hence, the term "moralistic." Only reluctantly do these parties
indulge in the political maneuvers of the time. They take a special
pride in standing aloof of immediate political gains and insist that
their mission is a long-range policy that cannot be accomplished
by simply taking over government. In the Baᶜth Party, for example,
this ideology has created two factions, one that aims at immediate
political action known as "the quick school" and popular among the
military, and the other faction which supports "popular action"

(al-ᶜamal al-jamāhirī) only in terms of a slow process of teaching and indoctrination (al-Razzāz, 1967: 31).[30] The chief concern of the moralistic faction is the creation of "the·new man" and not the attempt to control government for the purpose of changing society. Jalāl al-Sayyid, one of the early founders of the Baᶜth who left the Party after it was taken over by the military put it into these daring words:

> We believe that the Arab is a creature styled by God after one of His best models for man. We also believe that the Arab is clear of everything that soils man's glory. We read the classical books in Arabic in order to extract those high qualities which we believe are [should be] characteristic of the Arab, without realizing that there lives among the Arabs the laudable and the lamentable (al-Sayyid, 1973: 260).

The emphasis upon character and conduct and the molding of personality has made these parties popular among students and teachers (al-Jundī, 1969b: 50; ᶜUmrān, n.d.: 147). Concerned with the problems of daily life, ordinary men came to regard these moralistic parties as romantic, dreamy and impractical.[31] These parties address themselves to far-reaching, often utopian issues: Arab or Syrian (Greater Syria) unity, the creation of a new genera-tion, the logic and strategy of revolutionary change, the transforma-tion of personality—issues that may only indirectly pertain to the immediate interests of the populace (ᶜUmrān, n.d.: 153). It is no wonder that the founders of these parties came to be known in their actual role of teacher (muᶜallim) rather than as politicians (siyāsī). They consider it insulting to be called politicians.

The lack of a comprehensive program of action[32] and the mission-like activities of these parties limit their capacity for politi-cal mobilization. They have never been able to mobilize what ᶜUmrān (a once prominent Baᶜthist military officer) intuitively calls "the practical segment" of society composed of laborers, farmers, craftsmen, tradesmen, and retail merchants. These moralistic parties have been mostly active among "the abstract segment" com-posed of students, teachers, military officers, and civil administrators (ᶜUmrān, n.d.: 58). Within this "abstract" stratum of society, they seem to have appealed to some ethnic, social or minority groups. By and large, party members seem to have come mostly from the economically self-sufficient (mastūr) part of the better known families (al-Sayyid, 1973: 37).

Constellations of power (ḥizbiyyat), on the other hand, are composed of transient coalitions of community leaders, each of whom controls a specific but small group in his community. By virtue of

their internal organization, these constellations alienate politically a
great part of the mobile population—a segment which is expected
to grow with rural-to-urban migration, labor migration, or the opening of new cultivable lands. A constellation of power does not have
the quality of a political party, even though it may carry the name
of a party and act outwardly as if it were one. A constellation then
is a dynamic alliance between community leaders, each of whom
independently derives power from a single community or several
communal associations on the basis of a variety of assets: history
of pre-eminence in local affairs, patron-client relationships, factional
politics, personal services, mediation. The following a leader controls
at a time fluctuates with the power he commands in government
and vice versa. In this arrangement, the follower is tied to the leader
according to personal merits and relationships and not according
to an ideology or program of action.[33]

For this arrangement to continue, it is necessary that the
communal associations from which the leader derives power be
more or less stable. Any process such as urbanization, rural-to-urban
migration, migration of labor, any form of spacial or social mobility,
which disrupts socio-political relations, will weaken the link between
follower and leader and alienates the former from previous political
ties. Political alienation must not be confused with psychological
alienation that deals with the problem of adjustment of individual
personalities to a social system. This political form of alienation
refers to the situation whereby a person or group becomes incapable
of affecting, in one way or another, the decision-making process.
This kind of alienation must be explained by examining the changing
social structure of individual communities brought about by the
mechanization of agriculture, the expansion of the national market,
the introduction of cash crops and the diminishing importance of
subsistence economy, the rise of national industry, the extension of
a standardized national system of education, the enforcement of
land reforms and a host of other actions, measures and processes
that change the social order.

When major structural changes begin to take place in communities, the possibility of a community leader acting as an instrument of integration between local community and national polity
begins to wane, more so in those countries of the Middle East that
have historically experienced the practice of absentee landlords.
Herein is the main difference between Lebanon, on one hand, and
Egypt, Syria and Iraq on the other. Community leaders in Lebanon
have continued to act as instruments of socio-political integration

in the face of sweeping changes in the country. Many factors account for this structural continutiy—the small size of the country, proximity between village and city, the strong attachment to the community of origin, and the pluralistic character of the society that militates against the rise of national heroes. But the most outstanding factor of them all is the fact that in Lebanon, community leaders continue to interact with their following. If it happens that a part of the following migrates and settles in the city, leaders likewise spend part of the week in the city and part in the countryside. Like many a follower, a leader maintains one house in the city and another in the community of his origin, alternating residence between both and thus making himself available most of the time. This geographic mobility helps to maintain socio-political commitments.

On the other hand, community leaders in Syria, Egypt or Iraq, prior to military intervention in these countries, were usually absentee landlords who controlled resources but failed to act as instruments of integration at a time their countries were changing drastically. As a result, peasants in the countryside were much less affected by national policies than were urban people. Unlike peasants in Lebanon to whom public services and welfare projects and programs are extended through the political lobbying of community leaders, peasants in Syria, Egypt or Iraq have found it difficult to profit from public services or projects guaranteed them by law. It is obvious that the lack of community leaders linking ordinary citizens with the national polity and simultaneously transmitting public policies onto the local scene could be detrimental to peasant participation in the political process. The only link to the outside world for peasants in Syria, Egypt, or Iraq has been the military officer who has maintained roots in the community of his origin.

In national politics where administration is controlled by urban politicians who distribute the "national goods" to their various constituencies, the rift between civil administration and peasantry has deepened. This point must be stressed. In the early phase of a country's development, civil administration represents the mechanisms through which public services and welfare filters to the citizens. Whoever controls these mechanisms controls along with the redistribution of other things: the opening of roads, schools, colleges, hospitals, factories, the ability to affect employment, salaries, increments, markets, taxes, prices and the like. The advantages of bureaucratic office make civil administration an obvious ground for political competition among leaders whose interests it may serve. On the other hand, the military as a bureaucracy presents itself as the only effective means to reach the various segments of society, especially the peasant, and perhaps the tribal, segment.[34] In the post-independence era, the military tends to lose its appeal to the urban landed families, partly because of the growing opportunities in industry, commerce and agriculture and partly because the military itself becomes a more diffuse and national institution. The military ceases any longer to be a service for the select few and accordingly loses its value as a status vehicle for the privileged of society. These structural changes have implications for the role of the military officer himself. He becomes a new instrument of integration in place of the community leader who remains locked in the traditional struggle for power in the urban center. Writing about Syria, ᶜUmrān (n.d.), Zahr al-Dīn, (1966), al-Jundī (1969a and (1969b) and al-Razzāz (1967) depict the army officer as a link between the local community of his origin and the national polity. The new officer intercedes on behalf of the community in matters of employment, bureaucratic appointments and the channelling of public services and welfare projects. al-Jundī, who writes with a good deal of bitterness, maintains that the policy of nationalization of industry and commerce in Syria, which was enforced by various military regimes, was carried out in order to find jobs for the "caravans of unemployed peasants" (al-Jundī, 1969a: 88). This is one instance of the military taking over government after they have accumulated power and are recognized as an instrument of politics. Commenting upon what came to be known as "the reign of separation" (ᶜahid al-'infiṣāl) in Syria,[35] Zahr al-Dīn who was the commander-in-chief of the Syrian army between 1961 and 1963 and entrusted with the responsibility of de-politicizing the military, complains: "the army has become the state" (Zahr al-Dīn, 1966: 251). This means that the army takes on the state as its model for action. For instance, Zahr al-Dīn relates that at the Military Convention of Homs held in 1962 to put an end to conflict within the officer corps, the participants agreed to elect, rather than appoint or promote, officers to vacant military posts (Zahr al-Dīn, 1966: 220).

Practices of this type raise the issue of military-civilian relations. Given the historical inequality of access to education and new ideas in the Middle East, the military initially draws upon and even emulates the ideological sophistication of the civilian "big men." It has been noted by students of military sociology that soldiers often have a difficult time formulating an ideology of the revolution— 'Abd al-Nasser and the Egyptian experience usually being cited as the chief example. The military in the Middle East and other new nations generally learn from those whom Fanon referred to as "the national bourgeoisie." A great deal of how the military and civilian politicians relate, cooperate or conflict, will be a reflection of the social structure and its attendant distribution of economic rewards and assets. In a traditional system, where roles are broad, diffuse and general, not only may the civilian be hard to distinguish functionally from the officer-in-charge, but even where an analytical distinction can be made, it may gloss over an important sociological reality. The military and civilians have common reference points in the structural background of their traditional society. The military draw upon the civilian resources of power and authority and vice versa.

Such a structural obscurity of roles indicates that the military-civilian dichotomous model constructed from Western data has to be transformed into a continuum model whenever empirical attention is given to the range of societies of the Third World. There is a basis for a dichotomous conceptualization between military and civilian only at a level of advanced technology. What makes matters more complex is the fact that few in-depth studies of specific armed forces in developing areas are made (Bienen, 1971: 17). Like politicians, the military, far from embodying modernity, may be a true mirror of indigenous cleavages and constituencies; it may not transcend and even transform traditional divisions. Although army leaders may want to modernize, they may be just as bound by the demands and dictates of their primary communities as is any other group. The claim that the military is best qualified for the task of modernizing is questionable.

Ultimately, it is only the data on kinship, ethnic, tribal and village origins, and religious ties which will reveal the nature of military-civilian relationships and the capacity of either to carry out a modernizing program. Once this kind of data is stressed the term military is then necessarily "demystified" (Bienen, 1973: 2). The military as an institution of a primarily political nature should engender no more special attention than any other structure marked by leadership and the priority for decision-making. To single it out in a dichotomous relationship with the civilians is to overlook the power relations of the military with other political institutions and groups: labor unions, cooperative movements, political parties, cliques, charismatic personalities and religious specialists. An analysis of the interaction of the military with the various groups in society will contribute to our understanding of the internal divisions and factional disputes within the army itself. The army is not autonomous from a society still characterized by ties of ethnicity, kinship, tribalism and religion.

Prospects for Future Research

In this discussion we tried to examine the social bases for the military rise to power in the Middle East. Data on the coup d'etat are invaluable if we seek to comprehend the problem of power politics.[36] However, if we are to understand the historical basis and development of the army in politics we will have to view the total context of intervention beyond individual coups and counter-coups.

A clear distinction between the strategy of the coup and that of the developmental character of the military is necessary for a proper study of power and the evolution of authority in society. A military coup is always engineered by a faction tied together by any of a variety of links: friendship, educational background, kinship, ethnic or social origins. The peasant character of society and the partial socialization into the military profession produce structural continuity and ongoing factionalism in the military organization itself.[37] Munif al-Razzāz describes such a situation in the following words:

> The army is not a political party, nor does it acknowledge a single and unified political ideology, nor does it reflect the interests of a particular social class. The fact that a good part of the army comes from lower class background does not, by necessity, make it a "leftist" organization. The officer corps whose origin could at times be traced to lower class background, particularly peasantry, are by no means lower class people— this is particularly true nowadays when various Arab countries, both the revolutionary and the conservative, have been bestowing upon the officer corps all kinds of economic privileges and securities.
>
> Because the military is composed of various ethnic or social groups, it comes to reflect a wide variety of political outlooks. And by virtue of its own emphasis on discipline and obedience, it cannot possibly act democratically, which means that its capacity for political action is not determined by majority opinion. Individual coups are never engineered by the officer corps as a body; only a small number of officers who happen to be placed in key positions decide they should strike (take over government). Their decision, however, need not and does not always reflect public opinion, neither in the army nor in society. It is because of this that a coup may shift to the "right" or to the "left" according to the beliefs and convictions of individual officers (al-Razzāz, 1967: 38).

In order to consolidate its authority, the military faction that engineers a coup follows what seems to be a regular pattern: partisan officers are assigned key military and administrative posts such as the intelligence section and armored regiments, and more recently the air force, or ministries of interior, defense, and finance. Officers and officials who may constitute future opposition are purged, forced to retire, or are neutralized with diplomatic assignments. Other measures have become common practice: abolishing organized political action, establishing a new monolithic political party (such as in Egypt) or taking advantage of an already established one (such as in Syria and Iraq), controlling mass media, resorting to slogans stressing the common goals of the army and the people toward national unity, social development and the like. The circumstances of a coup diminish the efficiency of the army as a concentrated instrument of force, the outcome of which would be to encourage counter-coups. An officer who is uncertain of his future under a new regime or faction is apt to cast his lot with a group of trusted colleagues. A coup is not just a disruption and change in the state mechanism of control but also a realignment in the military organization itself. The fact that a coup, its ideology and future plan of action, unfolds amidst secrecy and among a small camaraderie promotes insecurity among the military men not directly involved in the take-over.

Should a junta be able to sustain the momentum of its coup, it will strive to protect itself through the creation of monolithic parties and political movements and the control of civil administration. In this process khaki becomes the uniform-of-the-day for technocrats, "doctors," heads of departments, diplomats, managers and civil administrators (Abdel-Malek, 1968: 177). At the same time, the army claims to be the instrument of national unity and the protector of the "homeland" (Haïkal, n.d.: 81; Kāmil, 1968: 59; ᶜAbed al-Jawād, n.d.: 22; Murād, 1972: 46; al-Saᶜīd, 1971: 18-23). Such claims came to be pronounced most clearly in Egypt where the emphasis on national unity as opposed to "social development" (Nasser, 1955: 42-43) and on the military as a profession rather than a "vanguard of change" (Haïkal, n.d.: 81) forced the regime to share power on the basis of a "national coalition" (al-tahaluf al-watanī) composed of peasants, laborers, soldiers, the educated (al-muthaqqafūn) and the national capitalists (al-Saᶜīd, 1971: 18-23). This policy of the regime of Nasser has generated criticism from the intellectual left, particularly in Syria and Lebanon, who saw it as an attempt to serve the interests of the *"petit bourgeois"* class, thus dwarfing the "leftist" movement in the Arab World (al-Adhim, 1969: 17; al-Razzāz, 1967: 40).

The fact that the military builds lasting political and state institutions demonstrates the historic and evolutionary character of military intervention. Whatever the political outcome of a given coup, military intervention as a social process has generated far-reaching structural change in Egypt, Syria and Iraq. It has redefined traditional loci of power, implemented a variety of socialistic measures, executed land reform and undertaken impressive projects in industry and agriculture. Some of the measures taken have been so socialistic in content that Ghassan Twaīnī, a prominent journalist in Beirut, has referred to the military as the *Caskaritariat* (derived from *Caskarī* which means soldier) of the second half of the twentieth century in the Arab World. Many of these developmental measures have taken strong root in society so that the trend seems virtually irreversible. The military regime in Syria, for example, which came to power between 1961 and 1963, was unsuccessful for an obvious reason. Being identified with the urban commercial segment of society (Zahr al-Dīn, 1966: 52), they were very unpopular with large parts of the army drawn mainly from lower class and peasant backgrounds. The two years they stayed in power (note that lack of popularity did not deter the success of their coup initially) were permeated with intrigue and conflict, open confrontations between politicians and military officers, and dissension within the officer corps. Out of this struggle for power within the Syrian military, however, has come the implementation of long-range policies of change. Social transformation, especially land reform has become the basis for political "one-upsmanship" between competing factions of the military.

The durability of the institutions the military build depend upon the extent to which they can accomplish their program of reaching and changing society. Such a program would involve the development of local industry and technological skills, the implementation of welfare projects and social security policies, and politicization through organized political action that cuts across various communities and groups. It is true that coups breed coups, but it is also true that everytime a coup succeeds there is an attempt to sustain it by implementing social reforms. Hence, the tendency to build lasting political and state institutions based upon organized political action and legitimate rules of succession. Military intervention, though generated by a struggle for power within the army, must be seen as a social process with far reaching aims.

In closing, we would like to indicate three areas of research which, if carried out, will greatly enhance our understanding of the military in Middle Eastern society. The military-civilian relationships must be examined with reference to the wider social context. Whether leaders—civilian or military—consort or conflict with one another can only be dealt with by examining the social structure in which they operate. Whether they constitute a single coalition or separate constellations of power is dependent upon the empirical facts of Middle Eastern community life.

The second area of research must focus on the structural characteristics of the army, data which go beyond the official statistics of information offices and selected interviews with army officers. It must include data on soldier-soldier, soldier-officer and officer-officer relationships; the system of military authority; the informal power structures within the army; and the meaning of old and new symbols by which the military leaders enhance internal control over the army and external control over society. Until this type of data— which we like to refer to as "the ethnography of the military"— becomes available no statement on the role of the military in society can be valid.

Finally, data dealing with the reintegration of the soldier returning to his community must be collected in order to evaluate the "modernizing" effect of the army experience. In this case, the ex-soldier must once again be seen within the context of the wider community. Even if the army is an agent of modernization we still must recognize the fact that it is society which provides the stuff to be worked.

Notes

1. Fuad I. Khuri is an Associate Professor of Anthropology at the American University of Beirut, and Gerald Obermeyer is an Assistant Professor of Anthropology at the same university. Data from our own field research has been integrated into this paper wherever deemed appropriate. Khuri has carried out research in peasant and suburban communities in Lebanon and Obermeyer in the Western Desert of Egypt (1969) and is currently engaged in research in the Yemen Arab Republic.

2. Much of the data for this paper comes from Arab writing on the military and therefore is primarily concerned with the Arabic-speaking countries of the Middle East. The Arabic literature on the military began to appear in the fifties. The Suez canal crisis of 1956 and the policies of nationalization, confiscation of property and land reforms, which were carried out by the military regime in Egypt, and later in Syria and Iraq, have triggered a growing interest in the military institution. The available literature is furnished mainly by the intellectual left, army officers, founders of political parties and journalists. The writings of the intellectual left focuses on the military as a vanguard of revolutionary change and are overwhelmingly ideological in content with little reference to empirical data. Here the army is treated as if it were a rational mechanism for change, a national hope, and a symbol of the "good" in society. There is little discussion of the internal organization of the army, the social groups of which it is made, and the effects of these groups on the performance of the military regimes. A representative sample of this kind of literature is the monthly

journal of al-ṭalīʿa ("The Vanguard") published in Egypt, the weekly of the same name published in Syria, as well as jaish al-shaʿb ("The People's Army") and al-jundi ("The Soldier") both published in Syria by the office of Morale of the Syrian army. Useful data of this sort are also found in Dirāsāt ʿArabiyya ("Arab Studies"), two separate journals one of which is published in Syria and the other in Lebanon.

The literature written by army officers, especially those purged of office, is very rich in data about the internal organization of the army, factionalism, and the nature of the struggle for power within the military. This literature is particularly significant for an analysis of the strategy of military intervention. The writings of former army officers such as ʿUmrān, Zahr al-Dīn, and Khalīl Mustafā of the Syrian Army, and ʿAmmāsh, Khaṭṭāb, and Ḥasan Muṣṭafā of the Iraqi Army, expose in some detail the intricate workings of the military. Unlike the literature on Egypt which seems to focus on the role of the military in revolutionary change, the literature on Syria deals mainly with the struggle for power within the army. This is partly due to the fact that the Syrian officer tends to dwell more on personal experiences than his counterpart in Egypt. The politico-ideological struggle between the civilian and military factions of the Baʿth in Syria—a game that has lasted more than a decade and ended with the victory of the military—has produced a valuable and comparative body of data on the military vis-a-vis other organizations in society. Perhaps ʿAflaq, al-Sayyid, al-Jundī, al-Razzāz, the founders of the Baʿth party, present the most analytic and critical accounts of the role of the military in Syria, and to a lesser extent, in Iraq and Egypt. The early leaders of the Baʿth party seem to have turned to scholarship once they lost control of their own converts—the officers.

More informative than other sources is the daily press of Lebanon. Non-partisan newspapers such as al-Nahār, al-Hayāt, and the French language l'Orient, offer a wealth of data on military organization, coups and their aftermath, vital statistics on officers, kin relations between them and their community origin, resistance to military rule and its sources, and a general evaluation of the military. This sort of data on the structure and dynamics of military regimes collected over a period of several years may help us to generalize about the army in specific situations and the reasons for their actions.

In addition to this written literature on the military, we interviewed a number of former army officers, diplomats of various Arab countries, journalists and political leaders living in Beirut who served and worked, at one time or another, in various Arab countries.

To all those who helped us in this endeavor, we submit our deep appreciation and gratitude. We would also like to acknowledge with thankfulness the influence Morris Janowitz has had in building our, especially Fuad I. Khuri's, interest in the sociology of the military.

3. See Rustow (1963: 9), Fisher (1963: 22), Campbell (1963: 108) and Halpern (1963: 271), who argue that military intervention in politics in the Middle East can be traced back to its historical and cultural roots.

4. See M.J. de Goeje's writings on the Caliphate originally published in the Encyclopedia Britannica, 11th edition, Vol. V; and T.W. Arnold's writings on the same subject in Encyclopedia Britannica, 14th edition, Vol. IV.

5. See T.W. Arnold's article on the ʿAbbāsid Caliphs originally published in the Encyclopedia Britannica, 14th edition, Vol. IV.

6. The Persian states included the Tahirids in Khurāsān (820-872), the Saffārids in Persia (867-903), the Sāmānids in Transoxiana (874-999), the Sajids in Adharbayjan (879-930), the Ziārids in Jurjān (928-1942). The Turkish states included the Tūlūnids in Egypt (868-905), the Hekids in Turkistan (932-1165), the Ikhshīdids in Egypt (935-969), the Ghaznawids in Afghanistan (962-1186). The Arabic states included the Idrisids in Morocco (788-985), the Aghlabids in Tunis (800-909), the Dulafids in Kurdistan (825-898), the Alawids in Taberistan (864-928), the Hamdānids in Halab and Mawṣil (929-1003), the Mazyalids in Ḥillah (1012-1150), the 'Uqaylids in Mawṣil (996-1096), the Mirdāsids in Halab (1023-1079).

7. See A. Adnan's article on Turkey originally published in the Encyclopedia Britannica, 14th edition, Vol. VI.

8. After an interview with a veteran of the Ottoman army in the First World War.

9. The British in Iraq favored the Assyrians and the Kurds (Hopkins, 1970: 25); the French in Syria favored Armenians, Kurds and Circassians (Torrey, 1963: 54).

10. This statement is more applicable to Syria and Lebanon than to Egypt or Iraq; see Be'eri (1970: 329-33) and Hurewitz (1969).

11. See Obermeyer, 1969.

12. In the various Palestinian Commando organizations, peasantry constitute the major element of combat units while townsmen and urlanites are more active in administration and public relations.

13. Soldiers and officers in Syria tend to come from peasant background (Be'eri, 1970: 339; al-Razzāz, 1967: 38), and in Iraq from urban settlements or towns (Be'eri, 1970: 335). This may be due to the fact that a large part of the Iraqi countryside is inhabited by tribesmen who refuse to serve in a regular army dominated by citymen or townsmen.

14. See al-Nahār Nos. 11815, 11816 and 11818 published on the 7th, 8th and 10th of July, 1973.

15. See Zahr al-Dīn (1966: 52, 134, 302, 362, and 419).

16. See ᶜUmrān (n.d.: 28, 51, 99, 188, 194), al-Jundī (1969b: 143-144), al-Razzāz (1967: 53, 63, 140, 159, 262, 263), al-Sayyid (1973: 210) and Be'eri (1970: 160).

17. See the publication of the Popular and Democratic Front for the Liberation of Palestine (1971: 5), Kāmil (1971: 12), al-ᶜAdhim (1969: 17).

18. These beliefs represent the views of those who advocate radical change in Arab societies as a way to overcome Israel. See, for example, the writings of Bitār (1965: 1970), Himādī (1968), al-Adhim (1967; 1969).

19. See Himādī (1968: 5-6), Naᶜāmah (1971: 6), and Bitār (1965: 16).

20. See the writings of ᶜAllūsh (1968: 45-65), Ibrāhīm (1968: 34-55), Dīrī (1969: 10-17), Tallās (1970), Rahmā (1972: 71-73), Kāmil (1968: 58-65), Yāsīn (1973: 24-30).

21. See al-Nafisi's work (1973) on the Shiᶜite tribes of Southern Iraq.

22. The Popular Democratic Front for the Liberation of Palestine (1971: 47).

23. Reference is made here to the coups d'etat of 1962 and the subsequent military intervention of Egypt in Yemen's civil war.

24. Reference is made here to the experiences of Libya under the reign of King Idris, Yemen under Egyptian influence, and Saudi Arabia at the present time.

25. Riyād Najīb al-Rayyis, who is a Lebanese journalist, reports that Jordanian officers are helping a number of emirates in the Gulf build a regular army similar in structure to theirs in Jordan (al-Nahār, March 21, 1973).

26. A possible exception to this would be the experiment of the United Arab Emirates to raise a standing army to replace the Trucial Scouts (see Barrat, 1972).

27. ᶜArīdī argues the point the the following words: "The army is the most advanced institution in society and therefore it is capable of changing society. Other institutions such as political parties and civil administration, by virtue of their internal structure, are subject to the influence of a variety of primary relations that weaken the role of these institutions in development. These non-military institutions are mere reflections of society and therefore incapable of changing it. By contrast, the military can be isolated from its social setting (here the authors disagree with ᶜArīdī) and then fashioned according to the knowledge of the age—a fact that makes the military the most effective instrument of change and modernization" (ᶜArīdī: 1968-79).

28. Henry Bienen argues: "When we understand the reasons for military intervention and as we explore the links between the military and other political institutions and social groups, we can better assess the prospects for the future evolution of the armed forces in society and we can better judge their capacity to deal with specific problems" (Bienen, 1971: 4).

29. A good example of the Nasserite groupings is "the Nasserite League of Action" established in Beirut after the death of Nasser. For details see Samir Haddād (1972) and Kamāl Shātīlā (1972).

30. Historically, the pursuit of immediate political goals came up after the Ba^{c}th Party had joined the Socialist Party of 'Akram al-Hurani in 1952. For details see al-Sayyid (1973: 90-95).

31. In his research in Lebanon, Fuad I. Khuri found that many affiliates to such parties desert them after marriage.

32. The socialistic measures undertaken by the Ba^{c}thist regimes in Syria and Iraq were adopted after military intervention. The same principle applies also to Egypt. For details see Abdel-Malek (1968) and Safran (1961).

33. For details see Fuad I. Khuri's work on leadership in two suburbs of Beirut in *From Village to Suburb: Order and Change in Greater Beirut,* (in press).

34. It is in this context that one should understand Nasser's famous statement: "If we, the army, do not do this job (take over government in order to modernize Egypt), who will?" (Nasser, 1955: 31).

35. This is the time (1961-1963) that Syria separated from Egypt and tried unsuccessfully to rebuild democratic institutions in the country.

36. Be'eri's work on *Army Officers in Arab Politics and Society* (1970) is an excellent example of this type of data. In Arabic, the work of ^{c}Umrān (n.d.), al-Jundī (1969b), Zahr al-Dīn (1966) or al-Razzāz (1967) are similarly rich.

37. Partial socialization into the profession may be a product of the peasant character of the military.

References

Abdel-Malek, Anouar (1968) *Egypt: Military Society.* New York: Vintage Books.

^{c}Abdel-Nāsser, Jamāl (n.d.) *Falsafat al-thawra* (the Philosophy of the Revolution), Cairo, Dar al-Ma^{c}ārif.

———(1955) *Egypt's Liberation: The Philosophy of the Revolution.* Washington, D.C. Public Affairs Press.

^{c}Abed al-Jawād, Mustafā (n.d.) $^c\bar{A}m$ fī dhil al-'infisāl (One Year in the Shadow of Disunity). Cairo: al-Dar al-Qawmiyya.

^{c}Abed al-Hamīd, Muhammad K. (n.d.) *ma^{c}rakat Sinā' wa qanat al-Suwāis* (The Battle of Sinai and the Suez Canal). Cairo.

'Abū-'Urās (1969) "al-^{c}askariyyūn wa al-thawra" (The Military and the Revolution), *Dirāsāt ^{c}Arabiyya,* Vol. 5, no. 11, (pp. 7-84).

al-Adhim, Sādiq (1969) "al-muqāwama al-musallaha wa al-mawāqif al-haīkaliyya" (The Armed Resistance and the Skeletal Stands), *Dirāsāt ^{c}Arabiyya,* Vol. 5, no. 10, (pp. 17-36).

Adnan, A.A. (n.d.) "Turkey." In *Provisional Readings in the History of the Arabs and Arabic Culture,* A.J. Rustum and C.K. Zurayk (eds.). Beirut: American University of Beirut (pp. 336-358; 402-405).

^{c}Allūsh, Nājī (1968) "al-harb al-sha^{c}biyya tarīq al-nasr al-wahīd" (The People's War is the only to Victory), *Dirāsāt ^{c}Arabiyya* Vol. 4, no. 7 (pp. 45-56).

^{c}Ammāsh, Sālih M. (1967) *al-wahda al^{c}askariyya: al-madmūn al-^{c}askari lil-wahda al-^{c}Arabiyya* (The Military Unity: The Military Meaning of Arab Unity). Beirut: Dār al-Talī^{c}a.

^{c}Arīdī, Bashīr (1968) "dawr al-jaīsh fī ^{c}amaliyyat al-tanmiyya" (The Role of the Army in the Process of Development), *al-Siyāsa al-Dawliyya,* Vol. 4, no. 13 (pp. 77-87).

Arnold, T.W. (n.d.) "Caliphate." In *Provisional Readings in the History of the Arabs and Arabic Culture,* A.J. Rustum and C.K. Zurayk (eds.). Beirut: American University of Beirut (pp. 155-164; 170-172; 179-181; 183-184).

Barrat, Richard H. (1972) "British Influence on Arab Military Forces in the Gulf—the Trucial Oman Scouts." An M.A. thesis submitted to the Middle East Area Program of the American University of Beirut.

Be'eri, E. (1970) *Army Officers in Arab Politics and Society.* New York: Praeger.

Berger, Morroe (1964) *The Arab World Today.* New York: Doubleday and Company Inc.

Bienen, Henry (ed.) 1971) *The Military and Modernization.* Chicago and New York: Aldine. Atherton, Inc.

Bienen, Henry and David Morell (1973) "Transition from Military Rule: Thailand and Nigeria." A paper read in the Conference on the Military in Chicago, October.

Bitār, Nadīm (1970) *mina al-naksa 'ilā al-thawra* (From Relapse to the Revolution). Beirut: Dār al-Ṭaliᶜa.

———(1965) *al-faᶜāliyya al-thawriyya fī al-nakba* (The Revolutionary Effect of the Disaster). Beirut: Dār al-'Irshād.

Campbell, John C. (1963) "The Role of the Military in the Middle East: Past Patterns and New Directions." In *The Military in the Middle East,* S. Fisher (ed.). Columbus: Ohio State University Press, (pp. 105-114).

Dīrī, 'Akram (1969) "al-madḥāhir al-madaniyya wa al-ᶜaskariyya lil-'al-difāᶜ al-madanī" (The Civil and Military Features of Civil Defense), *Dirāsāt ᶜArabiyya,* Vol. 5, no. 9 (pp. 10-17).

Fisher, Sydney N. (1963) "The Role of the Military in Society and Government in Turkey. In *The Military in the Middle East,* S. Fisher (ed.). Columbus: Ohio State University Press, (pp. 21-40).

Geoje de, M.J. (n.d.) "Caliphate." In *Provisional Readings in the History of the Arabs and Arabic Culture,* A.J. Rustum and C.K. Zurayk (eds.). Beirut: American University of Beirut (pp. 87-94; 109-111).

Ḥaddad, Samīr (1972) *al-mubarrirāt al-tārīkhiyya li al-ᶜaqīdat al-nāssiriyya* (The Historical Reasons for the Nasserite Ideology). Beirut: The Committee for the Teaching of Nasserism.

Hāikal, Ḥasanain M. (n.d.) *ma 'illadhī jarā fī sūriyya* (What Happened in Syria). Cairo: al-Dār al-Qawmiyya.

Halpern, Manfred (1963) *The Politics of Social Change in the Middle East and North Africa.* Princeton: Princeton University Press.

Hell, Joseph (n.d.) "The Arab Civilization." In *Provisional Readings in the History of the Arabs and Arabic Culture,* A.J. Rustum and C.K. Zurayk (eds.), Beirut: American University of Beirut (pp. 93-101).

Himādī, Saᶜdūn (1968) *'ārā hawl qadāyā al-thawra al-ᶜarabiyya* (Views Around the Affairs of Arab Revolution). Beirut: Dār al-Ṭaliᶜa.

Hindī, 'Ihsān (1964) *al-hayā al-ᶜaskariyya ᶜind al-ᶜArab* (Military Life among the Arabs). Damascus: al-Jumhūriyya Press.

Hopkins, Edward C.D. (1970) *Military Intervention in Syria and Iraq: Historical Background, Evaluation, and Some Comparisons.* An M.A. Thesis submitted to the Middle East Area Program of the American University of Beirut.

Hurewitz, J.C. (1969) *Middle East Politics: The Military Dimension.* New York: Praeger.

Janowitz, Morris (1964) *The Military in the Political Development of New Nations.* Chicago: The University of Chicago Press.

al-Jundi, Sāmī (n.d.) *Sūriyya: ra'idat kifāh* (Syria: A Pioneer of Struggle). Beirut: George Abi ᶜAkar.

———(1969a) *sadīqī 'ilyās* (My Friend Elyas). Beirut: Dār al-Nahār.

———(1969b) *al-Baᶜth* (The Baᶜth Party). Beirut: Dār al-Nahār.

Kāmil, Mishāl (1971) "baᶜd al-mulāhādhā hawl minhaj al-ᶜamal al-wantani li-daᶜm al-jabha al-iālhiliyya" (Some Observations on the Method of National Action for the Support of the Internal Front) *al-Ṭalīᶜa,* Vol. 4, no. 2 (pp. 11-17).

Khadduri, Majid (1963) "The Role of the Military in Iraqi Society." In *The Military in the Middle East,* S. Fisher (ed.). Columbus: Ohio State University Press, (pp. 41-51).

Khuri, Fuad I. (1969) "The Changing Class Structure in Lebanon," *The Middle East Journal* (1969: 29-44).

———(n.d.) *From Village to Suburb: Order and Change in Greater Beirut,* A manuscript that will be published by the University of Chicago Press.

Kirk, George (1963) "The Role of the Military in Society and Government: Egypt." In *The Military in the Middle East*, S. Fisher (ed.). Columbus: Ohio State University Press, (pp. 71-88).

Kishk, Muhammad J. (1969) *al-naksa wa al-ghaz al-fikri* (The Disaster and the Intellectual Invasion). Beirut: no publisher.

Khattāb, Mahmūd (1969) *al-wahda al-Caskariyya al-Carabiyya* (The Military Arab Unity). Beirut: Dār al-'Irshād.

'Ibrāhīm, SaCd al-Dīn (1968) "harb alttahrīr al-shaCbiyya" (The Populist War of Liberation), Dirāsāt CArabiyya, Vol. 4, no. 8 (pp. 37-55).

Murād, Zikī (1972) "harakat al-wahda al-sirāC fi al-tahāluf al-watanī" (The Idea of Unity and Struggle in the National Coalition), al-TalīCa, Vol. 8, no. 11 (pp. 45-49).

——— (1966) "hawl 'imkānāt al-thawra lil-jiyush fi thawrat al-tahrir al-watani" (Around the Revolutionary Probabilities for the Military in the National Revolution for Liberation), al-TalīCa, Vol. 2, No. 11 (pp. 40-48).

Mustafā, Hassan (1946) al-taCāwun al-Carabi al-Caskari (The Arab Military Cooperation). Beirut: Dār al-TalīCa.

Mustafā, Khalīl (1969) *suqūt al-jawlān* (The Fall of Gollan Highland) Amman: Dār al-Yaqīn.

NaCāmah, Salīm (1971) "risālat al-jabha" (Letters from the Front) Jaish al-ShaCib no. 990 (pp. 5-9)

Obermeyer, Geral J. (1969) *Structure and Authority in a Bedouin Tribe: The Aishaibat of the Western Desert of Egypt*. Ph.D. Dissertation, Indiana University.

The Popular Democratic Front for the Liberation of Palestine (1971) *hamlat 'aylul wa al-muqāwama al-falistīniniyya* (The September Attack and the Palestinian Resistance). Beirut: Dār al-TalīCa.

al-Qardāwi, Yūsuf (1971) *dars al-nakba al-thāniya* (The Lesson of the Second Catastrophe). No place of publication and no publisher.

al-Quwatlī, Shukrī (1970) Shukrī al-Quwatlī yukhātib 'ummatah (Shukri al-Quwatli Addresses His Nation). Beirut: Salīm Press.

Rahmā, SaCd (1972) "al-Rabit baina al-Camal al-siyāsi wa la-Camal al-Caskari" (The Connection between Political and Military Action), al-TalīCa Vol. 8, no. 11 (pp. 71-73).

al-Razzāz, Munif (1967) *al-tajriba al-murra* (The Bitter Experience). Beirut: Dār Ghandūr.

Rustow, Dankwart A. (1963) "The Military in Middle Eastern Society and Politics." In *The Military in the Middle East*, S. Fisher (ed.). Columbus: Ohio State University Press, (pp. 3-20).

SaCdāwi, Hassān N. (1956) jaish misr fi 'ayyām Salāh al-Dīn (The Army of Egypt during the Days of Salāh al-Dīn a-l'Ayyūbi). Cairo: Al-Nahdat Press.

Safran, Nadav (1961) *Egypt in Search of Political Community.*

al-SaCīd, RifCat (1971) "nadhariyyat al-tahāluf al-watani baina al-fikr wa al-tatbīq" (The Theory of National Coalition Between the Principle and the Practice), al-TalīCat, Vol. 4, no. 2 (pp. 18-23).

al-Sayyid, Jalāl (1973) *hizb al-BaCth al-Arabi* (The Arabic BaCth Party). Beirut: Dār al-Nahār.

Shātilā, Kamāl (1972) *al-nassiriyyat wa mafhūm al-yamin wa al-yasār* (Nasserism and the Concepts of the Right and the Left). Beirut: The Committee for the Teaching of Nasserism.

Tallās, Mustafā (1967) *al-kifah al-musallah* (The Armed Resistance). Beirut: Dār al-TalīCa.

Torrey, Gordon H. (1963) "The Role of the Military in Society and Government in Syria and the Formation of the U.A.R." In *The Military in the Middle East*, S. Fisher (ed.). Columbus: Ohio State University Press (pp. 63-69).

CUmrāh, Muhammad (n.d.) *tajribati fi al-thawra* (My Experience in The Revolution). No place of publication or publisher.

Vatikiotis, P.J. (1961) *The Egyptian Army in Politics.* Bloomington: Indiana University Press.

——— (1967) *Politics and the Military in Jordan: A Study of the Arab Legion 1921-1957.* London: Cass.

Wolf, Eric (1966) "Kinship, Friendship, and Patron-Client Relations in Complex Societies."
In *The Social Anthropoligy of Complex Societies,* M. Banton (ed.). London: Tavistock
Publications (pp. 1-22).

Yāsin, Muhammad H. (1973) "rafi^c mustawā al-^{c}amal al-tandhīmī ka 'asās li ta^{c}bi'at al-
jamāhir" (Raising the Standard of Organizational Action as a Foundation for the
Conscription of the Masses), al-Ṭali^{c}a , Vol. 4, (pp. 24-30).

Zahr al-Dīn, Abdel-Karīm (1966) *mudhakkarāti^{c}an fatrati al-'infisāl fī sūriyya* (My memoirs on the Period of Disunity in Syria). Beirut: no publishing house.

Zein, Zein (1968) *nushū' al-qawmiyya al-^{c}arabiyya* (The Rise of Arab Nationalism). Beirut:
Dār al-Nahār.

THE MILITARY IN FORMER
BELGIAN AFRICA

René Lemarchand

The job of the prophet is a thankless one. Whether based on guesswork, hunches or extrapolations, predictions are always risky, sometimes foolish. Futurologists of the African military, even in the best of circumstances, are in a peculiarly weak position. How to foretell the shape of coups to come, let alone of their outcomes?

Possibilities of error stem in part from the very nature of the military as an object of investigation, in part from the fact that the boundaries of predictions, are nowhere more difficult to define than in the realm of military behavior. The first point scarcely needs elaboration, except to note the difficulty of making intelligent predictions about the future when one lacks even the most rudimentary information about the present. Given the state of our ignorance concerning basic features of military organization—the size and ethnic distribution of the armed forces, their bases of recruitment, the over-/ all military budget and salary scales, or the methods of promotion, one wonders indeed whether there are sufficient empirical grounds for venturing anything but the wildest predictions.

Moreover, the realm of military behavior provides few readily identifiable, commonly accepted social variables for making predictions. To put it differently, the range of possible "if-then" propositions about military behavior is too wide to allow reasonably sound hypothetical statements about the future. Unlike what can be done in, for example, the realm of electoral behavior—where the connection between independent variables and dependent variables can be empirically tested over a period of time and used as a basis of prediction to tell how specific categories of individuals may vote in the future—no such scientific prediction can be made of how African armies, or specific elements within the army, may behave two, five or ten years hence. Though military coups, as some have suggested, may serve as functional alternatives to elections in much of the Third World, the electoral sociology of African armies offers little or no comparable predictability.

But a tentative forecast of military behavior in the forthcoming decade may still not be such a desultory exercise. Forcasting is but another name for political meteorology.[1] In this spirit, and emphasizing the very tentative character of our undertaking, we shall hazard some guesses about (climatic) trends in former Belgian Africa in the 1980s, concentrating on areas of potential turbulence associated with military pressures.[2] Specifically, our aim is to survey the conditions likely to prevail over the three successor states of former Belgian Africa (Zaire, Rwanda and Burundi) by taking into account (1) the conditions currently observable within each state, and (2) the changes that may be anticipated as a result of sequential variations. The first set of factors refers to cross-national discontinuities in the position of, and environmental constraints faced by the military in Zaire, Rwanda and Burundi; the second to the sequential trends that are likely to emerge at the national, regional and international levels over the next ten years. Our contention is that future conditions will be largely determined by the interactions among these factors.

The Political Meteorology of Former Belgian
Africa: Cross-National Discontinuities

The trains of thought developed in this discussion are grounded in several postulates about the relationship between the military as an institution and its wider societal environment:

1.   Short-run trends in patterns of civilian-military relations cannot be properly gauged without taking into account the environmental constraints operating within and across each of the national units included into our universe of comparison.

2.   Future boundary changes in patterns of civilian-military relations are likely to be conditioned in part (a) by elasticity of the relationships between environmental and institutional variables, that is, by the amount of change that can be expected to take place within the military as a result of the changes taking place within the environment, and in part (b) by the manner in which the military elites in each state are likely to perceive the threats or opportunities arising from such changing relationships.

3.   The interdependence of military actions and environmental variables may be seen to operate both at the domestic and international levels, hence validating the use of systems analysis to identify and assess the sequences of interaction likely to take place at the national and cross-national levels.

Before moving to an examination of interaction sequences, let us concentrate on some of the issues raised by the first two of the preceding postulates. In what ways are environmental discontinuities among the three states under investigation likely to affect the future capabilities and position of their respective military establishments? What implications does this hold in terms of military self-perceptions, threat perceptions and possible action patterns?

The answer to the first question is in part written into the enormous disparities of geographical scale, aggregate economic wealth, per capita income and industrial potential discernible between Zaire, on the one hand, and Rwanda and Burundi on the other. The total area enclosed within the boundaries of Zaire (906,000 square miles) is approximately 45 times the size of its two eastern neighbors put together; its GDP is roughly 200 times that of either Rwanda or Burundi, and its per capita income at least six times as high. The Zairian economy is already highly industrialized compared to most other African states; neither Rwanda nor Burundi have as yet built a modern economic infrastructure. Nor have they fully developed what little industrial potential they each have.

Staggering as these discrepancies in wealth and economic power are, their full significance becomes clearer still in the light of population patterns. Whereas Rwanda and Burundi claim one of the highest population densities in the whole of Africa with respectively 370 and 225 inhabitants per square mile, Zaire by contrast seems almost underpopulated (23.0 inhabitants per square mile). Given the paucity of economic resources and very limited environmental potential existing in Rwanda and Burundi, population pressures on their lands are evidently far more acute than in Zaire. The capacity of the lands to support major increments of population is simply much more limited.

In addition, there are crucial differences in social structure, on the one, and the more orthodox form of ethnic pluralism encountered in Zaire between the caste-like societies of Rwanda and Burundi, on the other.[3] In Zaire, where cultural pluralism has always taken the form of veritical cleavages among a multiplicity of discrete ethnic units. Rwanda and Burundi, prior to independence, were highly stratified societies, with power gravitating in the hands of a traditional aristocracy which also claimed the prerogatives of a ruling caste. Even though the advent of independence radically altered pre-existent patterns of power, releasing in each state new aspirations among up-and-coming generations of politicians, the result in Rwanda has been precisely the opposite of what happened in Burundi. In Rwanda, there occurred an abrupt shift of power away from the Tutsi minority to the representatives of the newly-enfranchised Hutu masses; in Burundi, power merely passed from one oligarchy (Ganwa) to another (Tutsi).

Although the foregoing broad discontinuities encompass but a small segment of the total environment, they nonetheless provide us with some clues to an understanding of how past and future trends may be connected. This is not to imply that a linear projection of such discontinuities is all that is needed to foretell the future, only that these constitute the basic parameters within which future patterns of interaction must be assessed.

To elaborate: The discontinuities displayed in Table I suggest a broad pattern of relationships between pairs of environmental and institutional variables, as between scale and economic infrastructure on the one hand, and military capabilities on the other; or between social structure and patterns of civilian-military congruence. In terms of future perspectives, however, the essential point to stress is the degree of elasticity characteristic of any such relationship in each of the three states under investigation—that is the amount of variation that is likely to take place within the military as a result of projected changes in the environment. For example: How much more advanced technologically will the *Armée Nationale Zairoise* (ANZ) be ten years from now, as compared with the *Armée Nationale du Burundi* (ANB) and the *Garde Nationale Rwandaise* (GNR) assuming that the current economic growth rates in each state will remain constant? What changes can one anticipate in the resource-base of the military elites of Rwanda and Burundi, as compared with the Zairian elites, given the very different degrees of elasticity of their respective social environments and economic potential?

The implication, in short, is that institutional variables alone are clearly insufficient as a basis of prediction. That each of the three states under consideration happens to fit the praetorian model outlined by Perlmutter—each in effect illustrative of a polity in which "the military tends to intervene and potentially could dominate the political system"[4] —is far less significant in terms of future perspectives than the range of variation that may be anticipated in each state with regard to the capabilities and resource-position of their respective military elites.

A mere glance at the size of their armed forces, training facilities and degree of technological advancement confirms some of the environmental disparities noted earlier between Zaire, on the one hand, and Rwanda and Burundi on the other. With a total of approximately 58,000 troops, the ANZ is almost ten times the size of the armed forces of Rwanda and Burundi put together, each claiming

TABLE I
Cross-National Discontinuities in Former Belgian Africa

	Zaire	Rwanda	Burundi
I. Environmental Variables			
1. Scale and Economic Infrastructure			
Area (in sq. miles	906,000	10,000	10,000
Gross Domestic Product at Factor Cost (in thousands of Zaires, BF and RF)***	1,025.40	* 16,433.00	** 12,604.00
Per capita Income (in US $)	195.00	35.00	30.00
Industrial Potential (Non-Agricultural Development Potential Index)	15	5	4
Economic Growth Rate	11%	2.5%	0.8%
2. Demography			
Total Population (in millions)	22.8	3.83	3.62
Population per sq. mile	23.9	370	225
Growth rate	2.3%	3.5%	3.0%
3. Social Structure			
Ethnicity	Poly-ethnic	Bi-ethnic	Bi-ethnic
Direction of Major Ethnic Cleavages	Vertical	Horizontal	Horizontal
II. Institutional Variables			
1. Military Capabilities			
Size of Armed Forces****	58,000	3,000	3,000
Percentage of national budget devoted to military expenditures	23.5%	24%	25.5%
Technological Capabilities	High	Low	Low
2. Resource-Base of Military Elites			
Legitimacy	Variable	Low	Mixed
Wealth	High	Low	Low
Status	High	Mixed	Low
3. Patterns of Civilian-Military Congruence	Diversified, fluid	Ethnic-Regional	Ethnic-Regional

Note: The figures above are compiled from the UN Statistical Yearbooks for 1970 and 1971,
  Africa 1973 (London 1973), and D.G. Morrison et al., Black Africa: A Comparative
  Handbook (New York, 1972); unless otherwise indicated the statistics in this table
  are for 1970.

(*) 1968   (**) 1965
(***) $1.00 is worth BF 87.50, RF 82.00, Z 0.50 as of February, 1974.
(****) 1974

an army of about 3,000 men. Given the rate at which the Zairian authorities would like to increase the size of the ANZ over the next ten years (aiming at an army of 120,000 men, a gendarmerie of 35,000 and a total of 3,500 officers for both the army and the gendarmerie), and in view of the severe limitations on any substantial increase faced by Rwanda and Burundi, the disproportions noted above are likely to become even more striking ten years from now.

Growing disparities can also be anticipated at the level of technological capabilities and training facilities. There is no equivalent, and probably never will be an equivalent in Rwanda or Burundi, of the highly sophisticated weaponry—ranging from armored vehicles to helicopters, from fighter bombers to troop carriers and amphibious vehicles of various kinds—which has already entered the arsenal of the ANZ. Nor would it be realistic to anticipate the development in either state of training facilities comparable to those offered in Zaire at the Kitona and Kotakoli centers, or of officers schools comparable to those offered in Zaire at the Kitona and Kotakoli centers, or of officers schools comparable to those recently set up at Luluabourg at the cadet, company commander and specialist levels. In view of the vastly greater resource potential available to the Zairian elites, and their determination to tap this potential for military purposes, one may anticipate a drastic widening of the gap between their overall military capabilities and those of their more disinherited neighbors to the east.

Just as the future capabilities of their armed forces must be assessed in the light of the relative elasticities of their economic and manpower potential, so also with the resource-position of their respective military elites. If access to economic wealth may be viewed as a source of future political power, both may in turn be converted into status and authority. Zaire emerges once again as the most favored nation. For not only is the volume of economic wealth available to the Zairian military far greater than in Rwanda and Burundi (a situation made manifest by the use of spoils and patronage, real estate deals and kickbacks on a scale unparalleled in Rwanda or Burundi) but the pressures for a redistribution of the military's wealth are not nearly as high. The economic pie in Zaire is likely to expand substantially in years ahead, rather the opposite is likely to occur in Rwanda and Burundi. In both smaller states economic scarcity and population pressures will most probably combine to narrow further the resource-base of their military elites not only in terms of wealth but of status and legitimacy. Coercion in each case will tend to predominate over legitimacy.

Although wealth may produce status and legitimacy, the relationship between them is by no means self-evident. In the case of Zaire economic success has had a very powerful feed-back effect on popular perceptions of military legitimacy. In contrast to what happened in Burundi (and may yet happen in Rwanda), where military rule has tended to coincide with a downward trend in the economy, the military in Zaire can legitimately claim to have achieved something of an economic miracle. Much of this miracle must, of course, be credited to circumstances unrelated to the advent of military rule but that is besides the point. What matters is that Mobutu is viewed as being largely responsible for it. The higher status enjoyed by the Zairian military is reducible to much the same phenomenon. That the rebellions of 1964-65 happened to be quelled with the help of European and South African mercenaries is irrelevant as long as the ANZ is being viewed as the sole artisan of a hard-won victory, and indeed as the instrument that ultimately brought the defeat of insurgent mercenary forces in the summer and fall of 1967.

Military performance takes on a rather different coloration in Rwanda and Burundi, as does the popular image associated with such performance. In the case of Rwanda the army was virtually non-existent at the time the Hutu revolution broke out, and in subsequent years military engagements against "counter-revolutionary elements" were generally conducted under the command and supervision of Belgian officers. External support in Burundi did not come from Belgium but from Zaire, and when the time came for the ANB to spring into action much of its energy was spent on rounding up and carrying to their graves truckloads of innocent school-children and university students. An estimated 80,000 Hutu lost their lives in the course of the repression triggered by the abortive, Hutu-inspired coup of April 1972, of whom only a tiny fraction can be said to have been actively engaged in subversive activities. Relatively little prestige, and considerable mutual hatred, is likely to accrue from such genocidal performance.

Reflective of the different resource-positions held by the military in Zaire, Rwanda and Burundi are the varied patterns of civilian-military congruence[5] that have developed in each state as a result of historical circumstances and environmental conditions. Although Rwanda and Burundi show a relatively high degree of civilian-military congruence in terms of ethnicity, between them the profile of elite ethnic identification is radically different. In Rwanda membership into the Hutu subculture, whether real or imagined, is the single most important criterion for recruitment into positions of authority within and outside the military. The

equivalent condition in Burundi lies in one's affiliation to, or identification with, the Tutsi minority. Yet, in each case, recruitment patterns are based on the systematic exclusion of a particular ethnic
group from all positions of authority. In effect in each state ethnicity
plays a determining role in the way in which the military define
environmental threats to its own corporate self-interests.

None of these generalizations apply to Zaire. Here the patterns
of civilian-military congruence are far more difficult to pin down,
involving a far wider range of reference-group identifications.
Regional, generational or class cleavages play far more important
parts than in Rwanda or Burundi in shaping the character of civilian-
military identifications. On the whole, ethnicity plays a rather marginal role.

On the strength of these disparities it is tempting to forecast
two major areas of potential turbulence—one resulting from the
spill-over of ethnic tensions across the boundaries of Rwanda and
Burundi, and culminating in a state of open warfare between them;
the other originating in Zaire, in the form of a reaction to the disturb-
ances developing between its neighbors. In the first case the source
of turbulence is likely to be a combination of the last two discontinuities—the existence of fundamental ethnic disharmonies within and
between the political systems of Rwanda and Burundi, and from the
inability or unwillingness of their military elites to come to grips with
the tensions arising from this situation other than through coercive
measures. In the second case, intervention is likely to result from the
extension of the arbitrating functions of the Zairian military into
the realm of inter-state politics, an occurrence made all the more
probable by the vast differences in military capabilities noted earlier.

The chances of these scenarios becoming reality depend on the
extent to which internal and external threat perceptions on the part
of the military, Rwanda as in Burundi, will reinforce each other,
prompting either state to engage in a type of pre-emptive strike
against its neighbor. The assumption here is that perceptions of hostility may transcend national arenas and acquire a momentum of their
own, ultimately leading to interstate violence. The other side of the
coin is that the mere anticipation of a Zairian intervention may
induce each of the potential belligerents to adopt a more flexible
stance towards each other.

Missing from this formulation, then, are the sequential relations
that may develop over the long run among these three polities and
which may yet give the lie to the apostles of apocalypse. Hence the
need to bring a different set of variables into the picture. Cross-

sectional discontinuities of the kind we just described can only provide the basis for a very rough and partial forecast. For a safer estimate of the future one needs to concentrate on those variables that involve sequential trends at the national, regional and international levels.

SEQUENTIAL TRENDS

Perhaps the most notable of such trends at the national level concerns the shift of reference-group identification (i.e., from ethnicity to class) already discernible in the armed forces of each state. As corporate membership in the armed forces of Zaire, Rwanda and Burundi become increasingly tied up with membership in a privileged economic group, self-perceptions within the military will tend to shift from "ethnicity" to "class" as the key contextual referent. Albeit in different degrees, and through varying circumstances, control in each state over the means of production already tends to gravitate in the hands of those who hold the means of repression; concurrently, elite status within the military is fast becoming identified with access to economic wealth.

This incipient transformation of military self-images and self-interests must be attributed in part to the impact of military technology on the wider society, a phenomenon which, according to Mazrui, can best be understood by reference to the growing technological gap between the military and the more "backward" rural sectors.

> Modern military technology in a relatively backward society tends to widen the gap of power between the unarmed citizenry on one side, and those who hold control over the new means of war on the other . . . Those who control the means of production—workers, managers and owners—are at their most powerful in relation to the soldiers in situations of technological complexity. They are at their weakest in relation to the soldiers in situations of rudimentary technology.[6]

The argument gains cogency in the light of the specific situational factors that have come into play in each of the states: the persistence within the military of socio-economic privileges of a traditional character (as in Rwanda), the systematic appropriation by officers and troops of the resources previously held by members of a particular ethnic community (as happened in Burundi after the massacres of 1972), and the deliberate extension of economic opportunities and pay-offs to senior officers (as has been and still is the case in Zaire). All have reinforced the saliency of "class" identifications within the military. Though the methods may differ from one state to the next, the long-range consequences are likely to be the same—an increasingly close association of military power with economic wealth, accompanied by the emergence of the military entrepreneur as the dominant element in society. This, in essence, is what Mazrui recently described as "the embourgeoisement of the lumpenmilitariat,"[7] a phrase that seems especially appropriate to describe the situation that has emerged in Zaire but which also applies, mutatis mutandis, to Rwanda and Burundi.

In both states, one may note parenthetically, this shift of reference-group identifications has been further accelerated by the manner in which military elites have recently perceived environmental threats to their corporate self-interests. In 1971 in Burundi, and in 1973 in Rwanda, challenges to the military have arisen from ethnic sectors that were least suspect of subversion—from Tutsi elements in Burundi, and from Hutu elements in Rwanda. Yet for this very reason in neither case were these threats defined in ethnic terms. Regionalism rather than ethnicity emerged as the essential component of threat perceptions. Concommittantly the tendency in each state has been for the military to slough off its ethnic self-image and to redefine its identity in terms of regional criteria. Regional self-perceptions within the military may thus be viewed as a transitional stage, though by no means an irreversible one, between "ethnic" and "class" identifications.

In short, the process by which the lumpenmilitariat achieves its embourgeoisement involves a variety of structural and conjunctural factors, and while their cumulative impact may differ from one state to the next, the ultimate consequences are bound to be everywhere the same—a growing coalescence of military technology and economic wealth, accompanied by an increasing concurrence of self-interests and self-perceptions among the military elites of each state. Cross-national solidarities within the military will tend to offset whatever discontinuities may persist, both at the national and cross-national levels.

Another component of temporal prediction, perhaps the most consequential in terms of its impact on future inter-state relations, refers to the mutual threats arising from the play of "external" forces at work in each state.[8] Basically, these threats stem from the flight of thousands of political refugees from their homelands, resulting in a three-way spill-over of anti-regime forces into adjacent national arenas. In each state domestic violence has generated massive involuntary migrations of individuals and groups into neighboring territories; each state has thus become host to a refugee community from one or the other of its neighbors. From 1959 on-wards thousands of Tutsi refugees from Rwanda have sought asylum in Burundi and Zaire; during and after the so-called "Congo Rebel-lion" (1964-1965), a sizeable minority of refugees from the Kivu and Katanga provinces have found asylum in Burundi and Tanzania. And since the Burundi massacres of 1972 tens of thousands of Hutus have left their homeland to seek protection in Rwanda, Zaire and Tanzania. The result has been to create in each state a "privileged sanctuary" for the launching of refugee-led guerilla operations against its neigh-bors, while at the same time exposing each of the host communities to the threat of military retaliations.

The implications of this situation for the security of these states concerned are nowhere more starkly revealed than in the seemingly endless series of infiltrations, border raids and guerilla attacks—some assuming the dimensions of full-scale invasions—that have taken place over the last decade. Since the massive slaughter of Hutu populations by the Burundi authorities in April and May 1972, followed by the exodus of an estimated 150,000 Hutu refugees into Rwanda, Zaire and Tanzania, something of a stalemate has developed between Rwanda and Burundi. Each in effect has had to rely on the guarantees offered by the other to prevent refugee groups from fighting their way back into their country of origin. The resulting equilibrium is nonetheless a very precarious one. Since neither state has as yet the capability to exercise totally effective control over its refugee population, the possibility of unintended warfare between them cannot be excluded, any more than the possibility of a Zairian intervention.

Yet the Zairian position is not solely reducible to that of a potential umpire, if and when open warfare should break out between Rwanda and Burundi. Far more perplexing is the role that the Zairian authorities might play in the event of unintended hostili-ties between Tanzania and Burundi. Judging by the extreme serious-ness of the diplomatic incident triggered by the mistaken strafing of a Tanzanian village by helicopters of the ANB in the spring of 1973,[9] the question is worth raising, even though the answer must remain speculative. What does seem reasonably clear, however, in the light of the arbitrating role devolved upon President Mobutu at the height of the Burundi-Tanzania crisis, is: (1) that Zaire will carry a decisive weight in any future confrontation in Central Africa, assuming in effect the position of an externally controlling state vis-a-vis both Rwanda and Burundi; and (2) that whatever interven-tionist move Zaire may wish to pursue in the future will be dictated as much by a desire to reduce the existing potential for civil war

in Rwanda and Burundi as by its determination to prevent the internationalization of domestic conflicts.

The sheer explosiveness of the situation we just described carries
fundamental implications for future patterns of interaction in Central Africa, emphasizing the need for some basic readjustments at
the institutional and diplomatic levels. The conditions of chronic
instability arising from the spill-over of anti-regime forces may in
time generate their own remedies, either in the form of a growing
interdependence of the security forces of each state, or in the form
of initiatives designed to encourage the growth of consensual relations among them. In the immediate future, however, the remedies,
or better the palliatives, are likely to be found in the guarantees of
external support which each state seeks to extract from outside
powers, African, European and American.

There is yet another significant variable in this analysis of
sequential relations, namely the probable impact of external dependencies on the perspectives and behavior of the military. The most
significant trend to note in this connection is the diversification of
dependency relationships rather than the continuation of existing
dependencies, especially with regard to military aid. For reasons
intimately connected with their domestic politics, as well as with the
domestic politics of their former colonial master, Rwanda and Burundi
are likely to become increasingly drawn into competing spheres of influence, with France seeking to enhance its military presence in
Burundi at the expense of Belgium, and the latter continuing to hold
a controlling position in Rwanda. Further reinforcing this line of
cleavage is Burundi's "Libyan connection," for which there is as yet
no counterpart in Rwanda, and which, if activated could possibly
alter the balance of forces between them. Although the trend in
Zaire is towards a multilateralization of external dependencies,
primary reliance for military aid will continue to be placed on the
United States, with France meeting only specific items on Zaire's
shopping list (such as fighter bombers and helicopters).

Such a diversification of international linkages could lead to
results opposite from those that might be inferred from the preceding discussion. The perspectives of the military in each state are
indeed likely to reflect for some time to come the diversity of
interests attached to French, Belgian and American commitments,
thereby seriously complicating the task of evolving a stable and dur-
able framework of regional cooperative relations. Moreover, continued injections of military aid in Rwanda and Burundi will most
probably raise the political expectations and military capabilities

of each state to a level scarcely compatible with the exigencies of
such cooperative relations, while doing very little to improve long-run
prospects of economic viability.

The paradox of this situation is that although foreign military
aid only serves to perpetuate the dependence of the recipient states
on external powers, the benefits accruing from such aid also serve
to enhance their national sovereignty at the regional African level.
Dependence at one level may thus act as a guarantee of independence
at another. Regional supranationality would undoubtedly minimize
the risk of external manipulation through bilateral military aid, yet
the very nature of the external forces at play in Rwanda and Burundi
makes regional supranationality on a tripartite basis all the more
difficult to achieve.

SCENARIOS OF THE FUTURE

The foregoing analysis suggests three possible lines of development—the first two predicated on the assumption of an extension of
domestic conflict across the national boundaries of Rwanda and
Burundi, the third in the nature of a mutually agreed upon formula
aimed at reducing the risk of a bilateral or multilateral confrontation.

(1) *Bilateral Confrontation: Zaire as an Umpire*

In this scenario the key emphasis is on continued perceptions
of hostility between Rwanda and Burundi, culminating in a state
of open warfare between them. The assumption, moreover, is that
the conflict will remain circumscribed to the initial belligerents, with
Zaire intervening in the capacity of a netural arbiter presumably for
the purpose of restoring the pre-existing balance of power.

The probable sequence of events in this scenario may be viewed
in terms of a dialectical ethnic conflict moving back and forth from
one domestic arena to the other. Repressive measures against the
Hutu of Burundi are likely to generate retaliatory actions against the
Tutsi of Rwanda, the latter in turn encouraging further repression
in Burundi, and so on into a cycle. With each ethnic crisis generating
its own momentum the point will soon be reached where conflict
is no longer manageable at the domestic level. At this stage several
possible alternatives may be envisaged: (a) a protracted trial of
strength between Rwanda and Burundi, leading to a unilateral settlement on the terms of whoever happens to gain the upper hand;
(b) a unilateral intervention on the part of Zaire, eventuating in a
negotiated settlement; (c) an internationalization of domestic con-

flicts in the form of a "client war," with Zaire and Tanzania each lending maximum support to their respective client states.

Given the nature of the interests at stake, and in view of the tremendous disparities of power and influence between Rwanda and Burundi on the one hand, and their immediate neighbours on the other, the first alternative is the least likely. A more probable outcome would be for Zaire to step in and either restore the status quo or act as an *amicus curiae* in the formulation and implementation of a negotiated compromise. Another possible outcome would be for Tanzania to jump into the fray and assert itself as the protector of Rwanda's national integrity against both Burundi and Zaire.

(2) A "client war": Rwanda vs. Burundi; Zaire vs. Tanzania

Here the plausibility of the scenario stems in part from the character of associational ties between Rwanda and Tanzania on the one hand, and Burundi and Zaire on the other, and in part from certain assumptions about the durability and strength of such ties.

Let us note, to begin with, Rwanda's recent reorientation towards East Africa in general and Tanzania in particular, a trend made manifest by a number of initiatives at the diplomatic level.[10] As one of the ten participants to the Economic Commission for Africa's "East African" subregion, Rwanda has agreed to the decision made in Lusaka in 1965 to eliminate all trade barriers between them by 1975. Although this would imply the restoration of free trade with Burundi, Rwanda's relations with Tanzania are bound to remain more friendly than with either Burundi or Zaire. The series of bilateral agreements recently concluded with Tanzania—ranging from the construction of a bridge over the Kagera to the construction of an all-weather road between Kigali and Tabora, and a joint Rwanda-Tanzania hydro-electric project near the Rusumo Gorge—bear testimony to Rwanda's overture to the east.

Burundi's relations with Tanzania, on the other hand, have undergone a rapid and serious deterioration since early 1973. As noted earlier, the mistaken strafing of a Tanzanian village by the ANB brought a near rupture of diplomatic ties between them. Although a severance of diplomatic relations was averted, tensions between them nonetheless persist. Meanwhile an all-out effort is being made by Burundi to strengthen its ties with Zaire and Uganda, each being regarded as potential allies in the event of a confrontation with Rwanda. Zaire's friendly dispositions were conclusively tested by President Micombero of Burundi in the spring of 1972, when Zairian troops were flown to Bujumbura to buttress the ANB's position during the recent Hutu-led rebellion. Furthermore, Uganda President Amin's threat in 1972 that he would not hesitate to "flatten the Rwandan capital of Kigali" if the circumstances required was received with understandable satisfaction in Bujumbura.

Projecting these trends into the future, it is easy to see why a local conflict might deteriorate into a wider confrontation. Yet the likelihood of such a scenario becoming a reality is extremely remote. Associational ties and supportive moves of the kind just described are clearly insufficient to warrant the intervention of either Zaire or Tanzania on behalf of their respective "clients," and in the absence of security agreements to that effect there is no reason to anticipate a full-fledged confrontation between Kinshasa and Dar-es-Salaam.

Moreover, largely missing from this scenario are the variety of countervailing pressures noted earlier in this discussion, in particular the existence of growing solidarities among the military elites of Zaire, Rwanda and Burundi. Whether arising from their shared consciousness of belonging to a privileged "class," from their own perceptions of the costs involved in an eventual confrontation, or simply from the restraining influences exercised by outside powers, European and American, the effect of such pressures on the attitude and orientation of the military cannot be dismissed. In these circumstances another alternative might be for the three states concerned to evolve a common framework of cooperative relations with a view to maximizing their chances of economic viability while at the same time reducing the risks of confrontation and hostility.

(3) *The Quest for a Modus Vivendi: Cooperation within a Hegemonic Framework*

The assumption here is that in years ahead a number of environmental and situational factors will generate pressures for at least a partial change in the relationships of the three states towards each other:

1. An explosive population growth in both Rwanda and Burundi, far exceeding the economic capabilities of either state and hence reinforcing the conditions of chronic instability and ethnic strife inherent in their respective social systems.

2. A growing awareness among the military elites of Zaire, Rwanda and Burundi of the threats posed to their security by the presence of anti-regime forces in the vicinity of their national boundaries, along with a common recognition by the elites of Rwanda and Burundi of the need to develop reliable techniques to avoid mutual destruction.

3. A concommittant realization in Rwanda and Burundi that the costs involved in a bilateral confrontation (Rwanda-Burundi) would far exceed the sacrifices required by a lessening of national autonomy for the sake of mutual security.

4. An increasingly clear commitment on the part of the Zairian authorities to the elaboration of new and constructive relationships with Rwanda and Burundi, and ultimately with the Congo.

These conditions are neither necessary nor sufficient for the emergence of a political-military union of Zaire, Rwanda and Burundi; from the standpoint of the national interest of the latter two, however, they are certainly sufficient to recognize the desirability of setting up a regional framework of cooperative relations, on a bilateral or tripartite basis.

If an initial assumption is that regional supranationality does not necessarily exclude the principle of national sovereignty, there is no reason to assume that the options facing the military elites of Rwanda and Burundi are reducible to independence in chaos or integration in harmony. While there is no denying the persuasiveness of the arguments in favor of a political union of Rwanda and Burundi with Zaire, there are strong disincentives in both smaller states to such a union. To expect the military elites of Rwanda and Burundi unilaterally to abdicate their political sovereignty for the sake of a better economic future would be just as naive today as it will be five or ten years from now. The differences between them cover a wide range of issues, reflecting both the character of their historical legacies and the ethnic confrontations triggered by the advent of independence. Nor should these differences obscure the existence of similar and other disharmonies between them on the one hand, and their neighbour to the west on the other. In these conditions there are few reasons to anticipate a radical transformation of the existing political status quo within the next decade, least of all a relinquishment of national sovereignty on the part of any one state.

Perhaps the most one can expect at this stage is a concerted effort to work out new types of cooperative relationships among them, in the economic, financial and educational spheres, hoping that such an attempt at functional integration may in time reduce the risks of political confrontation.

1. A tripartite security arrangement designed to bring the refugee populations of each state under the effective control of the host authorities.

2. The setting up of a customs union among the three states, perhaps along the lines of a Central African Common Market and involving

tariff preferences geared to the economic exigencies of each participant.

3.   An agreement on the utilization of certain common services and infrastructural facilities, ranging from airports and harbours to hydro-electric plants and roads.

4.   The establishment of cooperative links among the universities of Zaire, Rwanda and Burundi, followed up by similar links among various research institutes (IRSAC, INEAC, CEMUBAC) in each state.

In the long run it is hard to see how, even in the best of circumstances, that is assuming that the steps just outlined are in fact implemented, micro-states like Rwanda and Burundi can possibly survive the enormous demographic pressures with which they are plagued while at the same time resisting the attraction of a political integration with Zaire. It may be that someday cooperative links among them will take the form of a federation (in some ways reminiscent of the edifice that was once built by Belgium), with the security forces of Rwanda and Burundi reduced to the status of a constabulary apparatus. The immediate future will not be so simple, however. It will encompass a variety of actors, African and European, whose conflicting interests will be felt across a wide range of issues. The most one can hope for in these circumstances is that the resultant pressures might be contained within a framework of cooperation and reciprocal understanding rather than a framework of mutual hostility and persistent ethnic hatreds.

Notes

1. In Mazrui's words, "it admits into relevance seasonal weather conditons as variables behind specific socio-political incidents . . . (It is), in part, the literal utilization of climatic and weather conditons as a method of trying to predict political temperature and likely political events." The distinction between "prediction" and "forecasting" is further elaborated upon in M.Q. Sibley, "The Limitations of Behaviorism" in Charlesworth (1967: 60ff).

2. Mazrui (1968: passim).

3. For further information, see Lemarchand (1970).

4. Perlmutter (1969: 383).

5. For further elaboration on the concept of civil-military congruence and its implications for the analysis of civil-military relations, see Lemarchand (forthcoming).

6. Mazrui (1973: 1-12).

7. Mazrui (1973: 1-12).

8. Lemarchand (forthcoming).

9. Penza (1973) "Survivors of Burundi Raid Tell of Horror Tales." Daily News of Tanzania (March 29).

10. For further details, see "A New Era in Relations with Rwanda." Daily News of Tanzania (February 28, 1973).

PIETY AND PURITANISM UNDER A
MILITARY THEOCRACY: UGANDA SOLDIERS
AS APOSTOLIC SUCCESSORS

Ali A. Mazrui

In 1969 Pope Paul visited Uganda. He was the first reigning Pope
to visit black Africa. In 1971 General Idi Amin "returned" the visit.
He was the first Executive President of Uganda to visit the Vatican.
Behind both visits was the religious factor in Uganda politics. Neither
President Milton Obote—who played host to Pope Paul—nor President
Idi Amin were Roman Catholics. Obote was a Protestant, Amin a
Muslim. But their diplomatic courtesies with the Vatican were con-
nected with deeper issues in the political history of their country.

What were these deeper issues, and in what way do they relate to
Amin's role as a military ruler?

If Obote on independence was heir to the colonial administration,
Amin has in part become heir to the Christian missionaries. Uganda
under Idi Amin has re-entered the era of puritanism and fear of God
as principles of statecraft. If Max Weber's state was one which could
successfully claim a monopoly of the legitimate use of physical force,
Amin's state goes on to claim a monopoly of the legitimate use of
spiritual sanctions as well. The government under Amin has aspired
to create a devout society and to participate in transmitting the gift of
religious leadership. It is in this sense that Uganda soldiers might be
deemed to be "apostolic successors." Under Amin's inspiration, they
have at any rate became pretenders to that divine role.

Rudolf Bultmann has argued that the term "apostle" once
referred to all missionaries and was later narrowed down to the Twelve
desciples of Jesus in order to help establish the formal theory of
apostolic succession. It was not until the end of the second century
A.D. that "apostolic succession" was given a sacramental interpretation in the sense of uninterrupted transmission of a special gift of
consecration and sacred leadership, descended from one or more of
the original Twelve Apostles.

Our sense of "apostle" is the older one which refers to missionaries and messengers of God. A. Richardson distinguished between
apostles who had received their commission directly from the Lord,

such as the Twelve, and those who were emmisaries of local religious establishments. The distinction becomes difficult with General Idi Amin, since he claims to derive some of his policies from divinely-inspired dreams. But whatever sense of "apostle" might be appropriate for the General, his regime has included an important theocratic factor, partly derived from the impact of the Christian missionaries on Uganda society as a whole. Again, it is in this sense that Amin stands "in apostolic succession" to the European founders of the imperial religious culture of Uganda.[1]

Against a background of state sponsorship of religious ceremonies, the banning of mini-skirts, newly-imposed drinking hours, a ban on certain forms of "teenage dancing," and the enforcement of religious unity, several questions have arisen concerning the Second Republic of Uganda under Amin. Has Uganda under him been evolving into a military theocracy? Is the country experiencing an extension of the ethos of military discipline in the form of a puritanical mood? Has the Second Republic become the *Sacred* Republic? What does Uganda's experience tell us about the interplay and inter-relationship between politics, religion and the military?

There is little doubt that certain theocratic factors have indeed been at play in the political style of General Idi Amin since he assumed power. These theocratic elements are related to the triple capacity of the General in this regard—the General as a soldier, as a religious man, and as a political activist. But we propose further to argue in this paper that the origins of theocracy or neo-theocracy in Uganda do not lie merely in the military coup of 1971, but are more deeply rooted in the history of the country as a whole. The politicization of religion in Uganda has been a feature of the country's politics from way back in the colonial era, but has entered a new phase under military rule.

That is why the soldiers of the Second Republic are in an important sense successors to the early missionaries of Uganda. The early missionaries of Uganda were also profoundly sensitive to issues of piety, decency and propriety, and engaged in forms of moral censure which have had long-term consequences on the entire life style of the people of this country. The origins of the elaborate Kiganda dress, the *busuti,* and the ban on mini-skirts from one continuous moral thread in the history of this country. The ultra-modest *busuti* dress came into being partly in response to the moral puritanism of the early missionaries; the mini-skirt is disappearing in Uganda partly in response to the moral puritanism of the Military Government.

What we may be witnessing is a militarization of traditional

missionary activity, as new standards of decency, morality and propriety are set by the soldiers. The impact of the Christian missionaries
hold in spite of the fact that the General himself is a Muslim. The
General's own religious style and convictions are indeed based on the
Islamic religion, but the impact of the Christian missionaries was not
only on those they converted but on the society as a whole. Euro-
Christian standards were often the reference point for Christians and
non-Christians alike. Those Ugandans who were converted to Christianity acquired educational advantages, prestige and influence. The
socially prominent Christians influenced other Ugandans in a variety
of ways. And even when Uganda Muslims were being defensive in the
face of Christian influence, the Muslim reaction was itself a manifestation of Christian influence. Today, with a Muslim President in power,
the country has witnessed a remarkable interplay between the heritage
of politicized Christianity and the beings of military puritanism.

But there is an additional factor which this paper would seek to
bring out. And this lies in the degree to which a military theocracy
can have points in common with a socialist state in matters connected
with conceptions of decency and sexual discipline. Since 1971 Amin
has been moving to the left. In this regard we shall compare briefly
Uganda under General Amin with Tanzania under Mwalimu Nyerere.

What is a Theocracy?

First, what is a theocracy? For our purposes we define a theocracy as a political system which uses God as a point of reference for
policy-making and makes God the focus of political morality. Political wisdom in a theocracy is ultimately divinely inspired. The world
of politics and the world of religion in a theocracy are profoundly
intertwined.

For at least a year before the military coup General Idi Amin
was already beginning to make an impact as a religious man. He
attended special *Mauledis,* and had begun the sustained refrain that
he feared no one but God. There were times when President Obote
betrayed his anxiety about the style of the new Amin. Was the General beginning to build for himself a political base among the Muslims
of Uganda, adding to his already substantial following within the
armed forces? Or was his adventure in image-building among the
populace as a whole an exercise designed to give him extra protection
against Obote's arbitrariness?

A supreme game of political survival started between the General and his Commander-in-Chief, President Obote. In that supreme game Amin won. The Second Republic of Uganda came into being on January 25, 1971.

Soon the religious factor in Amin's personality as a political activist began to emerge. The General expressed an interest in establishing a Ministry of Religious Affairs. He was finally persuaded to establish a Department of Religious Affairs, but with a full Permanent Secretary at its head. Amin's language included a theme of religiosity. He organized a major religious conference at the International Conference Centre in Kampala, designed to bring the different and mutually suspicious denominations of Uganda into something approaching national harmony. Each major session of that conference, even when sub-divided into committee groups, was chaired by no less a figure than a Cabinet Minister. The Chairman of a session was seldom a member of the religious denomination over whose session he presided. That very trans-denominational technique of organizing a conference was itself an exercise in promoting a new attitude towards religion in Uganda as a nation. What began to emerge was that General Amin wanted to go down in history as the man who tried hard to come to grips with the religious factor in Uganda, and attempted to force national unity out of warring factions.

It was out of those initial moods that Amin appeared as a man committed to creating an ecumenical state in Uganda. An ecumenical state is to be distinguished both from a secular state and from a state with an established church. A secular state is one which systematically asserts that the duty of the state is to keep out of religious affairs, and insists that the churches should similarly keep out of affairs of state. A secular state tries to translate into reality the dictum that citizens should give unto Caesar that which is Caesar's and to God that which is God's. The United States is a secular state in this sense.

The United Kingdom, on the other hand, is not a secular state. The Head of State, Her Majesty the Queen, is also the Head or Governor of the Church of England. The Archbishop of Canterbury is appointed by the Prime Minister. Major doctrinal changes in the Church of England cannot be made without the approval of the British Parliament, either directly given or derivatively granted. There is no pretence in the British formal system of Government to separate Church from State. On the contrary, the very concept of an established Church is a repudiation of such a separation.

The third type of state is ecumenical. In this case the State neither favors one denomination against others, as the State does in England, nor does it keep out of religious affairs as a major constitutional imperative, as the federal government does in the United States. The ecumenical state by contrast maintains a role for Government in religious affairs, but not in favor of any one particular denomination. In the ecumenical state the thrust is towards state participation in serving as a referee among denominations, and in the systematic promotion of greater harmony. In the Middle East, Lebanon is an ecumenical state, elaborately institutionalized. Different denominations hold different ministries in Government; different denominations hold different percentages in Parliament. The Lebanese have since the 1920s attempted to provide their Christian and Muslim groups with a system of government that has institutionalized political balance based on religious affiliation.

General Amin seemed to have embarked on a similar policy when he first organized the religious denominations into a historic conference at the International Conference Centre. Among the denominations that turned up at the Conference, the Catholics were the most united internally. Though Amin later came to fear Catholic unity, he was initially impressed by it. Among the most divided internally were the Protestants and Muslims, each group having deep cleavages which went back several decades.

General Amin committed himself to promoting Protestant unity, Muslim unity, as well as unity between Muslims, Protestants and Catholics. When a certain section of the Anglican Church tried to make a bid to secede and form a dioces of its own, the Government of General Amin intervened. Amin's Government categorically asserted that the Anglican Church was to remain intact, and no sub-section was going to be permitted to secede. And when in 1971 Muslims were in disagreement as to when to celebrate Idd el Fitr, the Government of Idi Amin chose a common day for all Muslims to observe as Idd el Fitr, and threatened any Muslim attempting observance on any other day with unspecified retribution.

Uganda had witnessed a variety of forms of interference with freedom. But there was a danger that freedom of conscience might itself be interfered with for the best ecumenical motives in the world. And in fact the most serious risk of invading religious conscience so far has not been with reference to Christians, but to Muslims. The secessionist movement within the Anglican Church was an exercise in power politics within the Church, rather than a doctrinal issue of theological interpretation. But the issue of Idd el Fitr in its very simplicity, perhaps in its very frivolity, was a purely religious issue which concerned how long the Muslims observed the fast of Ramadhan, and on which particular day they were to break that fast. The fast of Ramadhan was a fast for simple people, based according to some on when the moon was sighted with the naked eye in the very country in which the fast was being observed; and according to other versions the month of Ramadhan was to be counted in precise astronomical calculations. Which side one belonged to was quite clearly a matter of deeply held conviction.[2]

But at what point does an ecumenical state become a theocracy? Both the state with the established church and the ecumenical state could become a theocracy when the center of the political system becomes markedly God-conscious in its policy formulation. Where the state merely tries to promote religious harmony, without directly engaging in defining the boundaries of spiritual purity and moral behavior, the state could be ecumenical without being theocratic. But where the State invokes God as the fountain of political morality, and specifies directions of moral puritanism symptomatic of religious fervor, the State has become not only ecumenical but also theocratic in spirit.

My own argument in this essay is to the effect that the roots of these theocratic trends lie in a fragile interaction between a nascent military puritanism, the personality of Amin, and the long-standing historic interaction between religion and politics in Uganda. Inspite of Amin's upbringing as a Muslim, the theocratic trends and the moral puritanism in his Second Republic of Uganda have, in historical terms, a Christian genesis. But the puritanical element under army rule has been reinforced by certain aspects of the military ethos itself, with its theoretical emphasis on "barrack austerity" and discipline. In reality the Ugandan army is not among the most disciplined and self-denying the world. Yet even that may help to explain Amin's search for a wider climate of discipline. Amin seems to feel that his army will sober up only when society as a whole becomes more sober.

Lastly, the personality of the General has itself played a part in defining the boundaries of these theocratic and puritanical elements. The General's style includes elements of religious leadership. He makes use of dreams and pre-vision as ingredients in political image-building. The utilization of dreams and inspired pre-visions is often more a characteristic of religious leaders than of political ones in the modern period. General Amin lies astride both traditions. Sometimes he defines a dream only partially, leaving the important factors undefined and adding to the mystery of what is forecast. Indeed the General cannot be excluded as a factor in his own right behind the theocratic trends in Uganda. He does claim a special divine gift—an apostle in uniform.

Some countries have Pilgrim Fathers among their Founders. Uganda can now count on one Pilgrim Dada in a formative period of its history.[3] Will the General go down in history as a religious unifier or was this particular "dream" too much for this rough-and-ready Muslim soldier? We shall return to this later in the analysis.

The Christian Origins of Uganda's Puritanism

But more important than Amin's religiosity is the deeper history of Uganda as a sacralized polity. Indeed, Amin's religiosity might itself have been profoundly influenced by that older interplay between religion and politics in the life of Uganda since the 1890s.

Professor B. A. Low once argued that Uganda's receptivity to Christianity was facilitated by the prior coming of Islam. Citing an argument of David Livingstone's brother-in-law, John Smith Moffat, Low shared the view that a new religion found it easiest to take root in a place where traditional values had already been disturbed. In the words of Moffat,

> . . . it is where the political organization is most perfect, and the social system still in its aboriginal vigor, that the missionary has the least success in making an impression. Where things have undergone a change and the old feudal usages have lost their power, where there is a measure of disorganization, the new ideas which the Gospel brings with it do not come into collision with any powerful political prejudice. The habits and modes of thinking have been broken up, and so there is a preparation for the seed of the word.[4]

Applying this reasoning especially to Buganda, Anthony Low suggested that the Christian missions would have encountered the prejudice of deep-seated Buganda traditional religions had the atmosphere for change not already been prepared for them by the Arabs. The first Arabs to enter Buganda were later expelled by Kabaka Suna. The Arabs were allowed to return by Suna's successor, Kabaka Mutesa I, at the beginning of the 1860s. The fortunes of Islam and the Arabs fluctuated. But the Arab intrusion was itself a preparation for what came later. In the words of Low,

> Though Islam had been the first to make its way in, Christian missionaries arrived at a singularly opportune moment. For Islam was not firmly entrenched, so that Christianity did not have to compete with another world religion—always a difficult matter; but Islam had set many minds agog; it had brought an era of change, and this helped to give Christianity its entree more particularly because the first question was usually whether

Christianity was a better version of religion than Islam—and here the
Christian denunciation of Arab slave dealings was clearly important.
Certainly the relatively exemplary character of the missionaries had its
influence.[5]

But in what manner did Christianity lay the foundation for the
theocratic styles of the Second Republic of Uganda under Amin? And
in what manner did this in turn relate to the problem of moral puritanism and its demands on individual behavior?

From this point of view the Christian impact on Uganda has to
be seen as a two-pronged impact. Uganda witnessed what might be
called the *Christianization of sexual relations;* and Uganda also witnessed the *politicization of Christianity.* The Christianization of the
world of sex prepared the ground for moral puritanism; the politicization of Christianity in Uganda initiated the theocratic process. Let
us take each of these two trends in turn.

The Christianization of sexual relations arose out of the widespread belief among the early missionaries that the world of sex in
African societies was a little too loose; that inadequate discipline was
exercised over sexual appetites. The missionaries were bringing the
Gospel to "heathen communities" steeped not only in superstition
but also in sinful desires. The first behavioral imperative therefore
was to control those areas of African life which helped to whet
those appetites and desires. Discipline was of the first order, and a
new regularity needed to be imposed. The new schools which came
into being proceeded to discourage important areas of African cultural life, on the assumption that these contributed to moral laxity
and sinful appetites. Africa experienced its own interrupted
symphony—the interruption of certain kinds of dance, music and
drama as these were banned by missionary intervention.[6]

Thus when in 1972 Amin banned what he called "teenage
dancing," he was as firmly within a Christian tradition in Africa
as he was within an Islamic one. Amin's regulation of drinking hours
in the Second Republic was also as firmly Christian and missionary,
as it was Islamic. Missionary disapproval of alcohol for Africans went
deeper than the American experience of prohibition. Behind it all
was the wider puritanism concerning "appetites," including disapproval of sexual longings.

Christian Origins of Uganda's Theocracy

But it is not merely the moral puritanism of the Second Republic that has its genesis in the missionary influence; it is also the
sacralization of the state.

Religion became politicized in Uganda in the modern period quite early partly because competitive proselytism was also competitive imperialism. The British became identified with Protestantism; the French with Catholicism; the Arabs with Islam. Proselytism might have been a competition for the souls of men; but imperialism was a competition for the control of societies. The Catholics became *Bafranza;* the Protestants became *Baingleza*—each denoting the national origins of the missionary thrust.

At first the Catholics and the Protestants were united as Christians against the Muslim threat. The most important unifying factor for Christians was Islam. Arab and European immigrants struggled for supremacy in Uganda towards the end of the nineteenth century. In the words of an official of the British East Africa Company in 1888 when Arab influence was on the ascendancy in Buganda: "These events render the question now paramount: is Arab or European power henceforth to prevail in Central Africa?"[7]

This was in many ways the time of maximum amity between Protestants and Catholics in Uganda. When Lugard came he managed to rally the Christian armies of both denominations, and put an end to the Muslim 'threat' and the power of the Muslim party. But in so doing Lugard "thus dissolved the last link binding the Catholics and the Protestants."[8]

The state was set for a continuing dialectic between Church and State, in the public life of Uganda. By the eve of independence religious affiliation was already an important factor conditioning people's political response. Uganda had at times already been viewed as "the Ireland of Africa," more susceptible to religious animosities than almost any other black African state. In the last elections held in Uganda, in 1961 and 1962, sectarian differences were evident. The Democratic Party became identified with the Roman Catholic Church and, though to a lesser extent, the Uganda Peoples' Congress under Milton Obote became identified with the Protestants.

And yet the ethnic factor in Uganda is always straining to reassert its primacy. With the emergence of Kabaka Yekka as the royalist party of the Baganda, ethnic loyalties momentarily superceded religious forms of solidarity. The 1962 elections showed a reduction in the influence of religion in the voting than the 1961 elections; but that might well have been mainly because Kabaka Yekka had come into being and competed in 1962, and ethnic loyalties within Buganda and against the Baganda affected the balance of support for the two other parties. The alliance between the so-called Protestant party, the Uganda Peoples' Congress, and the party of the Baganda, the Kabaka Yekka, helped further to obfuscate the religious dimension. After all the majority of the Baganda were Catholics—though in the ultimate analysis they were probably Baganda first and Catholics second.

By 1970 Obote was designing a new method of election which would dilute the ethnicity which had characterised the 1962 elections, and perhaps start a process which would help to keep tribal considerations out of the political behavior of parliamentarians. Obote emerged with a scheme known as *Document No. 5,* whereby each Member of Parliament was to stand for four constituencies. One of these constituencies was to be in the North, one in the South, one in the East and one in the West of the country. The Member of Parliament would thereby be compelled by the quadruple nature and multi-tribal composition of his electorate to look for areas of trans-ethnic interest and trans-regional popularity, rather than for platforms of a more parochial appeal. But the question arose with *Document No. 5* whether if Obote succeeded in de-tribalizing Parliament, he would by that same result re-sacralize it. Elections would be spared ethnicity, but at the cost of lending new importance to religion. After all, the voters had to choose their candidates by some criterion or another. In a situation where none of the two or three candidates standing was of their ethnic group, the second point of solidarity might well be that of denominational affiliation. Members of Parliament might once again be chosen, perhaps more clearly than ever, on the basis of whether they were Catholic, Protestant, or Muslim. A resurgence of sectarianism was feared should Obote's ambition to de-tribalize politics succeed. The fear arose precisely because the Uganda polity had for so long retained this heavy religious intrusion.

Theocracy and Neo-McCarthyism

Neo-McCarthyism is a style of political innuendo which seeks to discredit political opponents by associating them with communism. The song of neo-McCarthyism has been an important feature of the Ugandan scene, at least since the 1950s, and certainly featured prominently in the early years of the 1960s.

Milton Obote was often up against two accusations which normally should have been mutually incompatible. One accusation was that his political party, the U.P.C., was a Protestant Party; the other accusation was that the U.P.C. was leaning towards ungodliness and an atheistic ideology. Both accusations tended to come from supporters of the Democratic Party, and sometimes from people associ-

porters of the Democratic Party, and sometimes from people associated with the Roman Catholic Church itself. The fear that the U.P.C.
was moving Uganda towards a life of ungodliness offended that side
of the Democratic Party which stood for the consolidation of a devout
society. But the tactics of discrediting political opponents by such
innuendoes were themselves in conflict with the Democratic Party's
desire to remove sectarianism from the center of political activity in
Uganda.

Obote went through much of the first five years of Uganda's
independence with a deep cautiousness concerning the danger of neo-
McCarthyism. The last thing Obote wanted was to be portrayed as
a man who wanted to take God out of the value systems of the people
of Uganda. And even when Obote moved in a leftward direction in
1968, he repeatedly betrayed a great concern for religious approval.
He was keen to ensure that socialism should not be equated with
sin, and that it should in fact be deemed to be consistent with a
commitment to the service of God, as well as of the nation. His Holi-
ness the Pope visited Uganda against a background of the declared
aim of a move to the left under Obote's leadership. Symbolic gifts
were given to religious leaders. The face of Obote and the face of the
Pope competed for attention on hundreds of shirts worn around the
country and stacked in warehouses.

The furthest to the left Obote moved was on May 1, 1970 with
the Nakivubo pronouncements. In those pronouncements he
nationalized a number of industries, and declared plans to give
workers control in some sectors of the economic life of the country,
and peasants control in other sectors. The song of socialism was then
being sung at its most ambitious by the man who had once been all
too anxious to deny that he had ever gone behind the Iron Curtain.

As Obote stood there in Nakivubo Stadium announcing a series
of socialistic measures, the question was still with him whether this
move to the left might be misunderstood as ungodliness. Was there
a risk that neo-McCarthyism might once again sow the seeds of discontent and religious suspicion in the population? Obote rose to the
occasion in that very speech of Labor Day, 1970. The national motto
of Uganda provided him with a suitable line of reassurance. He concluded that historic speech with the simple sentence:

> Fellow citizens, I have decided upon the matters I have told you, 'For
> God and my Country'.[9]

With his "Move to the Left" Obote was in fact trying to move
Uganda from a country with politicised religion to a country with a

political creed. In this sense a political creed like socialism can be a
secular religion.

If Alexander Dubczek in 1968 was trying to give Czechoslovakia
"socialism with a human face," Obote in 1969 and 1970 was trying
to give Uganda "socialism with a divine face." Was Obote taking
Uganda towards a system of secular theocracy?

Behind the Obote experiment was Julius Nyerere's example in
Tanzania. And when Obote was overthrown, ideological tensions
developed between Nyerere and Amin. What must not be overlooked
was the shared link of puritanism and missionary styles between the
soldiers in Uganda and the socialists in Tanzania. It is to these links
that we must now turn.

Socialism as a Secular Theocracy

Of the three countries of East Africa the first to have had something approaching a state religion was Tanzania—but Nyerere called it
not a state religion but a "national ethic." Of course, Tanzania's
socialism has not carried the same passionate attachment to theological
issues that one sometimes finds among Marxist socialists. It is far
easier to portray communism as such as a kind of secular religion than
it is to portray *ujamaa.* Communism has, after all, definitely carried
in its history strong theological disputations on doctrinal matters.
Communism has also accumulated a collection of ideological ancestors
who command from followers a deep ancestor worship. Marx and
Lenin are not mere figures in the history of communism—in their very
death they continue to exert the kind of influence which wins deep
religious reverence.

Nyerere on the other hand has been all to conscious of the theological excesses of some schools of socialism. Nyerere has indeed
asserted that socialism is not a theology, and has described any attempt
to create a new religion out of socialism as "absurd." Marx was a
great thinker but not an infallible man. In the words of Nyerere:

> We are groping our way forward towards socialism, and we are in danger
> of being bemused by this new theology, and therefore of trying to solve
> our problems according to what the priests of Marxism say is what Marx
> said or meant. If we do this we shall fail. Africa's conditions are very
> different from those of the Europe in which Marx and Lenin wrote and
> worked. To talk as if these thinkers provided all the answers to our prob-
> lems, or as if Marx invented socialism, is to reject both the humanity of
> Africa and the universality of socialism. Marx did contribute a great deal

to socialist thought. But socialism did not begin with him, nor can it end in constant re-interpretations of his writings.[10]

Nyerere was prepared to be an admirer of Karl Marx, but not one of his worshippers. But was Nyerere himself becoming the center of a personality cult? Nyerere has not sought to become himself a prophet for popular reverence, or a founder of a new religion. On the contrary, there is a good deal of evidence to show the extent to which he has discouraged this trend towards a personality cult.

When all is said and done, however, there are in the very concept of *ujamaa,* as promoted by Nyerere, the seeds of a national secular religion. The atmosphere in Tanzania has increasingly discouraged even alternative schools to socialism, and to that extent the ideological monopoly bears comparison with theocratic righteousness. The one-party state itself was basically an attempt to institutionalize ideological monopoly. It certainly amounts to an assertion of ideological righteousness.

We might therefore say that until the advent of the Second Republic of Uganda, Tanzania was in an important sense moving in the direction of a secular theocracy, forging links with the African ancestors of socialism as practised in kinship systems, and seeking to bring to fruition a collection of gospels at the center of which was the *Arusha Declaration.* Kenyatta once described *Document No. 10 on African Socialism* in Kenya as the new Bible of the country. But if it was a Bible, it was more often honored in the breach than in the observance.

The same is not true of the gospel of Tanzania's socialism, with the central text of the *Arusha Declaration* itself. *Ujamaa* as a nostalgic link with African communalism seeks to introduce a little of the reverence of ancestors into Tanzania's socialism. *Ujamma* as a broad national ethic seeks to create a parallel code of behavior to that afforded by the traditional religions. *Ujamaa* as an exercise in documentary radicalism seeks to give this secular theocracy something approaching a holy scripture. There are Tanzanians who have walked more than a hundred miles as a form of prayer to the Arusha Declaration. Nyerere himself has walked such long miles on a pilgrimage to affirm the national ethic and its scriptural foundation, the Arusha Declaration.

Colin Leys, the former Professor of Political Science at Makerere University, was right to see in Nyerere a style very reminiscent of Gladstone in England. Gladstone was the grand moralistic statesman, tending in his style to see great spiritual issues involved in the banality of day-to-day politics. In the words of Colin Leys:

We have to understand Nyerere's style—the relentless magnification of the moral aspects of each and every policy decision—in terms of his need to sustain the moral basis of his own leadership, vis-a-vis both the party cadres and the public at large; it is his *stock-in-trade,* as it was also Gladstone's . . .[11]

But the analogy should go beyond Gladstone and include some of the founders of British socialism. The genesis of the Labor Party lies as much in Methodism as in Marxism. The genesis of Nyerere's puritanism may, in turn, lie as much in his socialism as in his "missionary" upbringing in colonial Tanganyika.

The national ethic of Tanzania before long was tackling not just the issue of who owned what but also the issue of who *wore* what. Even before the advent of the Second Republic of Uganda, Nyerere's Tanzania had already experienced debates on mini-skirts. It was in October 1968 that some girls wearing mini-skirts were manhandled by members of the TANU Youth League in Dar-es-Salaam. Riot police had to be called in to handle the youths. A resolution (entitled *"Operation Vijana")* was proposed to ban mini-skirts, wigs, and tight trousers from Tanzania with effect from January 1969, but younger members of the ruling party thought January was too far away and embarked on measures to speed up the change.

The Afro-Shirazi Youth League in Zanzibar soon endorsed the move by their sister organization on the mainland. In a resolution marking the close of a three-day seminar the Afro-Shirazi Youth League pledged they would work resolutely to eliminate such remnants of foreign culture in the country. In the background of these resolutions was the memory of Kariokoo market place, Dar-es-Salaam, a few days earlier when these youthful gangs stopped girls wearing mini-skirts and tight dresses and insulted them, and riot police carrying guns and teargas helped disperse huge crowds at the market place.

In a way, the excessive enthusiasm of the young militants helped later to promote greater toleration in Tanzania towards those who fell short of these rigorous standards. But what had happened was precisely the rapid extension of the fires of political puritanism from the socialist Cabinet to the private wardrobe, from issues of state to matters of taste.

The Masai and the Karamojong

Would all this puritanism have also manifested itself in Uganda had Obote continued on his own path towards socialism? Other

aspects of Tanzania's National Ethic had found an echo in Obote's
Uganda. Some of these questions can never be fully answered since
Obote was overthrown. What we do know is that Obote's successors—
the soldiers—now share certain forms of puritanism with Obote's
friend, Julius Nyerere.

The disapproval of the mini-skirt is not the only area of moral
sensitivity shared between the Military Government of Uganda and
the socialist Government of Tanzania. It is not even the only issue
connected with nakedness, real or asserted. Both the Socialist Government of Tanzania and the Military Government of Uganda have shown
a certain embarrassment over those traditions among their people
which accepted customary forms of nakedness and nudity. President
Nyerere's Government was concerned about the ancestral naked ways
of the Masai; and President Amin more recently has been concerned
about the naked ways of the Karamojong.[12] How much of the leaders'
embarrassment was Euro-Christian in origin?

The question which arises is what sort of factors were at play
behind this area of shared sensibility. Of course, objections to the
kind of nakedness implied by the mini-skirts were fundamentally
different from attitudes to the nakedness of the Masai and the
Karamojong. The denuciation of the mini-skirt was in part because
it was alien to African culture, an ominous and unwelcome intrusion
from a foreign universe of fashion. Yet to force the Karamojong and
the Masai to wear trousers and shirts was also to force them away
from their own traditions and customs into styles of imported attire.
While it is therefore arguable that the discouragement of the mini-
skirt in Tanzania and its ban in Uganda are motivated by a pursuit
of moral propriety and discipline, it is less persuasive to portray the
policies towards the Masai and the Karamojong in similar moralistic
terms outside the Euro-Christian missionary framework.

Where the mini-skirt and Nilotic nakedness might conceptually
touch is within the conceptual relationship between *cultural decadence* and *cultural retardation.* Cultural decadence is a stage of decay,
a situation which comes after the full flowering of a civilization.
Cultural retardation, on the other hand, implies being socially
arrested in one's development, stopping short of the full flowering
of civilization. Ancient Rome first rose to grandeur and then declined
and fell. The period of decline was a period of descent into decadence,
as values became diluted, as principles became abused, as moral
restraints became looser.

Social critics of capitalism see also a period of decadence setting
in in the entire capitalist civilization. Although many of those who

wear mini-skirts, or who profess to be hippies, are ideologically left-ists situated in Western countries, communist observers have been known to see in this very trend the beginning of the end of capitalist civilization, the rot setting in.

The mini-skirts become by this interpretation a manifestation of Western decadence; while the Masai blanket and Karamojong nudity are a manifestation of cultural retardation, defined in Euro-Christian terms.

We could therefore argue that for TANU Youth Wingers the attack on the mini-skirt was in part an attack on the cultural guise of capitalism. As for the motives behind the same policy in the Second Republic of Uganda, this came in a period of a general radicalization of foreign policy, with an expanding rhetoric of anti-imperialism. Opposition to the mini-skirt was in part an aspect of foreign policy, constituting a posture of resistance to cultural imperialism. Both the TANU Youth Wingers and the policy-makers in Amin's Uganda were extending their radicalism to encompass a particular form of attire.[13]

The policies concerning the Masai and the Karamojong, on the other hand, could be seen in terms of the pursuit of equal opportunity. Within the ideology of Tanzania this is even clearer. Nyerere's concern for the Masai included the worry that they would continue to be relatively underprivileged in Tanzania, unless certain important aspects of their life style were transformed. To get the Masai into the future stream of economic prosperity of Tanzania required at least a partial cultural transformation. Dress is one symbolic aspect which could be tackled first, in the hope that it would result in other changes of attitudes. Ataturk, the architect of modern Turkey, saw very clearly that the Westernization of the dress culture of Turkey could itself help to start a process of westernizing other attitudes in the life-style of the Turks. In some ways Ataturk oversimplified the connection between dress and other aspects of culture—but that there is a connection was itself a revolutionary premise from which Ataturk started.

Likewise, Julius Nyerere has concluded that dress for the Masai could not be separated from the issue of equal opportunity in Tanzania. The ability of the Masai to compete effectively in the job market was certainly connected with whether or not they wore anything. And in any case economic justice must not only be done, it must be seen to be done. And the visual aspects of economic justice range from whether people own cars, and if so which kinds, on one side, to the issue of whether they wear clothes and if so what kind, on the other.

If every Tanzanian were naked, this would itself be an assertion of equality. But since the great majority are already dressed, should the Masai be encouraged to enter that mainstream of economic culture?

The policies on the Karamojong in Uganda were less ideologically coherent, but an egalitarian factor was certainly present. General Amin certainly seemed to feel that the North as a whole in Uganda needed to establish parity of esteem with other parts of the country. And each section within the country needed to assert credentials of respectability and equal status. Amin's concept of egalitarianism was inter-regional and inter-ethnic. It might even be described as a nationally-oriented form of egalitarianism. Nyerere's egalitarianism, on the other hand, was clearly socialistically derived. But both showed a Euro-Christian influence in their origins.

Conclusion

President Amin and I were sitting together on a couch late in 1971 when I quietly raised the issue of religion. "Is it true, General, that you intend to bring up two of your children as Roman Catholics and prepare them for the priesthood?", I asked. The news had been announced publicly by Amin's Chief Justice at the time, Mr. Benedicto Kiwanuka. Justice Kiwanuka was himself a Roman Catholic.

When I raised the issue with the General a few days after Kiwanuka's announcement, my voice must have betrayed some surprise. It was as difficult to imagine a relatively devout Muslim committing himself to bring up a child of his as a Roman Catholic as it would have been to hear a Roman Catholic planning to have his eldest son converted to Islam and trained as a mullah.

General Amin turned to look at me and began saying rather defensively "It was the Chief Justice. . . ."! He never finished the sentence. He suddenly remembered that we were not alone. There were some Roman Catholic citizens within hearing distance in the same room. The General lowered his voice further and said: "We shall talk about this some other time."

Whether or not Idi Amin wanted to bring up any child of his as a Roman Catholic, it was clear that he did not want to deny it publicly inspite of the surprise the announcement had caused in Muslim circles in Uganda. What was at stake was Amin's ambition to forge Uganda into an ecumenical and yet devout society. Religious leaders of all denominations would have to share with him the burden of such a task. Was he also prepared to offer his children in the same apostolic cause? He left this latter question open.

Behind Amin's ambition was the momentum of Uganda's history since the 1890s when rival missionary groups started competing for the soul of the nation. We have sought to demonstrate in this paper that the origins of both the moral puritanism of the Second Republic and the evolving theocratic pattern are part of a tradition which has its genesis—inspite of the Muslim religion of General Amin—in the longer term impact of Christianity on Uganda. Sexual relations in African societies in Uganda, as elsewhere in the continent, became to some extent Christianized. They became subject to the puritanical restraints and inhibitions of missionaries, self-consciously committed to a cause to save Africa from some of its own presumed moral laxity.

The ban on mini-skirts is in part a child of cultural nationalism, and has been shared by radical countries like Tanzania. But it is also possible to see the disapproval of mini-skirts as part of the same tradition which had banned certain kinds of African dances, and led to the invention of the *basuti* as a style of modest attire.[14]

What should be noted is the additional puritanising effect of army rule. In reality Ugandan soldiers are normally over-indulgent rather than austere. General Amin himself used to be a heavy drinker at one time. He is now much more temperate, though not a total abstainer. But how is he to deal with the rest of his army? He has harangued them often on the virtues of moderation and discipline. He seems also to grope for societal sobriety as an answer to military inebriation.[15]

The other theme of this essay is the tradition of politicized religion in Uganda, and the strange dialectic it played when political parties came into being and the politics of electoral disputes entered the scene. We have argued that just as Islam once prepared the way for the reception of Christianity in Uganda in the nineteenth century, so Christianity in the twentieth century prepared the way for the religious style of the first Muslim President of Uganda. Uganda as a neo-theocracy did not emerge quite simply from the upheavals of January 25, 1971, but formed part of the flow of history which went back to Lugard, Mutesa I and beyond.

Amin was a self-conscious Muslim partly because the Uganda in which he grew up was so self-consciously sectarian. Historically, the Christians least patient with Muslims in Uganda were the Catholics. When in 1972 Amin found himself drifting towards religious intolerance, he became in turn more patient with the Protestants and

Muslims than he later became with Roman Catholics. He came to regard the Roman Catholic Church as the least African of the churches,
partly because it was a centralized church answerable to a European
religious pivot, the Pope. When Amin moved towards expelling mainly Catholic missionaries, and to denounce Catholic Archbishop
Nsubuga, Amin's ecumenicalism was struggling for breath under the
heavy weight of the sectarian history of Uganda.[16]

There are times when military heirs to church missionaries are
at the same time rivals to the missionaries. The competition is for
the soul of the nation. Religious leaders in Uganda—as in Zaire—are
up against a state which seeks to assert a monopoly of the legitimate
use of spiritual force. Yet to the extent that Amin stands for some
of the values of the old missionaries, history has indulged its own
ancient sense of humor once again. A rustic warrior from the womb
of the African countryside has symbolically presented his ecumenical
credentials to share in the gift of the apostolic succession.

Notes

1. Bultmann, (1952) and Ehrhardt, (1958).

2. For a report at the time about my protest concerning Idd el Fitr see *The Daily
Nation* (Nairobi). For my discussion of these issues in my fortnightly column see Mazrui
(1972).

3. President Idi Amin's decision to adopt the title of *Dada* (Patriarch or Father) was
inspired by a familial interpretation of a political system—that a polity is a family writ large.

4. Moffat to Unwin, September 4, 1869, in Wallis (Ed.) (1945: 70-71). Cited by Low,
Religion and Society in Buganda, 1875 to 1900 (Kampala: East African Studies, No. 8,
East African Institute of Social Research).

5. *Ibid,* Roland Oliver.

6. Welbourn (1965: 104-5, 114-5).

7. Oliver (1965: 133-134).

8. *Ibid.,* p. 142. Oliver (1962: 142).

9. For the full text of the Labor Day Speech of May 1, 1970, see either the *Uganda
Argus* or *The People* (Kampala), of May 2, 1970. The speech later came to be known as
Document No. 4 of the Move to the Left.

10. Nyerere (1968: 15).

11. Colin Leys, "Interalia—or Tanzaphilia and All That," *Transition* (Kampala) 7, 34: 53.

12. See for example the *Daily Nation* (Nairobi), (February 6, 1968) and *Daily Nation*
(Nairobi), (February 8 and 16, 1968). This issue is placed in a wider context in Chapter
XIV, Mazrui (1969: 281-305).

13. Nor should it be taken for granted that banning mini-skirts is peculiarly radical or
socialistic. Even before Operation Vijana got under way in Tanzania, President Banda of
Malawi had already expressed his distaste of the mini-skirt. The disapproval of the mini-
skirt has been championed by regimes as diverse as Dr. Banda's on one side and President
Nyerere's on the other, and by soldiers as diverse as the Greek colonels and the Ugandan
warriors.

14. Amin also banned long hair. For an earlier discussion see Mazrui (1971).

15. For a discussion of indulgence versus puritanism in another African army consult Price (1971: 416-19).

16. The Pope had finally to make a cautious appeal to President Amin for greater toleration towards servants of the Church. See The Times (London), (December 2, 4 and 5, 1972). Justice Kiwanuka—who had announced the story of Amin's children as potential Catholic priests—was openly kidnapped from his Court in September 1972 and reportedly killed. The Uganda government denied all responsibility for the Chief Justice's "disappearance" and inaugurated a search for him. It is virtually certain he is dead.

PERSONALISM AND CORPORATISM
IN AFRICAN ARMIES

Claude E. Welch, Jr.

Introduction

That the past decade has witnessed a significant expansion of the military's political involvement in Africa needs little documentation. The assassination of President Olympio of Togo by disaffected veterans of the French army, and the ouster of President Maga of Dahomey by General Soglo, hinted in 1963 that the armed forces could make, and unmake, governments. Now, more than a score of coups d'etat later, sub-Saharan Africa has become an area where analysts can trot out their favorite theories of the whys and wherefores of intervention.

Unfortunately, the "standard" explanations of military seizures of power find as many exceptions as confirmations in tropical Africa. A small army seems as well equipped to eject the occupant of a presidential palace as a large army.[1] Sixteen states on the continent have presidents who came to power by coups—including the heads of the states with the largest and smallest armies (Nigeria, 163,000 men; Central African Republic, 1,100 men).[2] Intervention has affected states with competitive party systems (Sierra Leone, Somalia), with highly mobilized single-party systems (Mali), with personalized rule disguised as single-party mobilization (Ghana), and with authoritarian personal rule (Libya). Countries of great affluence and of incredible poverty—to take the extremes, Libya with a per capita annual income of $1,500, and Upper Volta, with a per capita annual income of less than $40—equally have fallen under military sway. States of relative ethnic homogeneity (Somalia), ethnic polarization (Burundi), and ethnic fragmentation (Dahomey, Zaire), are headed by members of the armed forces. No theory of causation drawn from institutional, political or economic factors seems to encompass the diversity of military regimes in Africa.

Given this diversity, most students of African coups d'etat have turned to systemic explanations. Rather than search for a unicausal explanation, they suggest, we should recognize that the political settings of contemporary Africa offer no barrier to military intervention. Especially noteworthy, and frequently quoted, is Zolberg's

1968 article, "The Structure of Political Conflict in the New States of Tropical Africa." African states contain unintegrated, "syncretic" societies; severe constraints circumscribe the abilities of individual national governments to effect change; a shift has occurred from "power" to "force," owing to the politicization of residual cleavages, low governmental capabilities in the face of major tasks, and post-independence inflation of demands.[3] A coup d'etat, Zolberg argued, "can be viewed as an institutionalized pattern of African politics . . . and as a normal consequence of the showdown between a government and its opponents in a situation where the force at the disposal of the government is very limited."[4] He also suggested that contagion may encourage cycles of coups: "The success of one set of claimants encourages others to try."[5]

The nature of recent military interventions, however, suggests the need for significant extension and revision of this argument. Since June 1, 1968, there have been eleven successful coups d'etat in Africa:

TABLE I
Coups d'Etat in Africa 1968-1974

1968			1971		
	Mali	19, November		Uganda	25, January
1969			1972		
	Sudan	25, May		Ghana	13, January
	Libya	1, September		Malagasy Rep.	18, May
	Somalia	21, October		Dahomey	26, October
	Dahomey	10, December	1973		
1970				Rwanda	5, July
	–		1974		
				Upper Volta	8, February

Few of these seemingly sprang directly from cultural fragmentation, from what Zolberg characterized as the "politicization of residual cleavages." Even in those cases which seemingly turned on a lack of social integration—chronically-divided Dahomey, the Malagasy Republic, and Rwanda—there was at least one other major explanatory factor present which could have been independent of the particular socio-political context.

A brief description of the context in which each coup occurred will document these conclusions.

The Mali coup emanated from junior officers, fourteen of whom (ten lieutenants, four captains) constituted the "Military Committee for National Liberation"; *Le Monde* termed the conflict one of generations within the military, between the veterans of the former French colonial forces and the young.[6] In the Sudan coup, plotting was carried out, according to Major Farouk Osman Hamdallah (himself to be executed after an abortive counter-coup in July 1971), by members of a ten-year old underground organization within the armed forces.[7] The seizure of control had no direct links, accordingly, with such politically significant groups as the Communist Party, Madhist supporters, or southern organizations. The Libyan coup overturned a decaying monarchy (King Idris V was over 80 years old at the time of the seizure of control, and his nephew, the crown prince, was out of the country for medical treatment). Admittedly, both coups in Dahomey manifested elements of regionalism; however, conflicts among individuals and between generations of officers seem in retrospect to have been far more significant than cultural fragmentation in encouraging intervention.[8] Similarly, the triumph of General Amin in Uganda may be seen as the riposte of an ambitious individual, using his personal power base to stave off threats.[9] And Colonel Acheampong of Ghana issued a wide-ranging condemnation of "malpractices, corruption, arbitrary dismissal, economic mismanagement, and a host of other malpractices" when what became the National Redemption Council took power. Residual cleavages clearly were far less important than the conspirators' exclusion from positions of significance under the predecessor civilian government.[10] The change of government in the Malagasy Republic was a hand-over to Lieutenant General Ramanantsoa, in the face of student rioting in the capital, Tananarive; the military was confirmed in power October 8, 1972, by referendum. The scenario in Tananarive seemed quite similar to the deposition of President Yameogo of Upper Volta six years earlier, with urban unrest bringing the resignation of the president and the proclamation of a supposedly temporary period of military rule. The ouster of President Kayibanda in Rwanda bespoke strong regional tensions, with resentment allowing the return to political prominence of those from southern and western parts of the country. Finally, the bloodless coup of General Lamizana was carried out amidst growing bickering among the civilians in the mixed civilian-military government of Upper Volta.

Contagion across state borders seems to have played little part in these eleven coups. Those closest in time and space—the coups in Sudan, Libya, and Somalia—reflected domestic factors (e.g., the assassination of President Shermake; dissatisfaction with the civil

war in the south; fear of discovery by agents of King Idris), not comradeship or emulation among the respective leaders. What was of
greater significance were intra-military conflicts. In some respects,
these conflicts reflected what Zolberg called "the intergenerational
gap within the political sphere . . . in almost every other institutional sphere, including especially the civil service and the military."[11]
However, he tied this gap not to organizational strains internal to the
military, but to "the appearance of age-homogeneous movements and
organizations . . . which tend to maintain a distinctive sub-culture
and to act autonomously in the political sphere"[12] in other words,
as offshoots of residual changes. It might be analytically more satisfactory to view segments of the military as independent political
actors prior to intervention; and to consider changes internal to the
armed forces as crucial factors in the seizure of power. Zolberg's
model reflects the mid-1960s, when officers in tropical Africa were
first becoming aware of their ability to seize control, but were often
urged to do so by extra-military actors. By the early 1970s, active
and direct military involvement in politics required no urging from
other sectors of society. The armed forces had emerged as the leading
political actors.

My purpose in this paper is to suggest three pathways to military
intervention beyond the systemic weaknesses identified by Zolberg.
I shall concentrate on factors internal to the armed forces such as the
command structure, cohesion, and the ethos and effects of professionalization. The respective rubrics are personalism, corporatism, and
interventionary professionalization—all characteristics of the structure
of the military seen in isolation from its socio-political context.

One preliminary caution is in order. I assume that the military
establishment of each country exerts political influence. This influence derives from the inherent position of the military as a symbol
of sovereignty and as the main defender against external aggression,
from its share of government resources, and (in some states) from its
direct involvement in domestic pacification or civic action. It is admittedly difficult for the student of civil-military relations to un-
tangle where political influence shades into political participation,
and participation into political control. Some purportedly civilian
governments in Africa currently depend on substantial, if covert,
military support—Senegal stands as a main example. Conversely,
many, and probably most, post-coup governments in Africa are
"civil-military coalitions" rather than "military oligarchies," to
utilize Janowitz's terms. Only by co-opting civilians, particularly
bureaucrats, can officers exercise political responsibilities. For the

time being, the question can be posed: will civil-military coalitions become military oligarchies, thereby indicating a total shift from military participation in politics to military control over politics?

Problems in Classifying Military Regimes

Differentiations among influence, participation, and control cannot be readily drawn, much to the chagrin of scholars and policy makers. Hence, to ascertain the nature and extent of an individual military's members' involvement in politics, it is necessary to set up a spectrum, the poles marked civilian control of the military and military control of civilian institutions.

Several problems exist with existing schemes for classifying military regimes. Perhaps the first considerations are *definitional issues.* What precisely, is a military oligarchy? a civil-military coalition? Does one examine backgrounds of individual leaders, the positions they hold, the means by which they assumed control, their styles of rule, or other factors? Second are the problems of distinguishing sufficiently between *varying degrees of military involvement in politics.* What means short of intervention (blackmail, supplantment, and displacement) are employed? What distinctions exist among influence, participation, and control? Are these in fact appropriate categories for analysis?

Equally difficult is the identification of the *causes for changes* in the nature and extent of military involvement in politics. What processes of social, economic, and political alteration affect the military's roles in politics? What is the relative significance of internal (organizational) characteristics, as contrasted with environmental characteristics? What links, if any, exist between groups within the society and politically active members or segments of the armed forces? And what of the *policy choices made by so-called military regimes?* Do military backgrounds affect the ways in which individuals make and implement decisions? Do the belief systems inculcated within military establishments have a direct impact on policy choice?

Finally, there is the problem of assuming correctly the impact of historical and geographical constraints. Can scholars point to justifiable similarities between the caudillos of nineteenth century Latin America and military heads of state of contemporary Africa? Can area specialists (who stress common factors affecting states in a particular region), disciplinary specialists (who emphasize common methodological assumptions that cut across continents), and inter-disciplinary scholars (as are many in civil-military relations) adequately unite areal and methodological knowledge?

The classification of "military regimes" must embrace both organizational and societal characteristics. Most existing classificatory schemes emphasize one set. Huntington, for example, exclaims, "Military explanations do not explain military interventions."[13] Janowitz proposes to consider five types of civil-military relations; however, his emphasis on organizational format, skill structure and career lines, social recruitment and education, professional and political ideology, and social cohesion suggests an imbalance.[14] Finer speaks of levels of political culture, seemingly disdaining the internal means of operation that facilitate military involvement in politics.[15] Abrahamson discusses military professionalization with scant reference to the conditions under which a sense of corporate unity could result in heightened military involvement in politics.[16] Welch and Smith, developing a format suggested by Luckham, attempt to interweave socio-political characteristics (strength of civilian institutions and political participation) with organizational characteristics (the military's political strength and its institutional boundaries).[17]

Unfortunately, none of these formats has been tested at length against "military regimes" in Africa. It seems likely that the Welch-Smith format would be modified by clearer differentiations among arbiter, factional, and post-colonial "guardian" regimes. The types of civil-military relations examined by Janowitz could be further differentiated; "civil-military coalitions" might be subdivided, recognizing the differences among (for example) Upper Volta with its mixed civilian-military cabinet, Togo with the military-based head of state attempting to create a personal political movement, and Dahomey, with endemic cleavages cutting across all institutions and civil-military coalitions.

In the following pages, I shall sketch, in tentative fashion, a sequence of military involvement in politics—from "personalist" to "corporatist" regimes, with "interventionary professionalization" leading to expanded political roles for members of the armed forces. This sequence portends growing political involvement for African officers into the 1980s, although the resulting governments will more likely appear as military-civilian coalitions than outright military oligarchies.

"Personalist" Military Regimes

Personalist regimes, as the adjective suggests, center on the head-of-state/commander-in-chief. Among "personalist" regimes, I include Algeria, Burundi, Central African Republic, Dahomey 1965-67, Nigeria to mid-1966, Sudan 1958-64, Togo, Uganda, Upper Volta, and Zaire. Among the attributes of these governments are the following:

1. The act of intervention reflects, inter alia, (a) affronts to the institutional prerogatives of the armed forces, (b) personal challenges to the commander-in-chief, or (c) invitations from the head of state to the commander-in-chief to assume control.

2. The act of intervention is initiated by the ranking officer.

3. Given the extensive experience of the ranking officer with the armed forces, he will identify himself closely with their interests.

4. Both officers and civilians are named to cabinet positions; however, rapid and frequent changes in policy by the head of state are paralleled by equally rapid and frequent changes in cabinets.

5. To the extent that a national "ideology" is coined and propagated, it stresses the head of state.

Let us look at each in greater detail. Retrospect lends clarity to the search for institutional affronts. Unfortunately, there is no way to predict what may be interpreted as slights to the purported prerogatives of the armed forces. Villaneuva has graphically demonstrated that Peruvian governments that failed to increase appropriations for their armed forces fell victims to coups;[18] hence, budget slashes (as Prime Minister Busia should have realized) can uncork intervention. Certain danger signals can be noted: creation of paramilitary units directly responsible to the head of state without passing through the regular command structure; patterns of recruitment and promotion that might be interpreted as discriminatory; involvement of the armed forces in less desirable or less professional undertakings, such as subduing domestic opponents of the government; marked disparities in salaries or conditions of employment between officers and civil servants; dismissals of popular officers and the promotion of sycophants. It stands to reason that ranking officers may be especially resentful of perceived abridgements of military responsibilities.

Personal challenges have received little attention from academicians. Decalo aptly observes, "The main weakness of attempts to explain military interventions [sic] is in not placing sufficient weight on the personal and idiosyncratic elements in military hierarchies, which have much greater freedom and scope of action within the context of fragmented and unstructured political systems."[19] However, personal challenges, like institutional affronts, can be discerned far more readily with hindsight than within the prognosticator's crystal ball. And, to be certain, personal and institutional affronts cannot be readily distinguished, as in, for example, the dismissal of senior officers.

Intervention by the commanding officer may be encouraged by civilians. When a head of state confronts challenges to his rule that cannot be easily quelled, he may choose "temporary" abdication, tossing the reins of government to the head of the armed forces. An intractable deadlock or continued domestic strife (as in the Sudan in 1958 or the Malagasy Republic in 1972) can precipitate such a turnover.

As Table II shows, coup attempts led by ranking officers have far greater chances of success than coup attempts led by junior officers. Rank counts. Members of the military are schooled to accept and carry out commands. Field-grade officers who have intervened successfully have, on occasion, turned over control to their superiors, the outstanding examples being Major Nzeogwu's surrender to General Ironsi, or the emergence of Generals Ankrah and Siyad Barre following coups mounted by colonels. With the senior officer an active planner or supporter, no need exists to rally the support of a "swing man," as Needler noted for Latin America.[20]

Cabinet instability marks personalist regimes. In distributing positions, the new head of state indulges in time-honored exercises: reward the faithful; build support through incorporating as many regions and tendencies as possible; find congenial supporters. However, periodic government reshuffling testifies to the impotence of cabinets in such regimes. The focus of power is the leader himself. His vagaries are writ large in national policies. Consider, for example, the twists and turns of the Central African Republic, about which the editors of *Africa Contemporary Record* tartly wrote, "General Jean-Bedel Bokassa's rule continued to be characterized by an erratic direction of foreign affairs matched only by the impetuous changes in domestic decisions: all that changed even more frequently than the President's policies were his Cabinets."[21]

Similar observations can be made concerning "ideology." The head of state becomes the focus, the prime mover. Although campaigns may be announced for "authenticity," as in Zaire, or joining the people in an organic whole, as the RPT of Togo, it is the Mobutu or Eyadema of the individual state who counts. National unity figures prominently in official appeals—but the image evoked is that of the

TABLE II
Successful Military Seizures of Power in Africa.

State	Coup Date	Leader	Length of Service	Age at Coup	Regime Type
Algeria	6/19/65	Colonel Boumedienne	11 yrs.	40	P
Burundi	11/28/66	Major/Premier Micombero		26	P
Central African Republic	1/1/66	Colonel Bokassa			P
Congo-Brazzaville	11/2/68	Captain Ngouabi			C
Dahomey	10/20/63	Colonel Soglo			R
	11/17/65, 12/22/65	" "			P
	12/17/66	Major Kouandete			C
	12/10/69	Lt.-Colonel Kouandete			P
	10/ /72	Major Kerekou			C
Ghana	2/24/66	Colonel Kotoka			
		Colonel Ocran	19 yrs.	36	
		Major Afrifa	9 yrs.	30	
	1/13/72	Colonel Acheampong	13 yrs.	32	P
Libya	9/1/69	Captain (?) Gaddafy			C-P
Malagasy	5/18/73	General Ramamantsoa	42 yrs.	60	P
Mali	11/19/68	Lieutenant Traore		32	C
		Captain Diakhite			
Nigeria	1/15/66	Major Nzeogwu		32	
		Major Ifeajuna		29	
	1/16/66	General Ironsi			P
	7/29/66	NCOs			
Rwanda	7/5/73	Major General Habyalimana	12 yrs.	34	P
Sierra Leone	3/21/67	Brigadier Lansana			P
	3/24/67	Major Blake	8 yrs.		C
	4/ /68	Warrant Officers			R
Somalia	10/21/69	Colonels			C-P
Sudan	11/17/58	Lt.-General Abboud			P
	5/25/69	Colonel Numeiry			C
Togo	1/13/63	ex Sargeant Eyadema	8 yrs.	26	R
	1/13/67	Lt.-Colonel Eyadema	12 yrs.	30	P
Uganda	1/25/71	Major-General Amin			P
UAR	7/17/53	Colonel Nasser	17 yrs.		C-P
Upper Volta	1/3/66	Lt. Colonel Lamizana			
	2/8/74	General Lamizana			P
Zaire	9/15/60	Colonel Mobutu	7 yrs. (1950-6; 1960)		C
	11/25/65	Major-General Mobutu			P

benevolent, modernizing leader—not the strident, marching, organized, faceless image of corporatist regimes.

It is difficult to forecast the likely lifespan of personalist regimes. In large measure, they depend on the command structure remaining intact. The greatest threat comes from weakening of the acceptance of hierarchy. Should organizational strains and social cleavages within the society reinforce one another, military discipline and cohesion are threatened. Once the principles of rank and command are questioned, the way is open for further intervention. One might paraphrase Marx and Engels and call senior officers who seize control their own grave-diggers. The fact of ruling, as Bebler has documented,[22] opens divisions within the military. Direct involvement of officers in politics arouses expectations of rewards. The style of a general-turned-president may irritate his colleagues. Personal idiosyncracies, conflicts among generations of officers, and other types of organizational strain underlie continuing intervention. Support cannot readily be maintained, given the scarcity of resources and the errors new and inexperienced leaders make. Further intervention is thus the fruit of personalist regimes.

Personalist regimes brought military participation in politics to many African states—but the participation was confined to the ranking officer and his close associates. They may rule well or they may rule poorly; they may disengage themselves from extensive contact with their fellow officers or they may retain close identification with the armed forces: yet they cannot avoid reinforcing the idea that political power derives from coercive might. This is a lesson not lost on junior officers, the base from which corporatist regimes come.

Corporatist Regimes

Corporatist regimes begin with successful acts of intervention led by junior officers who, on reaching the political summit, stress unity in the face of severe divisions. Perhaps the most serious strains result from the impact of the coup d'etat on military hierarchy. Junior officers shoulder aside superiors as well as the civilian government. Corporate solidarity and cohesion are, as a consequence, severely threatened.

It should not be inferred that personalist regimes are models of corporate solidarity and cohesion; the differential rewards of ruling soon introduce or exacerbate organizational cleavages. However, what is striking is the emphasis on military cohesion in the absence or weakness of usual institutional means for ensuring compliance. The standard means is, of course, rank. Corporatist regimes are collegial, not hierarchical, though the coup leader holds a position of personal pre-eminence. Junta members are likely to hold the same rank or adjacent ranks; they mutually suffer from youth and limited experience.

The following features characterize corporatist regimes.

1. The act of intervention reflects varying combinations of societal and organizational tensions. Coups led by junior officers are more likely mounted against personalist regimes than against civilian governments.

2. Intervention is planned and carried out by a coalition of field grade officers, often with academy backgrounds or current academy postings.

3. Maintaining unity within the coalition necessitates rapid distribution of cabinet positions to coup supporters, and removal of potential opponents by means of retirement, exile, and the like.

4. Ideological themes of national unity predominate. The purported unity and goal orientation of the military serve as examplars to the entire political system; "revolution" appears as the catchword.

5. Collegiality cannot be easily maintained. One-man dominance emerges, the results of both military norms of command and heightened fragmentation within the junta resulting from the pressures of governing.

Let us again examine each assertion in detail. Isolating "The Cause" of a coup d'etat is a fruitless exercise. Personal, organizational and societal factors are intermingled. Public apologia for intervention may be replete with rationalizations rather than reasons—especially when the act springs from personal ambitions or animosities, rather than from high-sounding objectives of national reconstruction. For corporatist regimes, the most significant factor appears to be resentment against senior officers who have taken on political responsibilities, or who have compromised their standing within the armed forces by close identification with the incumbent, distrusted civilian government.

Corporatist regimes are indeed initiated against the "bigwigs" of the military and political hierarchies alike. Most corporatist regimes are headed by individuals, like Captain Ngouabi or Major Kouandete, who ousted superior officers—who themselves had previously seized political power. Some corporatist regimes are headed by individuals, like Lieutenant Moussa Traore, who believed their senior officers had compromised the position of the armed forces by accepting the decisions of civilian leaders. In most instances, the interests of the armed forces (as perceived by the junior officers) and the interests of the populace as a whole (again, as perceived by the junior officers) are intermingled. The armed forces must take up their responsibilities by ousting those at the top. The "Young Cadres" of Dahomey expressed these views strongly in December, 1967:

> Our seniors ignore the dissatisfaction of the masses and the suggestions emanating from the entire army. . . .The very people whom we had promised to defend and protect now hate and despise us. . . .This is why we, the young cadres of the army, aware that that the role of the whole army was in question; considering that our seniors in the army had disappointed the people and betrayed the national army; aware that it is the duty of us, the young army cadres, to restore the situation as well as the authority and dignity of the nation; decided in the higher interests of the nation to dissolve the Government of General Soglo.[23]

The "swing man" phenomenon, described by Needler for coups d'etat in Latin American, applies under certain conditions to intervention in Africa as well. Needler noted that the swing man "becomes the leading figure in the new government; yet he is the person who was least committed to the objectives of the coup, whose threshold to intervention was the highest of all the conspirators, and who was a last-minute addition to the conspiracy. . ."[24] He may in fact join the junta only after success has been achieved: Colonel Juxon-Smith was recalled from staff college in England to head the National Reformation Council in Sierra Leone. General Ankrah was approached only after Nkrumah had been ousted. Major-General Siyad Barre was not involved in planning the coup in Somalia, although he assumed command over the four main plotters (all colonels) when success was assured.

Successful intervenors raise themselves in rank as quickly as possible, retiring or exiling their superiors. Colonel Jaafar Nimeiry became Major-General and commander-in-chief hours after the coup. Captain Gaddafy[25] raised his rank to Colonel, assumed command,and had 250 officers, of the rank of major and above, arrested equally rapidly. Colonel Acheampong shuffled three major-generals (Addo, Aferi, and Amenu) into minor administrative positions, holding for himself the position of Commissioner of Defence and Chairman of the National Redemption Council, and arresting Lieutenant-General Afrifa, a chief architect of the 1966 coup. In the 1966 coup itself, Colonel Kotoka became Major-General and Commander of the Ghana army within three days of Nkrumah's overthrow, while Colonel Ocran and Major Afrifa respectively became Brigadier and Colonel.

Expansion of the coup-planning circle is an immediate task for successful intervenors. Many considerations must be juggled: region of origin, personal popularity, compatibility, rank, prestige. Shifting and tugging occur—usually behind closed doors. The Revolution Command Council in Libya remained veiled in shadows. In Somalia, the names of members of the Supreme Revolutionary Council (four generals, seven lieutenant-colonels, seven majors, and seven captains) were released a full ten days after the coup. As Table III indicates in Ghana, the selection process was even more public and ragged. Immediately after the coup the National Redemption Council was announced as having six members; the following day, it was expanded to nine; two furthermembers were named four days later. The Commissioner named two weeks after the coup provided graceful niches for six additional officers omitted from previous expansions.

The energies spent on coalition-building, and the fervent protest-ations of the need for unity, suggest that unity is a precious, scarce commodity indeed. The four methods suggested above—success by association of senior officers, promotions to achieve the patina of rank, retirement or reassignment of senior officers, and coalition-building—may only paper over significant splits. The appeals to all segments of the armed forces for support indicate that internal cohesion be severely tested by intervention—especially against ranking officers. It is worth recalling Janowitz's hypothesis: high internal cohesion results in greater capacity (1) to intervene in domestic politics, (2) to limit such involvement, and (3) to follow consistent policies; lack of cohesion "leads to unstable and fragmented involve-ment and to the likelihood of counter-coups d'etat after the seizure of power."[26]

What may be only a facade of cohesiveness does not preclude the junta from trumpeting the importance of national unity. The analogy of the serried ranks marching toward a set objective springs readily to the lips of junta leaders. "Revolution" becomes the watch-word. A transformation of attitudes is envisaged—particularly away from divisive, parochial loyalties based on region or kinship. However, these protestations, in the face of pressing issues and limited skills, result in little transformation. Military intervention, having been provoked in large part by divisions within the armed forces, can rarely get beyond healing internal splits to treating the problems of the society as a whole.

Military cohesion, weak prior to intervention, is further weakened by the complexities of governing. Corporatist regimes try to bring into being what has been severely challenged, and possibly totally undercut. These regimes reflect the fact of military participa-tion in politics—but the form of this participation shifts. Four possi-ble outcomes can be envisaged: (1) the emergence of a new form of

TABLE III
Changes in the Composition of the Second Ghanaian Military Regime

Name and rank	Ethnicity	First Broadcast 1/13	NRC 1/14	NRC 1/18	Commissioner as of 1/29
*Colonel IK Acheampong[1]	Akwapim	X	X	X	Defence; Finance and Economic Affairs
Major Gen. DK Addo[2]	Ga			X	Agriculture
Colonel JC Adjetey	Ga				Health
Major Gen. NA Aferi	Nzima	X		X	Foreign Affairs
*Major KG Agbo	Ewe	X	X	X	
Major Gen. DK Amenu[3]	Ewe				Transport & Communications
Major Kwame Asante					Labor, Soc. Welfare, Cooperatives
Brig. NYR Ashley-Lassen	Ewe		X	X	Trades, Industries & Tourism
*Maj. Kwane Baah	Brong	X	X	X	Lands, Mineral Resources
Lt. Colonel Barnor		X			
Brig. C Beausoleil (Air Force)		X	X	X	
Lt. Col. Benni					
Commander Boham		X	X	X	
Inspector JH Cobbina (Police)	Fanti		X	X	Internal Affairs
Colonel Victor Coker-Appiah	Fanti		X		Local Government
Colonel EA Erskine	Fanti		X	X	
Major RJ Felli				X	
EN Moore (civilian)		X	X	X	Attorney-General, Justice (Originally named 1/13)
Lt. Colonel PK Ntegbe					Education
Commander PF Quaye (Navy)	Ewe				
*Major A. Selormey	Ewe	X	X	X	Internal Affairs (deputy)

* Active coup leader.
1. Was promoted to Colonel two days prior to intervention.
2. Was briefly imprisoned after the coup, together with Lt. General Afrifa, Brig. Twum-Barima, Colonel Hamidu, and Colonel Osei-Owusu—all Sandhurst graduates whose promotions had been speeded by the Busia government.
3. Had been shuffled aside by Busia government as director of National Service Corps.

personalism, marked by the dominance of an individual leader; (2) extension of the ambit under the military's control, transforming the civil-military coalition into a military oligarchy; (3) gradual disengagement of the armed forces from direct political involvement, though they remain in the background; (4) disintegration of the armed forces as a coordinated entity, possible entangled with regionalism and civil war. The first and third outcomes may result in a re-emergence of civilian supremacy. More likely, however, is the second outcome. African armies will remain embroiled in the unseating and reconstituting of individual governments—these being a consequence of "interventionary professionalization," the third organizational factor we must consider.

Interventionary Professionalism

The ineluctable upshot of increased levels of military professionalization, in the absence of weakness of officers' beliefs that the armed forces should be subordinated to civilian control, is greater and more direct military involvement in politics.

Following Abrahamsson, we can distinguish two varieties of professionalization within the armed forces, organizational and behavioral. The former ("professionalization$_1$") emerged from the centralization of state authority and the industrial revolution and their concomitants, the decline of the nobility as a recruitment source and technological innovations. The latter ("professionalization$_2$") is an on-going process of socialization, including the homogenization of outlooks and behavior; Abrahamsson deems the constituent elements to be nationalism, pessimistic beliefs about human nature, alarmism, political conservatism, and authoritarianism.[27] He notes that professionalization$_1$ "refers to processes which have led to the establishment of the military as a *pressure* group, whereas professionalization$_2$ turns it into a pressure *group*."[28]

Professionalization is to be distinguished from "professionalism," particularly as employed by Huntington in *The Soldier and the State*. According to Huntington, the professionalism of an officer includes "an awareness that his skill can only be utilized for purposes approved by society through its political agent, the state."[29] Although Huntington does note exceptions to his definition, its overall consequences have been confusion—for in Africa many officers marked by corporateness, expertise, and social responsibility have found intervention an act appropriate to the political circumstances.[30]

Observers of African armed forces agree that low levels of professionalization (as Abrahamsson) and of professionalism (as Huntington) are characteristic. Only a handful of officers have enjoyed extensive academy training. The three states of Commonwealth West Africa with armies (Ghana, Nigeria, and Sierra Leone) respectively sent 78, 74 and 19 candidates to the Royal Military Academy, Sandhurst, between World War II and 1967; for the Mons Officer Cadet School (a six-month course), the respective figures were 43, 128 and 51.[31] However, training is unevenly distributed through the officer corps. Generally speaking, the younger the officer, the higher his qualifications—exception being made for the war-inflated Nigerian military.

As a consequence, there are latent fissiparious tendencies in all African military establishments. The causes have been touched on earlier in this paper—differences in training, in regional and ethnic origins, in personality. Intervention usually exacerbates differences. Although personalist regimes may mask cleavages under allegiance to the leader, and corporatist regimes may attempt to overcome them through retirements, promotions, and pleas for unity, coups d'etat result in increased tensions and organizational strains. Dahomey, with its six coups from 1963 to 1972, manifested the negative consequences of military fractionalization; the Dahomean armed forces had not yet manifested "professionalization$_2$," acting as a pressure *group.*

Although not currently characteristic of Africa interventionary professionalization seems likely to increase. Despite mounting evidence of differences within the armed forces "causing" coups d'etat, I believe that homogenizing tendencies will increase and that the presently discontinuous process of military socialization in Africa will become far more regularized. Greater homogenization will result from three factors. First, the establishment or further development of local academies will provide an explicitly national coloration to African armed forces. Organizational patterns developed under colonial auspices will be revised to suit the exigencies of the particular state. Even though a select portion of officers will continue to receive advanced training abroad, the great majority will gain their *formation* in their own country. Secondly, the revision of organizational patterns will be paralleled by altered missions. Under colonial auspices, the functions of the armed forces were simple: suppress domestic dissidence; serve as reservoirs of manpower in case of international conflict. Role expansion will provide the military a broader set of functions—most likely tied explicitly to "national reconstruction." These new functions point to the third factor, the acceptance of the armed forces as members of the political process. Recognized as a legitimate political actor, the military need have little fear about its institutional prerogatives being undercut by civilians. With such recognition by governments, a few discrete hints of military displeasure will accomplish what now results through full-scale intervention.

Interventionary professionalization, to summarize, leads to (1) greater emphasis upon institutional homogenity, this being facilitated by local academies, new missions, and acceptance of the armed forces as members of the political process, (2) formation of civil-military coalitions as the normal means of constituting governments, or of military oligarchies where the armed forces have sufficient manpower, and (3) a move away from primary reliance on supplantment or displacement of governments to pressure or blackmail, in order to achieve ends the armed forces deem necessary.

Where, in this set of assumptions, is the liberal, democratically-oriented, Western-inspired officer of whom Lefever and Price have written?[32] Gone, because the institutional dynamics of African armed forces and the increased localization of curricula and composition portend greater involvement with domestic politics, not reference to external models of appropriate comportment. The military in African states will become institutional political participants, using their position to safeguard "professional" interests. Less significant will be the fissions within the officer corps in sparking intervention. Once again, to turn full circle, the environment will become the area to which analysts of civil-military relations must turn their attentions.

Emerging Patterns

The 1960s witnessed a set of sudden, abrupt moves that shifted the armed forces of many African states from political bystanders to political participants. From having been adjuncts of colonial control, the military—or, more accurately, segments of the officer corps —vaulted into central decision-making positions. The 1970s is witnessing a shaking down of the military, with challenges to the command structure possibly leading (as in Dahomey, with its six seizures of power, or in Libya, with the drastic restructuring of the armed forces after the corporatist intervention led by Colonel Gaddafy) to homogenization by means of purge. The emergence of patterns of military participation in politics, because of interventionary professionalization will provide a more cogent explanation of the military's political roles than personal animosities, internal fission, or ideology.

Earlier, in this paper, I took for granted the systemic weaknesses delineated by Zolberg. These result in "praetorian" systems, in which military participation in politics can go far beyond that of a bureaucratic interest group. Political institutions are weak, lacking the authority to work out binding, allocative decisions seen as legitimate within the society. Violence and coercion serve as the chief levers for political change. These characteristics seem likely to mark Africa, and accordingly must be incorporated into an analytical framework for treating the political roles of the military. Equally, however, a framework must incorporate organizational variables, to which most of this essay has been devoted.

As mentioned above, Arthur K. Smith and I have elsewhere sketched a typology of military political roles (Welch and Smith, 1974). We distinguish between "civic" polities, in which the armed forces are controlled by the government (through either "subjective" or "objective" civilian control, following Huntington), and "praetorian" polities, in which the armed forces may exercise supreme political power (either as a coalition partner or as an independent actor). Four summary variables enter our analysis: strength of civil institutions; political participation; the military's political strength; and military institutional boundaries.[33]

1.   Political participation in Africa has dropped since the terminal stages of colonial rule—yet political awareness may be higher, and, more important, is increasing rapidly. Even though the mobilization brought through nationalist movements belongs in the history books, other indices of social mobilization are rising. Education statistics suggest that Africans now have a better than even chance of receiving primary education. The population of the continent as a whole remains primarily involved with subsistence agriculture and village life; however, urbanization is accelerating, and in some states more than a quarter of the populace live in towns or cities. Other measures of social mobilization point to the same conclusion; increased political awareness has not necessarily been complemented by broadened opportunities for political participation.

2.   Civil institutions do not function effectively and impartially in many African states. Corruption saps bureaucracies. Few political parties remain active. Military intervention has resulted in a near total ban on formal party activity. Trade unions can claim to represent only a small fraction of workers. The absence of institutional constraints on the political awareness of the armed forces figures heavily in the ease with which officers have been able to assume

control. In the absence of an overarching civil order, as Lee has argued, an army in Africa "is often tempted to behave independently of established government, as if it were a 'private army'."[34] Few countries are marked by parties enjoying widespread support (Guinea; Tanzania), or by extensive external involvement in the organization of the military (Ivory Coast). These current trends will not be reversed in the years ahead, although marginal improvements may occur in the effectiveness of the civil service.

3. The political strength of the military shows little sign of declining. Africa as a whole remains a lightly-armed continent, with a smaller portion of men under arms than any other continent. However, national expenditures on the military have risen markedly.[35] Efforts to court the favor of the armed forces enhance the military's sense of their political potency, as may the example of successful intervention elsewhere.

4. Boundary fragmentation likewise is increasing. Pressures from both sides—officers interested in expanding their political clout; "outs" interested in courting the new king-makers—link members of the armed forces far more closely with political processes than had been the case prior to independence, and in most states during the first three to five years of self-government.

The consequences of these shifts will likely—and unsurprisingly— be greater military involvement in politics. This involvement will not be limited to influence channeled through existing institutions with a facade of civilian control; rather, it will take the form of military *participation* in politics, or of military *control* of politics.

Military participation in politics will be signaled by the emergence of civilian-military coalitions. Politicians will continue to head the government, but they will rely increasingly on the support of co-opted members of the armed forces. Recognizing the precariousness of their positions, civilian leaders will cater to narrow military interests, seeking through relatively generous allocations from the public purse to stave off overt intervention. The armed forces not only can veto policies, but also can cater to corporate concerns. Astute use of "blackmail," as Finer suggested,[36] may involve intimidation or threats to keep civilians in line. Civilians will occupy the formal positions of power, but be unable to curb the participation in politics of interested officers.

Two forms of military control of politics can be distinguished: (1) when the armed forces ally themselves with various coalition partners; and (2) when the armed forces rule largely through their own personnel, remaining aloof from other groups and building popular support on their own behalf. The first may take the form of a military-civilian coalition, likely to be created under the auspices of a senior officer, and hence close to the personalist model sketched above. The second tends toward the corporatist model previously examined, in which the professionalization of officers seems to fit them for political responsibilities. The armed forces may seek to build their own political foundation; in the first form, they draw on coalition partners for popular acclaim.

The most willing partner in a military-civilian coalition may be the civil service. Bureaucrats and officers have many affinities, in style, in temperament, in *modus operandi*; Feit indeed has dubbed soldiers in developing countries "armed bureaucrats."[37] Evidence abounds of the links between bureaucrats and brigadiers. In Ghana under the National Liberation Council, for example, Pinkney sees civil servants playing central roles; it was they who "benefited most from the coup in the short run."[38] In Egypt, the longest-standing military regime of Africa, the relationship between officers and specialists has been a symbiotic one. According to Be'eri,

> The Officers are masters, but they do not rule alone . . . University graduates with a scientific education, engineers, the talented managers of former companies and economic and technical experts with initiative and resolution became the chief partners of the officers in power. . . . The rise of the officer class and the rule of the military is [sic] accompanied by the advancement of technocrats and technocracy.[39]

Pen and sword are natural allies; personalist and corporatist regimes alike will draw upon the expertise and purported political neutrality of civil servants and technical specialists.

To be sure, coups d'etat in Africa born of personal ambition, regional rivalry, or ethnic antagonism will not disappear. Greater military professionalization, however, adds further dimensions and complications to the task of understanding the political role of African armed forces. If the suggestions made above are accurate, officers will dominate African politics even more markedly than at present. The conditions under which military involvement in politics could be limited to the mere exercise of influence do not exist, and cannot easily be called into existence. Military participation in politics has already been achieved; military control of politics will characterize many African states in the coming decade, including some of those now under civilian rule.

Notes

1. Events quickly disproved Gutteridge's 1965 prognostication: "While the armed forces of Africa remain small in proportion to the total populations and to the areas of the countries. . .they are unlikely to be able to consolidate their positions and establish military regimes." Gutteridge, W.F. (1965: 143).

2. Booth, R. (1970: 12, 15).

3. Zolberg, A.R. (1968: 70-87).

4. Zolberg, A.R. (1968: 77-78).

5. Zolberg, A.R. (1968: 80).

6. Le Monde, 21 November 1968, cited in Africa Research Bulletin (Political), (1968: Col. 1235C) (Hereafter cited as ARB.)

7. ARB, (1969: Col. 1405C).

8. Decalo, S. (1973b: 449-78).

9. Decalo, S. (1973: 111-2).

10. ARB, (1972: Col. 2347B).

11. Zolberg, A.R. (1968: 75).

12. Zolberg, A.R. (1968: 76).

13. Huntington, S.P. (1968: 194).

14. Janowitz, M. (1964: 31-74).

15. Finer, S.E. (1962).

16. Abrahamsson, B. (1971).

17. Welch, C.E., Jr., and A.K. Smith, (1974: 35-42) Luckham, A.R. (1971: 5-35).

18. Villaneuva, V. (1969: 194).

19. Decalo, S. (1973a: 113).

20. Needler, M. (1966: 621).

21. Legum, C. [ed.], (1972: B473).

22. Bebler, A. (1973).

23. ARB, (1967: Col. 927C).

24. Needler, M. (1966: 621).

25. I have not found a biographical source on Colonel Gaddafy indicating his rank at the time of the coup, and have guessed at the rank he held.

26. Janowitz, M. (1964: 68).

27. Abrahamsson, B. (1971: 21-79).

28. Abrahamsson, B. (1971: 155).

29. Huntington, S.P. (1964: 15-16).

30. Leader, S.G.'s unpublished Ph.D. dissertation.

31. Lee, J.M. (1969: 126).

32. Lefever, E. (1970) and Price, R.M. (1971: 399-430).

33. The following four paragraphs are reproduced from Welch (1973: 16).

34. Lee, J.M. (1969: 22).

35. In his 1966 Adelphi paper, Wood estimated total military expenditures of independent African states as $1,020,296,000 (Rhodesia and South Africa excluded); as of 1968, the total jumped to $1,899,369,000. Wood (1966: 28-29); Booth (1970: 26).

36. Finer, S.E. (1962: 148-51).

37. Feit, E. (1973).

38. Pinkney (1972: 62).

39. Be'eri, E. (1970: 431).

PERU'S 'REVOLUTIONARY GOVERNMENT OF THE ARMED FORCES': BACKGROUND AND CONTEXT

Abraham F. Lowenthal

Peru's "Revolutionary Government of the Armed Forces" has now completed five years in power. Headed by General Juan Velasco Alvarado—the Army's top-ranking officer when he led the October, 1968, coup which toppled President Fernando Belaúnde Terry—the Peruvian regime has already attracted considerable attention. Military officers and civilian politicians in countries as diverse as Argentina and Ecuador, Bolivia and Brazil, Cuba and the Dominican Republic, Uruguay and Colombia, have expressed their interest in (and usually their admiration for) the Peruvian regime. Fidel Castro has acclaimed the Peruvian undertaking; Juan Perón has extolled it. *Peruanista* factions have been identified, and have sometimes identified themselves, in the armed forces of several South American countries.

The Peruvian regime is generally seen not as the typical Latin American *caudillo* government but rather as an essentially institutional effort. Although a government of force, Peru's military regime is regarded as relatively unrepressive, judged in light of the behavior of most of its neighbors. Although led by staunch anti-communist officers, many with considerable training in the United States, the Peruvian government has established friendly relations with several Communist nations as part of its campaign to escape external "domination," particularly by the U.S.

Most important, although it is the nation's force for order, the Peruvian military has promoted substantial change. Through a burst of legislative activity unprecedented in Peru, the military regime has set out to transform many basic areas of national life. Major structural reforms have affected land tenure and water rights, labor-management relations, the educational system, the state's role in the economy and in the communications media, the role of foreign enterprise in Peru's economy, and even fundamental concepts of economic and political relationships. Particularly noteworthy has been the regime's announced determination, vigorously reaffirmed on the government's fifth anniversary, to make predominant a "social property" economic sector based on collective ownership of the means of production and to move steadily away from capitalist

147

principles.[1] And the Peruvian regime has emphasized its aim to promote a drastic change in national values, to create a "new Peruvian
man," one dedicated to "solidarity, not individualism."

Peru's military regime has unquestionably put the country on
the world political map. Host of the "Seventy-seven," active participant in the Algiers conference of "non-aligned nations," frequent
spokesman for Latin American in the World Bank, chief proponent
of reform in the Organization of American States and in the inter-
American military system, host and leading supporter of the Andean
pact, current member of the UN Security Council, Peru has projected
itself into the international arena.

From several foreign perspectives, Peru's current process of
military-directed change is regarded with hope. For many on the
international left, Peru seems especially significant, particularly now
that the "Chilean way" has been abruptly closed. From this vantage
point, Peru's military regime is contrasted with that of Brazil. Leftist
intellectuals have lost their jobs and rights and some have suffered
torture in Brazil; many of their counterparts in Peru are advising the
regime or are at least sympathetic to it (though a few have been interfered with and some even deported). Bishops in Brazil condemn their
regime; Peruvian bishops generally support theirs. The Brazilian
regime promoted capitalist expansion, national and foreign, while
the Peruvian government announces its aim to move away from
capitalism and expropriates or nationalizes one foreign company
after another. And while Brazil ties itself ever more closely to the
United States, Peru (together with Chile under Allende) has led
newly invigorated attempts to reduce Latin American dependence
on Washington.

Many international lenders and even some investors, paradox-
ically, also regard Peru's experiment, on the whole, as positive. The
military regime has earned plaudits for its prudent fiscal management and for its willingness to strike specific bargains with foreign
companies on an individual basis. From this standpoint, Peru's
regime is contrasted with Chile's under Allende and with Castro's.
Whatever the short-term nuisance of renegotiating contracts and
absorbing nationalist rhetorical attacks, some foreign investors think
the military regime is "making Peru safe" for them, now and for
some time to come.[2]

Within Peru, however, the military regime's program is not so
widely acclaimed. Articulate observers from the left and the right
assail the regime for contrary flaws. Though the traditional (Moscow-
line) Communist party openly supports the military regime, many

on the left regard it as far from "revolutionary," but rather as an ally
of international capitalism, exploiting the Peruvian masses for the
sake of dominant minorities.[3] From the right, the military government's program is also viewed with deepening distrust. Even those
businessmen who had adjusted themselves to the agrarian reform, a
greatly extended state role in the economy, enforced profit-sharing
and worker-management schemes, and countless other changes they
might have resisted under other circumstances, found themselves
alarmed in 1973 by the sudden nationalization of the fishmeal industry (Peru's largest) and by the repeated, escalating stress on "social
property."[4]

   Despite its international stature, the Peruvian regime finds itself
almost bereft of conspicuous support at home. No group is likely
soon to have the force to displace or even seriously challenge the
military, but the government encounters serious opposition within
several important sectors: labor, business, peasants, students, and
professionals. One politically meaningful election after another
reflects anti-regime sentiment; opposition candidates have won the
recent polls held by sugar workers' and teachers' cooperatives as
well as the lawyers', doctors', and engineers' associations, and mili-
tantly anti-regime student groups hold sway in practically all
Peruvian universities. Some backing, particularly among the urban
poor and among highland peasants who have benefited from the
agrarian reform, is demonstrated from time to time, especially
through impressive mass meetings, but contrary evidence is even
more striking. General strikes in several provincial areas—including
Arequipa, Cuzco, and Puno—forced the regime to suspend constitutional guarantees temporarily in mid-1973 and again later that
year, and major anti-government demonstrations have occurred on
several other occasions.

   SINAMOS (the National System to Support Social Mobilization), established in 1971 partly to organize support for the government, has instead been the object of intensifying attack from all
sides, and even of some backbiting from within the regime. And
though the army is surely Peru's preeminent middle class institution,
middle class distress is increasingly perceptible. Housewives, bureaucrats, teachers, taxi drivers and secretaries are all grumbling.

   The contrast between international acclaim and domestic opposition is not the only paradox which characterizes the current Peruvian
regime. Detailed examination of its first five years would reveal a
number of apparent contradictions.[5] This is an avowedly nationalist
government which invites foreign investment into its most crucial

sectors; a regime which encourages private investment while moving away from capitalism and which undertakes structural reforms that leave most Peruvians largely unaffected; a government which mobilizes and depoliticizes simultaneously, which seems to radicalize in one area while retreating in another.

This is not the place to analyze Peru's regime nor to unravel its contradictions. For our purposes, suffice it to say that Peru's military rulers are undertaking and implementing a comprehensive reform program, albeit within class and sector parameters, which is significantly affecting the distribution of resources and rewards among Peruvians. This essay asks why: What accounts for the adoption by Peru's Armed Forces of a comprehensive reform program? My emphasis is on the national background and context of Peru's current process of military-directed change, and particularly on the interplay between the military institution's internal changes, Peru's wider social transformations, and the shifts in civilian approaches to Peru's long-standing problems.

There can be little doubt that most foreign (and even some Peruvian) assessments of the military regime have regarded it mainly in terms derived from the experiences of other countries, rather than from Peru's own past. Those who think primarily of other Latin American military regimes have understandably discounted the Peruvian government's professions of reform; they have consequently either been befuddled by what the regime seems actually to be doing or else quick to emphasize any evidence that it is doing nothing. Even those who, recognizing that armies vary substantially in their political roles, frame their approach to different regimes within a broader (often class-based) analysis find themselves puzzled by the Peruvian case, for the army's program unquestionably outruns what most middle-class Peruvians support.

Established conceptual boxes have not served well to characterize or explain the Peruvian process. Rather, familiar categories have led analysts astray, causing them to be so surprised at Peru's apparent non-conformance to their expectations that they have tended either to try to salvage their schemes by grasping at fragmentary evidence and ignoring contradictions, or to relax their critical scrutiny of the regime's ambiguities in deference to what seems to be a puzzling exception.

In seeking to explain the Peruvian military's policies since taking power, one may profitably concentrate on understanding Peru before 1968, analyzing changes both within the Peruvian Armed Forces and in the larger society within which it operates.

Victor Villanueva and Luigi Einaudi have focused on the Peruvian military's evolution.[6] They advance several explanations for the Army's recent course: the effects of recruiting and promoting middle class officers, primarily of provincial origin; the impact of the Army's extensive training program, particularly the course at Peru's equivalent of the National War College, the Centro de Altos Estudios Militares (CAEM), and the instruction at U.S. installations; the legacy of the Army's historic traumas and the consequent distrust by officers of civilians; and especially the experiences top-ranking officers suffered in putting down guerrilla uprisings in the mid-1960s. All these factors help account for the Army's approach in 1968, answering in part why Peruvian officers reject the landed elite, favor planning and an expanded state role generally, oppose politics and politicians, and see reforms as essential for national security.

Comparative data suggest, however, that none of these factors by itself—nor even all together—provides a sufficient explanation for the military's comprehensive reform program. Almost all officer corps in Latin American armies come predominantly from the provincial middle class, but few (if any) parallel the Peruvian Army's current stance.[7] The CAEM program is unusual among Latin American countries, but it is by no means unique. Most officers who have graduated from nearly equivalent institutions in Argentina and Brazil, for instance, have emerged with attitudes and policy preferences very different from those their Peruvian counterparts declare. Besides, not even the most extravagant proponents of education's impact would claim that a nine-month course for mature professionals, or even shorter exposure to foreign training, could fundamentally affect their values and behavior. And other armies in Latin America and elsewhere have emerged from battles with guerrillas determined to repress them, not eager to foster structural change.

When one considers the civilian context in which Peru's Armed Forces has acted, however, the fact that Peru's officers came to power in 1968 with a reform program is much less surprising. What is remarkable, indeed, is that the goals and means the current military regime espouses took so long to become an implemented government program.

In 1968 Peru was poor—probably the least developed of the larger Latin American countries, not just in per capita income but with regard to urbanization, literacy, mass media exposure, and other aspects of social development. A composite measure of "social mobilization indicators" prepared by David Scott Palmer ranks Peru sixteenth among the twenty Latin American countries considered, followed only by the Dominican Republic, Guatemala, Honduras, and Haiti.[8]

Property and income distribution were exceptionally unequal. Two percent of Peru's agricultural estates (many of them owned by the same individuals or families) accounted for some 76 percent of the country's land, while 89 percent of properties took up but 10 percent of the land.[9] One percent of Peru's population received about 31 percent of the nation's income; the top 10 percent obtained half the national total and the bottom quarter got only three percent.[10] This last group corresponded roughly to the residents of Peru's *"mancha india,"* the provinces of Ancash, Apurimac, Ayacucho, Huancavelica, Cuzco, and Puno. Eighty-seven percent of the persons over five years old in these six provinces spoke Quechua or Aymara at the time of the 1961 census, and more than half did not speak Spanish.[11]

Industry, exports, and credit—like land—were controlled by small groups, members of a reduced number of Peruvian families or else foreigners, tied in with international firms.[12] And national policies systematically protected the interests of Peru's dominant elites, domestic and international. Free currency exchange, protection for infant industries, incentives for foreign investments, tax regulations of various sorts, irrigation projects and water rights— all helped the rich and powerful retain their place.[13]

Peru before 1968 had not escaped challenge, of course. From the late nineteenth century figure, Manuel Gonzalez Prada, on writers had assailed the injustice of a society based on exploitation of the many by the few.[14] National and foreign observers alike had characterized Peru as a "beggar sitting on a throne of gold" and had argued that prosperity could only be achieved by a just and rational social reorganization. Oft-discussed remedies for Peru's acknowledged ills had been advocated for years by Church and lay thinkers, by Marxists and anti-Communists, by *Apristas* and by military men. All agreed that Peru needed to educate and incorporate its Indian masses, to redistribute property and its rewards more equitably, to expand production and markets, and to exploit Peru's resources to benefit the entire national population rather than just a few families or foreigners. José Carlos Mariátegui and Victor Raúl Haya de la Torre, Peru's internationally influential writers, coincided in their emphasis on these points in spite of their disagreement on others.[15]

Creating a stronger state and undertaking planning; establishing controls to assure that foreign investment serves Peru; ending, or at least reducing, dependence; reforming land tenure and general property distribution; extending and transforming education: these were all points of consensus among professionals, intellectuals, *tecnicos,* and even some industrialists, indeed among virtually all politically aware Peruvians not themselves directly dependent on perpetuating a pre-industrial land-based system of nearly feudal characteristics. Many differences remained among these sectors in 1968, but few, if any, opposed in principle the kinds of reforms the military regime announced it would undertake. It is instructive to note, for instance, that even *Accion Popular's* right-wing (as reflected in the Ulloa-dominated Cabinet of 1968) had pressed forward with measures designed to subordinate private interests to a strengthened state.[16] The 1962 and 1963 campaigns had included pro-reform appeals not only by Belaúnde's *Acción Popular* but also by *Apra,* the *Democristianos,* and the *Social progresistas,* and the prospective 1969 campaign promised more of the same.[17]

By 1968 structural reforms of the type the Economic Commission on Latin America (ECLA) had been proposing for years were, in Peru, an idea whose time had come. The concepts and rhetoric had been around a long time, attaining widespread legitimacy, and they were made more compelling by the facts of social and economic change, which had begun to accelerate in Peru after World War II.

From 1945 on, Peru experienced striking economic growth, urbanization, and general social mobilization. National economic production grew at an annual rate of close to six percent, fueled by a major expansion of copper and by the explosion of what quickly became the world's largest fishmeal industry.[18] Peru's population rose more than three percent a year, and the impact of this rapid growth was made even more dramatic by migration to Peru's cities, mainly to Lima. Thirty-five percent of Peru's population lived in cities in 1940; by 1967 the figure was 51 percent and still climbing fast.[19] Lima-Callao swelled to about three million, sprawling out over the city's vital agricultural land as well as over miles of flat desert. School enrollment, at the primary and secondary levels especially, climbed sharply during the 1950s and 1960s, pushing literacy rates up from 43.4 percent in 1940 to 81 percent in 1970, and feeding pressures to expand university facilities.[20] (This expansion, like that of income, was very unevenly distributed; few rural Indian children obtained more than two or three years of schooling, even in the 1960s.) Communications intensified and extended its ambit; by 1965 transistor radios dotted the Peruvian highlands, and television antennas were beginning to sprout in the shanty-towns of Lima and of other cities.

Pressures on Peru's elites began to mount from the increasingly urbanized and literate population, insistently seeking a larger share of the nation's resources. Rural and urban land invasions, guerrilla outbursts, student demonstrations, strikes, and increasing electoral support for reformist candidates reflected these demands.

No revolutionary coalition of the aggrieved had developed in Peru by 1968. No doubt this was in part due to repression, as Lima's elites managed to suppress individual challenges and to prevent the organization of concerted efforts among dissident groups. In part, however, Peru's revolution could be postponed, or avoided, because individual demands were being more or less satisfied.[21] The booming export-led economy permitted Peruvian governments from the end of World War II on to accede to specific pressures. Land invasions produced results: the acceptance and even the promotion of squatter settlements in the cities and the beginnings of land reform in the rural areas. Wages were raised in industry after industry and social security benefits were increased. Universities multiplied at a dizzying pace, from six in 1955 to at least thirty in 1968. Tens of thousands of housing units were constructed during the Belaúnde period alone, the number of hospital beds was doubled, electric power production multiplied and service was extended.[22] Each pressure was responded to on its own terms, however; little effort was made to devise comprehensive policies or to undertake structural changes. On the contrary, some concessions were granted with obvious disregard for their wider effects; Law 15215, providing an unrealistically rapid increase in teachers' salaries beyond the country's financial capacity, exemplified this problem.

While Peru's society changed, its political system did not keep pace. The land-holding "oligarchy" continued to exercise predominant political influence into the 1960s. Its power was clearly beginning to wane; for example, although almost all Cabinet officers of previous governments were from landed families, that group was represented by only two-thirds of Belaúnde's Cabinet officers.[23] But the "oligarchy" still dominated Congress, particularly by controlling the politics of the rural provinces, which accounted for 29 percent of the population and 27 percent of the seats but only 14 percent of the votes.[24] (Highland Peru was almost totally ignored, except in rhetoric, by Peru's politicians until candidate Belaúnde's extensive travels in the 1956 and 1962-63 campaigns. Even in 1963 residents of the densely-populated *sierra* were prevented by literacy requirements from becoming a major electoral force.) The significance of the oligarchy's entrenched hold on Congress was reinforced by the unusual importance of Peru's legislature in national politics; the Congress retained and exercised a system—unique in Latin America—permitting interpellation and even the censure of individual ministers.[25] With their control of Congress—plus their influence on the press, on access to credit, and on the interest associations—Peru's landed families assured themselves that comprehensive reforms would not advance.

The history of agrarian reform in Peru illustrates both how the consensus on structural reforms emerged, and how actual reform efforts prior to 1968 were thwarted.[26] Although the idea of land reform had been espoused for years by various intellectuals, landed interests successfully prevented it from becoming a matter for serious governmental consideration or even for significant public debate until the late 1950s. When domestic pressures and international trends made it impossible to avoid considering the land tenure problem any longer, the Prado regime in 1956 established a National Commission on Agrarian Reform and Housing. But the Commission's chairman was Pedro Beltrán, editor of *La Prensa* and Peru's leading apostle of classical economic liberalism, and five of eight members were either large landowners or their direct agents. The Commission's report was predictable; the recommendations consisted primarily of opening unused jungle lands for colonization and extending coastal irrigation projects.

When the peasant invasions of La Convención and Hugo Blanco's menacing successes convinced Peruvian army officers and others that land reform was needed to dampen a perceived threat to national security, the measure eventually decreed was limited to the geographic area actually suffering acute unrest. When the Belaúnde regime won election on a platform promising (among other items) a major agrarian reform, APRA opposition and the resulting Congressional bargaining substantially watered down the initial proposal. The eventual law, passed in 1964, circumscribed the potentially affected areas severely; subsequent provisions regarding financing and implementation assured that not even a limited reform could be rapidly effected. By 1968, therefore, the aim of substantial agrarian reform was no longer debated among Peruvian *tecnicos*; their concern, rather, was to obtain a government with sufficient strength and commitment to put such a reform into practice despite the opposition of Peru's landed families.

Proposals to strengthen the state and to assure that foreign investment would serve national needs had also been advanced but were even slower to become Peruvian public policy. Almost every writer on Peruvian problems in this century has emphasized the need to strengthen the public sphere, but Peru in the early 1960s was still a nation where taxes could be collected by a private banking firm which actually charged the government for the use of its own revenue![27] In the early 1960s Peru's Central Bank was still directly responsive to the private sector. The Peruvian state's share of national investment in 1960 was probably lower than that in any comparable South American nation.[28] And those with a stake in Peru's land-based economic and political system did what they could to keep the state weak. "Planning" as a concept was discredited in Peru, thanks largely to La Prensa's influence, long after it had been accepted elsewhere, and other terms of national debate on economic and social policy were similarly shaped by Lima's "oligarchy," at least until 1960.[29]

Things were changing in Peru by the late 1960s, but ever so slowly. The National Planning Institute was established in 1962 (by the caretaker military regime) but remained weak during the Belaúnde years. The Central Bank was somewhat restructured but stayed closely tied to dominant private interests. Public investment began to climb, but Peru's public sector was still weaker than that of any of Peru's neighbors, except perhaps for Ecuador.

As for toughening the terms on which foreign investment entered Peru, an aim Haya de la Torre had advocated since at least 1928, Peruvian governments after 1950 actually bucked the general Latin American nationalist trend.[30] One concession or incentive after another was granted by Peru to foreign investors in mining, petroleum and manufacturing. By the 1960s, Mexico, Brazil and Argentina had long since nationalized their petroleum companies. In Peru, however, IPC was not only private and foreign but even enjoyed sub-soil rights unique (and questionable) under Peruvian law. Special tax advantages were also exercised by Conchan (itself half owned by a U.S. company), the other main oil refining and distribution enterprise in Peru. The Peruvian mining code of 1950 was universally considered one of Latin America's most generous to foreign investors, as was the 1952 Petroleum Law, and the special provisions of the Toquepala copper contract were particularly favorable to the foreign investor, Southern Peru Copper Corporation. Industrial incentive laws were similar; the automobile assembly industry, for instance, drew thirteen companies to Peru in the 1960s for a total market of less than 20,000 vehicles a year. Here, again, change occurred in the 1960s, as Peru gradually imposed stricter reinvestment obligations, higher taxes, and other requirements.

More sweeping reforms, however, were always frustrated by the hold the landed elite continued to exert on the political system.

By 1968 Peru was considerably "behind" most of its neighbors with regard to various economic and political reforms. Ready consensus existed among *tecnicos,* civilian and military, regarding what needed to be done. A considerable and obvious policy vacuum was waiting to be filled.

It should not have been surprising that the military regime eventually occupied that space. Already, in their short-term takeover of 1962-63, top Army officers had shown their disposition toward reform, a disposition underlined by the Armed Forces' widely understood support for the Belaúnde platform.[31] Army officers shared with their civilian brethren in the middle class the desire to break the "oligarchy's" hold, a desire which underlay the birth, during the 1950s, of Belaúnde's *Acción Popular,* the Christian Democratic movement and the *Movimiento Socialprogresista.* All took essentially the same approach; the Army officers, taught at CAEM by civilians from these groups, were by no means alone.

Nor should it have been surprising that Peru's Armed Forces in 1968 had both the sense of legitimacy and the clout to proceed at once with a reform program. Throughout the 1950s and 1960s, while civilian political institutions were proving increasingly anachronistic and were being questioned by Peruvian critics of several political persuasions, the Armed Forces was growing in size, strength, capacity and coherence.[32] Imbued—at CAEM and other military schools, in the intelligence service, and through their military journals—with a "new professionalism," Peru's officers looked to the problems of national development as a legitimate and high priority battleground.[33] Their sense of competence often reinforced by success in university studies and other civilian spheres, Peru's officers felt confident they could tackle long-deferred problems.

Their way was relatively unimpeded at the start. Peru's still relatively low level of prior social mobilization and participation, the weak and dependent nature of Lima's industrial bourgeoisie, the dwindling economic base of Peru's rural elite, and especially the general disrepute which civilian politicians had achieved—all left Peru's officers virtually unchallenged as they took over. Only APRA, the Army's historic nemesis, was vociferously opposed. And APRA— by 1968 mainly a party of old men and their memories—could easily be outflanked, especially by the immediate nationalization of IPC, so long an issue in Peruvian politics, and then by the agrarian reform.[34]

That Peru's armed forces came to power talking about comprehensive structural reforms, that it really intended to undertake them, and that it was able to begin doing so with relative ease are much more easily understood when one considers the national background and context of the military takeover. Personal leadership, contingent circumstances, the international environment—these and other factors undoubtedly influenced the Peruvian regime's initial approach and its subsequent evolution. But the fundamental fact, which this essay seeks to underline, is that Peru's military rulers entered power prepared institutionally to overcome an evident gap between Peru's socio-economic reality and its political institutions and public policies. Whatever the final outcome of Peru's "revolution," that first task has already been achieved.

Notes

1. The evolution of the "social property" concept is analyzed in Knight (1974).

2. See, for instance, Ferrer (1970) and Utley (1973).

3. See Quijano (1971) and Letts (1971), as well as the first four issues of *Sociedad y Politica*, a journal published in Lima in 1972-1973 and closed down by the regime in September 1973.

4. The pages of *El Comercio* and *La Prensa*, Lima's two best-established daily newspapers, were filled with communiques and letters along these lines after the fishmeal nationalization in May 1973.

5. For an extensive discussion, see Lowenthal (1974), Cotler (1971).

6. Einaudi (1969, 1973); Villanueva (1962, 1968, 1971, 1972).

7. See Fitch (1973: 248-249).

8. Palmer (1973: 7-9).

9. See Quijano (forthcoming).

10. Webb (1973).

11. Cotler (1968).

12. Malpica (1968) provides a compendium, inaccurate in some details but useful as a general view, on the holdings of Lima's major families and firms. Cf. Bourricaud (1969).

13. Bourricaud (1970).

14. Gonzalez Prada (1946). Cf. Plank (1958).

15. See, for instance, Haya de la torre (1936; 1961) and Mariategui (1971). Alexander (1973) provides much of Haya's work in English translation, as does Kantor (1966).

16. See Jaquette (1971) for a good discussion of the Ulloa period and its significance.

17. Cf., for instance, Alianza Acción Popular–Democrata Cristiano (1963), Cornejo Chavez (1960, 1962), and Salazar Bondy (1973) for summary statements reflecting the views of Acción Popular, the Democristianos, and the Social progresistas. See also Martinez (1962).

18. See Banco Central de Reservas del Peru (1966).

19. Larson and Bergman (1969: 137).

20. Drysdale and Myers (1974: 8).

21. Chaplin (1968).

22. Hoyos Osores (1969).

23. Stephens (1971: 103).

24. Cotler (1968).

25. McCoy (1971).

26. The following paragraphs draw on Bourricaud (1970), Carroll (1970), Petras and Laporte (1971), and Strasma (1973).

27. Jaquette (1971).

28. Hunt (1971: 391-2).

29. Bourricaud (1970) discusses the oligarchy's remarkable success at controlling the agenda for public discussion in Peru. Cf. Hunt (1971).

30. Hunt (1974).

31. See North (1966), Payne (1968) and Villanueva (1963).

32. Einaudi and Stepan (1971).

33. Stepan (1973).

34. Epstein (1972) discusses the impact of the military regime's early measures on the support for Apra.

This essay, originally presented orally at the Inter-University Seminar, is drawn from Chapter One of Abraham F. Lowenthal [ed.] (forthcoming) *Continuity and Changes in Contemporary Peru* and is published here with the permission of Princeton University Press.

The author gratefully acknowledges support for his research from the Council on Foreign Relations and the Center of International Studies at Princeton University, as well as the helpful comments received from discussants at the Inter-University Seminar, members of the Peru Seminar at the Center for Inter-American Relations in New York, and friends in Peru.

II.

POLITICAL-MILITARY SYSTEMS

The Socialist States

ARMED FORCES AND SOCIETY IN YUGOSLAVIA

Robin Alison Remington

> *'All that is foreign book-learning, my good fellow,' answered Stiković,*
> *'which vanishes before the living impetus of awakened nationalist forces*
> *among the Serbs and then among the Croats and Slovenes also, through*
> *tending to one aim. Things do not come to pass according to the fore-*
> *casts of German theoreticians but advance in complete accord with the*
> *deep sense of our history and racial destiny.' From Karageorge's words:*
> *'Let each kill his Turkish chief,' the social problem in the Balkans has*
> *always solved itself by the way of national liberation movements and*
> *wars. It all moves beautifully logically, from the less to the great, from*
> *the regional and tribal to the national and the formation of the State...*

Andrić (1967: 250-1)

The Yugoslav state rose from the ashes of World War I, was
dismembered in the onslaught of World War II, and rose again bat-
tered but more firmly united than before by the Yugoslav Communist Party. The party—led, sometimes driven, by a Croatian locksmith
peasant, Josip Broz, turned revolutionary who became, under the
name Tito, one of the most important statesmen in postwar Europe
as well as its most controversial communist leader[1] —fought an
indigenous battle of national liberation. Unlike most of their East
European comrades, who rode to power on the wake of the Soviet
Army,[2] Yugoslav communists followed Chinese methods that were
yet to succeed in China. Nor were they unaware of the relevance of
their model.

As Dedijer quotes Pijade:

> Daddy Mosha had issued stern instructions to all brigades on how to
> behave when passing through any village. The honor of the partisans
> must be preserved. 'The people are water, a partisan is a fish; fish cannot
> live without water.' That principle of the Chinese partisans holds here
> too.[3]

Such a pattern of revolutionary take-over had the advantage of
creating a large constituency that looked to the party for leadership.
Still, the integrating nature of partisan resistance notwithstanding,[4]
and despite Stiković's optimism about the awakened nationalism of
Serbs, Croats, and Slovenes "tending to one aim," one must be

163

exceedingly careful in talking of *the* Yugoslav military or even a
Yugoslav society. For Yugoslavia is a mosaic of five non-state nations
(each with its own history, tradition, political culture) struggling to
come to an as yet uneasy modus vivendi and dozens of national
minorities. The Yugoslav nation is at worst a fiction; at best it is very
much in a zig-zag process of becoming one nation, in which observers
and participants alike have trouble distinguishing between one step
forward and two steps back.

The south Slavs share a common, visceral knowledge of the
rigors of foreign domination.[5] Since Yugoslavia is the heart of the
Balkans, a pivotal intersection between East and West, they are well-
versed in the running battles of international crossroads. The Slovenes
were first under Charlemagne, then German (Austrian) domination
until the end of World War I. The Croats, taken over by Hungary
in return for autonomy under a Croat governor in 1102, lived in the
memory of an independent Croatia while looking to Austria for protection from the Turks. The Serbian empire dates from 1077. Under
the Nemanja dynasty in the glorious days of Tsar Dušan (1331-1335)
Serbia included Albania, Bulgaria, Macedonia, and much of Greece
—only to submit to the Turkish yoke after the battle of the Kosove
in 1389. The Montenegrins, Serbs who retreated to the black mountain from which they took their name, fought a guerrilla resistance
until fighting itself had become the way of life so eloquently described by Milovan Djilas:

> So it has always been here: one fights to achieve sacred dreams, and
> plunders and lays waste along the way to live in misery, in pain and death,
> but in one's thoughts to travel far. The naked and hungry mountaineers
> could not keep from looting their neighbors, while yearning and dying for
> ancient glories. Here war was survival, a way of life, and death in battle
> the loveliest dream and highest duty.[6]

By the 19th century Serbian history reads like a serialized epic
of repression and revolt under the leadership of simultaneously
feuding families: Karadjordje in 1804, Milos Obrenović who fought
brilliantly in the Balkan wars of 1912-1913, heroically in World War I.
Never had the idea of a Yugoslav state been so popular. The Croatian
parliament voted to end its tie with Hungary and to cast its lot with
the Council of Croats and Slovenes negotiating for a united, federal
Yugoslavia in which each nationality would retain significant autonomy,
    Serbs, still in the euphoric haze of victory, wanted not a federal
Yugoslavia, but a Greater Serbia. The government signed without

enthusiasm the Declaration of Corfu creating a South Slav state in which in principle its peoples would be equal: The Kingdom of Serbs, Croats, and Slovenes.

Not surprisingly, these incompatible goals led first to conflict, then chaos. By 1923-24, Croatia was virtually in insurrection. The Croat party was outlawed, its leader Stjepan Radić in jail. Released in 1925, Radić died violently, killed by a Montenegrain over an insult during parliamentary debate in the Skupština. King Alexandar suspended the constitution and declared a dictatorship. Thus by 1929 Yugoslavia was in fact a police state under Serbian direction. Croatia suffered harsh martial law that did not alleviate but rather exacerbated national unrest bringing into existence the notorious Ustashi terrorist extremists who were at least in part responsible for the assassination of Alexandar in France (1934) and whose quisling independent Kingdom of Croatia set up by Hitler under Ante Pavelić in 1941 reaped a genocidal revenge on Serbs within its reach.

Since Alexandar's son Peter II was under age, Prince Paul acted as regent. Paul brought Yugoslavia closer to the Nazis in a last ditch effort to avoid a war the country was in no condition to fight. Desparately maneuvering to keep both his throne and the country together, he also in 1939 agreed to sign a sporazum (agreement) granting greater autonomy to Croatia. With the Tripartite Axis pact on March 25, 1940, his efforts were swept aside by an army coup. Reason had succumbed to the passion of resistance. Germany invaded, slicing Yugoslavia into pieces parcelled out to those of its neighbors Hitler wished to woo. Never had the attempt to build a united Yugoslavia been as cherished as when Hitler brutally aborted these efforts.

How are such Byzantine maneuverings related to contemporary relations of Yugoslav armed forces to society? The Balkan answer would be that a tree is the product of its seed. Today is rooted in yesterday. In the Balkans, that yesterday is at least as important as today; for some it is more real than tomorrow.

First, from the perspective of deeply held historical attitudes, military roles come easily to Serbs and Montenegrins (according to the 1971 census they comprise roughly 8.6 million out of 20 million Yugoslavs, about 40 percent of the population). These roles are accepted as the natural duty of a man in a political culture that has always prized heroism and leadership.

Secondly, Croats have tended to rely more on political tactics— negotiation, passive resistance, obstructionism—than on armed struggle.[7] Moreover, behavior of the predominately Serbian Yugoslav

Army during the interwar years did nothing to strengthen either fraternal feeling or a liking for the military. Indeed, many Croats viewed the army coup against Prince Paul as directed largely against his promise of Croat autonomy.

Thirdly, and on one dimension perhaps most dangerous, interwar repression brought to life the fanatical Ustashe terrorists, whose atrocities during World War II stand to this day as one of the most fundamental barriers to building common trust among the nations of Yugoslavia while their emigré sympathizers insidiously continue to escalate tensions by hijacking airplanes, random bombings, attempted instigation of uprisings within the country—all combined with inflammatory nationalist propaganda and attacks on Yugoslav representatives abroad. Such low level violence can recreate a blood feuding mentality that undermines all compromise until arbitrary resolution from above seems the only feasible alternative.

For many years Tito has played the role of mediator, using his personal authority to break stalemates by forcing through his own preferred solution. The problem is obviously biological; President Tito is 81 years old. He cannot be the indispensable lenchpin holding the country together for much longer. Despite—some might go so far as to say because of—recent party reforms, the party may well prove incapable of strong centralized interventions without him. The method of reform—forced resignations of popular republican leaders, spiraling party purges, increased repression and harrassment of all opposition under a variety of slogans: "anarcho-liberalism," "technocratism," and, most recently, "pseudo-humanism"[8]—risks weakening party legitimacy by substituting unknown, potentially mediocre cadre for republican leaders with identifiable constituencies. Although such a move has the advantage, for those who consider it such, of strengthening control from the center, it can also lead to a token (in all likelihood itself factionalized) collective leadership that without the authority of Tito increasingly substitutes force for persuasion to achieve resolution of differences.

Thus speculation on "after Tito, what? " has for some years focused on the army, suggesting (1) that Tito will not tolerate chaotic conditions and with the help of the army and support of 80 percent of the masses will install a semi-military central government to establish order. Or (2) that the army with Soviet support, will seize power once Tito becomes incapacitated or dies.[9]

In a country with a history of military intervention, where for centuries, at least in Serbia, the military has played a direct, often brutal role in the political process,[10] such speculation is grounded in more than academic futurology. Even if the problem is "national specific," it has wide implications for the nation in question, for the currently flourishing European detenté, and for an understanding of the relationship of party organization to other potentially powerful political forces in Eastern Europe.

Therefore, as tentative and preliminary as the following analysis is, it is a step toward sorting out inadequate data on an incredibly sensitive question[11] —what we actually know about the function of Yogoslav armed forces, their composition, and their relation to the extremely complex, multi-ethnic society of which they form one identifiably cohesive interest group. In doing so I will focus on three crises of the past five years in which the Yugoslav armed forces came dramatically into the spotlight. First an external crisis—the threat to Yugoslav security stemming from "allied socialist" military invasion of Czechoslovakia in 1968; second, an internal crisis during which President Tito himself referred to the danger of civil war and the duty of the army to defend socialism internally as well as at Yugoslav borders[12] —the Zagreb student strike of December, 1971, with its consequences for the League of Croatian Communists; and third, the role of the military during a small but symbolically threatening invasion of a band of Ustashe terrorists in the summer of 1972.

First, however, it is useful to look in general at army-party relations as they developed during the prelude to revolution (the period of partisan struggle) until the first of the three crises in question, that of August, 1968.

The Army and the Party in Socialist Yugoslavia

It is not exaggerating to say that a virtually symbiotic relationship between the Yugoslav party and the armed forces developed during the partisan struggle itself. In a sense the army was the child of a marriage of convenience between party and peasantry, that despite its unromantic nature had a certain compatibility. During wartime the bulk of the army and party alike were politically backward peasants with often only ten days of political training organized on the run by each company. Dedijer has estimated that 99 percent of the fighting men were peasants, adding bluntly,

> We must fling wide the gates of the Party. When a man has carried a rifle eight months, and fights like a hero he has the qualifications of a party member.[13]

The implications of such a policy for party membership and for the very nature of the party is clear. Statistics, particularly those that are broken down into what could be considered the wrong categories for a specific research purpose, can be extremely misleading. However, Horvat indicates that in 1946, 130,000 (50.4 percent) of the party were peasants—a figure that had increased absolutely to 331,000 (42.8 percent) and declined slightly in percentage in 1952; he added to this category "students, military, pensioners, others" as 30,000 (11.7 percent) in 1946; 47,000 (6.1 percent) in 1952. This gives one an idea of the composition of the rank and file.[14] In 1946 very many of those peasants undoubtedly came into the category of Dedijer's men "who carried a rifle eight months," even if they subsequently left the military to return to the land. In the second category, both students and pensioners of the late 1940s were frequently former partisans (either young or wounded, somtimes both). Even if one assumes that workers and members of the state bureaucracy (known as employees) were not among party members who were former partisans—by no means a certain or fair assumption—in 1946 approximately 62.1 percent of the party most likely had had some military experience and could have been expected to be justly proud of the Yugoslav army.

The manner in which Moscow's attempt to impose its own military advisers on the Yugoslav army exacerbated "differences" which escalated into an open split by 1948 has been well documented.[15] By the early 1950s fear of a Soviet invasion had led to a massive conventional military build-up with an estimated near half-million men under arms. With several notable exceptions,[16] Tito's party and army stood solidly behind him. Not, one might suspect, because they understood what had gone wrong in a situation that the party leadership presented as a mammoth misunderstanding with their Soviet comrades, but because Tito and the central core of the party leaders had bought their political credibility in battle. On the whole, the Yugoslav party cadre backed their leadership not for reasons of democratic centralism or even of political expediency. They stood firm in 1948 because during the years of partisan struggle party and army leadership had amounted to almost the same thing.

There is little reason to think that this relationship had changed dramatically by 1952, when Horvat estimates membership as 42.8 percent peasants, 6.1 percent students, military and others. It is still reasonable to assume that of this 48.9 percent the vast majority had some military experience or had come from a family in which at least one member had seen action in the liberation war/revolutionary struggle. Moreover, the category of employees (members of the state or party apparatus in which Horvat sometimes confusingly includes "career military men") undoubtedly included former peasant-soldiers who instead of returning to the land had taken advantage of the preference they were being given in terms of education to become upwardly mobile. At that time the threat to the nation had a kind of tense reality,[17] so that no one, at least openly, dared to question that 22 percent of the national income was devoted to defense.

After the Soviet-Yugoslav rapprochement of the mid-1950s, as the top leadership's phalanx-like image crumbled in the public aftermath of Milovan Djilas' "falling away," it became less and less clear what such a defense budget was buying. Particularly under the impact of the Economic Reform of 1965, questions that 10 years before would have been unthinkable were being asked even in the Skupstina, where in December, 1966, the former Minister of Defense Ivan Gosnjak was told to take a second look at his proposed budget to see if he could not be more economical, also some probing inquiries were made into why officers' pay should be increased more than the national average.[18]

According to Johnson, by 1968 less than 6 percent of the national income went into defense expenditures, while the size of the armed Yugoslav People's Army had shrunk to roughly 200,000 men. These figures make even more understandable the decision to opt for a "mixed" defense with emphasis on territorial units during those crucial months following the August invasion of Czechoslovákia by Prague's allies.

Impact of Czechoslovakia 1968 on Yugoslav Military Strategy

By 1968 there was a deceptive complacency in Belgrade on the delicate question of relations with the Soviet Union.[19] Perceived threats from the East had declined so as to be almost nonexistent. Stalin had died and with him died implacable Soviet hostility for Tito and Titoism in any form. Khrushchev even went so far as to return to the slogan of the "people's democracies" in the immediate postwar period, recognizing the legitimacy of "national roads" to socialism in his attempt to bring Yugoslavia back into the fold. True, no one would claim it had been a problem-free process. The polemics see-sawed, sometimes wildly, as in 1958 during what is now known as the "Second-Soviet-Yugoslav dispute." Still relaxation in which Moscow seemed to see its minimal East European interests in broad outlines lulled the Yugoslavs into a false sense of security. Rumania had achieved an unimagined freedom of foreign policy maneuver.[20] In late 1967 Brezhnev had refused to intervene in Czechoslovak internal affairs, thereby tacitly sanctioning Novotńy's fall; initially Dubček seemed an acceptable substitute.

Yugoslav sympathy for the goals of the Prague Spring soared. Despite nervousness at the increasingly hostile response of Moscow and the more orthodox East European regimes (particularly East Germany and Poland), Belgrade's euphoria during those months of liberation paralleled the mood in Prague and Bratislava. For Tito, even if less than for Dubček, win or lose, the stakes were high.

The depth of Yugoslav trauma at the actual violation of Czechoslovak territorial integrity by allied socialist troops came from the bitterness of shattered expectations intensified by the knowledge that from the Soviet view Tito was both an accomplice before the fact and a willing supporter of Dubček's deviation from Moscow's version of common socialist principles.[21] The LCY attacked the invasion of Czechoslovakia as a gross violation of socialist norms, offered its support to the KSC and the Czechoslovak people in their struggle for independence, and reminded all parties that in case of need the Yugoslav army was ready to defend Yugoslav borders.[22] Moscow responded by polemicizing against "Yugoslav defenders of nationalism;" and more seriously with the theoretical rationalization known to the West as the Brezhnev doctrine.[23]

Insisting that the concept of sovereignty among socialist states must not be understood abstractly, this doctrine held that among these states international law must be subordinated to class struggle. In sum, Moscow reserved the right to intervene militarily or otherwise if developments in any given socialist country threatened either socialism within that country or the basic interests or other socialist countries as defined by Moscow.

From the moment of its birth, the Brezhnev doctrine put forward to justify Soviet troops on Czechoslovak soil directly threatened Yugoslav national security. Moscow's minicold war against Tito was on again. The political climate worsened. The tone of Soviet-Yugoslav exchanges sounded remarkably like those of 1948,[24] although in fairness polemics never reached the flood of vindictiveness of the early postwar years.

Any lingering doubts as to what the Brezhnev doctrine meant to Yugoslavia could not have survived Gomulka's detailed restatement at the Fifth Congress of the Polish United Workers Party in November:

Yugoslavia, while maintaining a policy of so-called nonalignment, can maintain it only in the shadow of the Warsaw Pact states. If other socialist states followed the steps of Yugoslavia, then, in a situation in which Europe did not have any collective security mechanism, each of these countries would represent an open gate to all kinds of imperialist and reactionary intervention, pressures and chaos. . . .[25]

At a minimum this interpretation returned Yugoslavia to the status of an isolated exception, barred from the mainstream of European socialism. It was a role the Yugoslavs had learned to handle, if not to like. The problem was that the Yugoslavs tended toward a much more extreme interpretation: that, contrary to the Belgrade and Moscow Declarations between the governments and parties of Yugoslavia and the USSR in 1955 and 1956, Brezhnev and company were serving notice that when in the Soviet view socialism as defined by Moscow was threatened, Soviet troops might again be used.[26] Today the victim had been Czechoslovakia; yet the KSC had not adopted policies perceptibly more controversial than those daily carried out in Yugoslavia. In analyzing the invasion, if in little else, Belgrade might well be tempted to agree with Peking that what the Soviets appeared to want was not a socialist community but a colonial empire with Russian overlords.[27]

Not surprisingly, therefore, from August, 1968, until Brezhnev himself disowned the "Brezhnev doctrine" as a "western fabrication" on his visit to Yugoslavia in September, 1971,[28] national security in Yugoslav eyes meant primarily Yugoslav military security in the face of an unambiguous threat.

The response was an immediate retreat to the tactics of 1948. Tito moved to consolidate his base. Domestically this led to revitalizing the party and reviving the concept of partisan popular resistance. Known as "General (total) People's Defense,"[29] this strategy should be considered an outgrowth rather than a straightforward reincarnation of the theory of "all people's war" that provided conceptual underpinning for the Yugoslav partisans during World War II. Notwithstanding Tito's explanation of the new military policy as the experience of people's liberation war applied in present conditions,[30] it differed in purpose, circumstance and possibilities. For the concept of "people's war" as developed by Mao Tse-tung, contributed to by Che Guevara, was primarily a recipe for revolution. In that sense the struggle against the foreign invader is also a struggle for mobilizing the people into a militarized mass insurrection designed both to liberate the country and to seize power—to simultaneously destroy the pre-existing system and carry out a social-political revolution.

In 1968 the Yugoslav revolution, despite heated debates about the content of that revolution, was a fact. Tito's partisans had taken power a full quarter of a century ago. Partly as a result of the popular myths stemming from the mass nature of partisan struggle, the Yugoslav Communist Party had consolidated its position (unlike the other East European parties) with the advantage of both power and authority, i.e., recognition of that power as being based on accepted mutual interests between the party and the people rather than on the regime's control of superior coercive instruments.[31] The object of "general people's defense" was not to make a revolution but to defend one—not to destroy the existing system but to preserve it.

This difference brought its own duality. On the plus side, the regular armed forces provided a solid core around which irregular guerrilla units could form. Thus, the Yugoslav People's Army (JNA) had an integral place in strategic planning, thereby allowing military planners to think in terms of a "mixed" force combining elements of both traditional and partisan strategies. Secondly, territorial defense units are more economical than massive conventional military build-up, something that—given the already extensive demands on Yugoslav resources, the dubious success of the 1965 Economic Reform, and the political undesirability of outside assistance even it it had been available—was not likely a minor consideration. For the extensive decentralization of the mid-1960's had added a domestic political limitation in the form of unwillingness of the non-Serbian republics to see a reconcentration of power in Belgrade.

Moreover, even if the political-economic liabilities of returning to the conventional, large-scale standing army of the 1950s had not existed, that kind of build-up offered pathetically little protection against the highly mobile forces that had marched into Czechoslovakia virtually without advance warning. Such a threat required effective mobilization capability with a speed that would leave little time for transmitting centrally-made decisions. To the Yugoslavs, recent experience seems to prove that the weakness of modern conventional armies is not in taking territory; the problem is rather in controlling that territory to political advantage. As Dr. Savka Dabčević-Kučar put it, "history teaches the obvious unequivocal lesson, especially exemplified in the revolutionary and people's liberation wars in our times (particularly in Vietnam. . .) that armed people's might, up-to-date equipment, and force of numbers have not always been decisive factors."[32]

Therefore, the thrust of the deterrence value of total people's defense was to come in upping the cost of occupation. In short, unlike the theory of "all people's war," total people's defense was designed primarily to avoid war, not to fight it. The doctrine was based on the belief that if they wish to remain sovereign, small and medium-size states must be able to defend themselves rather than relying on outside aid. It assumed that with national will and the mechanisms for involving the entire population in resistance, such a state can withstand attack.

Such a strategy also, however, makes certain assumptions about the relationship of the country's armed forces to its society, or in the Yugoslav case, to its multi-national societies. It assumes a united will to resist and a population that knows what it is fighting for, not just whom it is fighting *against*. It assumes that professional and non-professional soldiers can "mix" well, whether or not the country is actually under attack. In short, it assumes that "national" issues that have proved "to matter" with extraordinary intensity in many other Yugoslav arenas will not matter when it comes to restyling the armed forces.

Whether or not such assumptions are warranted is still in question, but the evidence that is in is by no means totally encouraging. Public material is sparse on the reaction of senior regular officers to relinquishing their role as *the* Yugoslav military institution for an arrangement in which the territorial units are legally coequal rather than subordinate to the regular army. Although interpretation is largely a matter of reading esoteric arguments between the lines, Rusinow has made a convincing case that reservations did (quite likely still do) exist among the traditional military elites.[33]

Further, using regular reserve officers in command posts of the territorial units has ethnic ramifications. Despite efforts to recruit among Slovenes and Croats, traditionally the Yugoslav army is largely (estimates vary from 70-90 percent) Serbian, meaning that Croatian and Slovene units were in some unavoidable cases commanded by Serbs, a situation in itself fraught with friction as the nationality tensions rose during 1971-1972.[34] This brings us to the second instance in which the Yugoslav army came sharply into the limelight in recent years; a nationality crisis escalated, although not in any sense caused by, the Zagreb student stirke in November-December 1971.[35]

The Role of Yugoslav Armed Forces During Internal Crisis

Despite the historically proven ability of the South Slavs to unite against any actual invader, despite the myths of national (ethnic) equality and a loose agreement on the fundamental ideological tenets of self-managing socialism, the scars of the genocidal civil war fought simultaneously with the struggle against German invaders (at least in the case of the party, towards social revolution) are still raw. Fear is the factor underlying an ideological debate in which Serbs argue that class interests must have priority over national interests, in contrast to the Croat position that both class and national interests must be considered. Croats (and to some extent Macedonians, Slovenians, and the Albanian majority in the Kosovo) fear the emphasis on class interest is only a new incarnation of Serbian hegemony. The Serbs fear first that nationalist should read "separatist," that what the Croats really want is out—secondly, that it could all too easily happen again in one lifetime. They fear for the lives of the 700,000 Serbs still living in Croatia who make up 15 percent of the republic.

This becomes a basis of tension within Crotia as well as between the Serb and Croat republics. Thus what to do about protecting the rights of Serbs living in Croatia is a corollary of the conflict over whether Yugoslavia must have a strong central government as the Serbs insist (an attitude condemned by the Croats as unitarianism) or whether the country can survive as a genuinely multinational federation. Then for Serbia there is conflict no. 2: what to do about the Albanians in the Kosovo, with their enormous growth rate, (29 percent since 1961), who are pushing to gain republican status.

The deeper problem has another dimension—an international one. For with Yugoslavia's split with Moscow in 1948, Tito demanded both *national* emancipation from the Soviet Union and *socialist* emancipation of the YCP from Soviet domination of ideology; i.e., from now on Yugoslav socialism must be of a self-managing nature, an idea which predictably upped the legitimacy of inputs from below and, despite recent attempts to return to old ways, seriously undermined democratic centralism. No matter how one slices, it is impossible to have things decided at both the top and the bottom simultaneously. In terms of the national question this made it increasingly difficult to preach national communism at the international level and prohibit greater decision-making power at the republic commune level.[36]

For years Tito himself was the rather unwieldy answer to this problem. There was more than a little truth to the joke that Yugoslavia was a state the size of Wyoming with a personality cult the size of China. Unfortunately, Tito's personality cult served both to guarantee state and party unity and to block any genuinely negotiated settlement. Even he recognized that in principle such a system was untenable. Hence, the mammoth 1971 constitutional amendments, which in practice began as Tito's rather uncomfortable attempt to stagemanage his own succession.[37]

The amendments themselves were politically negotiated. Rather than being drafted by a commission of legal experts as had the constitution of 1963 and in earlier amendments, these were drafted by a mixed commission of political leaders and legal advisers. The process took two months. Tito presided at the final meeting; yet in the end what he got surely was not what he had intended. These amendments designed to solve the problem of succession had become much more than that. The process had been swept forward by the demand once again for a genuine participatory federalism, a division of federation-republican and state-party authority. In the process it seemed at first that the federation had all but disappeared. Although it retained responsibility for defense, foreign policy, and a "united market" (no one seemed quite sure what "united market" meant) one might almost say it had "withered away."

Inter-republican committees were set up to negotiate political and economic conflicts of interest. The rule was decision by consensus so that in effect everyone had a vote. A collective presidency consisting of 23 members (three representatives from each republic, two from each of the provinces) was to replace Tito, who was allowed by amendment 36 to retain his position as president for life.

Not too surprisingly, there was soon a stalemate precisely on the issue that closed Zagreb University four months later—the foreign currency system—a system whereby in the Croat opinion an extremely large percentage of the foreign exchange that came into the country via the Croatian coast was drained off into Belgrade banks. The enterprise was allowed to keep only 7 percent of hard currency earned on export of goods, 40 percent on tourism. That had long been a sore point in Zagreb and one on which Tito had publicly supported the Croatian leadership during his visit in September, 1971. Still nothing happened. On November 23, 24 faculties at the university and various high schools struck to "exert pressure on these forums whose duty it is to reform the plundering foreign exchange regime and which are today unwilling to do so."

Within a number of days the strike involved an estimated 30,000 students. According to the Tanjug version of the student proclamation, this was a peaceful, nonviolent action. The proclamation warned of possible provocations, urging students not to go into the street. It also extended support for the League of Communists of Croatia and its president, Dr. Savka Dabčević-Kučar.

At this point such support was decidedly unwelcome. Miko Tripalo, 45-year-old representative of Croatia to the new Collective Presidency, personally warned the students that their actions could have tragic consequences, that they were already dangerous. He urged them to return to lectures before they put the whole policy of the Croat party in jeopardy. As Tripalo had prophetically warned while speaking in Zadar, "tactics of revolutionary struggle should not be determined in a thousand places."[38]

Although deaf to pleas for cutting short their action, the students on the whole stuck to their pledge of nonviolence, even, according to Radio Zagreb, to the extent of throwing the leader of an "ultraleft" faction calling for more radical views out of a meeting of the philosophy faculty. Although individuals did discuss the more extreme issues of Croat membership in the United Nations and an *independent Croatian army* (italics mine), the joint proclamation limited itself to reform of the foreign exchange system, something Tito himself had promised two months before when he said, "this question must be solved, irrespective of who resists it."

Close on the heels of the student strike came a purge of the Croatian Communist Party that Tito justified as necessary to avoid civil war. He spoke with great seriousness of the danger of foreign intervention. "Counter-revolutionary forces" were blamed for the strike. Tito personally conferred with retired generals and said bluntly that the duty of the army was to defend Yugoslav socialism internally as well as at the border. He added pointedly: "We will never allow anyone else to maintain order in our country," a clear allusion to the "Brezhnev Doctrine" used to justify Soviet and East European invasion of Czechoslovakia in August 1968.[39]

Security is as much a state of mind as an actual condition. Political decisions may or may not be based on fact. They are always based on a political leadership's perception of the fact. Seen in this light the fact that as early as June, 1971, 54 percent of the high-ranking Yugoslav army officers interviewed thought the main threat to the country came from "nationalism and chauvinism," rather than from external aggression, had more than marginal significance.[40]

Tito showed himself ambivalent on the question of what was or was not the main danger, enough so to confuse both the republican leadership involved and leave subsequent political analysts divided as to what he thought or intended.[41] However, clearly, he leaned heavily on the army throughout the crisis and has subsequently made even more explicit that if order (the exact meaning of which remains a matter of conjecture) is not restored, "I will step in and make order with *our* army."[42]

To my mind, the relation of all this to the striking students was almost incidental. It is a question not of students but communist party members. Tito had been speaking about the need to purge and remake the Yugoslav party well before November 23. It was a demand he repeated at the conclusion of the "Freedom" military maneuvers in early October (October 8), warning those "who undermine brotherhood and unity" that, "if we cannot persuade them politically, we will adopt administrative measures."

In brief, twenty-five years after the revolution Tito was trying to force a political party that had become absorbed in the problems of consolidation and running the country into the small disciplined core of revolutionaries that had taken power. The problem was (and is) that revolutionaries who have become bureaucrats may live in the afterglow of revolution but they are still bureaucrats. Moreover, many of the younger cadre did not belong to the "club of '41" (those first fighters who had actually taken power). They had begun as bureaucrats or technocrats who considered economic persuasion more to the point than ideological purity and rather impatiently thought the answer to political problems could be found in economic reform.[43]

Just as with all living organisms, bureaucracies require frequent pruning, but the process becomes mired in conflicts of interests between the inertia of bureaucratic expansion and desire at the top to reestablish control. Therefore, it is not surprising that there are signs that at a minimum some sectors of the party fought back or that Yugoslavia is still being convulsed by Tito's "administrative measures." Signals of the army's role in this struggle appeared as early as April, 1971, when a leading general said that *only* in a case where the *constitutional order* was threatened would the army become an instrument for solving internal difficulties.[44] Subsequently, Tito went so far as to claim that the army was "innocent" of nationalist tendencies.[45]

Thus, what had happened to date seemed to be a variant of Lendvai's unknown informant's number 2 hypothesis in which Tito used the support of the army but was still intent on preserving the dominant position of the party. As Tito said to the LCY second party conference, "The party and not the army is the chief guardian of the revolution. The army's task is to defend the borders . . ." This was considerable backtracking on his blunt insistence of December 22 that the Yugoslav army must be prepared to defend the achievements of the revolution internally as well as at the borders.

Tito's retreat, the shifting emphasis on the relationship to the JNA to internal crisis, came in part because "the crisis" in question

was under control; his cherished party reform seemed to have moved
one step forward with the streamlining of the LCY Executive Bureau
at the conference. Perhaps another significant consideration was a
slightly veiled warning coming from one of the Yugoslav president's
oldest comrades, Dr. Vladimir Bakarić, who for years has continued
to play the role of "godfather" to the Croat Party even after he went
to Belgrade as a member of the LCY Praesidium in 1966. Bakarić
himself had been instrumental in undermining Tripalo, his former
protege, and had appealed to conservative veterans' organizations in
that process.[46]

Nonetheless, he openly expressed his distaste not only for speculation that the army would take over after Tito's death but for a
dominant role of the military in principle. In his oft cited interview
with *Frankfurter Rundschau* shortly after the purge of the Croat
party, the Croat leader emphasized that:

1. "Even the army cannot inherit Tito's authority."
2. There was "potential danger" from the army, because no one could
   say how it would act in similar crises in the future.
3. The army "could create many political troubles"; but that at the
   present time, "it is making no efforts to seize power."
4. Any "attempt by the army to seize power would unleash a civil
   war. . .we too organize our army. . ." [an apparent allusion to the
   territorial defense units].[47]

Indeed, it may have been Bakarić's pointed intervention in the
discussion that prompted Tito, on December 22 (after the strike had
ended, after the brief spasm of rioting following the removal of the
popular LCC party leadership had been contained without so much
as toppling the glittering Christmas trees in Zagreb's Republic
Square),[48] to put forward his own view not only on the role of the
army, but on its relationship to the political vanguard that in theory
occupies the "leading role," the communist party.

Our army's primary task is to defend the country from foreign enemies.
However, it should defend the achievements of our revolution, if needed,
from internal enemy too.[49]

Western commentators typically assumed that Tito's main intent
was to publicly upgrade the role of the army in achieving internal
solutions.[50] His emphasis on party organization within the armed
forces was taken to imply army influence on the party—an increased
place for the JNA in Yugoslav policy making—rather than party control of the army. Such a difference of interpretation makes a world
of different both in one's conclusions about the speech itself, and in

one's perception of who will run the post-Tito show in Yugoslavia. Before going into what at this point is my own highly tentative opinion, it is important to keep in mind the pattern of Yugoslav army-party relations over time and the implications of "total people's defense" for that relationship.

General peoples' defense had received a great public relations treatment; yet it was not a new idea. For years a submerged tug-of-war had been going on within party and army alike on precisely the question of territorial defense. Although it seems to have been accepted as necessary, the centralism imposed on the army in the late 1940s had been less than totally welcome. Throughout the war Croats and Slovenes had fought in their own units, used their own language and been commanded by their own chief-of-staff.[51] Integrating these units into a centralized organization with Serbo-Croat as the official language of the army was facilitated by an urgently felt external threat. Nonetheless many Slovenes and Croats continued to live in the memory of their "own" army.

These forces surfaced well before 1968, for example, when U.S. military assistance grants to Yugoslavia were ending in the late 1950s, emphasis on the role of partisan and territorial forces increased, thereby legitimizing the "federal" position. In this sense the 1963 constitution made a tentative compromise. The Federation remained responsible for organization and preparation of the army, whereas republics, communes, and "other" social political communities shared in setting up civil defense, pre-military training, and general preparation for defending the nation.[52] It was, still, a solution that left the JNA *the* military organization in Yugoslavia.

The shift to total peoples' defense in 1968, therefore, was a shift of major significance for the relationship of the professional military both to the territorial defense units (that became with the National Defense Law of February 1969 legally "coequal") as well as a move with wide ramifications for the relations of the armed forces to Yugoslavia's multiethnic society. On the most basic level, it suddenly involved ordinary citizens in military matters in a big way. The new National Defense Law under which it became treason not to fight the as yet potential invader brought home the seriousness with which at least "some people" viewed the change.

What it meant in practice is still open to question, although those indications that, in my view, should be taken most seriously came during the mini-invasion of Yugoslavia by a band of Utashi terrorists in the summer of 1973.

Low Level Terrorist Violence: A Complicating
Factor in the Relation of Armed Forces to Society

Ever since Stephan Radić was shot in the Skupština by an out-
raged Montenegrin member of that parliament, the already strained
inter-ethnic relations have been exacerbated by low level, terrorist
violence. Among the most bizarre of these instances was the infiltra-
tion of 19 Utashi guerillas deep into Bosnia in late June 1972. The
intruders met resistance that turned into a running gun battle, leaving
15 of the guerillas dead, 13 members of the Yugoslav forces who
hunted them down dead, and the entire country in a state of psychological seige. Of the invaders, who claimed to be members of the
"Croatian Revolutionary Brotherhood," four were captured and subsequently three executed, with the fourth sentenced to 20 years in
return for his cooperation.

Although it is not totally clear to what extent which forces
were involved, the most detailed Yugoslav account to date credits
"security units" and "units of territorial defense" with most of the
fighting, asserting that "13 members of the territorial units of the
people's defense lost their lives bravely. . .the liquidation of the
terrorists confirmed the vitality of the organization of all people's
defense. . . ."[53]

On the one hand, this can and has been seen as a victory for the
new military strategy. Questions were raised both in and outside of
Yugoslavia,[54] as to the "amateurishness" of the operation, indeed
why it took more than a month from knowledge of arrival of the
terrorists to getting rid of them, and why at such a high cost? Certainly the TDU's demonstrated both worth and vulnerability in the
only situation other than simulated war games (such as October 1971
"Freedom Maneuvers") where they have seen action.

On the other hand, the sensitive issue of just what "all people's
defense" means for the regular army is graphically demonstrated by
differences in emphasis on the part of contributors to Mladenović's
collection. Take for example the following statements:

> Observed from this aspect, this country's system of general people's
> defense is an integral part of self-managing socialist society, reflecting the
> resolve and determination of the working people, the nations and national-
> ities of Yugoslavia, to defend with all forces and means the freedom,
> independence and sovereignty of Yugoslavia and all the achievements of
> the liberation war and revolution of the Yugoslav peoples. *The socialist
> substance of our defense efforts is the defense of socialist social relation-
> ships and the full sovereignty of the peoples and nationalities living within*

the framework of socialist Yugoslavia. . . . It is clear to the peoples of Yugoslavia that each nation and nationality can enjoy national independence and sovereignty only in an integral Yugoslav community, that no nation can be free itself without the others. Unless all the nations of Yugoslavia are free and independent, no single one of them can be so.

Only within this context is it appropriate to consider the role and tasks of the Yugoslav army as a factor in self-managing society which, together with the entire armed force of society, guarantees the independence of the entire community and of each individual nation.[55]

All nations and nationalities in Yugoslavia are aware that their national independence and sovereignty are viable propositions only if they are united. This awareness and knowledge were built up in the not so distant past, especially during the people's liberation struggle, and are being substantiated today: no single nation or nationality in Yugoslavia can be free on its own. That is why *the Yugoslav People's Army epitomizes the interests of all as their common army and a national army of each of our peoples. . . . Yugoslav society is monolithic because* it is consistent in promoting self-management, equality and free socialist development, as all decisive moments in our recent history have shown. For this reason, *there is no ground in our society to fear the alleged emergence of separate, national armies.* The Yuguslav peoples already have their army, forged in the revolution through joint efforts and sacrifices. It is an instrument in the defense of freedom and sovereignty of all nations and nationalities in Yugoslavia and of each one separately.[56]

This certainly does not mean that it is not necessary to strengthen the army, modernize it and keep it capable of warding off any surprise blows. It simply means that our people are profoundly conscious that the consolidation of the socialist social system and socialist relationships in our country, the steady promotion of awareness about the significance of that system for the present and future of our peoples, represent an extraordinary socio-political force which, in case of attack, would materialize into military power as well.[57]

Since this book was published in 1970, it is a safe guess that it went to press in 1969. The implications of such differences became more and more explicit as the sense of threat decreased. Nor was the division by any means purely along national lines. There was, for instance, the attack of the JNA Chief-of-Staff, Lt. General Viktor Bubanj, himself a Croat, on the idea of republican armies as "disastrous" from a military point of view.[58] By June, 1971 (certainly not at a high point of Soviet-Yugoslav "normalization," considering former Foreign Minister Tepavac's symbolic trip to Peking),[59] the army spokesman in the Party Presidium was insisting not only that "unitarist and nationalistic" behavior must be resisted regardless of its source but also that a "united strategy and command, of the Yugoslav People's army must exist."[60]

Conclusions

In short, by the 1970s it is fair to say that party-army relations had moved from the closeness of the postwar years to an increasingly complex interaction in which the professional military was faced with a declining budget, limitations on its manpower, loss or at least a changing nature of political influence, challenges to its formerly privileged position on the pay scale, and a situation in which factionalism within the party itself had led to growing demands that the army be dismembered into its six components.

In such circumstances, the hypotheses in Frank Margiotta's excellent paper on the reasons for the recent unique pattern of nonintervention by the military where there was a long history of predatory military interventions in the political process would seem to have more than a little relevance in the Yugoslav case.[61]

I.   the military had been psychologically and materially satisfied and therefore felt no need to intervene to improve their status or rewards.

II.   the military has been politically involved and has participated in the orderly running of the country; thereby reducing the incentive for an ambitious military elite to intervene in the political process by alternative political rewards.

Both hypotheses would apply even more strongly to Yugoslav armed forces which had been created by the party (rather than the party being an outgrowth of the army as in Mexico) until the ousting of Alexander Ranković, formerly thought of as Tito's most likely successor, secretary of the LCY secretariat and permanent president of the Veteran's Union.

As Antić has put it:

> The most prominent 'veterans' were at the same time the most prominent party members. . . . It could be said that during all this time Yugoslavia's power pyramid was composed of three interwoven elements, with the veterans at the base, superimposed by the state and party apparatuses. The top party leadership selected politically reliable veterans for the army, administration, security and economic structures. This was the time when 'first fighters' were offered the most responsible and best positions in the country.[62]

This is not to say there were not exceptions or even that it was a conscious policy decision. Rather than being what Antić makes seem (I am sure unintentionally) a rational, orderly, methodical process by which the party controlled the army, the relationship was an extension of deeply rooted social patterns in Yugoslavia and much of the rest of the Balkans, where kinship, fictive kinship and comradeship in battle, impose strong, almost tangible obligations on all parties that it is hard for outsiders coming from highly mobile societies where one's social life is often a matter of colleagues (or friends that become so because they are colleagues) to understand. There was a natural impact of traditional society in which both before and after the revolution time-honored "ways in which tings are done" continued to influence the political process. As I was so often told, "Ko nema vezi, nema nista": literally, "He who is without connections has nothing." Therefore, in my opinion, the relationship that maintained between the party and army for so much of postwar Yugoslav political life was not planned, it just grew, in response to threat, out of a political culture that was fertile soil. Had it been otherwise, the party would have avoided the pitfalls inherent in the shift to "total people's defense" at all costs.

Yet, political leaders, in and outside of communist states, do not control their external political context. Ironically, the "allied socialist intervention" in Czechoslovakia that brought with it the peak of national unity in Yugoslavia in the 1960s[63] also strengthened the hand of those who wanted decentralization and liberalization, i.e., the basic principles of self-management, to apply to the armed forces. It fed into an on-going struggle between those favoring increased importance for territorial defense units, return to partisan strategies, and incidentally more autonomy for the republican leadership in matters of defense. In the past proponents of more decentralization in military had lost.[64] However, now for all the reasons described in the section dealing with "total people's deterrence" as a concept, they were temporarily on top.

And as fragmentary as the evidence is at this point, it still, to my mind, persuasively suggests that a professional military elite supported from below by Veterans' organizations fought back even against those within its own ranks who had been persuaded.[65] The question to my way of thinking is not "will the military intervene in politics when Tito goes? " There is reason to think that the military is already up to its neck in a perhaps uncoordinated but equally damaging intervention on the most important political question in Yugoslavia today. It is not a question of party-army relations. It is a question of the impact of the interests of the armed forces on (1) the way in which party conflicts at the highest level are resolved and (2) the future nature of the party itself. The implications become even more serious when one realizes that for at least party of the highly sensitive period in question, the army was, to put it bluntly, footing the bill for the party.

> Ever since the Ninth Congress (1969), the activities of the Presidium have been financed chiefly from membership fees paid by the members of the League of Communists in the Army. These membership fees are not collected according to republics, but are ceded to the Presidium just as the membership fees paid by our missions and their employees and officials abroad.[66]

The army did not publicly "intervene" in the Croat crisis of 1971. Yet there are some signs that it may have been individual, if not collective, intervention by members of the armed forces that led Tito to resolve the crisis in what many Yugoslavs even outside Croatia considered a sledgehammer fashion.[67] Nor was such influence on Tito unimportant in the forced resignation of the chairman of the Serbian party, Marko Nikezić, in October, 1972. This is not the place to outline the strategy by which Nikezić lost his post.[68] It is, however, important that "veterans accepted the (Tito's) letter with the greatest enthusiasm. They are supporting the party line without reserve. Their faith in the party now is again confirmed."[69]

Such support (what I would call subliminal intervention) may be instrumental in determining the scope of Tito's cherished party reform that continues to convulse Yugoslav political life in the days leading up to the 10th LCY congress (at this postponed once again, now set for April 1, 1974). It could have a potentially determining effect upon just what kind of party Yugoslavia is left with when "Tito goes." The nature of that party, its links to a genuine constituency or the lack of them, will in turn determine the extent to which the party relies on the army, or to put it more bluntly this process will determine the extent to which party and army in Yugoslavia once again become virtually the same thing under very different conditions, and with different implications for the future of that maverick socialist state than in the immediate postwar years.

Therefore, to my mind, the popular dichotomy between army and party as the controlling force in post-Tito Yugoslavia is a false one. The danger is not a military coup in which the army would throw out the party. I doubt that the important core of military leadership so much as thinks of its aims as incompatible with those of the party; I would suspect rather that the military elite in question considers itself a righteous defender of the correct and proper party line. In such circumstances, the most likely scenario, far from being a coup in any traditional meaning of the word, is that the representatives of the

armed forces within the party would adopt "a leading role" within
the LCY itself: that to be dramatic or perhaps pedestrian depending
on one's view, the army would become the Vanguard of the party.

Notes

1. For the more intersting biographies of Tito, one should see Auty (1972), Dedijer
(1953); and Halperin (1958).
2. This is not to say there were not differences among the other East European
countries both on the dimension of the relation of the local communist party to society,
the role (and image) of the party as leading or participating in a national resistance, and
relations with the Soviet "liberators." In Poland, for example, some Polish communists
stayed in Moscow, others fought with the underground. Also, although it is generally
ignored, the Albanians fought their national liberation struggle very much along Yugoslav
lines and with Yugoslav advisers. See Dedijer (1951).
3. Dedijer (1951:39).
4. Strongly emphasized by both Johnson (1962) in his chapter, "Peasant Mobilization
in Wartime Yugoslavia"; and Zaninovich (1968).
5. For historical background see: Clissold (1966); Heppell and Singleton (1961); and
Wolff (1956).
6. Djilas (1958): 39).
7. An exception to this would be the peasant uprising under Matija Gubec in 1573,
Clissold (1966: 25). Auty considers the impact of heroic tales about Gubec an important
childhood influence on Tito, Auty (1972: 9).
8. Anderson's account (1973) of a new wave of "ideological purification" on the road
to the League of Communists of Yugoslavia's (LCY) controversial 19th party congress
slated for early 1974. *The New York Times* (September 24, 1973).
9. Lendvai (1971) quoting an unnamed editor of one of Yugoslavia's "most influential"
newspapers, *The Financial Times* (May 25, 1971).
10. Take the tragic rule of Alexander Obrenović. He dismissed his regents, (allowing
them to choose between being his guests or prisoners) with the aid of the army to which
he swore an oath of fidelity. He and his wife died, slaughtered during a drunken army
mutiny in 1903. For a grippingly detailed account, West (1941: 543-561).
11. When I was in Yugoslavia as a visiting scholar at the Belgrade Institute of International Politics and Economcis, 1970-1971, working on a study of Yugoslav attitudes
toward European security, it was generally agreed that I should interview at least one ranking military officer on the strategic aspects of my topic. That interview turned out to be so
complicated to arrange for the Institute that we eventually settled on a military commen-
tator, i.e., a journalist with close ties to the army but no longer actually connected with the
armed forces.
12. Tito speech to the 30th anniversary of the Yugoslav People's Army (JNA), December
22, 1971.
13. Dedijer (1951: 68).
14. Horvat (1969: 199).
15. Bass and Marbury (1959). Yugoslav spokesmen made this comparison quite explicitly:
Borba (August 31, 1968); also Kommunist (September 12, 1968). For direct attacks on Tito
see the reporting of Yankovitch, Le Monde (September 19, 1968).
16. The only potential nucleus of an opposition leadership loyal to Moscow, Andrija
Hebrang, leader of the Croat Communist and a strong critic of the crash five year plan then
in progress, and his ally Minister of Finance, Streten Zujović, who had spoken in favor of
conciliation with the Soviets at the key meeting of the Yugoslav party's Central Committee

April 13, 1948, were immediately expelled from the party and arrested. Hebrang died in jail, said to have committed suicide after confessing to having committed treason following his earlier arrest by Ustashi police in 1942. Zujović was released and even allowed to rejoin the party two and a half years later after public confession in the party press. The only other major threat would appear to have come from Tito's brilliant chief of staff, General Arso Jovanović, who reportedly was shot leaving the country. Halperin (1958: 69ff and 92).

17. White Book on Agressive Activities by the Governments of the USSR, Poland, Czechoslovakia, Hungary, Rumania, Bulgaria, and Albania towards Yugoslavia (1951).

18. According to Statisticki Godisjak SFRJ 1966, military expenditures for 1966 were 5.6 percent of GNP and 56.4 percent of the federal Budget. See also Reports from the *London Times* (December 24, 29, 1966).

19. The following section draws heavily on my article "Yugoslavia and European Security," Orbis (Spring 1973).

20. Remington (1971: 56ff).

21. In the context of the Czech crisis I. Pomelov restated "Common Principles and National Characteristics in the Development of Socialism," Pravda (August 14, 1968); Current Digest of the Soviet Press, (CDSP) (September 4, 1968, pp. 3-5).

22. Resolution adopted by the Central Committee of the League of Communists of Yugoslavia, Borba (August 26, 1968); English text in Remington (1969: 361-367).

23. First put forward by S. Kovalev, Pravda (September 26, 1968).

24. Bass and Marbury (1959).

25. Trybuna Ludu (November 12, 1968).

26. See Milenkovitch (1968-1969), "Soviet-Yugoslav Relations and the Brezhnev Doctrine."

27. "Total Bankruptcy of Soviet Modern Revisionism," Peking Review (August 23, 1968).

28. Arrival toast, Borba (September 22, 1971). The Soviet leader did not at any time reject the principles underlying that doctrine however. On the contrary, he restated them in his speech at the Zemun factory by saying, "the foreign political line of the CPSu is clear and consistent. We firmly protect the interests of socialism against all its enemies." Borba (September 23, 1971).

29. Among the more useful of the rapidly growing Yugoslav explanations of this concept are the proceedings of the 18th session of the LCY Executive Bureau, Aktuelna pitanja svenarodne odbrane [Contemporary Questions of National Defense](Belgrade, 1971) and Drljević (1969: 456-477). Some of the more authoritative statements have been collected in Mladenović (1970) For western analyses, see Johnson (1971), and Rusinow (1971).

30. Tito speaking to the 15th anniversary of Ljubljana University, Borba (December 12, 1969).

31. Distinction made by Johnson (1962: 156ff)

32. In "General People's Defense—A Form of Self-Defense by the Citizens," Mladenović (1970: 50) [ed.].

33. Series of articles by Bubanj, Narodna Armija (July-August, 1971), also a long interview by Bubanj in Nedeljne informativne novine (NIN) (July 25, 1971), quoted by Rusinow (1971: 3).

34. Seventy percent was the figure given by Bakarić in his interview with the German press, Frankfurter Rundschau (December 17, 1971). For analysis see Larrabee (1972). The method of financing the territorial units certainly would not have alleviated the problem, for the territorial defense force is financed at the commune (opstina) and republic level out of assembly budgets and enterprise funds, although the current 5 year plan indicates that eventually .5 percent to 1 percent of the national income will go to such defense in addition to the current JNA budget. Dozet, "Narodna odbrana u Drusvenom" (National Defense in the social plan) Kommunist (January 13, 1972). For analysis Johnson (1962: 56).

35. The best existing analysis of these events even if I would disagree with some of its interpretations is Rusinow's four part study, "Croatia in Crisis," (1972). Other valuable but less detailed accounts include Larrabee (1972) and Rubinstein (1972).

36. Stanković, lecture to St. Anthony's College, Oxford (October 21, 1971).

37. Tito speech concerning the need for such amendment, Borba (September 21, 1970); also his further insistence, Borba (December 14, 1970).

38. Tripalo speech (November 24, 1971).

39. Tito to 30th anniversary of the JNA, Borba (December 23, 1971).

40. NIN (June 20, 1971).

41. At the end of his speaking tour of Croatia in September 1971, Tito had said, whether or not he had concluded, that the stories of Croat nationalism getting out of hand were "completely absurd"; Borba (September 16, 1971). This statement itself seems more than a little puzzling given his unpublished warning to the Croat party in July 1971, released the following May as a part of an ex post facto explanation of or rationale for the December events in Croatia, Politika (May 9, 1972). Whether or not the May 9 version is a rewriting of history as some have suggested, it does flatly contradict his early public assessment of the situation.

42. Tito's unpublished July 1971 speech, referred to above. Underlining mine.

43. Nor was such thinking limited to "technocrats." As the leading figure of the Croat League of Communists put it as early as 1966, "If the Economic Reform does not work, nationalism will become question number one." Bakaric (March 1966) quoted by Lendvai (1969: 51).

44. Misković to Narodna Armija (April 22, 1971).

45. Tito's interview with the Hungarian language newspaper in Novi Sad, Magyar Szo (May 22, 1971).

46. For example at the end of October Bakarić had spent several days in Sarajevo holding talks with the president of the Bosnian party, Branko Mikulić, also a Croat who had on a number of occasions reacted angrily to nationalistic propaganda coming from Croatia. More important, there was an opening to gain support from below. The wiley grandfather of Groatian communism stumped based organizations, warning in Split on November 26 of "an organized nationalist group which is on the offensive" Borba (November 3, 1971). Not surprisingly Tripalo responded with charges of exaggeration and "undemocratic" forces that wanted to restrain mass support for the party. He explicitly accused "underground forces" of systematically stumping some municipalities in Croatia "especially using *the war veterans associations*" to carry out their action, to change the LCC line and create an artificially tense situation in Croatia. Politika (November 11, 1971).

47. Bakarić interview in Frankfurter Rundschau (December 17, 1971).

48. See Eric Bourne to the Christian Science Monitor (December 22, 1971).

49. Tito to 30th anniversary of JNA (December 22, 1971).

50. This is the view taken, for example, in Antić (1972).

51. See Dedijer (1951), and Auty (1972).

52. Yugoslav Constitution 1963, Article 252.

53. Belgrade TANJUG in English GMT (April 12, 1973); almost simultaneously speaking to the celebration of the liberation of Posuje, Dzemal Bijedić, president of the Federal Executive Council said:

> Events have confirmed that the concept of all-people's defense is inherent in our total social being and that it represents at the same time the logical continuation of the heritage of all-people's revolt and of the socialist revolution . . .
>
> Borba (April 13, 1973)

The importance attached to this action at the highest level was evident even at the time when Jure Bilic, member of the LCY Presidium, stressed that there had been not one case of "members of the territorial units which took part in the liquidation of the terrorist groups abandoning their posts during the action." (Belgrade TANJUG Domestic service in Serbo-Croat, 1702 GMT July 19, 1972.)

54. For analysis see The Economist (August 5, 1972).

55. Mitja Ribičič (a Sovene), "The Armed People in Defense of Socialism and Independence," in Mladenovic (1970: 31 and 33). (Italics added.)

56. Mijalka Todorović (Serb), "The Essence of the Concept of General People's Defense," in Mladenovic (1970: 44). (Italics mine.)

57. Dr. Savka Dabcević-Kucar, "General People's Defense–A Form of Self-Defense by Citizens," in Mladenovic (1970: 48).

58. Politika, December 20, 1970.

59. After more than minor Soviet-Yugoslav tensions including claims by Croat extremists in West Germany that Moscow supported their demands for an independent Croatia, The Times, London (April 19, 1971), and rumors of Soviet demands for a base on the Yugoslav Adriatic either at Split or Pula, Tepavac made a trip to Peking in June 1971, more likely a political gesture of defiance than to seek a credible ally. For Yugoslavs and Soviets both believe that in a conflict situation Chinese aid in the Balkans would prove minimal (especially for a socialist country as ideologically corrupted as the Yugoslavs are in the Chinese view). As Chou-En-lai so tactfully put it in talking with a Zagreb newspaper interviewer, "distant waters cannot quench fire." Vjesnik (August 28, 1971).

60. Col. General Djuro Lončarević to Serbian C.C. Plenum June 30, 1972, Borba (July 1, 1972).

61. Margiotta (1973). Wiatr distinguished between two types of party control from above, through subordination of the army command and from below, through party organizations on various levels of military organization. In that they are not isolated from the civilian power center, civil-military relations tend to be harmonious except in the case of factionalism within the party in which different factions may then turn to the military for support. I am grateful to Professor Wiatr both for calling his article to my attention and for his kindness in commenting on this paper.

62. Antić, RFE Background Analysis, "Political Influence of Yugoslav Veterans" (April 10, 1973).

63. At that time party membership increased particularly among students and other young people and Tito himself even went so far as to pronounce the "national problem" as having been solved. Borba (September 22, 1969).

64. For example General Rade Hamović who wrote an article for the Soviet military press Krasnaya zvezda stressing the advantage of territorial warfare on the grounds that the operational cost of conventional armies is too expensive, The Economist (January 28, 1967), had been relieved of his post by summer of 1967. I am grateful to Adam Roberts (forthcoming) both for drawing the above example to my attention and for letting me read the manuscript version of his chapter on Yugoslav defense policy.

65. There is the case of General Janko Bobetko, a 53 year-old Croat General that it was rumored was to become commander of the Zagreb military district before the fall of the Croat leadership in December 1971. Whether or not he was trying to "take over the army" in Croatia as some charged, Bobetko had made explicitly stated that "society" should acquire full control over the army, i.e., that the army must become an integral part of self-managing society. Vjesnik (March 18, 1971). Bobetko was suspended from his military post pending a full investigation of his political activity and purged from the Croat Central Committee.

66. "Forms of Financing the Activity of the Presidium and the League of Communists," Borba (February 29, 1972).

67. After an interview with President Tito on May 12, 1972, Pribechevich wrote in an article on the Marshall's 80th birthday that at a secret meeting in Bosnia in November, "Yugoslav army leaders showed Tito suppressed TV reels of Croatian Communit mass meetings, with only Croatian flags and with Croatian nationalist and anti-Tito slogans, songs shouts and signs. Then Tito struck." The New York Times (May 25, 1972). This seems to support the implication of reports that just a few days before the final decision to get Tripalo out, "63 former prominent veterans, former generals and high party and state functionaries" sent Tito a letter demanding a firm stand against all those responsible for the chaotic political situation in Croatia. See Politika (December 9, 1973); for the excellent analysis of the broader problem of veterans and their influence on politics, Antić (1973).

68. Take Bakarić's somewhat ambiguous, delayed support for Tito and the Executive Bureau's letter of September 18 that began the drive culminating in the purge of the Serbian party:

> The LC of Serbia was blamed for proceeding too slowly and incorrectly. But this problem indeed concerns us all. The problem is not to force some order among them (the Serbian party) but. . .the question of *how the military and we* (LCY) stand in this fight. . . . (italics mine)

Borba (October 21, 1972).

69. Politika (March 16, 1973).

ARMED FORCES AND SOCIETY
IN ALBANIA

Peter R. Prifti

Like Yugoslavia, the contemporary Albanian state grew out of a fierce, costly Partisan struggle during World War II. Albania achieved communism via a successful guerrilla resistance against the Italian and German occupation forces, and the defeat of domestic opposition forces which, toward the end of the war, collaborated increasingly with the Fascist armies in the country. Throughout the war, not a single Soviet soldier set foot in Albania. Indeed, it was only in August of 1944, just four months before the liberation of the country, that an advisory military mission from Moscow arrived in Albania,[1] which is not to deny that substantial ideological inspiration for Albanian Partisan efforts came from faith in the inevitable triumph of the Red Army over Hitler's *Wehrmacht.*

However, the major source of influence on the organization and growth of the Albanian Communist Party and Army alike was the Yugoslav Partisan struggle, led by Tito. That influence stemmed in part from similarity of conditions of struggle; in part from a conscious effort by the Yugoslavs to aid the Albanians militarily and politically. First, both Albanian and Yugoslav traditions of guerrilla warfare developed over many centuries in resistance to Turkish domination with the backbone of the Partisan Army in each case being the peasantry. Both the Albanian and the Yugoslav Communist Parties were also fighting on two fronts. Tito had to fight Mihailovic's Chetnik forces; the Albanian Communists had to contend with two groups, *Balli Kombetar* (The National Front), a moderately liberal group opposed to communism and monarchy alike; and *Legaliteti* (Legality), a smaller group dedicated to the return to power of King Zog, Albania's exiled prewar monarch.[2] Finally, close collaboration between Yugoslav and Albanian Partisan forces throughout the war led to a nearly symbiotic relationship. This was not to end until Stalin's break with Tito in 1948, when Yugoslavia was expelled from the Cominform and ostracized within the socialist camp.

In principle—and to a large extent, in fact—the operations of the Partisan forces were based on a dual structure, one military, the other political. At the head of each fighting unit stood a military officer and a representative of the party, the political commissar.

Together they coordinated and directed the activities of the troops, and were jointly responsible for the troops' combat efficiency and ideological education. The seriousness of the ideological input is indicated by the fact that military ranks were not introduced in the Partisan Army until May, 1944. This too was a political move, aimed at upgrading the image and authority of the Partisans, in order to counter the propaganda of their enemies to the effect that the Partisans were nothing but bands of mercenaries.[3]

The Albanian Communist Party—now known as the Albanian Party of Labor (APL)—was anxious to develop correct and productive relations with the armed forces. Accordingly, only its best cadres were assigned to carry out political work in the army. Policies concerning rank and file membership in the party were much in line with Dedijer's picturesque description (Remington, 1974). In Albania, too, a man's fighting record often served as his credentials for party membership. Thus, on the one hand, the war served as a channel through which party cadres gained military experience. On the other hand, the battlefield became the testing ground and filtering process which determined the composition of the rank and file membership. This process inevitably influenced the postwar government of Albania, including Party-Army relations.

Certainly, at this period, Margiotta's hypothesis regarding the Mexican army would hold (Margiotta, 1973). Throughout the war the rank and file in the Partisan Army explicitly enjoyed equal rights with their commanders and political commissars "to take part . . . in the political life of the country," and in the solution of problems confronting the Army.[4] Moreover, the leadership that emerged from the Partisan war was the same leadership which took control of the Albanian nation and state after the war. At the time of the First APL Congress in 1948, of the nine members of the Politburo, five held the rank of General, two had been very active militarily during the war, one was a commissar. Only one, Spiro Koleka, did not seem to have held a military or political post of consequence in the Partisan Army.[5] Further, among the 12 members of the Party's 21-member Central Committee who were not members of the Politburo, the majority had military experience with the Partisan forces.

This shared Partisan experience was undoubtedly a factor which made for relatively harmonious postwar relations between the Party and the Army. Another factor was that Partisan Army leaders, now in two positions of power within the Party and Government, had the chance to take part in, and influence the nation's political life, instead of being left out and deprived, more or less, of the fruits of victory. The realization on the part of Army and Party leaders that they faced new and grave political, social, and economic challenges in the postwar period—possibly even military challenges—tended to unify the two groups. They were as yet far from secure in their power, and had great need of each other. Finally, communist doctrine dictated the primacy of politics, and the vanguard role of the Party in the affairs of state, which meant that the Army must in principle subordinate itself to the Party and its program.

All of these factors appear to have made for stability in Party-Army relations in Albania over the past three decades. But the success has not been complete. Party-Army harmony and stability have been threatened time and again, leading to charges of betrayal, anti-Party plots, arrests and purges of a number of powerful figures, both within the Party and the armed forces. These difficulties inevitably paralleled the crises in Albania's intra-Party relations, with significant implications for the Albanian military.

Not surprisingly, trouble marked the years 1944-1948, the period of extensive Yugoslav influence in Albania. Belgrade's policy toward Albania produced a profound split within the Albanian Party of Labor, which was bound to affect the Army as well. Albanian spokesmen accuse Yugoslavia of seeking to subvert the Albanian Army. Thus:

> Under the influence of the Trotskyite Yugoslavs, the Army's Political Directorate aimed at . . . [forcing] the withdrawal of Soviet advisors, and the extinction of our army's and country's independence. The men chiefly responsible for these serious errors . . . [were] comrade Kristo Themelko, Politburo member and Chief of the Political Directorate, and comrade Pullumb Dishnica, deputy director of the Political Directorate.[6]

The same source adds that at that time the Politburo went so far as to "accept [a proposal for] the unification of the Albanian and the Yugoslav armies. . . ."[7] The unification did not occur, due to the Stalin-Tito break in June of that year. In the aftermath of that break, both Themelko and Dishnica fell from power. The expulsion of Tito from the Communist bloc was followed immediately by the rupture of the Albanian-Yugoslav alliance. This brought to an end Albania's first close alliance with a communist nation.

Albanian sources contend that the attempt of the Yugoslavs to manipulate Albania's Army was part of an overall plan to control the Party, the economy, and the national security organs, with a view to gaining total control of the country. But while they had considerable success in manipulating the Party hierarchy, they apparently were unable to make important inroads in the Army hierarchy, for there were no major shake-ups in the armed forces following the split with Yugoslavia. The presence of Soviet military advisors in Albania at the time may have acted as a brake to any inclinations by Army leaders to seek closer ties with Yugoslavia. Moreover, the two leading figures in the Partisan struggle, Enver Hoxha, Supreme Commander of the Armed Forces; and Mehmet Shehu, the outstanding field general of the Partisan forces, were two of the leading opponents of Yugoslav policy on Albania. There had been some friction, too, between Albanian and Yugoslav Partisans during the war, which presumably had a negative effect on the thinking and attitude of most influential Army leaders toward Belgrade.

Freed from Yugoslav influence and pressures, and the resultant tensions and divisions within the country, the Albanian leadership threw its lot with the Soviet Union, at that time the much-heralded savior of Albania from the Italo-German Fascists, and now from the "Yugoslav revisionists." The Soviet Union became the model for Albanian socialist construction, and also of Tirana's armed forces. When Albania joined the Warsaw Pact in 1955, the country became a part of an international defense system. Belgrade shunned military blocs, and sought rather to enhance Yugoslav national security and international influence by cultivating a third force in international affairs, the non-aligned nations.

For twelve years (1948-1960), Moscow trained and equipped the Albanian Army. By 1960, Albania's defense arsenal bristled with modern artillery pieces, tanks, MIG planes, a dozen submarines, and even a number of Soviet missile batteries. Hundreds of Albanian officers, among them the current Defense Minister, General Beqir Balluku, went to the Soviet Union to study Russian and "the military art of Stalin."

However, as with Yugoslavia in the 1940s, tensions developed between the Albanian leadership, headed by Enver Hoxha, and the Soviets. Stimulated by such developments as Khruschev's reconciliation with Tito in 1955, the "revisionist" 20th CPSU Congress in 1956, and the attack on Stalin and the "cult of personality," these tensions intensified with the emergence of the Sino-Soviet dispute. The refusal of the Albanians to accept unquestioningly the Soviet vision of the communist utopia, Khrushchev's views on proper intra-party relations, or the CPSU line on Stalin, led to a total break in Soviet-Albanian relations in December, 1961.

Militarily, the effect of the split with Moscow was a weakening of Albania's defense posture, and Tirana's declining participation

and eventual exclusion from the Warsaw Pact. These developments
were soon reflected in Albanian Party-Army relations. In May of 1961
—a few months before the open break—there was a trial in Tirana of
an alleged counter-revolutionary group, headed by Rear Admiral Teme
Sejko, Commander of Albania's naval forces. According to a Yugoslav source, Sejko was arrested, tried and shot because of his failure
to prevent the Soviets from withdrawing their military craft and
armaments from Albania.[8]

The break with the Soviet Union left Albania militarily exposed,
as well as politically and ideologically isolated from the mainstream
of European socialism. To repair the damage, Albanian leaders turned
toward the East, forging an ever closer alliance with Maoist China.
Although the underlying principle of this alliance was a common
ideology—an uncompromising, militant struggle against Western
imperialism and Soviet revisionism—its importance for Albanian
military policy was more concrete. The Chinese now began to fill
the military vacuum created in Albania by the departure of the
Soviets.

When the Warsaw Pact countries, led by the Soviet Union, invaded Czechoslovakia in 1968, Albania formally withdrew from the
Warsaw Treaty Organization, and further strengthened her military
ties to China. In a message of approval of Albania's move, Mao Tse-
tung pledged to come to Albania's defense in case anyone, meaning
the USSR, dared to attack her.[9] In this respect, Albania and China
became implicit allies of Yugoslavia—a development that was reflected in improved diplomatic relations among the three countries,
despite ongoing ideological hostilities[10]—since the Yugoslavs also
feared a Soviet attack at the time, and began to take steps to prepare for such an eventuality (Remington, 1974).

Since 1968, the Albanians appear to have adopted a defense
policy similar to that of Peking in theory, terminology, and tactics.
They stress the principle of self-reliance in national defense, the
superiority of man over weapons, and above all the invincibility of
"the people's war." However, effusive praise of Peking aside, these
ideas were not an innovation of the Chinese communists. Rather,
this is a concept of warfare that on the rugged terrain of Albania
has proved its effectiveness from the Middle Ages—when Albania's
national hero, Skënderbeu, fought and defeated the Ottoman Turks—
to World War II, when Albanian Communists led the masses in a successful struggle for national liberation. It is the type of warfare that
brought victory and political power to the communists in Albania,
Yugoslavia, and China. All three countries share a common military

experience, which plays a large, even dominant role in their current defense thinking in at least two major respects: the stress laid on the principle of self-reliance, and the concept of "the citizen army," or the massive involvement of the entire population in the nation's defense.[11]

Conclusion

The evidence at hand reveals a history of recurrent tensions in Army-Party relations in Albania, which from time to time erupted into open conflict and led to purges of a number of military leaders, and civilian personnel connected with the military. Nonetheless, the military has not sought to play the dominant role in postwar Albanian society. The Party has at all times been in command in governing the country, at the same time making sure that representatives of the Army can speak with a political voice. For example, although the Army has always acknowledged the leadership role of the Party, and subordinated itself to it, the two top Army leaders, General Beqir Balluku, Minister of Defense; and General Petrit Dume, Army Chief of Staff, both hold posts in the all-powerful Party Politburo—the former is a full member, and the latter is a candidate member. Nor is it irrelevant that both of these men fought with Enver Hoxha during the Partisan war, and have shown a strong personal loyalty to him throughout the postwar period. For in Albania such informal ties often cut across potential conflicts of interest. Therefore, it seems likely that the established pattern of mutual trust and close collaboration between Hoxha and Balluku—between the most powerful figures in the Party and the Army at present—will continue in the foreseeable future.

Notes

1. History of the Party of Labor of Albania, (1971: 216).
2. *Balli Kombetar* was founded in November, 1942, and headed by Mithat Frashëri; *Legaliteti* was organized by Abaz Kupi in September, 1943.
3. History of the Party of Labor of Albania (1971: 290, 563).
4. History of the Party of Labor of Albania (1971: 161).
5. The five generals were Enver Hoxha, Tuk Jakova, Mehmet Shehu, Xhafer Spahiu, and Hysni Kapo; Liri Belishova, Spiro Koleka and Beqir Balluku had distingusihed military backgrounds; Gogo Nushi was a top-level commissar.
6. PPSH Dokumenta Kryesore, I (1960: 392).
7. PPSH Dokumenta Kryesore, I (1960: 391-392).
8. Cardhaku, (1965).

9. Zëri i Popullit (September 19, 1968).
10. Prifti (1971: 26-30).
11. Johnson (1962: 156-176). The Albanian penal code against draft resistors was severe. The penalty for such resistance in times of war was at least ten years in prison, and even death. See Kodifikimi i Përgjithështëm i Legjislacionit në Fuqi (1961: 550-551).

THE PUBLIC IMAGE OF THE POLISH MILITARY: PAST AND PRESENT

Jerzy J. Wiatr

In 1973 Polish cinema-goers applauded the "biggest film success" since World War II: the new Polish movie "Hubal." Artistically well done, the film became a success not because of its artistic value but because of its message. "Hubal" is based on a true episode in the Polish campaign during the Second World War. After the thirty-six day Polish defense in September and early October 1939, a cavalry unit commanded by Major Henryk Dobrzanski (whose pseudonym was "Hubal") continued fighting—undertaking guerrilla warfare until its final defeat in June 1940. It was a unique experience—a regular military unit fighting in uniform against the armed forces of the Third Reich long before the popular guerrilla became the "third front" of the war. Militarily hopeless, the fighting had its psychological importance. "We are the bridge between Autumn and Spring," explained Hubal as the rationale for his stubborn refusal to dissolve his unit. "Spring" meant, of course, the victorious French-British offensive that never materialized. Thirty-three years after Hubal's death, Poles of all generations have been given the opportunity to revive his hopes and efforts by watching a film which has reconstructed the historical truth in an almost unaltered version.

Traditions

The popularity of "Hubal" symbolizes an interesting psychological phenomenon. Formed under conditions of the military struggle for national liberation in the nineteenth century, the national consciousness of Poles has traditionally given a very high rating to such military values as courage, patriotism, honor. The Polish national hero is typically a military man, distinguished by his sacrifices in the struggle for the future of his country. He is not necessarily victorious. In fact, the greatest national heroes of modern time have been those whose destiny it was to suffer defeat and death at the hands of enemies. Tadeusz Kosciuszko, a hero of the American War of Independence, defeated by the Russians in his unsuccessful uprising of 1794, imprisoned and then exiled; Prince Joseph Poniatowski, commander-in-chief of the Polish armed forces under Napoleon, the only foreign Marshall of the Empire, killed in the Leipzig battle of 1813; General Jozef Bem, twice defeated hero of the Polish and Hungarian uprisings of 1830/31 and 1848 respectively; Romuald Traugutt, the "dictator" of the Polish national government during the uprising of 1863, hanged by the Russians in Warsaw in 1864; General Jaroslaw Dabrowski, the Polish commander-in-chief of the Paris Commune of 1871, killed in battle at the end of the revolution, formerly one of the central figures of the left wing of the Polish uprising of 1863—these are some of the best known symbols of Polish military struggle for national independence, who albeit unsuccessful, all left a dominant imprint on the psychology of the Polish nation.

The traditional national hero was a military man, but not necessarily a professional soldier. The nation, deprived of national state and of its armed forces, learned how to admire its military heroes regardless of whether war was their profession or only the case for which they abandoned their permanent, civilian interests. In fact, the very character of national uprisings tended to obscure the difference between professional soldiers and military amateurs; the latter once more became central figures in the heroic underground fighting of 1939-1945.

The "romantic" tradition[1] tended to admire heroism regardless of its immediate effects. In fact, it was the defeated hero who was the focus of popular sympathy. When the positivists argued against "hopeless" military efforts, Stefan Zeromski, one of the greatest Polish writers of early twentieth century swore that:

> Polish poetry alone shall never betray, never defame thee, Soldier. She alone will never be afraid of thy dreams and deeds. Even if thy case is lost, she will keep faith with thou. . . . In thy hands, stiff and only in death helpless, she will put her golden dream, the dream of so many generations of youth—the dream about knight's sword.[2]

Defeat is not a defeat, since the struggle itself produces immortal values. When at the end of "Hubal" the body of Major Dobrazanski is carried away by the German soldiers, one thinks about Zeromski's "golden dream." It is the struggle itself, not necessarily the victory, that has the highest value.

The romantic tradition, however, equated heroism not with every military struggle but only with the just struggle for noble aims. In the twentieth century, the national independence of Poland, as well as liberty of all oppressed, became the symbolic central values of national heroism. Kościuszko, Bem, Dabrowski—heroes of Polish uprisings as well as of American, Hungarian or French revolutions respectively—symbolize this trait of the traditional image of the Polish military. In other words: the traditional image was that of the liberating hero, who wins appreciation by his sacrifices rather than by his victories, and whose main contribution is the example he gives to future generations. Interpreted against this background, the success of the film "Hubal" can be seen as proof that some traditional elements of the Polish image of the military still function as components of national consciousness.

The Second World War in the Eyes of Post-War Generation

The reconstruction of the public image of the Polish military in earlier times is inevitably based on impressionistic analysis of literary sources, memoirs and similar "soft" data. The situation is, however, different in respect to the contemporary attitudes toward the military traditions of the Second World War. Since the early 1960s, the subject has been studied through public opinion polls sponsored jointly by the Military Political College and the Public Opinion Research Center. The results of these studies are consistent with the hypothesis that the public image of Polish military in World War II retains certain traditional characteristics, albeit combined with new elements. Since the Second World War remains the most important military experience in the living memory of the nation, attitudes toward this tradition are of greatest importance for understanding the transformations of the public image of the military.

The war experience itself was a combination of four principal military activities carried by the Poles and identified by the contemporaries as the Polish contribution to final victory. They differed both in their military character and in their political content, making the interpretation of public attitudes toward the military tradition of the Second World War a fascinating subject. These four military activities were:

1.   The Polish military campaign in September and early October 1939, with the defense of Warsaw, Westerplatte, Hel and the battle at river Bzura as the best known episodes;

2.   The activities of the Polish armed forces under the government-in-exile on the side of the Western allies from 1940 until the end of the war. Narvik, Battle of Britain, Tobruk, Monte Cassino, Falaise belong to the most famous battles in which these forces distinguished themselves;

3.   The activities of the Polish forces organized in 1943 on the Soviet soil by the Union of Polish Patriots, a left-wing association with considerable Communist influence. These forces fought until the final defeat of Nazi Germany and at the end of the war constituted the fourth biggest allied military force in Europe, after the Soviet, American and British forces. Lenino, Kolobrezeg, and Berlin belong to the list of their best known battles; the present Armed Forces consider themselves the continuation of these units;

4.   The activities of Polish underground and guerrilla, both non-Communist (in majority) and Communist, during the Nazi occupation with the Warsaw uprising and the guerrilla battle in Janowskie Forests—both in 1944—as the best known battles.

During the early years of post-war period the official historiography tended to down-grade the traditions of the non-Communist military contribution in 1939, in the West and in the underground. It was only some time after 1956 that a more balanced and fair judgement which gives credit to all manifestations of military struggle during the Second World War, has been approved as part of official policy.[3]

The first public opinion poll concerned with the evaluation of Polish military traditions was taken in June and July 1961 by the Public Opinion Research Center in collaboration with the Department of Sociology, Military Political College.[4] The sample—a quota sample—consisted of 2385 adult men, 18-65 years old, from all social strata of the Polish population. The survey was concerned with a wide range of problems relating to the evaluation of Polish armed forces, with special emphasis on the respondents' opinions about contemporary forces, obligatory military service and similar topics. This part of the survey indicated a generally positive attitude toward the armed forces with a tendency toward positive correlation between age and evaluation of the military, and negative correlation between education and the evaluation of the military. The respondents also favorably compared the contemporary forces with the pre-war Polish military, particularly on such dimensions as the attitude of officers toward the subordinates, cultural life, educational and professional opportunities offered by the military service.

One of the open-ended questions asked for identification of the "most glorious military traditions" in Polish history. Approximately eighty percent (80.7%) of all respondents identified at least one military tradition from the time of the Second World War. By type of military activities identified as the most glorious, this can be divided as follows:

— Polish armed forces in the West—25.0%
— Polish armed forces in the USSR—21.0%
— Polish campaign of 1939—14.3%
— Underground fightings including the Warsaw uprising—12.5%
— World War II without specification—7.9%.

To evaluate fully these results, it is important to note that only 22.3 percent of all respondents indicated military traditions from the period prior to the partitioning of Poland at the end of eighteenth century, 15.9 percent mentioning national liberation fighting against the partitioning powers, and only 1.1 percent, citing the war against the USSR in 1920. These results show clearly that the recent experience of the Second World War is considered the most important and the most glorious military tradition in Polish history. It also shows that, very much in line with the time-old pattern, contemporary Poles consider as glorious not only the victorious battles, like Monte Cassino, Lenino, Berlin, but also the lost ones, like Westerplatte or Warsaw uprising. It is the military heroism, rather than victory, that matters. Finally in spite of political differences so deep during the war, contemporary Poles tend to value highly various military traditions regardless of their political characteristics. "Western" and "Eastern" military contributions were given almost equal share among the "most glorious" traditions of the nation.

An additional question illustrative for the public image of the Polish military called for comparing Polish soldiers with other armed forces on three dimensions: courage, discipline and training. We were, of course, aware of the fact that most of the respondents had very little information on the subject. However, it was the pattern of national stereotypes that we were interested in. The majority of respondents favorably compared Polish soldiers with the others. Poles were listed as the most courageous by 71.5 percent of all respondents; the best disciplined—by 13.5%; and the best trained—by 12.8 percent. Comparisons between nations look as follows:

rank	"most courageous"	"best disciplined"	"best trained"
1.	Poles /71.5%/	Germans /54.3%/	Germans /24.8%/
2.	Russians /15.9%/	Russians /13.6%/	Russians /24.7%/
3.	Japanese /6.2%/	Poles /13.5%/	Americans /17.9%/
4.	Germans /1.4%/	British /5.5%/	Poles /12.8%/
5.	Americans /0.3%/	Japanese /3.7%/	British /9.0%/
	others 3.4%	5.4%	4.0%
	no opinion, no answer 1.3%	4.0%	6.7%

It is interesting also that the respondents tended largely to identify the same six nationalities, albeit in different proportions depending on the question. Although the sterotype of Poles was generally favorable, it was much more strongly so on the dimension of courage than on the other two. Finally, one can see an indication of the impact the Second World War had on the military stereotypes of the Poles. No similar poll was taken before the war, yet one can hardly imagine similarly low evaluation of the French after their glorious victory of 1918.

In December 1965 the Public Opinion Research Center in collaboration with the Social Studies Laboratory of the Political Department of the Armed Forces conducted a special poll on the public evaluation of Polish contribution to the victory over Nazism.[5] The quota sample consisted of 1902 respondents, men and women, 16 years of age and older, from all social strata. The survey demonstrated that the public is greatly interested in the history of the Second World War and actively seeks information on this subject. In addition, parallel surveys were conducted with the samples of teachers, high school students, university students and soldiers.

Asked about the relative importance of various nations contributions to the victory over Germany the respondents could identify more than one country. They gave the following answers:

1. Soviet Union—69.3%
2. United States—36.1%
3. Poland—20.9%
4. Great Britain—6.7%
5. France—0.4%
6. "All countries fighting against Germany"—21.9%
7. No answer—2.3%.

Asked directly about the relative importance of the Polish contribution 70.9 percent of the national sample considered it as substantial; moreover, 16.6 percent of the sample considered the Polish contribution as "decisive" for the outcome of the war. Whatever the historical truth might be, these results are consistent with the hypothesis that retrospectively the Poles are proud of their behavior and role in the Second World War. Sixty-one percent (61.4%) of the sample declared that the best policy during the war was the one of active, uninterrupted struggle against Germans. Only 7.4 percent of the sample favored the policy of conserving national forces and waiting for the end of the war without active armed struggle; this category included mostly old women of low education. One can conclude that in spite of very high war losses the Poles retrospectively consider the policy of active, military resistance as the best one—this again is consistent with traditional patterns of Polish national consciousness. One can consider this an important characteristic of Polish national character, the one which more than anything else explains Polish collective behavior in modern history.

Against this background it is easy to understand why the war time military traditions were given such high evaluation. The pattern of relative evaluation of traditions emerging from the 1965 study is to some extent different from that found in the earlier poll. Most of the Poles identified as the most highly valued Polish military contributions to the victory over Germany the following activities:

1. Underground fighting in occupied Poland—45.0%
2. Polish armed forces formed in the USSR—38.2%
3. Polish campaign of 1939—31.5%
4. Polish armed forces in the West—19.9%

In addition 25.7 percent of all respondents declined to identify any of the fronts on the ground that all of them had equal importance. Moreover, the percentages do not total 100, since the respondents could choose more than one alternative.

Another interesting pattern was revealed by which of the battles fought by Poles during the World War II proved to be the best known. In the first three places were battles identified with soldierly heroism rather than with strategic importance: Monte Cassino (May 1944 in Italy), Westerplatte (September 1939) and Warsaw Uprising (August-October 1944). Only thereafter came the battles of considerable strategic importance like Lenino (October 1943), Berlin (April 1945), the defense of Warsaw in September 1939 and others.

The comparison of the public opinion polls indicates that the most important factor determining Polish evaluation of the military past is heroism rather than political or strategic success—with high evaluations for both the traditions of victories and those of defeats. Respondents also tend to greatly value military contributions made by nonprofessional fighters. This is consistent with the national tradition of popular uprisings, guerrilla warfare and conspiracies and may provide the nation with a psychology favorable for all-national military and civilian defense.[6]

The Public Evaluation of the Military as a Profession

I have mentioned before that the 1961 public opinion poll demonstrated a generally positive evaluation of the Polish armed forces by the civilian population. Poles are proud of their military forces and consider obligatory military service not only a matter of obligation but also of honor. It is a popular custom to organize good-bye parties for the new draftees as well as cordial receptions for soldiers returning home. Civilians are frequent visitors in military barracks and special programs of cooperation between military units on the one hand and factories or schools on the other are under way. Although Polish forces did not fight after the end of the Second World War except in semi-civil war against the armed underground (1944-1947), their training and experience are frequent topics in the mass-media and are followed with great interest. Recently, for instance, the part played by the Polish unit in the United Nations Emergency Force in the Middle East allowed the military to popularize among the public its new role as a peace keeping force with international obligations.

Public opinion polls consistently show that the Polish military has relatively low prestige, both compared with other professional groups in the Polish society and compared with the prestige of the military in other countries. Comparative secondary analysis showed for instance that the prestige of Polish military is lower than any of the foreign militaries for whom comparative data were available.[7] My interpretation of these findings stressed the impact of industrialization on the rapid changes in popular values indicating at the same time, that the Polish pattern of non-professional military fighting could also be a factor. Indeed, in a nation in which every generation of civilians has produced war time heroes, one may be less inclined to award high prestige to the military profession than is the case among other more fortunate nations whose military history has been mostly that of wars fought by regular armies.

Another factor, however, is the evolution of the armed forces themselves.[8] The combined effect of political changes after the World War II and of the rapid expansion of the size of the military after the outbreak of the Korean War was to emphasize recruitment of politically reliable workers and peasants, rather than of those with professional competence. For a short time indeed, the military became, compared with other professions, the path of easy promotion and lower educational requirements. This did not last long. In late 1950s the armed forces launched a campaign to improve the quality of their professional corps. Formal educational requirements again became of great importance and in short time the professional officers became a group with good professional and general training. The evolution of military technology tended to accelerate this process even further.[9] Selected comparisons between the educational standards of the professional officer corps in 1957 and 1971 provide good illustrations of this trend. In 1957 only 6.6 percent of all officers had graduated from military and 7.8 percent from civilian colleges, while 57.4 percent of all officers lacked secondary education. In 1971 35 percent of all officers have college education (10.7 percent from civilian colleges) and all the others have secondary or junior college education; by the end of 1975 it is expected that the proportion of officers with full college education will reach 60 percent.[10]

Has this trend resulted in higher prestige for the military profession among the civilian population? Empirical studies available now do not indicate such a change. The question, whether an increase in prestige will come later, is purely speculative and cannot be dealt with in a scientific way. It is, however, quite possible that the relatively low prestige of the professional military will coexist with a high evaluation of the military values of heroism: both as traditions of the past and as norms for future behavior in case of international conflict.

Lasting peace is, however, the most likely future for the Polish generations to come. In this context the military changes its role. From active fighters to guardians, from heroic amateurs to well educated professionals—these are the two most important directions of the changing role of the military. In its new role the military is in fact accepted by the public, albeit without such exaggerated prestige as it enjoyed before the Second World War. After all the dramatic experiences of her history, Poland has now become more similar to other nations. Her military enjoys no exceptionally high prestige, even when its contribution to national safety and well being is fully appreciated.

Considering the most likely hypothesis of continuous detente in Europe, one can visualize the future attitudes of the Polish population toward the military as a combination of the heroic military traditions of the past with better understanding of the modern role of armed forces—both as guardians of peace and as the useful school for younger generations. It is, on the other hand, unlikely that the Polish military will return to the elevated prestige and spiritual influence it used to enjoy before World War II. Its role now is viewed as part of the role played by the whole system of state institutions: political, educational, economic and others. This transformation seems to be one of the lasting changes in the public image of Polish military.

Notes

1. Compare Bromke (1967).

2. My translation of Zeromski (1905).

3. In late nineteen-fifties, however, one of the most vivid cultural controversies was started by a group of writers, theater and film directors and journalists who frontally attacked the traditions of military heroism as no longer useful or important. Albeit some of the artistic manifestations of this trend are of a very high value, this line of "anti-heroism" went much too far and was rejected by diminant trends in Polish culture and in Polish public opinion.

4. Compare Gesek, Szostkiewicz, and Wiatr, (1962: 97-142). In Polish with an English summary.

5. Compare Olczyk (1967).

6. Systematic comparisons with other countries might reveal more universal implications of these Polish findings. Yugoslav experience, albeit different in many respects, shares some of those characteristics. It was, therefore, of a great help to me that I was given an opportunity to read Dr. Robin Remington's chapter in this volume on Yugoslavia, as well as to discuss with her the similarties and dissimilarities of these two cases, before this volume was finalized.

7. Compare Wiatr (1969). The countries compared were Denmark, the German Federal Republic, Indonesia, Pakistan, Philippines, Poland, Sweden and the United States.

8. See Wiatr (1968).

9. Compare Graczyk (1971).

10. Compare Graczyk (1972). In Polish.

THE CIVIC SOLDIER IN CUBA

Jorge I. Domínguez

Two major patterns of civilian control over the military have been identified.[1] One, subjective civilian control, maximizes civilian power over the military by increasing the power of a governmental institution (such as parliament) or of a social class (such as the bourgeoisie) or of a political party (such as the Communist party) over the military institutions. The other, objective civilian control, maximizes military professionalization, that is, the increase of military expertise, responsibility and corporate autonomy.

Civilian control over the military is not a worldwide norm. Among economically underdeveloped states and new states with relatively weak political institutions in particular, military control over civilian institutions often prevails. Two basic types of military intervene in politics.[2] The arbitrator military tend to have no independent political organization, little interest in constructing an independent political ideology, and are often content merely to supervise leading civilians in government. When arbitrator armies take over power directly, they set a time limit on their trusteeship and hand the government back to "acceptable" civilians. The arbitrator accepts the existing social order, and places relatively high value on civilian government. The ruler military tend to have, in contrast, little confidence in civilian rule, reject the legitimacy of the existing social order, have little expectation of returning to the barracks after they take power, construct an independent and sometimes change-oriented ideology and may develop an independent political organization.

These and similar formulations[3] assume that one can identify with some precision civilians and military, that there is actual or potential conflict between them, that civilians are always capable of governing the country, and that the military scope of activity is so defined that unusual behaviors (such as taking over the government or performing normally civilian unskilled labor) can be identified, isolated and analyzed. One can, therefore think about a praetorian polity, a militarized society, or a politicized army.

AUTHOR'S NOTE: The original version of this essay was presented at the Inter-University Seminar on Armed Forces and Society, held in Chicago, October, 1973. I am grateful to Abraham Lowenthal, Alfred Stepan, other seminar participants and Timothy Colton for comments on that version.

The central hypothesis of this essay is that Cuba is governed in large part (though not exclusively) by civic soldiers, that is, military men who actually rule over large sectors of military and civilian life, who are held up as symbols to be emulated by all military and civilians, who are the bearers of the revolutionary tradition and ideology, who have civilianized and politicized themselves by internalizing the norms and organization of the Communist Party and who have educated themselves to become professionals in military, political, managerial, engineering, economic and educational affairs. Their civic and military lives are fused. It is, therefore, inaccurate to speak of civilian control over the military, military control over civilians, the politicization of the military or the militarization of society as if the civic and military spheres were clearly distinct.

The civic soldier is the key political role in Cuba.[4] Civic soldierly behavioral patterns are expected of about two-thirds of the occupants of top elite positions. Most civic soldiers were socialized into their role during the insurgency against Batista in the 1950s and during the counter-insurgency against anti-communists in the early 1960s. This type of warfare, more than any other, tends to fuse military and political roles in the battlefields. Civic soldiers head both military and civilian agencies in Cuba and, just as military agencies have civilian tasks, civilian agences have military tasks and use military symbols and organization. Therefore, the sent roles of a military commander or the Minister of Education or a sugar harvest administrator include both civilian and military elements. While the sent role of a military commander may have more military elements, there are still strong civilian elements.

This has important implications for the nature of political conflict and adaptive behavior. First, there is relatively little evidence (though there is some) of conflict between persons in distinct civilian and military roles. Conflicts in various issue areas tend to occur between civic soldiers; the more "pure" civilian minority of the leadership tends to split, too, so that there are rarely clear civilian and military sides to a dispute. Second, there is *no* issue area in which civic soldiers are totally disinterested. Civic soldiers are engaged in disputes in military, political, economic, artistic, educational, and social deviance issue areas. When conflict occurs, for example, over the defense budget, civic soldiers are found on both sides of the dispute. Thus the presence of conflict in the military issue area can co-exist with the civic soldier role, though it may increase role pressures.

Third, the civic soldier role, theoretically, seems fraught with objective role conflict. How many resources will be diverted from the defense to the industrial investment budget, when both goals are prescribed by the Party leadership to which one belongs (intra-sender conflict)? If one is in charge of a motorized brigade, does one emphasize training for combat or for a mechanized harvest, that is, does one respond more to the strict military or strict economic organizations (inter-sender conflict)? The leadership has addressed itself primarily to the second type of role conflict by seeking to prevent extreme organizational specialization, and by relying on long standing interpersonal bonds from the shared guerrilla experience. Thus the Ministry of the Armed Forces will demand both economic and military performance: but what is the field officer supposed to do when he must apportion his own time? One may continue theoretically to expect inter-sender role conflict. The civic-military fusion creates a host of potential role conflicts. But, empirically in Cuba, the meager evidence suggests thus far little conflict between different organizational senders. The organizational pull of the Armed Forces and Education Ministries clash little by preventing extreme organizational specialization. The civic soldier concept has permeated many organizations, too. And too little is known about intra-sender conflict.

Fourth, because the civic and the soldierly elements of the role are equally legitimate, organizational adaptation is facilitated. For example, if the defense budget is threatened because threats to the state decline, it is feasible to stress more the non-defense elements of the civic soldier role. The objectives of the military institutions include both elements; as H. A. Simon argued, loyalty to the organization will support opportunistic changes of emphasis to promote organizational survival and growth; the legitimacy of civic soldiership facilitates the shift. Blau has argued that the attainment of organizational objectives (e.g., military security) generates a strain toward finding new objectives (e.g., politics, or economics). It can be hypothesized that organizational growth is a specific goal of the military institutions or, at the very least, that the prevention of organizational decline is certainly such a goal. The civic soldier concept helps to legitimize a shift in objectives or missions of the military organization as perceived by the entire elite. In turn, the ability to shift objectives, as Huntington has argued, adds to the organizational age of the military organization so it becomes more institutionalized.[5]

In this essay, we will pay attention only to the military as an institution of government, emphasizing the strictly military, the socioeconomic and the political objectives or missions of the armed forces from the view of the party-military relationship. We will pay little attention to the military as a re-socializing institution or as a symbol or norm for civilians (especially for children) or to matters purely internal to the armed forces such as training, schools.[6] Thus we consider the civic soldier hypothesis in order to explain the fusion of civilian and military aspects of governing Cuba.

Background

Cuba has experienced three distinct periods of civil-military relations. The first, from qualified independence in 1902 until the 1933 revolution which overthrew President Machado, emphasized subjective civilian control. The military served in large part as a Presidential political machine, insuring the victory of the President's party at the polls in return for participation in a system of widespread and institutionalized graft. The military also defeated insurrections by the opposition after the elections. These insurrections were usually minor, designed to provoke U.S. interference to annul the elections. There were no military coups during this period.[7]

The second period, from 1933 until the 1958 revolution which overthrew President Batista, emphasized arbitrator military behavior. There were two successful military coups, in September 1933 and in March 1952, but no military rule. The military placed their chosen civilians in power, including a thoroughly civilianized Senator Batista in 1952. In 1936, the military forced Congress to impeach the President and replace him with the Vice President. From 1933 to 1940, effective political power was held by the Commander-in-Chief of the Army, Colonel Fulgencio Batista, who often removed civilian Presidents. But a military officer on active duty never served as President of the Republic. All military coups attempted between 1940 and 1952 failed.

Batista relied on existing political parties, whose ideas he borrowed, in both periods of effective rule 1933-1944 and 1952-1958. Though he eventually developed a political organization, it was not the military's, but his own. As Army Chief in the 1930's, he toyed with corporatist political ideology but abandoned it swiftly. He expanded the role of the military extensively into civilian areas, especially education and public health, yet he kept the military out of economic tasks. He emphasized the more effective distribution of resources, such as education and public health, which did not require taking from some social groups to give to others. In literacy and public health, the military supplanted civilians and brought no skills which could not have been provided by civilians if resources had been channeled through civilian rather than military agencies. A technically or managerially competent military, stressing development, was *not* the role performed; rather, the military were the distributors of basic values by using "cheap labor" through enlisted men.[8]

During the course of the 1940s, the scope of army "non-military" activities was sharply restricted, as many educational and health functions were transferred from military to civilian agencies. The Batista government in the 1950s turned to repression of the opposition but without militarizing the social system. The President chose to risk defeat in combatting the insurgency rather than disrupt the economy. He allocated troops to protect enterprises, and to guarantee production, rather than to facilitate military offensive operations.[9] At the end of the Batista regime, therefore, the scope of military activities was restricted, the weight of the military on the national economy and life was limited (as shown below) and attitudes toward the armed forces were negative.

The third period, from 1959 until the present, is the rule by the revolutionary government headed by Fidel Castro. It fits none of the theoretical categories. While one can identify a ruling elite and "pure" civilians, it is not always easy to identify the "pure" military. A large majority of Cuba's contemporary ruling elite have military rank. There is no identifiable alternative "pure" civilian elite capable of ruling the country without the military politicians. There is only limited evidence of civil-military conflict, not only because the "pure" civilian share of the elite is small, but also because the military's decisive political role is perceived to be legitimate. Finally, the scope of activity of the military is not well defined, and it is becoming more ill defined with the passing of time.

The Military Mission of the Military

The "military" mission of the Cuban military has been to provide for external defense and to suppress internal challenges to the authority of the government. Since the early summer of 1960, the Soviet nuclear shield has protected Cuba against U.S. attack. The Cuban armed forces are responsible for sub-nuclear defense. The major external attack was the Bay of Pigs invasion in 1961. Since then, though with declining frequency, various exile groups have launched hit-and-run attacks on the island or have landed small parties, which have typically been captured quickly.

Cuba's external defense, in practice, rests with the Navy, equipped to intercept landings and prevent hit-and-run raids with the air and the anti-aircraft defense forces, equipped to intercept exile bombings of the island, and with the Frontier Corps, which serves as the first line of territorial defense against a successful landing, prior to calling the regular army units. Cuba's other military capabilities are not necessary to the daily practice of external defense. In 1970 total navy size was between 6,000 and 7,500; the size of the air force and the anti-aircraft defense units was between 12,000 and 20,000. The army had about 90,000. In short, the bulk of Cuba's military force is not externally but internally oriented.[10]

Cuba faced internal war, with some interruptions, from December 1956 through 1965. Since then, the pockets of internal resistance have been few and have been eliminated quickly. From December 1956 to January 1959, Batista's forces fought against the insurgency led by Castro and allied organizations. During the second half of 1960 insurgents rose against Castro's government, primarily in the Escambray mountains at the center of the island, in Las Villas province. This was followed by the Bay of Pigs invasion in April 1961. The defeat of the invasion and the containment of the Escambray insurrection slowed down the internal war, which resumed in 1962. In July 1962, the government created the Anti-Bandit Struggle Corps throughout the island (Lucha Contra Bandidos, or LCBs). Although the LCBs undoubtedly fought against some bandits, their clear target was political insurrection against the revolutionary government.[11]

Table I shows the military burden. National income estimates between the 1950s and the 1960s are not strictly comparable. Budget statistics, however, are even less comparable. The budget is vastly larger after 1959 than before because it encompasses operations for a socialized economy. Therefore, the national income estimates are preferred.

Table I shows that the highest level of military expense weight on national income in pre-revolutionary Cuba came in the period through 1940, when the Batista-led armed forces were engaged in fairly extensive activities beyond the strict military mission. But the weight of military expenses declined to a low point just as Batista staged his coup of March, 1952. Among the first measures after the coup were pay raises for all military forces. Although the military budget grew during the Batista regime, its weight on national income remained virtually unchanged because the economy also grew. In 1958, as his government was threatened with widespread insurrection, the Batista government still registered a very low commitment of

TABLE I[12]
The Military Burden, 1940-1970

	Military Expenditures				Military Personnel (in thousands)	
	Millions current pesos[a]	Millions current dollars[b]	% of national income[a]	% of GNP[b]	Regular forces[c]	Regular and paramilitary forces[b]
1940	19		4.5			
1949-50	40		2.6			
1951-52	42		2.2		25	
1958	50		2.3		29	
1961		175		7.6		270
1962		200		8.0		280
1963	213	200	6.5	7.4	300	285
1964	223	200	5.6	6.7		175
1965	214	220	5.5	6.9		175
1966		230		6.6		175
1967		250		6.3		175
1968		300		6.0		200
1969		250		5.0	116	200
1970		290		5.6	110	200
1971						
1972	365					

a. From Cuban government data
b. From ACDA data
c. From various sources cited in footnote 12

national resources to military ends. In contrast, the Castro government has committed a share of national income which is two or three times larger than Batista's.

Table I shows a reasonable (though not exact) correspondence between the ACDA estimates and the computations based on direct Cuban government data. In particular, both sets of data point to a decline in the weight of military expenditures on the economy after 1963, as the intensity of internal war declined and the economy recovered from its near-collapse of 1962-63. The decline in the economic weight of the military was steady throughout the second half of the 1960s, to be interrupted only by the rise in activities by the military in connection with the 1970 sugar harvest.

Cuba's regular armed forces grew from 24,797 when Batista took over on March 10, 1952, to 29,270 on the day he fell (in addition, Batista created army and navy reserves amounting to 18,542 by

December, 1958). The revolutionary government had 300,000 regular forces, with a reserve of approximately the same size, at the peak of the insurrections against its rule. Table I shows the shrinking of the size from 1963 to 1970, to correspond with the reduced threat to the government's survival.

Table II shows detailed estimates of deaths from domestic violence in Cuba. The table was computed from the *New York Times Index* for the second edition of the *World Handbook of Political and Social Indicators*, and slightly adapted for use here. It suggests that deaths from domestic violence were almost five times higher in the insurrection against Batista than in the insurrection against Castro.

The deaths for the 1950s are probably overstated, and the deaths for the 1960s are probably understated. For example, a disaggregated independent count of the *New York Times Index* for 1958 shows 1169 soldiers, 1408 rebels or other identified oppositionists, 52 unidentified persons who were probably rebels or oppositionists, and 17 innocent persons reportedly killed. These total 2594 deaths, close to the 2500 in Table II. In addition, the *Times* reported 1000 persons killed in the last major battle of the war (Santa Clara); evidently, the *World Handbook* coders took this round number to mean no more than "a lot of people" and left it out of the body count.

However, the number of soldiers reportedly killed typically came in round numbers (mainly three batches of 200, 300 and 600) announced by the rebels. The government, in turn, reported upwards of 650 rebels killed in four reports between November 14 and 25. Therefore, two-thirds of the deaths from domestic violence in 1958 were reported in round numbers, or were suspiciously clustered together. There are other grounds for suspicion. On June 4, 1958, the *Times* reported the rebel announcement that 200 soldiers were

TABLE II[13]
Deaths from Domestic Violence

Year	Deaths		Year	Deaths
1952	5		1959	16
1953	74		1960	92
1954	1		1961	203
1955	9		1962	45
1956	172		1963	311
1957	638		1964	35
1958	2500		1965	11
	Total 3399+			Total 713

killed in recent battles. Yet, in 1966, the revolutionary government opened the files of Batista's armed forces and showed that the total number of officers and enlisted men killed in action or by terrorists between January and June of 1958 was 162.[14] The report of 200 soldiers killed in a few weeks is grossly overstated. On the other side, Castro's forces numbered no more than 300 in mid-1958; no more than 2000 in early December, 1958, and no more than 3000 by the end of the month. If Batista's armed forces had killed 650 rebels in mid-November, they would have wiped out a third of the rebel force and assured Batista's victory. As for the alleged 1000 dead in the battle of Santa Clara, the rebel forces, led by Guevara, numbered only about 300. The bombardment of a part of the city by the Air Force killed few civilians. And Batista's forces, with very few exceptions, were surrendering in large numbers.[15]

The only detailed account of the total number of persons dead in the 1950s lists 898 killed, of whom 275 were Batista supporters—civilian and military killed in action or by terrorism during the seven years.[16] Yet is is now known that the number of officers and enlisted men killed between January, 1957, and May, 1958, was 289.[17] If one could add civilians and military, especially for the last six months of 1958, the number would surely rise.

In sum, the number of deaths for 1958 in Table II should probably be cut in half to eliminate exaggerated reports of casualties by both sides. But one should also add a couple of hundred people killed in the battle of Santa Clara. The number for 1957 should shrink, too. Thus approximately 2000-2500 persons (or two to three times the 898 reported in the only detailed count ever published, which itself was demonstrably understated) were killed on both sides during the insurrection against Batista.

Questions can also be raised about the validity of data for the 1960s in Table II. For example, on September 11, 1963, the *New York Times Index* notes exile reports of 198 casualties, probably all coded as deaths. The newspaper text shows only 168 deaths, of which 144 were soldiers and 24 were anti-Castro insurgents. If such reports were accurate, the revolutionary government would have been overthrown long ago. The *Index* report for this day accounts for almost two-thirds of the deaths for the year and almost two-sevenths for the 1960s.

Alternative data, however, suggest that Table II's order of magnitude for the 1960s (in the absence of a regular, on-site *Times* correspondent) has erred on the low side. In the first half of the 1960s there were two insurrections against the Castro government in each of the six provinces. There were at one time as many as 179 insurrectionary bands. The revolutionary government estimated the size of this armed opposition at 3591 (dead plus captured), and has reported about 500 military deaths from the Anti-Bandit struggle, independent of other military deaths from other actions or terrorism. Anti-government forces numbered 1000 at their peak.[18] Because the government won and the insurrectionists lost, more insurrectionist than government deaths may also be expected. Indeed, one gets into the same range (2000-2500 deaths) for the 1960s as for the 1950s.

In sum, the number of regular troops committed by the Cuban government against insurrection was ten times greater under Castro than under Batista; the reserve forces under Castro were ten to fifteen times greater than under Batista; the level of fighting was probably the same. Batista's government lost; Castro's government won. Revolutionary government in Cuba could not have survived without the military's effective performance in their strictly military role.

Once survival of the revolution was assured, broad shifts in the posture of the military occurred. In the early 1960s, the Cuban military had a large standing force but with limited professional competence. The military could defeat an internal insurrection or exile landing, but would have had to rely on Soviet protection against a major external attack. By the late 1960s, the desire for greater strategic autonomy joined the wish to reduce the burden of the military on the Cuban economy. The size of the standing force shrunk; the military share of national income declined. But the actual military budget remained high and rose moderately. The new funds were used for the modernization of inventories and the professionalization of the officer corps. The new Cuban strategic doctrine emphasized more self-reliance on a modernized and professionalized "small" standing force *plus* a capability for full and swift mobilization of the reserves.[19]

The shift in strategic doctrine, therefore, provided more autonomy at less economic cost. The real cost to the civilians—and gain to the military was the expansion of military training and military control over the lives of young and middle-aged adults. Civilians were militarized. But another trend began simultaneously. The armed forces became much more involved in activities which were not strictly military. Their socio-economic and political missions became paramount. The military were civilianized. More appropriately, it is arguable that these joint trends have led to civilian and military role fusion in many areas, and to the diffusion of the civic soldier concept within both military and civilian sectors.

The Socio-Economic Mission of the Military

Upon the suppression of the insurgency by 1965, the military searched for new or expanded roles. One was the supervision of social deviants and their presumed rehabilitation, the other was the promotion of economic growth. It had been foreseen for some time that the military would perform such roles. In 1963 the compulsory military service law was discussed and implemented. Although external and internal defense were its foremost military justifications, there were additional public justifications. Armed Forces Minister Raúl Castro argued that a three-year military tour of duty for draftees was justified in order for the military to perform in missions other than external defense and internal order:

> If we emphasize military training alone, if we want but an army, we can have them [the draftees] for two years. . .[but] because we believe that the armed forces should help in national production. . .[we intend to make] a bit lighter the burden of military expenditures on our people, that is, we must work during a part of the service, first of all in the sugar harvest . . .[20]

Secondly, the lazy, the corrupt, the homosexual, the religious proselytizer (especially Jehovah's Witnesses) would be drafted into special military units. They would be given no weapons; they would be socially "rehabilitated." Although it was emphasized that the compulsory military service was not designed primarily for this purpose, this would be a subsidiary benefit.[21]

When the internal armed challenge to the revolutionary government was defeated and the objective of state security achieved, the military sought to find new organizational objectives to promote organizational growth by emphasizing the non-defense elements of the civic soldier role. In November 1965, the Army High Command proposed the formation of Military Units to Aid Production (Unidades Militares de Ayuda a la Producción—UMAP) and Prime Minister Castro agreed. UMAP would be nourished by the often arbitrary draft of social deviants. Deviancy included "bad" work habits, intense religious beliefs, homosexuality, and all those traits not in strict accord with a public perception of the "good citizen." As the first UMAP draftees arrived, they were treated so brutally that some of their officers were court martialled and convicted.[22] The initial brutality by military officers was brought under control by one of the leaders of the revolution against Batista, Ernesto Casillas, who headed the UMAP in its formative months. Casillas' work was so satisfactory to the leadership that his next assignment was Army Chief of Staff and Deputy Minister of the Armed Forces.

UMAP remained through two sugar harvests (1965-1966, 1966-1967). It was not universally applauded. The Cuban Union of Writers and Artists protested to Prime Minister Castro, because many intellectuals and members of the universities were sent to UMAP as alleged homosexuals. Although the Prime Minister had approved UMAP and spoke well of it as late as March 1966, the scandalous treatment of UMAP draftees was unacceptable, and UMAP was eliminated after the end of the 1967 harvest. This decision was resisted by the Army High Command, whose journal ran articles in four different issues in the spring of 1967 defending UMAP's record.[23] The defeat of the military establishment on this issue highlights both the decisive role of Prime Minister Castro—a civic soldier—and the limits on military expansion. The military would still recruit and train "good revolutionaries." Their positive socializing mission would continue. Their repressive, "rehabilitative" mission was sharply curtailed.

The military expanded their role in economic production more successfully. Even in the early 1960s, when the strict military mission was paramount, military units contributed to production. LCB units in the Escambray mountains in the fall of 1963 helped the peasants. This work was also part of the counter-insurgency strategy in this threatened area. Similar LCB work with the peasants occurred elsewhere in 1962, 1963 and 1964.[24] As in the case of UMAP, the major expansion in the economic role of the military came only after the external and internal military threats declined. Economic objectives flowed also from emphasizing the non-defense aspects of the civic soldier role, were thereby legitimized, and contributed to military organizational growth.

Table III shows military participation in sugar harvests. Cutting sugar cane requires limited skills. This use of the military, therefore, does not stress military technical or managerial skills, though these would be used in other ways in the harvest. The chief military contribution in cutting cane was to guarantee a cheap labor supply in conditions of labor scarcity. Though the specific tasks were different, this use of the military was similar to Army Chief Batista's in his role expansion programs of the 1930s, except that the role expansion of the 1960s emphasized growth, that of the 1930s, distribution. Normal military participation (1968, 1969, 1971) was just over 40,000 men, somewhat over one-third of the armed forces. The 1970 harvest was extraordinary. Cuba sought to produce ten million tons of sugar; it actually produced 8.5 million tons, the largest harvest in its history. Almost two-thirds of the armed forces cut cane in 1970.

TABLE III[25]
Military Participation in the Sugar Harvest

	Number of soldiers	% (range)
1968	51,000	44-47
1969	38,000	32-35
1970	70,000	60-64
1971	43,000	37-40

Unlike Batista's military in the 1930s, whose technical and managerial contribution to economic growth was minimal, the revolutionary armed forces also took on important technical and managerial economic roles in the late 1960s to promote growth.[26] This began in 1967, when the Air Force took charge of 60 airplanes devoted to aerial fumigation and fertilization of agricultural areas. In the fall of that year the Army formed a motorized brigade to take over mechanized or motorized equipment, first to open up new fields for cultivation and subsequently for the sugar harvest. By the spring of 1969 all farm machinery was under military authority. Officers and enlisted men who had worked in tank or motorized military units were shifted to the new brigade. Since the fall of 1968, the Che Guevara Brigade was organized into 36 sub-units throughout the six provinces. Its Commander-in-Chief Raúl Guerra Bermejo, was also a member of the Party's Central Committee. The Brigade retained a strict military organization and hierarchical chain of command, but it operated entirely in the economic field. It took over all the machinery formerly administered by the State Farms and civilian personnel.

In the giant 1970 sugar harvest, the military cut 20 percent of the sugar cane harvested. They organized and operated the Henderson combines, which sought to mechanize the cane cutting. The military coordinated the cane loading at strategic locations; and supervised the transportation of cane for the sugar mills in the more important eastern provinces. They operated all tractors and cane lifters. They built roads, railroad tracks and temporary housing. The military brigade Luis Turcios Lima, of the Eastern Army, won the coveted title of National Heroes of Labor. The harvests since the late 1960s— and especially in 1970—have been directed from a national command post, linked to the field through provincial, regional and municipal posts. The symbolism is strongly military: the harvest is a battle, a struggle, portrayed as no less essential to the survival of the revolution than the real military battles of the earlier 1960s.

Contrary to some expectations that the military economic role expansion fever of 1967-1968 would subside, it continued and became institutionalized with each subsequent harvest. There is now nothing unusual about military participation in Cuba's annual battle of the sugar harvest. The military have yet to prove that they are more successful than civilians in rescuing the Cuban economy, but their commitment to large scale economic participation and the general acceptance of such participation are now unquestionable.

The growing economic role of the Cuban military gave it a new mission. It has also blunted a criticism that the armed forces were an excessive burden on the Cuban economy. The previously cited 1963 speech by Armed Forces Minister Raúl Castro suggests that this concern was prevalent even when it was clear that the government needed the military for survival. This criticism was stronger in the mid-1960s, as the insurrection against the government was defeated and the military's economic role had not yet expanded. The old objectives had been achieved. Until new ones were found, the organizational health of the military organization was at stake because of the pressures of civic soldiers heading civilian agencies. In 1966 the military agreed to cancel purchases of helicopters and military transport aircraft in order to divert such resources to the purchase of the airplanes for aerial fumigation; and the transfer of no less than 250 pilots on active military service to aerial agricultural service was justified on similar budgetary grounds.[27]

In mid-1967, however, the reductions in the economic weight of the military budget and in military manpower had not yet satisfied some critics. The military responded in two ways. One was the sharp increase in economic activities that has been described. The other was the renewed assertion of the priority of the military budget. Raúl Castro noted on July 22, 1967, that the country may have to "sacrifice even some aspects of its social development in construction work in order to earmark more of our resources to prepare the country for a war whose outbreak we cannot foresee." By January, 1968, after the military's economic role had expanded, Fidel Castro acknowledged the priority of the military in the allocation of scarce strategic resources such as petroleum.[28]

Tables I and II show how the conflict was resolved. The defense budget rose 20 percent and military manpower rose 14.3 percent from 1967 to 1968. The armed forces, therefore, registered the largest annual increase on either indicator for the entire decade. However, military expenditures as a percentage of Gross National Product continued to decline. The military budget grew, but at a rate slower than the economy in a good year (1968). And almost one-half of all military personnel in the regular army had to cut sugar cane in 1968. Though the defense budget retrenched in 1969 to the 1967 level, it almost reached the 1968 level again in 1970, and reached a new height in 1972.

Other communist and non-communist armed forces have also engaged in what is variously called the peaceful uses of military forces, civic action programs, non-military uses of the military or productive work. The scope and domain of the Cuban military's involvement in social and economic tasks is, however, vast compared to many other reported instances of this kind of military behavior.[29] Among communist armed forces, the Soviet military have strongly and repeatedly emphasized professional, strictly military concerns; they have argued that modern military technology requires their full attention to military tasks. But even in the early years of the Soviet revolution, there was little of the kind of role expansion into non-military employment that the Cuban armed forces have embraced.[30] This may have resulted from a regime decision or from military resistance. The point is that role expansion did not occur.

The closest parallel to the Cuban performance is the Chinese military. The Chinese military's reported involvement in the Great Leap Forward was probably comparable to the Cuban military's reported involvement in the Giant Harvest of 1970. A remaining difference with the Chinese is that a significant number of military officers in the Chinese army resisted such role expansion into social and economic tasks, and argued, as did their Soviet colleagues, that the profession of arms was a full-time profession.[31]

There is very little evidence of comparable resistance within the Cuban military. On the contrary, the evidence strongly suggests that the military have entered their non-economic tasks with eagerness and enthusiasm. The only instance when the Cuban military may have resisted involvement was in the 1970 harvest. As Table III showed, their participation in that harvest was clearly extraordinary; in 1971, they reverted quickly to their "normal" rate of participation. There are indications that Fidel Castro wanted, but did not get, additional military participation in the 1970 harvest.[32] Noting that limited exception, the generalization is that the Cuban military have and want a very large involvement in social and economic tasks. One reason for this important difference is the Cuban military's efforts to redesign their mission to remain useful to society, to protect their budget, and to promote their organizational growth in size and function. This explanation, while necessary, is not yet sufficient to distinguish between Cuban and other comparable armed forces. What sets them apart is a set of political variables.

The Political Mission of the Military

The political mission of the Cuban military has four components. First, the internalization of the structure of the Communist Party, so that the corporate autonomy of the military institutions is preserved and party-military conflict contained. Second, the elimination of historical cleavages which plagued the armed forces prior to the revolution: conflicts between commissioned and non-commissioned officers, and between professional and non-professional commissioned officers. Third, the political indoctrination of recruits, and the weeding out of military men with undesirable traits. And fourth, the organization of modes of party organization and control, and the development of leadership cadres that can be exported to the civilian sectors and, in particular, to the top elite. It is at this high level that the fusion between the civic and military tasks of the soldier is climaxed by placing the civic soldier in charge of the highest commands in both the party and the military. The military commander is not a mere technician of arms, but also a political officer; the party national leader is not only a politician but also an officer with technical and managerial competence for civilian and military work.

The civic soldier hypothesis does *not* apply for the early years (1961-1962) of party-military relations. This period ended with a large scale expulsion of members in 1962 (most of the expellees were members of the pre-revolutionary Communist party, faithful to Moscow and not especially close then to Castro's movement) and the large scale recruitment of new members.[33] The party's crisis was caused primarily by a confrontation between Fidel Castro and pre-revolutionary Communists, not by civil-military friction. But the latter was a contributing factor and steps were taken to correct the problem. The bitter memories of civil-military relations in 1961-1962 spurred the civic soldier concept.

During 1961-1962, the party sought control over the armed forces. Political instructors were trained in the Osvaldo Sánchez School for Revolutionary Instruction of the Revolutionary Armed Forces, and then assigned to military units. These political instructors lacked any military training or operational field experience. There was a separation of political and military tasks in the military units. Military commanders strongly opposed both the division of command

and the imposition of political instructors outside the military chain of command. These early political instructors explicitly copied the experience of political commissars in the military from other communist countries. One result of the great purge of the party in 1962 was the abandonment of this system. Beginning early in 1963, prospective students for the Osvaldo Sánchez School were drawn directly from the military ranks, particularly officers. The curriculum in the school was revamped so that 40 percent of the time would be spent on military topics.[34]

By the end of 1963, party recruitment and organization in the military began.[35] There was a trial run in the Mountain Corps (compañías serranas) of the easternmost province, to be followed in December 1963 by the beginnings of party organization in the regular units of the Eastern Army. The formation of the party in the military has observed this procedure. All members of a military unit are classified into eight ranks, from soldier to commanding officers. Each rank has an assembly—directed by a Commission of political instructors appointed by the party's political bureau in the armed forces—to elect "exemplary combatants" (except that all commissioned officers are automatically assumed to be "exemplary combatants"). The exemplary combatants are then interviewed individually by the Commission. Exemplary combatants meet also as groups with the Commission, separately for each of the eight categories of military rank, for criticism and self-criticism. The Commission members select new party members after discussing the candidates among themselves and with ranking officers. The new members are presented to the rest of the unit, and to the party cell (núcleo) which is established in the military unit, and includes all party members regardless of military rank. Party officers are elected at the cell level in the unit and progressively upward in battalions, armies, etc.

At the outset, neither the military orders of the officers nor the officers' own personal and political behavior could be criticized in the party cell. By the mid-1960s, this rule held only during the course of the first year of party formation in the military units. By the second year of party formation in a military unit, though military orders and regulations issued by the officers could still not be questioned in the cell, the personal and political behavior of the officers could be criticized, regardless of the military ranks of the officer and his critic. However, the officers and their orders could at all times be criticized by higher ranking military officers and by political instructors assigned to higher ranking military units.

Political work in the armed forces was directed by the National

Commission of the Party in the Armed Forces, whose chief was Raúl Castro—Armed Forces Minister, Deputy Prime Minister, and Second Secretary of the national party. The political instructors are not elected, but appointed by the National Commission upon the completion of their training. There are two political channels within the armed forces. One is the party, organized from the bottom up; the other, from the top down, is the set of Political Sections in the military units, at all levels of aggregation, composed of the political instructors. The two channels, however, are merged in two ways. First, the political instructors and all party members belong on equal footing to the party's political organs at each level of military organization. Second is the principle of the unified command.

In contrast to the early 1960s and possibly to other communist countries, "command and party go forward together; they are not parallel. The content of the party's work is determined according to the Work Plan of the military unit, according to the specific tasks which it is expected to perform. There is no separation of activity between military and party obligations."[36] Party organization within the military is hierarchical. The upward flow of criticism is difficult, but possible. Innovation remains at the top. Though the party penetrates the military, the military has also penetrated the party. The party in the military is led by the military high command, not by party cells or agencies outside the military. The party in the military is self-contained. Non-military party members have no authority over the party in the military. Party criticism in the military is, at once, criticism within the party, criticism of the military by the party, and criticism of the party by the military, because party and military are fused.

The formation of the party in the military was complete by the end of 1966. The party's formation moved geographically from the eastern to the western provinces, and hierarchically from the bottom up. The last military sector to organize party cells was the National Headquarters of the Army Chief of Staff. By the fall of 1970, 69.6 percent of all officers in the armed forces belonged to either the party or the Communist Youth Union. By the summer of 1973, the proportion rose to 85 percent. The 15-member Advisory Commission of party members to the Political Bureau of the Armed Forces in 1970 was composed entirely of commissioned officers, of whom 7 were *Comandantes* (the highest rank in the Cuban military). In the fall of 1970, 69 percent of the members of the party in the military were commissioned officers. Enlisted soldiers and draftees were a larger, though unspecified, proportion of the membership of the

Communist Youth Union.[37] The high overlap between the officer corps and party-youth union membership further facilitates the fusion of party and military.

Though such membership overlap is a necessary condition for fusion, it is not sufficient. In the Soviet military, the proportion of military officers who have belonged to the party has varied over time: 32 percent in 1924, 65 percent in 1928, 86 percent in 1952, 90 percent in the early 1960s, 93 percent in 1966 when 80 percent of the total personnel of the Soviet armed forces were in the party or in the Communist Youth Union (mostly the latter).[38] And yet, there has been repeated conflict between the party and the military throughout Soviet history.[39] What is crucial, beyond the overlap, is the militarization of the political instructors within the armed forces, the internalization of politics by the military officers, the principle of unified command which preserves, in practice, the military chain of command, the self-containment of the party within the military so that the corporate integrity and autonomy of the military are not threatened, and the presence of civic soldiers at the core of the top elite and in charge of both military and civilian organizations. Thus, in the Soviet Union, even when political commissars and military commanders coalesce on a specific issue,[40] the central organs of the party have limited representation from either of them. In the absence of fusion in the top elite, conflict between central civilian party organs and military leaders and units can continue.

The chief problem in the party-military relationship in Cuba has not been partisan interference with military matters, but the lack of fulfillment of political programs in military units. Military commanders tend to leave political matters to the political instructors. In the spring of 1968, according to the Army Chief of Staff, the net result was not the agglutination of power in the hands of the political instructors, but rather the downgrading of political work within the armed forces. Military commanders were urged to become responsible for the political education of all their subordinates, even if the daily political tasks were implemented directly by the political instructors.[41] At the military unit level, therefore, there did not seem to be a politico-military conflict.

The proportion of soldiers and non-commissioned officers in the party in the military—almost one-third—is comparatively high. In the Soviet military, the proportion of soldiers and non-commissioned officers fell as low as 3 percent of all military party members in the 1940s.[42] The relatively high proportion in Cuba can be explained as a part of the democratic commitment of the revolution within the armed forces.

The revolutionary leadership has also been aware of the historical cleavage between commissioned and non-commissioned officers in the Cuban military prior to the revolution. Though such cleavages are latent in most military institutions, Cuba experienced a comparatively rare event: On September 4, 1933, army sergeants and corporals headed by then Sergeant Fulgencio Batista overthrew the government and the officer corps. Sergeant Batista promoted himself to Colonel, and other Sergeants and Corporals were equally promoted. Many former officers gathered at the National Hotel to fight back; Batista's forces attacked and killed 14 officers, wounded 17, and took the rest prisoner.[43] Subsequent Cuban military leaders have been concerned lest anything resembling those events should re-occur.

The second major cleavage within the military prior to the revolution existed between professional officers, who had received formal military training in Cuba or abroad, and non-professional officers who owed their position to their participation in military coups and shrewd politicking. In the 1950s about one-sixth of the officers were non-professionals including Generals Juan Rojas González, Luis Robainas, Martín Díaz Tomayo, Pilar García, and Roberto Fernández Miranda.[44] The revolutionary government sought to prevent the re-occurrence of such a cleavage through its promotion policy.

Table IV shows that no less than three-quarters, and typically none-tenths, of all professional officers promoted and graduating cadets are members of either the Communist Party or the Communist Youth Union. Among the officers promoted, party membership is widespread; among the cadets, Youth Union membership is even more pervasive. The share of officers or cadets promoted with any rebel army experience is declining to zero. Party membership has become a prerequisite for promotion to the upper ranks of the military, and Youth Union membership for promotion from the cadet level. The sharp conflict between party and military of the early 1960s in part occurred because so few military men were in the party. By the 1970s, however, the policy for officer promotion was guaranteeing near-perfect overlap between military officership and party membership. Politically connected officers would also be military professionals and vice versa.

A second aspect of the promotion policy was to send military officers with very low levels of formal training to military school to acquire professional skills. According to Fidel Castro, it would become policy to promote only those who had had professional training in military schools; but, in the late 1960s, those officers with operational experience but no school training were still being

TABLE IV[45]
Professional Military Promotions and Party-Communist Youth Membership

Ranks and dates	N	% in rebel army	% in party	% in Youth Union	% party + % Youth Union
April 1968					
First Captains	35	100.0	94.3	0.0	94.3
Captains	56	100.0	100.0	0.0	100.0
All lieutenants	1757	33.7	69.3	8.8	78.1
March 1969					
Graduate Cadets	414	1.2	48.5	48.5	97.0
August 1969					
Graduate Cadets	731	N.A.	N.A.	N.A.	89.0
August 1970					
Graduate Cadets	1304	N.A.	N.A.	N.A.	87.0
August 1973					
Graduate Cadets	N.A.	N.A.	N.A.	N.A.	95.0

N.A. = not available

promoted. However, the problem of professionalizing the military was quite severe. For example, the Ignacio Agramonte School for Officers in the city of Matanzas required officers to have completed the fifth grade of elementary school prior to admission. Throughout most of the 1960s, this rule was frequently broken. It is not until the spring of 1967 that all new students admitted to the school had prior schooling equal to a sixth grade education. The military were not very different from—and actually a bit ahead of—the rest of the political leadership. In 1969, 79 percent of all national party members lacked a sixth grade education.[46]

In sum, the revolutionary government sought to politicize the entire officer corps, but especially the younger officers who had good professional training but little or no operational experience. It also sought to professionalize, and partly politicize, those non-professional officers with a great deal of operational experience. These joint promotion policies sought to reduce the historical cleavages which had weakened the Cuban military in the past.

The main tasks of the party are to support the authority and enhance the prestige of the military chain of command. The party is expected to strengthen troop morale and combat preparedness through propaganda, political education, and surveillance, not only during uneventful periods of military life, but also in the midst of tactical maneuvers. Political instructors accompanied the LCB units in their struggle against internal insurrection in the early 1960s.

There are additional pay-offs from party work in the military. The process of party formation in the military yielded a lot of information about the troops and the officer corps, which could subsequently ease decisions concerning promotion or forced retirement. The system of criticism and self-criticism institutionalized this pay-off and led to greater discipline in the military. The process of party formation activated latent support for the government, and exposed opposition. The introduction of the party established political criteria for promotion beyond normal military criteria.[47]

Moreover, the party in the military organized a program of *captación*. Party and Youth Union members are assigned a number of military men for their supervision. They were expected to "find out about his anxieties, find out about his personal or family problems," engage in political education, and take the tutee to political meetings and activities. The program was supposed to uplift morale, discipline and education. Its by-products, according to Raúl Castro, included repression of homosexuals and of deeply religious soldiers. The program also stimulates competition within military ranks for promotions, through separate political activity amidst soldiers, NCO's, and commissioned officers. When serious problems appear, a court martial may be in order. Service on all military tribunals is limited to party and Youth Union members. In the fall of 1970, when the second all-military party National Meeting gathered, among the chief criticisms of the weaknesses of party work in the military were the insufficiency of criticism and self-criticism and greater need to survey the personal needs of members of the armed forces—suggesting that both programs had yielded rich results in the past and that more was wanted.[48]

.   This concern for the individual and for small group ties within the military in Cuba is similar to findings about the Chinese army in the early 1950s. Both leaderships took an active interest in the development and control of small group ties. Political judgments were made to control interpersonal relationships and to erode their autonomy. Autonomous, small group social cohesion would not be allowed to threaten the political and military capabilities of the armed forces. Here the interests of party and military clearly went hand in hand.[49]

The previous political missions of the military are largely operative within the military organizations. Another mission, in contrast, aims to export political models and personnel from the military to the rest of the political system. The military experience in forming the party preceded the formation of the party in most of the civilian central administrative agencies. While the party in the military finished its process of construction by the end of 1966, the construction of the party in most of the civilian ministries only began in the spring of 1967. The party drew on the experience of party building in the military and, in particular, on the principle of unified command. As the party began its organization in the civilian ministries, its national Secretary of Organization, Armando Hart, noted:

> There cannot be dual leadership in a central State organization. The maximum authority of the party, in each branch of the State apparatus, will be that of the minister or president of the organization, who works under the direction of the Party Central Committee and Political Bureau. If in any case this should turn out to be impossible, we will have to consider the demotion of the executive. . .[50]

The party in the military also developed a regular practice of holding assemblies to evaluate its work in the military units. These assemblies were held at all levels of command virtually every year. National meetings to evaluate party work in the military were held in 1966 and in 1970.[51] This regularity in the party's organization within the military would serve as a model for non-military branches of the party. Though there had been provincial (civilian) party assemblies since the early days of the party,[52] the especially impressive feature of the party in the military—and a contribution for export to the civilian sectors—was the seriousness and relative regularity of party work in the military.

Finally, the military have developed cadres that can be and have been exported to the civilian sectors. Table V shows the military shares of the Central Committees of the Communist parties in China, Cuba and the Soviet Union. The data for Cuba have been divided into "total" and "strict." The "total" statistic includes all those members of the Central Committee with military title and rank. The "strict" statistic includes only those members of the Central Committee who were primarily engaged in military affairs most of the time, including political work within the military. Military for these purposes also includes the Ministry of the Interior and internal security. The difference between the "total" and "strict" statistics is a measure of the export of cadres by 1965 from the military to the civilian sectors, that is, of the diffusion of civic soldiers in Cuban public life. Under either version, the military share of the Cuban Central Committee is very high, and it was greater in 1965 than 1962. In

TABLE V[53]

**Military Shares of the Central Committees of the Communist Parties
of China, Cuba and the Soviet Union: Selected Years**

	% military	N
China,[a] 1949-1950	38.1	168
China,[a] 1962	24.6	171
China,[b] 1969	51.2	170
China,[b] 1973	31.8	195
China,[a] 1973	31.3	319
Cuba,[b] 1962, total	56.0	25
Cuba,[b] 1962, strict	28.0	25
Cuba,[b] 1965, total	69.0	100
Cuba,[b] 1965, strict	51.0	100
Soviet Union,[b] 1956	7.5	122
Soviet Union,[b] 1966	8.2	195
Soviet Union,[b] 1971	10.2	235

a = all members; b = full members only

1962, the Central Committee in fact had not yet been established:
it was then called the National Directorate of the United Party of the
Socialist Revolution; it was obviously quite small.

Since 1965, men who had been classified as "strict" military at
the time have not taken on new tasks in the civilian economy. For
example, former UMAP Chief and former Army Chief of Staff
Belarmino Castilla would become Minister of Education; his successor
as Chief, Diocles Torralba, would join Castilla in late 1972 in the
super-Cabinet which was organized to direct all Cuban government
policies. Lesser military lights have followed the same path. The process of export of cadres from the military to the civilian sectors, which
had begun in the early 1960s, has continued to accelerate through
the early 1970s. Leaders are trained in the military ranks; as they
have matured, and as the strict military mission of the military has
become less important, civic soldiers have shifted their attention to
the civilian sectors. In the central ministries as well as at various levels
of the "civilian" party ranks one finds civic soldiers again and again.
Of the eleven men in the Political Bureau and the Secretariat of the
Central Committee, the highest organs of the revolution, there are
seven *Comandantes* who fought in the insurrection against Batista,
but who increasingly devote their attention to the widest range of
matters.

In the 1950s, the military share in a modern, complex, mature communist political system such as the Soviet Union was small. The Soviet pattern—about 10 percent of the Central Committee coming from the military, with a range between 7 percent and 13 percent— was set by the late 1930s. Prior to that time, the military share of the top elite had been much less.[54] The Table shows that the Chinese case is more complex. We noted in the discussion of social and economic role expansion that the Chinese case came closer to the Cuban, and it is useful to spell out similarities and differences.[55]

First, as Table V shows, the normal participation of the military in the top elite is much higher in Cuba than in China. The "normal" rate of military participation in the Chinese Central Committee is about one-third, well above the Soviet, well below the Cuban cases. The 1969 Central Committee, at the end of the Cultural Revolution, is exceptional. The participation of the Cuban military in central decision making is apparently more stable and institutionalized than in China. There has been no purge of the Cuban military comparable to the effects of the Lin Piao affair. Second, as the discussion of social and economic role expansion indicated, there has been resistance by professional Chinese officers to engage in non-military tasks. Cuban military officers have welcomed such role expansion. In China, professional resistance to role expansion existed also just prior to, during and after the Cultural Revolution. The entry of the armed forces into the Cultural Revolution was no military coup, it was the result of a decision by the political leadership. The People's Liberation Army (PLA) did not set out to expand its role, as the Cuban armed forces did between 1965 and 1968; power gravitated to the PLA and its role expanded. The impetus came from outside the military. During the Cultural Revolution, the professional vs. political dispute was less salient, but it simmered beneath the surface. The professional officers still opposed the large scale involvement of the PLA in politics. An important element in the anti-Lin Piao coalition was the professional commanders who had opposed political involvement and favored its reduction so that the armed forces could concentrate again on professional military tasks. Thus, though both the Cuban and the Chinese military have engaged in role expansion, Chinese professional officers have resisted while Cuban professional officers have favored it. The impetus in China was primarily external to the military organization; it was both internal and external in Cuba.

Third, the Cuban armed forces have institutionalized the export of political models and cadres to the rest of the political system. In 1964, Chinese were publicly called upon to "learn from the experience of the PLA in political education and ideological work." The PLA did, indeed, become a model for the rest of the political system. But the "learn from the PLA campaign" lasted only four or five months. During the course of the Cultural Revolution, though the PLA played a decisive role, the export of political models to the rest of the political system was not emphasized. The PLA intervened generally to restore order. It exported middle and low level cadres who became regional or local political leaders through the Revolutionary Committees. But in the years since the Cultural Revolution there seems to have been a gradual restoration of civilian rule and a retrenchment of the export of cadres from the military to the political system (some of it reflected on Table V). Thus the Chinese case shows some elements of the civic soldier concept, but not all elements simultaneously. And, whereas the Cuban civic soldier pattern is quite stable, the Chinese clearly is not. Though some Maoists may have had a civic soldier model in mind, though they may have intended its implementation, it was not, in fact, achieved to the degree that it was in Cuba.

A Paradox

Cuba is governed, in large part though not exclusively, by civic soldiers. The leaders of the insurrection against Batista were socialized then into the fusion of civilian and military roles. They have remained the top government elite and have turned the civic soldier concept into a dominant norm in civilian organizations. The Cuban military organization has undertaken, both simultaneously and sequentially, important tasks in the Cuban revolution. As the strictly military mission or objective faded, social, economic and political missions became more important. The result has been the gradual spread of civic soldier roles within the military organization. Therefore, a government led by civic soldiers has sought to diversify and induce convergence of goals and structures in civilian and military organizations.

Since the beginning of the 1960s, Cuba has not had an alternative civilian elite within the system capable of governing it. There is also relatively little evidence of conflict between persons in distinct civilian and military roles. Conflict occurs not only amidst civic soldiers; civilians, too, divide. For example, some leading old-Communists and cultural bureaucrats are evidently in agreement with new-Communists in the armed forces concerning the decadence of many Cuban intellectuals.[56] There are, of course, conflict in the "military issue area." However, these conflicts as in other issue areas (budget, harvest participation, UMAP); are settled by civic soldiers. Conflicts in this issue area may have been less severe than in other issue areas, such as economic policy and incentives policy.[57]

Organizational survival and growth were achieved by reemphasizing the continuing legitimacy of old objectives and finding and implementing new, non-defense objectives within the civic soldier role. The civic soldier concept legitimated role expansion. The military organization has not faded away, but organizational boundaries have become blurred. Organizational survival and growth led leaders of the military institution to seek to expand organizational objectives in the mid-1960s as strategic security seemed assured. Strategic doctrine shifted to emphasize civilian mobilization rather than a standing army. Social, economic and political roles were sought and obtained. The UMAP affair was but a minor setback in a story of organizational success. The broadened scope of organizational activity assured organizational survival, and promoted growth in size, functions and resources.

At the same time, inter-sender role conflict was reduced by reversing the organizational specialization of the military. The sent roles of subordinates would be less incompatible because the military organization became more compatible with civilian organizations. The role pressures on civic soldiers serving in civilian agencies were reduced too. They no longer had to argue to reduce the budget of their former comrades-in-arms, because the military organization now performed civilian tasks. Party structures learned from the military experience; party hierarchies were populated by civic soldiers. These changes were, therefore, generally welcomed by the elite because they reduced intra-elite disputes, role pressures on civic soldiers in civilian agencies, and inter-sender role conflict for subordinates. They may, however, have increased intra-sender role conflict, about which, unfortunately, little is known.

It has become fashionable to write about the militarization of the Cuban revolution. That approach has suggested that the events of the late 1960s were drastically different from earlier ones; in fact, a continuum of behavior, with an admitted acceleration in recent years, is closer to the facts. But the concept of militarization is inappropriate in itself, because it fails to identify the special political quality of the soldiers who are clearly so important. These are soldiers who went to military school *after* they had become military commanders and ministers of state,[58] and who have had extra-military concerns from the day they learned that the insurrection against Batista required not only military but also political skills. The Cuban civic soldier, therefore, is different from military men in both Communist and non-Communist countries because of his eagerness and conviction that military and political tasks require a fusion of personnel and methods.

Yet the civic soldier is a soldier still, and Cuba's reliance on him bespeaks important failures of the revolutionary government. The need to employ the armed forces in the sugar harvest highlights the failure of economic production, and the inability to handle labor supply problems. The use of military methods in the political field has stifled criticism from the bottom of the system, has shut off the upward flow of political communication, and has curtailed the adaptability of the political system. The thorough use of military techniques in the 1970 harvest ended with a quasi-strike by labor in the summer of 1970 and emergency measures to correct a serious problem by the Labor Confederation.[59]

The successful development of the civic soldier concept in Cuba has occurred in the context of political and economic failure. Nor has the civic soldier's performance in economic production been any more successful than that of civilians. The problems are too profound to rely as exclusively as the Cuban leadership has on the fusion of military and political methods into a single, unified tool. The various tasks of the revolution require various tools, but the Cuban leadership has yet to implement an approach that makes separate and distinct use of political, economic and military tools according to the ends pursued.

Notes

1. Huntington, (1957: 80-85).
2. Perlmutter, (1971: 314-324).
3. Germani and Silvert, (1961); Janowitz, (1964); Huntington. (1968: Chapter 4).
4. The usage of role theory in this and the following paragraphs follows Kahn, [et al.], (1964: 11-35).
5. Simon, (1961: 118); Blau (1955: 195); Huntington (1968: 13-17); and Starbuck (1965).
6. For these topics, see San-Martín and Bonachea (1972).
7. Adam y Silva (1947); Chapman (1970).
8. Batista (1944: 58-59), 62, 82-85, 123-124, 127); Cuba's Three Year Plan (1937); Consejo Corporativo de Educación, Sanidad y Beneficencia (1939: 5-6, 8, 82, 106); and Chester (1954); Perez (1971).
9. Suárez Nuñez (1963. 89-90, 94-98, 170).
10. Institute for Strategic Studies, (1970: 76); Subcommittee on Inter-American Affairs of the Committee on Foreign Affairs, House of Representatives (1970: 37, 125-126); and Subcommittee on Inter-American Affairs of the Committee on Foreign Affairs, House of Representative (1972: 6, 18-19, 22) and Blutstein [et al.] (1971: 439).

11. Suárez Amador (1970: 4-5); see also Verde olivo, 4, 46 (November 24, 1963), and Granma (March 5, 1966: 8 and March 13, 1939: 8).

12. Entries under B are taken from U.S. Arms Control and Disarmament Agency (1971) (Washington: U.S. Government Printing Office, 1972). Entries on Military expenditures under A have been computed from the Cuban Economic Research Project (1965: 455, 461, 621), for the pre-revolutionary period; and for the revolutionary period from Junta Central de Planificación (1966: 13); and "Economic Policies and Growth," Mesa Lago (1971: 319, 331); Granma Weekly Review, August 6, 1972, p. 4. Entries on military personnel under C are taken from Reyes (1966: 23, 27-28) for the 1950s; and from Granma Weekly Review (December 12, 1971: 6)for 1963; Blutstein (et al.) (1971: 439) for 1969; and Institute for Strategic Studies (1970: 76), for 1970.

13. Taylor and Hudson (1972): 110-111).

14. Reyes (1966: 24).

15. Thomas (1971: 1024-1025, 1042).

16. Thomas (1971: 961-963, 1044).

17. Reyes (1966: 24).

18. Castro, R. (1967: 11); Granma Weekly Review (June 13, 1971: 2-3) and (December 12, 1971: 6).

19. Castro, R. (1973: 28).

20. Verde olivo, 4, 47 (November 24, 1963: 19).

21. Verde olivo, 4, 47 (November 24, 1963: 19-20, 52; and "El proyecto de ley del servicio militar obligatorio," Cuba socialista, 3, 28 (December, 1963: 85-87).

22. Granma (April 14, 1966: 8).

23. Granma (April 14, 1966: 8) and (March 14, 1966: 4); Verde olivo, 7, 43 (October 30, 1966:14-15 supplement) 8,11 (March 19, 1967: 34-38); 8,12 (March 26,1967: 27-30); 8,18 (May 7, 1967: 19-21); 8, 19 (May 14, 1967: 36-39); see also Yglesias (1968: 274-302).

24. Verde olivo, 4, 47 (November 24, 1963: 10-11); 4, 4 (January 27, 1963: 52-53); 11, 28 (July 12, 1970: 5); Granma (March 5, 1966: 8).

25. Granma Weekly Review (July 18, 1971: 9). The range of military participation has been computed by using the data on the size of the armed forces in Table I for 1969 and 1970 for the 1968-71 period in Table II.

26. Castro, F. (1967: 6-7); Vascos (1968: 6-7); Verde olivo 10, 45 (November 9, 1969: 7-9, 62); 11, 4 (January 25, 1970: 32); "Algunas tareas cumplidas por las FAR en 1970," in Verde olivo, 11, 52 (December 27, 1970); Dumont (1970: 417-420); and Karol (1970: 444-450, 534-544).

27. Política internacional, 4, 16 (Fourth quarter, 1966: 214-215).

28. Castro, R. (1967: 22); Granma Weekly Review (January 7, 1968: 3).

29. See, for example, Hanning (1967).

30. Kolkowicz (1967: 36-79, 309-321).

31. Gittings (1967: 29-32, 176-201); Joffe (1965: 80-87).

32. Karol (1970); Dumont (1970); and Suárez (1972: 12, 19-20).

33. Domínguez and Mitchell (1972: 4-6).

34. Verde olivo, 4, 7 (February 17, 1963: 6-7).

35. Causse Pérez (1965); Castro, R. (1966); Verde olivo, 4, 44 (November 2, 1963: 35-41); 4, 50 (December 15, 1963: 3, 12); 4, 51 (December 22, 1963: 3-10, 58-59, 66).

36. Yasells (1967: 11).

37. Verde olivo, 7, 52 (December 13, 1966: 4); 8, 51 (December 24, 1967: 12); 11, 40 (October 4, 1970: 8, 10); Granma (March 1, 1966: 4); Bohemia, 65, 31 (August 3, 1973: 28).

38. Garthoff, (1968: 247, 253).

39. Kolkowicz (1967).

40. For a fascinating discussion of this behavior, see Colton (1974).

41. Quoted in Gutierrez (1968: 11).

42. Kolkowicz (1967: 74).

43. Aguilar (1972: 187-188).

44. Suárez Nuñez (1963: 64, 91-92).

45. Computed from Politica Internacional, 6, 22-24 (Second half, 1968: 93); Granma Weekly Review (March 16, 1969: 7, and August 31, 1969: 1); Verde olivo, 11, 34 (August 23, 1970: 8); Bohemia, 65, 31 (August 3, 1973: 27).

46. Verde olivo, 9, 17 (April 28, 1968: 5-6); 8, 19 (May 14, 1967: 7); 8, 20 (May 21, 1967: 18); Granma Weekly Review (July 20, 1969: 10).

47. Causse Pérez (1965: 54-55); Granma Weekly Review (January 10, 1971: 10-11, and January 24, 1971: 10-11); Granma Weekly Review (March 5, 1966: 8).

48. Castro (1966: 56-57); Verde olivo 10, 2 (January 12, 1969: 29); 11, 40 (October 4, 1970: 8-9).

49. George (1967: 26-55); Janowitz, "Social Cohesion under Prolonged Stress," and Little, "Buddy Relations and Combat Performance," in Janowitz [ed.] (1964).

50. Granma Weekly Review (May 14, 1967: 11); Bridgham (1973); Joffe (1973).

51. Granma (May 20, 1966: 5); Yassells (1967); "Sección política de la Marina de Guerra Revolucionaria," Verde olivo 9, 2 (January 14, 1968); "Primera asamblea de balance del Partido Comunista de Cuba en el cuerpo blindado," Verde olivo 9, 7 (February 18, 1968); Gutierrez (1968); "Asamblea de balance del partido en el Ejército de Oriente," Verde olivo 10, 5 (February 2, 1969); "Balance del partido en el Cuerpo Ejército de Camagüey," Verde olivo 10, 42 (October 19, 1969); "Segunda asamblea de balance del Partido Comunista de Cuba en una unidad en Matanzas," Verde olivo 10, 42 (November 2, 1969); "Segunda asamblea de balance del partido en el Ejército del Centro," Verde olivo 10, 44 (November 2, 1969); "Segunda asamblea de balance del Partido Comunista de Cuba en el Estado Mayor General," Verde olivo 10, 49 (December 14, 1969); "Segunda reunion del partido en las Fuerzas Armadas Reudicionarias," Verde olivo 11, 40 (October 4, 1970); "Primera asamblea de balance del partido," Verde olivo 8, 51 (December 24, 1967).

52. Méndez (1964).

53. Klein (1962: 66); Joffe (1973: 457); computations based on China News Summary 483 (September 6, 1973). Donaldson (1972: 394); and a biographical file on Cuban leaders kept by the author.

54. Colton (1974).

55. The following comments on China are based mainly on Joffe (1965: 57-72); Gittings (1967: chapters 5, 8, 11, 12); Bridgeham and Joffe (July-September, 1973); Nelson (1972); Domes (1970).

56. Karol (1970: 394-395); Benedetti (1972: 520-524); Casal (1972: 458-464).

57. Domínguez (1971); and Silverman [ed], (1971).

58. Granma, July 24, 1968: 1, makes reference to courses taken by Political Bureau members, Comandantes Castro, R., Valle, and Valdes.

59. Dominquez and Mitchell (1972).

THE STUDY OF CHINESE MILITARY POLITICS: TOWARD A FRAMEWORK FOR ANALYSIS

Jonathan D. Pollack

Introduction

Few recent changes in the study of contemporary China have been more pronounced than the sudden, and still growing, interest in the role and behavior of the People's Liberation Army (PLA) within the Chinese political system. While ten years ago only a handful of scholars were working in this area, the current situation and the outlook for the immediate future is for a substantial outpouring of research. The recent appearance of William Whitson's long-awaited history of the Chinese high command (Whitson and Huang, 1973), ongoing analysis by scholars in Europe, Asia and the United States, and an anticipated flood of doctoral dissertations within the next few years all suggest that the PLA has moved to center stage in thinking and writing on contemporary China.

Unquestionably, the principal factor explaining this increased interest was the greatly expanded political participation of the PLA and its leaders in Chinese domestic politics during the 1960s, eventually culminating in direct intervention to restore order and help reconstitute the structure of power during the Cultural Revolution of 1966-69. These developments catapulted China's military elite into a focal and possibly dominant policy-making position, a trend apparently reversed by the high-level military purge of 1971 and more recent leadership changes. Specific political events, therefore, rather than an inherent interest in the subject matter, explains the attention given to the PLA over the past decade.

This circumstance also helps account for the most conspicuous inadequacy in this body of literature: its almost total lack of analytical context. The novelty of the topic, coupled with an intense interest in explaining sudden changes—and explaining away prior formulations—gives much of the published research a tentative, unfinished quality frequently not reflected in the certainty espoused by its authors. There are, to be sure, a large number of accounts which provide adequate descriptions of events and issues as they have developed, particularly for the political concerns of the 1960s. But this pursuit of instant analysis has produced a prevailing norm of hyperfactualism, often supplemented by what Stanley Hoffmann in another context has acidly termed *"ex post facto* omniscience." Not unlike the circumstances of the Cultural Revolution itself, today's verities and certainties become tomorrow's foolish thoughts and discarded assumptions. Thus, in spite of a considerable growth in interest, researchers do not seem much closer today to an explicit understanding of the conditions and circumstances (beyond the specific, situational factors) which seem likely to affect the prospects for and dimensions of future military participation in Chinese politics.

More generally, the dominant research tasks of recent years have been ones of description and topicality rather than synthesis and criticism. There has been no attempt thus far to evaluate this growing literature—whether to summarize its findings, to assess its overall quality, or to consider its possible relevance to an audience wider than the limited number of individuals who study contemporary China. This essay will hopefully help fill such a gap. Indeed the dimensions of Chinese military policy identified in this paper are not the product of any scholarly consensus, but rather represent an attempt to impose a degree of order on an otherwise unstructured body of literature. This essay proposes a new tentative framework for analysis which might be used to focus and guide future work.

Therefore there will be several recurring major questions. What topics have received the most attention? Does the research to date suggest agreement among scholars on any key questions? How and to what extent have issues of more comparative concern been addressed? What conceptual and methodological tools have been employed? And, does the research of recent years suggest that students of the Chinese military will avoid talking only to themselves?

Two principal conclusions emerge from this survey. First, the major trends discernible in published studies indicate a number of conceptual and methodological deficiencies specific to the research itself. Second, there is an almost total isolation from work in related areas which are highly relevant to the field's concerns. In the concluding section some further research possibilities will be proposed that might help overcome these difficulties. First, however, the principal findings of recent research will be considered.

Military Participation in Chinese Politics

The virtually complete neglect of the PLA as an actor within the political process until the events of the 1960s reflected a belief that in China's post-1949 institutional structure, the Army mattered little in terms of power and policy-making. Military leaders had, of course, played an active role in the transitional administrative framework of 1949-54, when decision-making was shared on a regional basis by party, governmental, and military elites. Yet once these structures were dissolved, the overt political role of the military receded greatly. Only in recent years have scholars acknowledged the multiple responsibilities assumed by the PLA, if on a discontinuous basis, since the earliest years of Communist rule.[1] Three dimensions of military participation in politics have been particularly important: (1) the PLA's behavior as a political elite and its relationship to other principal actors (a relevant issue only since the early 1960s); (2) the resource and technological demands of the military sector and its impact on the Chinese economy as a whole; and (3) the economic and administrative responsibilities assumed by the Army in Chinese society.

THE PLA AS A POLITICAL ACTOR

The principal issues dominating recent scholarship have been the evolving powers, political orientation and status of the Army vis-a-vis other major elites, in particular its entanglement in the events and aftermath of the Cultural Revolution. To some analysts, this deepening involvement in domestic politics was the logical outgrowth of policies initiated by Party Chairman Mao Tse-tung in the early and mid-1960s. At that time, Mao had begun to question the political reliability and ideological rectitude of leadership within the Chinese Communist Party (CCP), as well as sense his growing isolation within the policy process. Mao—apparently in need of an institution to compete with Party organizations and in order to reestablish his own political beliefs and preferences—turned increasingly to the PLA and more particularly the Minister of National Defense, Lin Piao (Solomon, 1971: 436-448). Since assuming this position in the fall of 1959, Lin had been extremely active in pursuing organizational reforms within the PLA, both to resurrect its efficiency and political reliability (at the time severely undermined), and to re-emphasize its revolutionary traditions, seemingly at the expense of more professional military considerations.

The success of Lin's efforts, most scholars agree, was instrumental in convincing Mao to turn to the PLA. Political control systems modelled on those resurrected in Army units were initiated in both party and governmental hierarchies, and campaigns for emulation of the PLA were encouraged throughout Chinese society (Powell, 1965). Lin and other military leaders, especially those within the Army's General Political Department, also gave great emphasis to political and ideological incentives, both in military work and in broader political and economic developments, as well as stressing the continued relevance of Mao's writings on guerrilla warfare. When the Cultural Revolution was formally initiated in August, 1966, Mao had become closely identified with the Army leadership, and they, with him. The PLA's principal journal, *Chieh-fang-chun Pao, (Liberation Army Daily),* for example, had by this time become a far more accurate gauge of Mao's preferences and policy intentions than its CCP equivalent, *Jen-min Jih-pao (People's News).* The consensus among scholars, however, is that the Army leadership did not actively seek the political power which befell it. Rather, it appears that Mao's attempt to establish a rival to the CCP had led Lin and his associates— perhaps at first reluctantly but later with greater enthusiasm—to enter the national political arena for the first time since the Communist accession to power (Powell, 1968b; Joffe, 1971).

The events of the Cultural Revolution and details of the PLA's behavior and impact are far too complex to be discussed here at any length;[2] instead, some of the major trends will be briefly discussed. In retrospect, perhaps no consequence of the Cultural Revolution proved as significant as the Army's activation as a major political force. Mao's deeply-held beliefs concerning civilian control of the military, first undermined by his own efforts to supplant the CCP as a leadership elite, were severely tested and threatened in the actual course of political conflict. No doubt his increasing reliance on military support, particularly during the latter half of 1967 and into 1968, was the product more of circumstances than of design. But the practical effect was the same, with individual PLA leaders and military units at several levels assuming increasingly powerful, if somewhat ambiguous and highly unstable, political roles. Military organizations, unlike the CCP, were largely insulated from attack and involvement during the initial phases of the Cultural Revolution. In subsequent periods, however, PLA units were ordered to intervene on behalf of the Cultural Revolution Left (the Red Guards and associated groups), and later still charged with protecting industrial plants, maintaining order amongst rival Red Guard factions, and in some cases disarming and forcibly suppressing rebel groups. These activities produced verbal attacks on some PLA leaders, in particular the regional military commanders frequently assigned these responsibilities. In addition, some national level leaders were purged, allegedly for their reluctance to commit the PLA to such widespread political involvement; one disgraced veteran commander, Ho Lung, was even accused of conspiring with several purged Party officials to overthrow Mao.

However, the effect of these attacks on the PLA as a whole, were minimal. Individual military leaders and regular army units were given progressively greater responsibilities for maintaining order and reviving political and economic administration at the local level, first through military control committees and later through top-heavy military representation on the Revolutionary Committees, the new provincial governing bodies organized primarily during the first half of 1968 (Domes, 1970). Further, the proportion of military members on the provincial party committees reconstituted later was even higher. Lin had also emerged as Mao's closest political associate and, eventually, constitutionally-designated successor. By the time of the CCP's Ninth National Congress in April, 1969, the PLA seemed firmly entrenched both in Peking and the provinces as the dominant political force, with military representation on the new Central Committee at an all-time high of 65 percent, two-thirds of whom were professionally-oriented commanders. Thus, while the declared intent of the Cultural Revolution may have been to destabilize and revamp existing political structures, events and circumstances increasingly compelled the central leadership to rely on a conservative ground force military elite—individuals intent on restoring a semblance of stability and order in the areas affected by political strife.

Equally important, it is unlikely that these military leaders were favorably disposed to the uneven and erratic political and internal security responsibilities they had been ordered to assume. Indeed, on one occasion, Ch'en Tsai-tao, Commander of the Wuhan Military Region, felt sufficiently exercised by orders from the central elite that he forcibly detained (quite possibly, for their own protection) two major emmissaries from Peking and sided with local factions opposed to the Peking-backed Red Guard units. On this occasion, the airlifting of PLA personnel and a show of force by naval units, as well as the personal intervention of Premier Chou En-lai, proved necessary to remove the recalcitrant commander. Yet his fellow regional officers, apparently convinced that Ch'en had transgressed the boundary between indirect dissent and open defiance, did not rally to his defense.[3] Most expressions of disatisfaction seem indeed to have been covert rather than overt—for example, circumventing or freely interpreting policy edicts emanating from the top leadership, intervening in most circumstances on behalf of the more status-quo political and economic forces in the provinces, and probably voicing private displeasure over the activities of military men in Peking more inclined to a leftist posture. It is probable, for example, that the large-scale purge during 1967 of the PLA's General Political Department was prompted at least partly by the anxiety of regional commanders.

This is not to suggest, as some analysts have hinted rather darkly, that China in 1969 was moving into a period of indirect military rule or even incipient warlordism. Detailed research instead suggests that while regionalism may have been of considerable importance in analyzing intra-military politics, it could not adequately explain military interactions with other political actors—in particular the dominant coalition in Peking, regardless of its political coloration. As one careful study has shown (Nelson, 1972a), the main ground force units were and are responsive only to orders from Peking, not from the military regions or provincial military districts. And, while a conscious attempt was made to keep these troops apart from the factional strife of local-level politics (no doubt because of their primary concern with national defense), the political leadership in Peking did not hesitate to introduce them when circumstances seemed overly threatening in the fall of 1967. Moreover, there is no evidence that these units or their commanders—many of whom became entrenched in post-Cultural Revolution political and economic administration—were at all disloyal to the central governing elite.

Events since 1969 have also demonstrated that civilian control over military leaders and military units, while momentarily in doubt during some of the Cultural Revolution's darker days, remains very much in effect. In spite of the autonomy and localist tendencies attributed to the regional commanders, their loyalty to the political center did not waver in the 1971 purge of Lin Piao and a large number of his military associates; they may even have provided vital support for Mao Tse-tung at that time (Bridgham, 1973; Joffe, 1973). Nor did their support constrain the central leadership from eventually moving against these individuals, as well: in January, 1974, a whole-sale shift of the regional leaders, some of them entrenched in specific locales for 20 years or more, was executed without apparent dissent (Durdin, 1974). And, while numerous factors might explain the death and political disgrace of Lin Piao, the central issues seem to have been Mao's determination to rebuild Party structures decimated during the Cultural Revolution and his apparent intent to reduce severely the political role of the PLA (Bridgham, 1973; Lelyveld, 1974). Military membership on the new Central Committee named at the 10th Party Congress of August, 1973, for example, was cut from 65 percent to 31 percent, of whom almost half were working in national-level offices in Peking, approximately twice the previous portion.[4] Thus the apparent intent of those currently dominant in Peking is a considerably reduced political role for the military in future years, with an emphasis on a "return to the barracks" orientation (Robinson, 1973).[5]

This review of the Army's experiences during the 1960s underscores the novelty of the PLA's political responsibilities in terms of earlier behavior. As virtually all researchers imply, the most appropriate mode of analysis for these events is that of high politics, a mode which ignores or minimizes the influence of variables less situationally defined. However, this approach seems unduly restrictive and oversimplified in view of some of the PLA's broader and less strictly political involvements. Several of these involvements will now be discussed.

THE ECONOMIC CONTEXT OF MILITARY POLICY-MAKING

As a large military organization, the Chinese Army requires considerable resources for which it must compete with rival economic needs and interests. Functioning within a command economy where economic scarcity has been a given for 25 years, its claim to resources is subject to economic as well as political fluctuations. Moreover, the scientific and technological demands of modern weapon systems necessarily create special manpower and resource requirements which must be justified to economic planners and political decision-makers.

The lack of adequate data (China has not issued any statistical series since 1959) has unfortunately limited research on patterns of defense spending. The available figures for the 1950s, when combined with cruder derived estimates for the 1960s, nevertheless provide some insights. Clearly, a major objective in economic policy-making during the initial decade was to reduce progressively the proportion of resources allocated to defense, with corresponding increases in revenues earmarked for economic development, welfare allocations, and other categories. At the time of the Korean War, military outlays claimed more than 40 percent of the Chinese budget. By the end of the 1950s, this percentage had been reduced to 12 percent (Godaire, 1968: 157).[6]

Several mehods were employed to achieve this reduction. After the signing of the Korean armstice in 1953, a major demobilization of PLA manpower was begun, with a simultaneous effort to steer this labor pool toward more productive economic tasks. More importantly, Soviet economic assistance—in modern military hardware, heavy industrial goods, technological inputs, and whole factories—provided a major stimulus both for impressive industrial performance in China during the 1950s and for the beginnings of a modern military capability (Cheng, 1964; Eckstein, 1966: 135-182; Gittings, 1967: 132-152). Thus, although the absolute level of military expenditure remained virtually constant during this period, China was able to enhance its military power considerably without hampering heavy industrial expansion or more general economic rehabilitation and growth.

Growing Sino-Soviet friction during the late 1950s, however, substantially undermined this economic strategy. The withdrawal of Soviet technicians and economic advisors in 1960, and the virtual cessation of military aid at the same time, coupled with a Chinese decision in 1958 to develop an independent military capability, necessitated considerable redirection in both economic planning and military acquisitions. In addition, a severe decline in economic performance in the early 1960s produced a major retrenchment in Chinese industrial investment. The burgeoning advanced weapons program, however, remained among the few items of highest priority (Ashbrook, 1972: 24). As a result, foreign trade calculations were increasingly influenced by technological needs in national defense and heavy industry, with Japan and Western Europe becoming the principal suppliers (Usack and Batsavage, 1972). In spite of these difficulties and setbacks, China's defense industries had by the late 1960s scored impressive gains in vital areas, particularly in the nuclear weaponry program, in the indigenous production of jet fighters, and in a variety of conventional weapon programs (Cheng, 1971). That Chinese policy-makers regarded these defense concerns as critical also seems clear in light of a sustained (if not entirely successful) effort to insulate scientific and defense research personnel from the events of the Cultural Revolution.

Yet, however vital defense concerns might have been, the extraordinary demands placed upon available resources probably constituted a highly divisive issue, both in intra-military budgetary politics and in economic policy-making as a whole (Halperin and Perkins, 1965: 29-47; Barrett, 1967; Hsieh, 1970; Horner, 1972). For example, P'eng Teh-huai, China's first Minister of National Defense, was dismissed in 1959 when defense spending as a percentage of state expenditures was at an all-time low. He had been personally associated with attempts to reduce the military budget during

the mid-1950s (Hsieh, 1962), but at the time of his political eclipse
had become a severe critic of Mao's economic policies (Union Research Institute, 1968). Inferential evidence thus suggests he may
have been vulnerable to criticism both from military clients and from
Party spokesmen. The expenses incurred in the military modernization program of the early and mid-1960s, however, expanded the
military budget to a point where it is now estimated to consume
10 percent of China's annual gross national product (Ashbrook,
1972: 45). The consequences of these resource demands have also
become more apparent now that China's advanced weaponry program
has begun to move from prototype development into serial production of specific defense items.[7] Unquestionably, China's defense
doctrine and strategic policy choices will continue to be influenced
by domestic economic and technological considerations (Whitson,
1972a).

Given these assumptions, resource considerations would also
affect what otherwise would be treated as strictly political concerns.
This seems likely in light of several anomalies of the PLA's involvement in domestic politics during the 1960s. Lin Piao's vigorous
repoliticization of the Chinese Army, for example, took place while
considerable efforts were being made in both nuclear development
and the upgrading of Chinese conventional defense capabilities.
The simultaneous presence of these decidedly contradictory tendencies indicates that as Minister of Defense, Lin had to balance highly
divergent intra-military preferences. The more professionally-
oriented commanders, for instance, may not have strenuously ob-
jected to repoliticization within some sectors of the PLA so long as
they were not subject to similar pressures and were faring well in the
military budget (Joffe, 1971: 366-369; Gillespie and Sims, 1972:
200; Harding, 1972). Similarly, the Air Force, while the most elitist
and professionally-oriented of the military services, contains some
of the most staunchly Maoist officers within the PLA, no doubt due
partly to its exceptional dependence on leaders in Peking for military
hardware and supplies. Overly strict dichotomies in categories of
analysis (for example, posing military disputes as ones between professional and political considerations) tend to ignore very real economic considerations which apparently affect the stance of different
leaders on important issues.

ARMY AND SOCIETY

China's armed forces, as many observers have noted, are distinguished by their regular involvement in a wide variety of social and

economic tasks. While there is considerable precedent in the non-
military responsibilities of military elites in other modernizing systems
(Janowitz, 1964: 75-106), the sustained nature of this participation in
Chinese society seems particularly pronounced. The reasons for this
involvement derive from several factors—administrative and economic
necessities, organizational traditions, and quite possibly intra-military
and Party-Army politics. At an administrative level, it is apparent that
military personnel have demonstrated political reliability and leadership abilities superior to those of many civilians, suggesting their considerable value for production tasks and for demanding work assignments. The PLA Production and Construction Corps, for example, has
been deployed to politically sensitive areas since the regime's earliest
years, most notably in Sinkiang. During the mid-1950s, when the
PLA reduced manpower by several million, the demobilized veterans
became Party members in large numbers and emerged as a key source
of political leadership at the local level (Schurmann, 1968: 135).
Efforts at professionalization and regularization for those remaining
within the PLA, however, greatly reduced the military role in social
and economic tasks. Emphasis on these assignments has varied considerably since that time, with major emphasis coming in 1958-59
and again in the mid-1960s when the PLA became a model for civilian
society as a whole (Joffe, 1965). When Cultural Revolution activities
threatened to disrupt agricultural and industrial production, a substantial military intervention again resulted (Powell, 1971).

The degree to which this involvement in essentially civilian
tasks became an issue of substantial contention among the PLA
leadership remains somewhat unclear, although some evidence suggests that it is still divisive. Apparently many of the more politically
inclined in the high command still view these non-military tasks as
a basic means of assuring and maintaining close links between the
army and society, a relationship carefully nurtured in two decades of
revolutionary experiences (Gittings, 1967: 176-201). The periodic
fluctuations in the Army's assigned tasks suggests that neither Party
nor Army policy-makers have been able to conclusively resolve this
issue. Institutional considerations also indicate that a final decision
for or against such involvement is unlikely to emerge. On most
occasions, only lower-level PLA units (the militia, garrison and public
security units, and the production and construction corps), have been
assigned responsibility in the civilian area (Nelson, 1972b). These
sectors have always fared worst in terms of career mobility, intra-
organizational status and the quantity and quality of military equipment. Thus the alleged usual complaint voiced by military com-

manders (specifically, that time spent on civilian productive tasks represents a net loss for more important military responsibilities, such as national defense training) may be somewhat overstated.

In the context of both intra-military politics and Party-Army relations, therefore, this issue may be more manipulative than real. This conclusion may also pertain to the focus of militia activity, the importance of which has also varied considerably over time. No doubt the emphasis given domestic political mobilization and militia training has been affected by the degree of perceived external threat (Gittings, 1967: 74-98, 202-224; Griffith, 1967: 265-278). But there is evidence that very few of those serving have been assigned genuine defense tasks, given military training, or issued weapons. Instead, militia members have provided a readily available labor pool with very close ties to local leadership, both military and political. Perhaps more importantly, the ability of Party personnel to affect militia policy represents a significant lever by which the non-military leadership apparently attempts to influence decision-making in the PLA. Further research into this question could be expected to clarify its precise meaning and consequences.

The PLA and Foreign Policy

As noted in the previous section, military organizations in China have been and remain closely wedded to a domestic political and social context. National security issues, however, have also been major concerns since the earliest years of the People's Republic. The East Asian region has ranked among the most volatile of international sub-systems since World War II, and Chinese military power, whether by proxy or by direct involvement of Peking's armed forces, has been closely linked to much of this international conflict. The considerable enhancement of PLA military capabilities in recent years has further solidified China's role as a major regional power. Thus analysis of past PRC strategic calculations and military performance, as well as tentative projections in both these areas, assumes considerable importance.

CAPABILITIES AND STRATEGIC DOCTRINE

Of the major themes stressed in discussions of China's national defense orientation, principal emphasis has been on China's limitations as a military actor. In purely strategic terms, China's leaders have had to acknowledge their clear inferiority and vulnerability, first in relation to the United States and more recently vis-a-vis the Soviet Union. Whatever pretensions the military high command may have had of assuming a more global strategic posture (and this argument itself seems highly doubtful), the numerous uncertainties and constraints affecting Chinese defense policy worked potently against them. From the first months of the regime, the military leadership has been confronted with a vastly superior and hostile military presence at or near China's borders, sometimes coming from more than one source. In one sense, this state of affairs has been comparable to the situation faced by the Chinese Communists in two decades of revolutionary struggle—that is, being confronted by an enemy with far superior capabilities. This necessitated reliance on tactics calculated to overcome one's own weaknesses and probe the vulnerabilities—psychological as much as military—of one's opponent. The close correspondence between Mao's writings on guerrilla warfare and Chinese perceptions of threat in recent international politics represents more than a paean to his strategic and tactical insights; in a real sense, the situations are comparable (Bobrow, 1964, 1969; Tsou and Halperin, 1965; Powell, 1968a; Huck, 1970; Boorman, 1972; Whitson and Huang, 1973: 458-497). However, the problems since 1949 involve more than strategic inferiority, as economic, technological, and organizational limitations have created even greater difficulties. Nor are these problems distinct; they require a coordinated and integrated solution. To a considerable extent, the need to resolve this entire set of issues has defined the context of China's strategic postures and weapons acquisition policies since the Korean War.

Of the numerous conflicts which have arisen in the course of this defense effort, none have proved more significant than those created by China's earlier close links to the Soviet Union. During the mid-1950s, substantial Soviet assistance enabled rapid progress toward modernization and professionalization within the armed forces. No matter how welcome this contribution, Soviet aid created patterns of organizational and economic dependence that Mao, as well as some military leaders, began to question. Should the PLA continue to rely on assurances of Soviet military assistance and the Soviet nuclear guarantee, thus enabling Chinese policy-makers to pay far closer attention to more general economic tasks? Or should the Chinese military risk short-term vulnerability and instead develop the economic and scientific base needed to create an autonomous network of defense industries, which would assure a defense capability free from Soviet interference? This "quick fix" vs. "long-term" dilemma has surfaced on several occasions since the mid-1950s; each time the commitment to an autonomous defense posture has been reaffirmed (Hsieh, 1962, 1970).[8] But there have been negative consequences of this decision: lengthy delays in acquiring a fully operational, modern military capability; a costly long-term resource commitment to the development of advanced weaponry; and perhaps most importantly, greatly heightened intra-organizational conflict (Joffe, 1965: 91-106; Bridgham, 1970: 215-220).

In articulating a defense posture with which to accompany these emerging capabilities, the Chinese have continued to stress their vulnerability vis-à-vis both the Soviet Union and the United States, thus providing a rationale for nuclear development. Despite having achieved at least a minimal operational capability by the early 1970s, there is still very little evidence of corresponding adjustments in strategic doctrine beyond the themes that have dominated since the early 1960s (Halperin, 1968a; Pollack, 1972).[9] Thus Chinese postures have tended to lag somewhat behind their military achievements, suggesting that current attitudes are substituting for a more explicitly transitional military strategy.

Available evidence on recent military developments and force deployments indicates that the predominant orientation in Chinese strategic planning remains regional security, with special concern for acquiring a retaliatory capability against Soviet cities. This is supported by recent deployments of both MRBM's and IRBM's at or near China's borders with the Soviet Union and the development of bomber-based delivery capabilities. A continued interest in a tactical nuclear capability should also not be ruled out (Hsieh, 1971). And, despite recent improvements in both naval and air capabilities, both primarily suggest an upgrading and sophistication of existing coastal and air defense systems, with only a very modest striking power beyond Chinese territorial limits (Beecher, 1972a).

Thus China's military orientation in the early 1970s represents a "restatement" of a highly defensive posture. This policy may have resulted as much from domestic considerations as from strategic analysis. Development of more broad-based, externally projectable military capabilities would no doubt be highly destabilizing in strategic terms, but the consequences for economic and organizational arrangements within China would be even more profound. This problem is illustrated by the recent easing of tension along the China coast and the enhanced possibility of conflict on the Soviet border, which have led to reduced air force allocations and an upgrading of conventional ground unit capabilities. The Chinese media have described this as a renewed preference for "steel" over "electronics," suggesting the close relationship between military postures and more basic economic and technological strategies. There have also been difficulties in implementing a program of military dispersal and decentralization. In spite of a declared intent to pursue such a policy as early as the mid-1950s, most Chinese heavy industrial and national defense production facilities remain highly concentrates, (Blaker, 1972).

In sum, as suggested earlier, calculations concerning the efficacy of Chinese national security measures must be judged in terms of the continuing interrelationship of strategic, economic, and organizational concerns. This seamless web of military policy is not easily subject to change, thereby suggesting a continued relevance for policy projections at least through the 1970s.

THE USE OF FORCE

China has deployed and used military force at or beyond its borders on ten separate occasions between 1950 and 1974.[10] Close analysis suggests that PLA troop deployments have almost always been in response to military crises deemed threatening to Chinese security. When these situations involved either the United States or Soviet Union, Chinese military behavior has been closely coordinated with diplomatic moves aimed at either deterring or limiting the particular conflict (Whiting, 1968; Robinson, 1972). Similar behavior was also evident during the Sino-Indian border dispute of 1962. More generally, the Chinese leadership has committed itself to the use of force only when Chinese actions could be carefully controlled, strictly limited to the security objectives of the particular case, and subject to ready reversal should circumstances warrant (Tsou, 1959; Hsieh, 1962, 1968b). There is no evidence that China's occasional resort to military power has been unduly reckless or provocative, although some might interpret the Chinese preference for pre-emptive attacks as such. There are two apparent reasons for this circumspect behavior. First, China's crisis performance seems the logical outgrowth of the military vulnerabilities discussed earlier. Second, the potential uncertainties in the response to Chinese-initiated moves, most especially in dealings with the superpowers, have constrained China's armed forces from pursuing actions that might threaten to enlarge conflict situations beyond the capacity or intent of the PRC to deal with them.

Despite this record, there has been a growing interest in whether or not Chinese commitments to the use of force have been the subject of elite conflict or debate. Since virtually all research on Chinese foreign policy has been geared to a national actor frame of reference, it is exceedingly difficult to offer any judgments on such speculations. More definite answers may be possible when studies on domestic-foreign policy linkages in Chinese crisis behavior are completed. To the extent that hypotheses or evidence have been offered, two principal interpretive strains have emerged. Elite conflict purportedly occurred when portions of the leadership questioned the wisdom or necessity of a specific involvement (with Korea, India and the Sino-Soviet border dispute the most likely possibilities), or when conflict situations became embroiled in bureaucratic divisions or alliance politics (the Quemoy episode of 1958 and the Vietnam escalation of 1965-66). To date, only the Vietnam case has been extensively considered on either basis in published research, no doubt due largely to the publicly-expressed differences between Lin Piao and the then Chief of Staff, Lo Jui-ch'ing.[11] Without a more substantial body of evidence or systematic testing of hypotheses, however, these ideas represent intriguing but unsubstantiated conjectures. Persuasive evidence of the impact of elite politics on foreign policy outcomes has yet to be assembled, and seems a likely task for future research.

Lines of Cleavage in the Military High Command

Implicit in much of the research discussed in the preceding pages is a concern with the sources of conflict and change in military policy-making. While this issue has not yet been pursued in systematic fashion, it is at least being discussed with increasing frequency. Of the interpretations and explanations attracting scholarly attention, four seem particularly suggestive. First is the notion of persistent conflict between revolutionary traditions and professional military values —what in "organizational labels" has been termed a debate between commissars and commanders. Second, some have argued that long-standing patterns of interpersonal and/or organizational affiliation can largely explain elite behavior during the past several decades. Third, there is some evidence, now only beginning to be explored, that an officer's political and professional orientation is strongly affected by the service sector with which he is affiliated. Finally, certain research findings suggest the importance of the institutional structure of the PLA itself. As one analyst has noted, however, these explanations usually appear in mixed rather than in pure form; thus it seems unlikely that an undiluted set of historical or contextual factors would govern elite behavior (Whitson, 1972b). Yet, to the extent that these models or hypotheses suggest divergent sources of explanation and rely on different types of evidence, they are worth closer consideration.

COMMISSAR VS. COMMANDER

The most frequent interpretation of within-military conflict concerns the values espoused by China's military elite under circumstances of organizational change (Joffe, 1964, 1965; Gittings, 1967; Whitson and Huang, 1973: 436-457). The debate centers on the legacy of the PLA's historical experiences and its relevance to China after 1949. Most analysts agree that the success of China's revolutionary armies, given the low status and negative connotations of military power in China's past, derived largely from the close social and economic bonds forged with the civilian population and the organizational responsiveness to Party edicts based on an extensive political control system (Johnson, 1962: 71-91, 123-155; George, 1967; Gittings, 1967: 99-118). This has also been Mao's personal conception of the organization and use of military power since the earliest years of the Red Army.[12] These values, however, have been severely undermined by the growth since 1949 of a professionalized military force isolated both physically and politically from Chinese society. The commander vs. commissar orientation has been further reinforced by highly distinct career channels, with little crossover except at the highest levels of military leadership. As in the Soviet Union, the salience of political concerns within the armed forces has waxed and waned with the degree of military professionalism espoused by Party and Army spokesmen. The degree of political control within the PLA, however, has not always corresponded to the extent of concern expressed over external military threats to China.

Several qualifications to this argument ought to be noted. It seems highly unlikely that these values have surfaced in as pure a form as some analysts imply. For example, there have been leadership purges in which political commissars were accused of maintaining an overly professional orientation. More importantly, the General Political Department's formal responsibilities include duties which involve major military tasks, such as assessing combat readiness, overseeing aspects of military research and development, and evaluating officer performance (Dick, 1972). Particularly during the 1950s, the resort to the PLA's historical experiences seems best explained as a primary means by which Party leaders have intervened in military affairs, thereby constraining the organizational autonomy of China's armed forces. Army commanders, for example, have voiced considerable resentment over the dual institutional structure and system of political accountability imposed upon them, in particular when they have interfered with the performance of military duties.[13]

As an overall issue of policy debate, however, numerous key questions have yet to be answered. More attention needs to be paid to the specific role of Mao Tse-tung within these conflicts. Many scholars assume that Mao has been a key actor in attempting to resurrect traditional Party concerns within the PLA. Yet, particularly when compared to issues such as education and agricultural policy, there are very few known instances since 1949 of Mao's active intervention in military affairs.[14] What should be closely considered is the frequent resort to Mao and his military theories as a symbolic device, as compared with concrete participation in this recurring debate. For this type of question, scholarship thus far has not provided much guidance.

INTERPERSONAL ASSOCIATIONS: FIELD ARMIES AND MILITARY GENERATIONS

There has been considerable effort in recent years to uncover networks of personal affiliation in the PLA which predict to subsequent political behavior (Whitson and Huang, 1973: 498-517). This research proceeds essentially on two assumptions. First, biographical data on China's current military leadership indicate that many officers have fought and worked together in specific units since the Army's earliest years. These relationships were more formally recognized in the designation of five Field Armies during the Chinese civil war, each with a separate command structure and, to a lesser extent, autonomous military responsibilities within a selected area of China. After the Korean War, these military units were returned to specific provinces and regions where they have generally remained since that time. Equally important, a considerable portion of each Field Army's leaders, rather than circulating from area to area, remained in one particular locale. Thus, at a minimum, these officers developed strong personal ties to provincial governing elites. The distribution of command positions in Peking and the thirteen military regions has led to further suggestions that one's Field Army designation provided the basis for informal political loyalties and formal division of spoils. This assumption seemed strengthened by evidence that certain military leaders (most notably, one-time Acting Chief of Staff Yang Ch'eng-wu and Lin Piao) attempted during the Cultural Revolution to aggrandize their own power positions by appointing former Army associates to key positions. Field Army affiliations can also to a certain extent explain post-Cultural Revolution provincial political assignments (Bennett, 1973). Thus, there is some reason to assume the existence and continued vitality of personalistic ties within Chinese military politics.

A related argument has concerned the period and circumstances of entry into the Chinese Army (Whitson and Huang, 1973: 416-435). According to William Whitson, China's military leadership can be divided into eleven military generations, each with distinct "organizational memories" based on differences in combat experiences, exposure to varying types of military thinking, and the historical circumstances of the period involved. As recently as 1967, 96 percent of the top 450 positions in the PLA were filled by military leaders who had held commands as early as or before 1936. Thus, given the extraordinarily low rate of leadership turnover, these formative experiences remain central elements in defining subsequent perspectives on a host of key issues.

Neither of these arguments, of course, is unique to the Chinese case (Janowitz, 1960: 257-302). Their persuasiveness, however, has been severely undermined by more extensive evidence, some inherent conceptual limitations, and concrete political behavior. A recent critique of the Field Army hypothesis has raised serious questions about credibility (Parish, 1973). Whitson's finding of a more or less equal division of spoils in military commands, for example, which he interprets as a conscious attempt to maintain a balance of power among the five Field Armies, can more easily be attributed to random behavior, and thus constitutes an artifact of his data. There are also higher percentages of the leadership showing inter-regional mobility than were originally calculated.[15] In addition, there is as much or more evidence contradicting the argument of long-standing personal loyalties as there is to support it. And, most importantly, it has yet to be demonstrated that Field Army affiliations have produced common views on major military issues which remain undiminished to the present day. Indeed, with the exception of some Cultural Revolution evidence, scholars know almost nothing about military elite behavior since 1949, let alone the distribution of attitudes and preferences within the high command.

The generational hypothesis seems somewhat more persuasive,

based both on elite socialization research more generally, and on the available evidence in the Chinese case. Yet here, too, significant problems exist. Undeniably, an officer's earliest professional experiences may critically affect his subsequent beliefs, but it seems equally likely that more recent events have exerted an equally great effect. The jarring nature of commanders' encounters with American military power during the Korean War has been carefully documented (George, 1967: 163-189); the destabilizing experiences of the Cultural Revolution may have had a similar effect. Socialization is an ongoing process affected greatly by factors such as one's specific organizational responsibilities and position within a bureaucratic hierarchy. Changes in military tasks and political circumstances also tend over time to diminish the relevance of personal ties and historical experiences. Therefore, other possible interpretations derived more from present-day organizational context must be considered, even if they remain little researched and inadequately understood.

SECTORAL DIFFERENCES

One interpretation only faintly visible in research to date is that stressing inter-service rivalries as a good predictor of policy preferences and budgetary allocations (Whiting, 1971; Whitson, 1972b, 1972c: 135-266). Given what is known about intra-military behavior in other political systems (Huntington, 1961), it seems reasonable to expect similar patterns in China, particularly as military needs move into more complex, sophisticated weapons systems which demand greater resource allocations. Evidence for this phenomenon, however, is scattered and only intermittently available. Thus, any attempts at analysis must rest heavily on inference and indirect evidence of rival strategic postures, variations in resource allocation, and differences in overt military behavior. It may not even prove possible to disaggregate policy preferences much beyond the level of what Franklyn Griffiths has termed competing "tendencies of elite articulation" (Griffiths, 1971). One dramatic example is the conflict, discussed earlier, between a "quick-fix" strategic posture aimed at rapid acquisition of modern air defense capabilities (associated primarily with the General Staff) and one stressing long-term economic growth which would eventually contribute to the acquisition of more diverse modern military systems (the prevailing Ministry of National Defense position) (Hsieh, 1962, 1968a; Harding and Gurtov, 1971).

Publicly available evidence on military capabilities offers further guidance on who wins and who loses in Chinese military budget politics.[16] The Chinese Air Force has reportedly been the primary recipient of advanced military hardware during the upgrading of PLA capabilities undertaken in the mid-1950s and again in the mid-1960s (Bueschel, 1968; Mogdis, 1972). The increasing salience in recent years of the Soviet threat, however, has shifted expenditures away from the Air Force and into the ground forces, now with key defense responsibilities along the Soviet border. Changes in strategic posture must thus be carefully considered for their possible impact on the internal distribution of military power. In the case of the Sino-Soviet border conflict, Chinese decision-makers have been sufficiently alarmed to devote a major portion of the current military modernization effort to weaponry and delivery systems intended to deter a Soviet attack or to confront an invading force with considerably enhanced fighting power. Thus the forces arrayed along the border now include a significant number of troops redeployed from other regions, most notably the coastal areas opposite Taiwan, where the probability of conflict has been reduced (Beecher, 1972b). The major commitment of regular ground force units has also displaced militia and paramilitary forces, who have moved to areas further inland, where alternative responsibilities for them must be found.

The extent to which such changes in unit deployments and weapons priorities have caused controversy among military elites is very difficult to determine. If allowances are made for the lead times involved in the acquisition or production of military hardware, and to a lesser extent the shifts of military units, the timing, circumstances and issues related to divergent military postures might be more accurately identified. Consideration to sectoral differences as a working assumption thereby provides an alternative frame of reference which should help explain variations in policy and their consequences. But definitive assessments must await more sustained media attention than has been evident thus far.

LEVELS OF MILITARY DECISION-MAKING

Events in China during the 1960s demonstrated the necessity for viewing PLA participation from the perspective of institutional structure. The Cultural Revolution afforded a rare opportunity to examine overt military elite behavior, with events indicating diffusion of power, variations in responsiveness and reliability, and intersecting institutional claims and prerogatives less apparent in earlier years (Domes, 1970; Gittings, 1970; Heinlein, 1972; Nelson, 1972a). As one study has shown (Gittings, 1967: 280-302), China's armed forces are imbedded in a highly complex system of organizational hierarchies further complicated by the parallel political control systems extending to the lowest levels of the PLA (George, 1967; Gittings, 1967: 306). Numerous questions thus emerge. Can lines of authority and patterns of communication be identified within and across these bureaucratic hierarchies? How substantial are the differences between the formulation and implementation of policy? At what levels are the conflicting pressures and responsibilities of military officials most evident? To what extent did the PLA's activation as a political force during the 1960s undermine or alter more formal lines of command and control?

At a systemic level, very little thought has been given to the Army's position and performance within the policy process as a whole. What are the PLA's resources as a political actor, and how is its influence brought to bear? Is the Army usually aligned with particular forces and interests and opposed by others? How great a role do military decision-makers play in the formulation of economic policy? A fair amount is known about the allocation of decision-making power in military affairs during the early 1960s (Powell, 1963; Gittings, 1967; 280-288); to what extent do these patterns still hold after the tumultuous events of the last decade? How secure is Party domination of the Military Affairs Committee (the most authoritative military policy-making body) after a period when CCP legitimacy and supremacy was severely undermined? Does the Ministry of National Defense in any sense constitute a rival institution? Questions of this sort, while not easily answered, comprise an essential research agenda requiring careful consideration. More substantial conclusions and projections about the distribution of power within the PLA and the Army's influence in Chinese politics as a whole are unlikely in the absence of such research.

Conclusion: Some Future Directions

The study of Chinese military affairs now commands the attention of a considerable number of specialists on contemporary China. As has been suggested throughout this paper, the results generated by this research effort have been mixed. While far more is known than a decade ago, major limitations and problems continue to undermine the value of what has actually been reported. Rather than dwell further on these weaknesses, it seems appropriate to consider some new directions researchers could take to compensate for these difficulties.

An inherent and inescapable problem is that of data-availability. Students of contemporary China, as with any society, are prisoners of their sources, but the circumstances in this case seem particularly trying. Analysts must depend very heavily on information that the Chinese government and its subordinate institutions choose to make public, not all of it useful to the concerns of contemporary scholarship. These materials can be supplemented by the uneven and unpredictable availability of sources not officially sanctioned by the regime, such as Cultural Revolution materials, internal documents secreted out of the Mainland, or the occasionally reliable accounts of those leaving the PRC. Relatively rich biographical materials can also be added to these sources, but the total array of evidence is not impressive, even when compared with the range of available materials on the Soviet military. Yet, few scholars have confronted these problems directly and considered carefully the kinds of analysis and research methods that might still prove appropriate or feasible. They have rather retreated into the huge volume of unprocessed documentation, thereby assuring that a conceptual and methodological barrenness will continue to plague work in this area.

What alternatives exist? Even with the problems created by the quantity and quality of evidence, more innovative research strategies would clearly prove helpful. One largely untapped possibility is the use of quantitative content analysis. Research on China necessarily depends heavily on mass media materials, and those who rely on such sources implicitly assume the general accuracy and less than total manipulatability of content. No doubt considerable problems are created by over-reliance on such an approach, but its discriminating usage has produced considerable insight into the expressed perceptions and preferences of Communist political elites (Lodge, 1969; Grow, 1973). Similarly, other types of quantitative analysis could be further developed as possible indicators of conscious policy choice, particularly economic data that shed light on the importance attributed to military needs (Eckstein, 1967). Greater attention to refugee interviewing, despite its numerous shortcomings and pitfalls, might also furnish insight into issues such as the PLA's role in Chinese society.

More important than methodological problems, however, is the almost total conceptual isolation from related fields of inquiry. Notwithstanding the considerable handicaps encountered in studying contemporary China, virtually no effort has been made to place post-1949 military attitudes and behavior in a broader theoretical context. Comparative concerns, then, currently matter little or not at all to

most of those studying the PLA. Only when researchers attempt to
extract generalizations from their own findings and communicate
with specialists on other political systems will this situation begin to
change. At least four issue-areas would permit significant and provocative comparison with the contemporary Chinese case; each will now
be briefly discussed.

The first basic requirement is simply to recognize the need for
comparison. In spite of a lingering assumption that China somehow
remains *sui generis,* the close correspondence between the themes
found in research on the PLA and the concerns raised in more general treatments of military behavior is quite striking (Janowitz, 1964;
Hopkins, 1966; Huntington, 1968: 172-263). Regardless of the data
problems, the relevant issues being addressed by each group are
simply too comparable not to be compared—for example, military
attitudes toward political participation, the professional ideology of
military elites, the internal organization of the military, the links of
military elites to civilian leadership, and the relationship between
domestic and foreign policy responsibilities. These issues constitute
the heart of any comparative effort, particularly insofar as the experiences of military elites in other new nations are considered.[17]
As comparative theoretical efforts pay very little attention to the
military role in Communist systems (the assumption apparently
being that Communist military elites lack sufficient autonomy to
be altogether interesting), some mutual awareness would also be
useful in this area. It is possible, of course, that Communist military elites represent a distinct subset which cannot be accomodated
within any existing framework, in which case comparisons strictly
among Communist systems are necessary. Whichever option seems
more appropriate, students of China will continue to lack even
minimal theoretical guidance unless the hypotheses and findings of
others are more closely consulted.

Among other possibilities, the experiences of the Soviet military
also provide a very rich source of ideas. To some extent, this is already evident in published research (Hsieh, 1962; Ford, 1964; Joffe,
1965; Garthoff, 1966; Gittings, 1967: 119-131, 158-175; Whitson
and Huang, 1973: 24-100). In spite of this work, far more could still
be done. Numerous issues in the history of the Soviet armed forces
are virtually identical with ones that the Chinese military elite has
had to confront—for example, the Party-Army relationship, the consequences of changing military technology and professionalization
for political control, the economic context of military affairs, and
the more general military role in foreign and domestic policy formula-

tion (Kolkowicz, 1967). Less fully understood is the considerable contribution of Soviet military thinking and organizational models to the qualitative changes occurring within the PLA during the mid- and late 1950s. Wholesale professionalization and regularization of China's armed forces occurred at the time of maximum economic and military cooperation between China and the Soviet Union, with the two issues being closely intertwined. The consequences of this organizational legacy are still evident, as the continuing if less direct influence of Soviet organizational doctrines within the PLA remains a highly divisive issue. As a case study in the cross-national diffusion of political ideas and institutional forms, Sino-Soviet military relations has seen far too little attention.

Perhaps no body of social science literature seems more likely to influence future work on military policy-making than recent research on organizational behavior. Approaches to the study of institutional change, the impact of environment on organizational behavior, role conflict within organizations, and patterns of organizational decision-making—all would allow fruitful new insights into Chinese military experiences both before and after 1949. Yet, here, as elsewhere, students of the PLA have not exhibited much interest, again reflecting the general unfamiliarity with (and resistance to) social science theorizing on the part of most China scholars. The availability of evidence appropriate to these and other organizational perspectives makes the creative synthesis of theory and data a more realistic and reasonable objective. Comparative insights could also be generated at this level of analysis.

The alien nature of work in comparative military policy, Soviet military experiences, and organization theory can to a certain extent explain why few students of the PLA have considered any of these alternative approaches. Each of these fields, in effect, is divorced from the training and background of a specialist in modern China studies. However, it is totally surprising that so few of these individuals have considered the conduct of the PLA even in light of China's past experiences with military power. As a number of recent historical studies have shown, the role of the military in China, particularly during the late 1800s and early 1900s, was closely associated with the efforts of newly-mobilized elites to confront the problems of imperialist encroachment, political and economic decay, and widespread societal disintegration. These and other problems demanded attention to modernization and economic transformation (in particular, its consequences for enhanced military power), political re-integration, and the mobilization of new human and material resources. Military elites

were among the most active and innovative of these modernizing
political elements. Thus, somewhat ironically, the literature on China
which seems most relevant to scholars concerned with the military
as agents of change, comes for the most part not from political scien-
tists or sociologists, but from social and military historians. Anyone
trying to find similar issues addressed in the context of post-1949
politics will be greatly disappointed.[18]

The lack of attention to these concerns, then, suggests that
despite all the writings of recent years, no firm sense now exists of
the personal commitments and professional implications involved in
the pursuit of the military occupation as a career in contemporary
China. Yet, the PLA elite, particularly those of the earliest military
generations, is itself not unaware of the historical connotations of
military power in China since the late 1800s.[19] Thus, the implicit
assumption of a *tabula rasa,* whether beginning with the Red Army's
historical experiences or with the onset of Communist rule, has
detached scholars from a central element in the personal and professional evolution of China's current military leaders. Instead, a somewhat bloodless quality prevails in the recent literature: while the
issues and events seem real, the individuals often do not. The total
neglect of this question surely constitutes one of the severest limitations in the works that have been discussed.

The past decade has seen a rush to compensate for the lack of
attention given to Chinese military affairs in earlier years. Thus it is
perhaps unrealistic to expect that this flurry of work would have
produced studies synthesizing the various historical, organizational,
and political influences on the behavior of China's military leadership. When the severe data problems and the lack of theoretical
sophistication are added to this consideration, it is even less surprising that this has remained a largely ill-defined and unsystematic
area of inquiry. The rooting out of much factual information, while
an obvious necessity, must now be supplanted by a firmer sense of
perspective and analysis if the chief issues underlying Chinese military politics in future years are to be adequately understood. For
the moment, scholars are ill-equipped to deal with these topics.
Thus the tasks for the immediate future seem clear: integrating
research work far more explicitly with studies of military elites in
other social and political contexts; linking recent findings with China's
own past; and moving away from the incidentals of events into a
larger interpretive context with which to analyze the perspectives and
behavior of China's current military leaders.

Notes

1. Consult and compare, for example, the successive editions of Franz Schurmann's pioneering analysis of China's economic and institutional evolution since 1949 (Schurmann, 1966, 1968). The original volume completely omitted the Army from its analytical scheme, an error which Schurmann candidly admits only became apparent with the advantage of hindsight. The second edition, however, includes the PLA as one of the three key institutions of state power within China.

2. For a representative sample of some of the principal interpretations to date, consult Domes (1968); Chien (1969); Joffe (1970); Powell (1970); Chang (1972); and Whitson and Huang (1973: 364-415). These publications also represent the basic sources for the analyses in this section.

3. Virtually all analysts agree that this series of events marked a major turning point in the Cultural Revolution, with a noticeable decline in the fortunes of more radical leaders in Peking. For the most thorough analysis to date, see Robinson (1971).

4. My thanks to William Parish for furnishing these preliminary figures on the composition of the 10th Central Committee.

5. These conclusions, however, rest heavily on the state of the political climate in Peking, particularly in view of the increasing emphasis being given to renewed radicalization in early 1974. Should events similar to those of 1966-68 transpire, the military leadership would most likely again prove responsive to the central political elite, even if overt intervention violates their apparent preference for limited political involvement.

6. Unfortunately, as several students of the Chinese economy have noted, it remains most unclear what specific items are included within this category. Most scholars still are willing to accept these statistics as useful working figures in spite of their limitations.

7. This issue, for example, surfaced in August, 1971, in a "steel vs. electronics" debate, with the former then judged to be more important. For further consideration, see the discussion on military capabilities in Part III and sectoral differences in Part IV.

8. The possibility that China's opting for an independent military posture may have derived more from necessity than choice should not be ruled out. Soviet military assistance had already declined considerably by the late 1950s, and further support (such as the nuclear assistance promised in an October, 1957 national defense agreement that according to Chinese statements was reneged upon in 1959) may have been contingent upon the Chinese leadership (or perhaps Mao personally) making what were considered unreasonable assurances of support for Soviet policies or to Soviet leaders, Conclusive judgments on this issue await more sustained consideration of the military dimension of Sino-Soviet alliance politics. For some earlier findings, see Hsieh (1964), Clemens (1968: 13-42), and Halperin (1968b).

9. During 1973, however, there was increased attention to arms control measures, provided they did not result from U.S. and/or Soviet sponsorship. In this context, China has declared its support for a treaty proposing a nuclear-free zone in Latin America. The treaty was formulated by a conference at which neither the United States nor the Soviet Union participated.

10. This compilation and analysis closely follows Whiting (1972), who mentions nine instances. I have added to his list the January, 1974 air and naval battles between China and South Vietnam for control of the Paracel Islands. While the conflict arena and military forces deployed were somewhat novel, the overall pattern of Chinese behavior seems generally consonant with prior actions.

11. For several accounts based exclusively on the analysis of esoteric communications, see Ra'anan (1968) and Zagoria (1968), neither of them very persuasive in light of subsequent research (Harding and Gurtov, 1971; Yahuda, 1972). The Harding and Gurtov study is particularly suggestive in terms of intra-organizational politics in the PLA contributing to this "foreign policy debate."

1960) *The Professional Soldier.* New York: The Free Press.

he Military in the Political Development of New Nations. Chicago: University
Press.

n Doorn [ed.] (1971) *On Military Intervention.* Rotterdam: Rotterdam
Press.

4) "The Conflict between Old and New in the Chinese Army." The China
London) 18 (April-June): 118-140.

*rty and Army—Professionalism and Political Control in the Chinese Officer
9-1964.* Cambridge: Harvard University East Asian Research Center.

The Chinese Army in the Cultural Revolution: The Politics of Intervention."
ene (Hong Kong) 8, 18 (December): 1-25.

The Chinese Army Under Lin Piao: Prelude to Political Intervention," pp.
J.M.H. Lindbeck (ed.) *China: Management of a Revolutionary Society.*
niversity of Washington Press.

The Chinese Army After the Cultural Revolution: The Effects of Inter-
The China Quarterly (London) 55 (July-Sept.): 450-477.

(1962) *Peasant Nationalism and Communist Power—The Emergence of
ary China, 1937-1945.* Stanford: Stanford University Press.

(1967) *The Soviet Military and the Communist Party.* Princeton: Princeton
Press.

974) "The Ghost of Lin Piao." New York Times Magazine (January 27):
26.

964) "China's Secret Military Papers: 'Continuities' and 'Revelations'." The
rterly (London) 18 (April-June) 68-78.

69) *Soviet Elite Attitudes Since Stalin.* Columbus, Ohio: Charles E. Merrill
Co.

nd A.D. Biderman (eds.) (1968) *Mass Behavior in Battle and Captivity—The
Soldier in the Korean War.* Chicago: University of Chicago Press.

972) "The Role of the Chinese Communist Air Force in the 1970's," pp. 253-
W. Whitson (ed.) *The Military and Political Power in China in the 1970s.* New
Washington: Praeger Publishers.

(1972) "Mainland China's Evolving Nuclear Deterrent." Bulletin of the
ientists 28, 1 (January): 28-35.

72a) "Military Forces in the Cultural Revolution." The China Quarterly
51 (July-Sept.): 444-474.

"Regional and Paramilitary Ground Forces," pp. 135-152 in W.W. Whitson
Military and Political Power in China in the 1970s. New York and Washington:
blishers.

1973) "Factions in Chinese Military Politics." The China Quarterly (London)
er-December): 667-699.

1972) "Chinese Attitudes Towards Nuclear Weapons, 1964-9." The China
(London) 50 (April-June): 244-271.

1955) *The Rise of Chinese Military Power, 1895-1912.* Princeton: Princeton
Press.

olitico-Military Relations in Communist China.* Washington: U.S. Department
xternal Research Staff (October).

Commissars in the Economy: Learn from the PLA Movement in China."
ey 5, 3 (March): 125-138.

"Maoist Military Doctrines." Asian Survey 8, 4 (April): 239-262.

"The Increasing Power of Lin Piao and the Party Soldiers, 1959-1966." The
rterly (London) 34 (April-June): 38-66.

The Party, the Government, and the Gun." Asian Survey, 10, 6 (June): 441-471.
Soldiers in the Chinese Economy." Asian Survey 11, 8 (August): 742-760.

12. Space does not allow us to discuss the highly controversial argument espoused by William Whitson to the effect that Maoist military conceptions have been anathema to most members of the Chinese high command since the Army's earliest years. As a large part of Whitson's thesis derives from extensive interviews with several key Party members purged during the 1930s who are avowedly hostile to Mao, his evidence must be regarded as somewhat suspect. Nevertheless, his argument is forcefully and extensively presented, and merits careful consideration. See Whitson and Huang (1973: 24-100, 436-457).

13. For a revealing account of this issue in the context of the Korean War, consult George (1967). For additional evidence on questions of organizational morale and effectiveness, see Lewis (1964), Cheng (1966), and Meyers and Biderman (1968). Unfortunately, insufficient time and space prevent us from considering these issues more fully.

14. Michel Oksenberg should be credited with this observation. Powell (1963) also notes that, on the basis of the available issues of the *Kung-tso T'ung-hsun (Bulletin of Activities)*, a secret PLA publication acquired by U.S. intelligence, Mao does not appear to be a regular participant in the formulation of military policy. For a translation of these documents, see Cheng (1966).

15. The sudden shift in January, 1974 of virtually all the regional commanders, allegedly when their power was never more secure, weakens this argument even more.

16. For a comprehensive statement of what was publicly known in late 1971 about China's emerging defense arsenal (with particular emphasis on the nuclear program), see Murphy (1972). Other major sources include the annual Department of Defense Posture Statements, compilations by the Institute for Strategic Studies (London), and occasional inspired press leaks.

17. See, for example, the essay by Henry Bienen and David Morrell in this volume. For studies of the experiences of military elites after political independence, consult Van Doorn (1969) and Janowitz and Van Doorn (1971).

18. Space limitations prevent us from addressing this issue more extensively. For some of the more import works on the role of military power in Chinese politics during the late 1800s and early 1900s, see Powell (1955), Gillin (1966), Sheridan (1966), Rawlinson (1967), Ch'en (1968), Hatano (1968), Wilbur (1968), Young (1968), Chi (1969), and Pye (1971). My thanks to Michel Oksenberg for suggesting the relevance of this literature and in noting the inattention to these historical issues in the analyses of more recent developments.

19. Consider, for example, the personal sketches of China's military leaders found in Whitson and Huang (1973). Many of these officers trained and fought in warlord armies and even participated in the Revolution of 1911. Personal experiences such as these unquestionably affected their subsequent perspectives on the uses of military power.

References

Ashbrook, A.G. (1972) "China: Economic Policy and Economic Results, 1949-1971,"
    pp. 3-51 in Joint Economic Committee, Congress of the United States *People's Republic
    of China: An Economic Assessment.* Washington: U.S. Government Printing Office.
Barrett, J.W. (1967) "What Price China's Bomb?" Military Review 47, 8 (August): 16-23.
Beecher, W. (1972a) "Improved Missile in China Reported." New York Times (February
    1): 1, 6.
———(1972b) "Shift in Strategy by Peking Seen." New York Times (July 25): 1, 14.
Bennett, G. (1973) "Military Regions and Provincial Party Secretaries: One Outcome of
    China's Cultural Revolution." The China Quarterly (London) 54 (April-June): 294-307.
Blaker, J.R. (1972) "The Production of Conventional Weapons," pp. 215-227 in W. W.
    Whitson (ed.) *The Military and Political Power in China in the 1970s.* New York and
    Washington: Praeger Publishers.

Bobrow, D.B. (1964) "Peking's Military Calculus." World Politics 16, 2 (January): 287-301.

———(1969) "Chinese Communist Response to Alternative U.S. Continental Defense Postures," pp. 151-213 in D.B. Bobrow (ed.) Weapons System Decisions. New York and Washington: Praeger Publishers.

Boorman, S.A. (1972) "Deception in Chinese Strategy," pp. 313-337 in W.W. Whitson (ed.) The Military and Political Power in China in the 1970s. New York and Washington: Praeger Publishers.

Bridgham, P. (1970) "Factionalism in the Central Committee," pp. 203-235 in J. W. Lewis (ed.) Party Leadership and Revolutionary Power in China. Cambridge: Cambridge University Press.

———(1973) "The Fall of Lin Piao." The China Quarterly (London) 55 (July-September): 427-449.

Bueschel, R. (1968) Chinese Communist Air Power. New York and Washington: Frederick A. Praeger.

Chang, P. (1972) "The Changing Patterns of Military Participation in Chinese Politics." Orbis, 16, 3 (Fall): 780-802.

Ch'en, J. (1968) "Defining Chinese Warlords and Their Factions." Bulletin of the School of Oriental and African Studies (London) 31, 3: 563-600.

Cheng, C. (1964) Economic Relations Between Peking and Moscow: 1949-63. New York: Frederick A. Praeger.

———(1971) The Machine-Building Industry in Communist China. Chicago and New York: Aldine-Atherton.

Cheng, J.C. [ed.] (1966) The Politics of the Chinese Red Army. Stanford: The Hoover Institution.

Chi, H. (1969) The Chinese Warlord System: 1916 to 1928. Washington: American University Center for Research in Social Systems.

Chien, Y. (1969) China's Fading Revolution—Army Dissent and Military Divisions, 1967-1968. Hong Kong: Center of Contemporary Chinese Studies.

Clemens, W.C. (1968) The Arms Race and Sino-Soviet Relations. Stanford: The Hoover Institution.

Dick, G.G. (1972) "The General Political Department," pp. 171-183 in W.W. Whitson (ed.) The Military and Political Power in China in the 1970s. New York and Washington: Praeger Publishers.

Domes, J. (1968) "The Cultural Revolution and the Army." Asian Survey 8, 5 (May): 349-363.

———(1970) "The Role of the Military in the Formation of Revolutionary Committees." The China Quarterly (London) 44 (October-December): 112-145.

Durdin, T. (1974) "Dramatic Military Shifts in China." New York Times (January 4): 3.

Eckstein, A. (1966) Communist China's Economic Growth and Foreign Trade. New York: McGraw-Hill Book Co.

———(1967) "Arms Control and the Vulnerability of Communist China's Economy to External Inducements," pp. 86-105 in E. Benoit (ed.) Disarmament and World Economic Interdependence. Oslo: Universitetsforlaget.

Ford, H.P. (1964) "Modern Weapons and the Sino-Soviet Estrangement." The China Quarterly (London) 18 (April-June): 160-173.

Garthoff, R.L. (1966). "Sino-Soviet Military Relations 1945-66," pp. 82-99 in R.L. Garthoff (ed.) Sino-Soviet Military Relations. New York and Washington: Frederick A. Praeger.

George, A. (1967) The Chinese Communist Army in Action. New York: Columbia University Press.

Gillespie, R.E. and J.C. Sims (1972) "The General Rear Services Department," pp. 185-213 in W.W. Whitson (ed.) The Military and Political Power in China in the 1970s. New York and Washington: Praeger Publishers.

Gillin, D.G. (1966) Warlord: Yen Hsi-shan in Shansi Pro ton University Press.

Gittings, J. (1967) The Role of the Chinese Army. New

———(1970) "Army-Party Relations in the Light of the in J.W. Lewis (ed.) Party Leadership and Revolution bridge University Press.

Godaire, J.C. (1968) "Communist China's Defense Est tions," pp. 155-165 in Joint Economic Committee, Economic Profile of Mainland China. New York an

Griffith, S. B. (1967) The Chinese People's Liberation Book Co.

Griffiths, F. (1971) "A Tendency Analysis of Soviet P Skilling and F. Griffiths (eds.) Interest Groups in S University Press.

Grow, R.F. (1973) The Politics of Industrial Developm Organizational Strategy as a Linkage between Nati Michigan: Unpublished Ph.D. Dissertation.

Halperin, M.H. and D.H. Perkins (1965) Communist C Harvard University East Asian Research Center.

———(1968a) "Chinese Attitudes Towards the Use and 135-157 in P. Ho and T. Tsou (eds.) China in Crisi Chicago Press.

———(1968b) "Sino-Soviet Nuclear Relations, 1957-1 (ed.) Sino-Soviet Relations and Arms Control. Car

Harding, H. and M. Gurtov (1971) The Purge of Lo Ju Strategic Planning. Santa Monica, Calif.: The RAN

———(1972) "The Making of Chinese Military Policy, The Military and Political Power in China in the 1 Praeger Publishers.

Hatano, Y. (1968) "The New Armies," pp. 365-382 tion: The First Phase, 1900-1913. New Haven: Y York

Heinlein, J. (1972) "The Ground Forces," pp. 153-1 and Political Power in China in the 1970s. New Y

Hopkins, K. (1966) "Civil-Military Relations in Deve Sociology 17, 2 (June): 165-182.

Horner, C. (1972) "The Production of Nuclear Weap The Military and Political Power in China in the Praeger Publishers.

Hsieh, A.L. (1962) Communist China's Strategy in t N.J.: Prentice-Hall, Inc.

———(1964) "The Sino-Soviet Nuclear Dialogue: 19 8, 2 (June): 99-115.

———(1968a) The Military Confrontation in Asia: T Calif.: The RAND Corporation P-1104/9740 (A

———(1968b) Communist China's Military Policies, Calif: The RAND Corporation P-3960 (Novemb

———(1970) Communist China's Evolving Military S Institute for Defense Analyses P-646 (June).

———(1971) "Communist China's Nuclear Missile P The China Quarterly (London) 45 (Jan.-March)

Huck, A. (1970) The Security of China: Chinese A Strategy. New York: Columbia University Press

Huntington, S.P. (1961) The Common Defense. Ne

———(1968) Political Order in Changing Societies.

Janowi

———(1
of C

———an
Uni

Joffe, E
Qua

———(1
Cor

———(1
Curr

———(1
343-
Seat

———(19
venti

Johnson
Revo

Kolkowi
Univ

Lelyveld
15, 1

Lewis, J.
China

Lodge, M
Publis

Meyers, S
Comm

Mogdiz, I
266 in
York

Murphy,
Atomi

Nelsen, H
(Lond

———(197

(ed.) T
Praege

Parish, W.
56 (Oc

Pollack, J.
Quarte

Powell, R.
Univers

———(1963
of Stat

———(1965
Asian S

———(1968

———(1968

China Q

———(1970

———(1971

Pye, L.W. (1971) *Warlord Politics: Conflict and Coalition in the Modernization of Republican China.* New York and Washington: Praeger Publishers.

Ra'anan, U. (1968) "Peking's Foreign Policy Debate, 1965-1966," pp. 23-71 in P. Ho and T. Tsou (eds.) *China in Crisis,* Vol. II. Chicago: University of Chicago Press.

Rawlinson, J.L. (1967) *China's Struggle for Naval Development, 1839-1895.* Cambridge: Harvard University Press.

Robinson, T.W. (1971) "The Wuhan Incident: Local Strife and Provincial Rebellion During the Cultural Revolution." The China Quarterly (London) 47 (July-Sept.): 413-438.

---(1972) "The Sino-Soviet Border Dispute: Background, Development, and the March, 1969 Clashes." American Political Science Review 66, 4 (December): 1175-1202.

---(1973) "Alternative Modes of Military Involvement in Chinese Society During the 1970s." Chicago: Paper Delivered at the Annual Conference of the Inter-University Seminar on Armed Forces and Society (October).

Schurmann, F. (1966) *Ideology and Organization in Communist China.* Berkeley and Los Angeles: University of California Press.

---(1968) *Ideology and Organization in Communist China,* Revised Edition. Berkeley and Los Angeles: University of California Press.

Sheridan, J.E. (1966) *Chinese Warlord: The Career of Feng Yu-hsiang.* Stanford: Stanford University Press.

Solomon, R.H. (1971) *Mao's Revolution and the Chinese Political Culture.* Berkeley and Los Angeles: University of California Press.

Tsou, T. (1959) *The Embroilment over Quemoy: Mao, Chiang and Dulles.* University of Utah: Institute of International Studies.

---and M.H. Halperin (1965) "Mao Tse-tung's Revolutionary Strategy and Peking's International Behavior." American Political Science Review 59, 1 (March): 80-99.

Union Research Institute (1968) *The Case of P'eng Teh-huai, 1959-1968.* Hong Kong: Union Research Institute.

Usack, A.H. and R.E. Batsavage (1972) "The International Trade of the People's Republic of China," pp. 335-370 in Joint Economic Committee, Congress of the United States *People's Republic of China: An Economic Assessment.* Washington: U.S. Government Printing Office.

Van Doorn, J. [ed.] (1969) *Military Profession and Military Regimes—Commitments and Conflicts.* The Hague: Mouton.

Whiting, A.S. (1968) *China Crosses the Yalu.* Stanford: Stanford University Press.

---(1971) "China: The Struggle for Power." The New Republic (December 4): 19-21.

---(1972) "The Use of Force in Foreign Policy by the People's Republic of China." The Annals of the American Academy of Political and Social Science 402 (July): 55-66.

Whitson, W.W. (1972a) "Domestic Constraints on Alternative Chinese Military Policies and Strategies in the 1970s." The Annals of the American Academy of Political and Social Science 402 (July): 40-54.

---(1972b) "Organizational Perspectives and Decision-Making in the Chinese Communist High Command," pp. 381-415 in R.A. Scalapino (ed.) *Elites in the People's Republic of China.* Seattle: University of Washington Press.

---(ed.) (1972c) *The Military and Political Power in China in the 1970s.* New York and Washington: Praeger Publishers.

---with C. Huang (1973) *The Chinese High Command—A History of Communist Military Politics, 1927-71.* New York and Washington: Praeger Publishers.

Wilbur, C.M. (1968) "Military Separatism and the Process of Reunification under the Nationalist Regime, 1927-1937," pp. 203-263 in P. Ho and T. Tsou (eds.) *China in Crisis,* Vol. I, Book One. Chicago: University of Chicago Press.

Yahuda, M. (1972) "Kremlinology and the Chinese Strategic Debate." The China Quarterly (London) 49 (Jan.-March): 32-75.

Young, E.P. (1968) "Yuan Shih-k'ai's Rise to the Presidency," pp. 418-442 in M.C. Wright (ed.) *China in Revolution: The First Phase, 1900-1913.* New Haven: Yale University Press.

Zagoria, D. (1968) "The Strategic Debate in Peking," pp. 237-268 in P. Ho and T. Tsou (eds.) *China in Crisis,* Vol II. Chicago: University of Chicago Press.

    I am greatly indebted to Catherine Kelleher both for encouraging me to undertake this essay and for her numerous suggestions on improving its content. David M. Lampton also provided a number of valuable comments and criticisms based on an earlier draft.

Bibliography

ADAM Y SILVA, R. (1947) La gran Mentira. La Habana: Editorial Lex.

AGUILAR, L.A. (1972) Cuba: 1933. Ithaca: Cornell University Press.

Aktuelna pitanja suenardone odbrane. [Contemporary Questions of National Defense] (1971) Belgrade.

ALEXANDER, R.J. (1973) Aprismo: The Ideas and Doctrines of Victor Raul Haya de la Torre. Kent, Ohio: Kent State University Press.

Alianza Accion Popular-Democrata Cristiano (1963) Bases Para El Plan De Gobierno. Lima.

ANDRIC, I. (1967) The Bridge on the Drina. New York: Signet Classics.

"A New Era in Relations with Rwanda," Daily News of Tanzania (February 28, 1973).

ANTIĆ, Z. (1972) "National Structure of the Yugoslav Army." Radio Free Europe Background Analysis (April 12).

———(1973) "The Political Influence of Yugoslav Veterans." Radio Free Europe Background Analysis (April 10).

"Asamblea de balance del partito en el Ejercito de Oriente," Verde olivo, Volume 10, 5 (February 2, 1969).

ASHBROOK, A. (1972) "China: Economic Policy and Economic Results, 1949-1971," pp. 3-51 in Joint Economic Committee, Congress of the United States, People's Republic of China: An Economic Assessment. Washington: U.S. Government Printing Office.

AUTY, P. (1972) Tito. New York: Ballantine.

AYIDA, A.A. (1973) "The Nigerian Revolution 1966-1976." Presidential Address to the Nigerian Economic Society Annual Meeting.

Banco Central de Reservai del Peru (1966) Cuentas Nacionales del Peru, 1950-1965. Lima.

BARRETT, J.W. (1967) "What Price China's Bomb?" Military Review 47, 8 (August): 16-23.

BASS, R. and E. MARBURY [eds.] (1954) The Soviet-Yugoslav Controversy, 1948-1958: A Documentary Record. New York: Prospect Books.

BATISTA, F. (1944) Revolucion Social o politica reformista. La Habana: Prensa Indo-americana.

BEBLER, A. (1973) Military Rule in Africa: Dahomey, Ghana, Sierra Leone, and Mali. New York: Praeger.

BEECHER, W. (1972a) "Improved Missile in China Reported." New York Times (February 1): 1, 6.

———(1972b) "Shift in Strategy by Peking Seen." New York Times (July 25): 1, 14.

BENEDETTI, M. (1972) "Present Status of Cuban Culture," in R. Bonachea and M. Valdes [eds.] Cuba in Revolution. Garden City: Anchor Books.

BENNETT, G. (1973) "Military Regions and Provincial Party Secretaries: One Outcome of China's Cultural Revolution." The China Quarterly (London) 54 (April-June): 294-307.

BIENEN, H. (1974) Kenya: The Politics of Participation and Control. Princeton: Princeton University Press.

———[ed.] (1970) The Military and Modernization. Chicago: Aberton-Aldine.

———[ed.] (1968) The Military Intervenes: Case Studies in Political Development. New York: Russell Sage Foundation.

BLAKER, J. (1972) "The Production of Conventional Weapons," pp. 215-227 in W. W. Whitson [ed.] (1972c).

BLAU, P.M. (1955) The Dynamics of Bureaucracy. Chicago: University of Chicago Press.

BLUTSTEIN, H.I. [et al.] (1971) Area Handbook for Cuba. Washington, D.C.: Government Printing Office.

BOBROW, D. (1964) "Peking's Military Calculus." World Politics 16, 2 (January): 287-301.

———(1969) "Chinese Communist Response to Alternative U.S. Continental Defense

Postures," pp. 151-213 in D.B. Bobrow [ed.] Weapons System Decisions. New York and Washington: Praeger.

Bohemia (1973) 65, 31 (August 3).

BOORMAN, S.A. (1972) "Deception in Chinese Strategy," pp. 313-337 in W.W. Whitson [ed.] (1972c).

BOOTH, R. (1970) "The Armed Forces of African States." Adelphi Paper 67. London: Institute for Strategic Studies.

BOURRICAUD, F. (1969) La Oligarquia en el Peru. Lima: Moncloa-Campodonicio.

———(1970) Power and Society in Contemporary Peru. New York: Praeger Publishers.

BRAIBANTI, R. (1959) "The Civil Service of Pakistan: A Theoretical Analysis," South Atlantic Quarterly, 58: 258-304.

———and Associates (1966) Asian Bureaucratic Systems Emergent from the British Imperial Tradition. Durham: Duke University Press.

BRIDGHAM, P. (1970) "Factionalism in the Central Committee," pp. 203-235 in J.W. Lewis [ed.] Party Leadership and Revolutionary Power in China. London: Cambridge University Press.

———(1973) "The Fall of Lin Piao." The China Quarterly (London) 55 (July-September): 427-449.

BROMKE, A. (1967) Poland's Politics: Idealism vs. Realism. Cambridge.

BUESCHEL, R. (1968) Chinese Communist Air Power. New York and Washington: Praeger.

BULTMANN, R. (1952) Theology of the New Testament.

CARDHAKU, B. (1965) "The Gravediggers of a Revolution." Rilindja (March 4).

CARROLL, T.F. (1970) "Land Reform in Peru," AID Spring Review of Land Reform.

CASAL, L. (1971) "Literature and Society," in C. Mesa Lago [ed.] Revolutionary Change in Cuba. Pittsburgh: University of Pittsburgh Press.

CASTRO, F. (1967) "Briganda invasoro Che Guevara." Verde olivo 8, 44 (November 5): 6-7.

CASTRO, R. (1967) "Graduacion del III curso de la escuela basica superior General Maximo Gomez, 22 de Julio, 1967." Ediciones Or 17 (1967): 11.

———(1973) "Las FAR rinden profundo y sentido homenaje al vigesimo aniversario." Bohemia 65, 31 (August 3): 28.

———(1966) "Problemas del funcionamiento del partido en Las FAR." Cuba Socialistas 55 (March).

CAUSSE PEREZ, J. (1965) "La Construccion del Partido en las Fuerzas Armadas Revolucionarias de Cuba." Cuba Socialista 5, 47 (July).

CHAKRAVARTI, N.R. (1971) The Indian Minority in Burma. New York and London: Oxford University Press.

CHANG, P. (1972) "The Changing Patterns of Military Participation in Chinese Politics." Orbis 16, 3 (Fall): 780-802.

CHAPLIN, D. (1968) "Peru's Postponed Revolution," World Politics. 20 (April): 393-420.

CHAPMAN, C. (1970) A History of the Cuban Republic. New York: Octagon Press.

CH'EN, J. (1968) "Defining Chinese Warlords and Their Factions." Bulletin of the School of Oriental and African Studies (London) 31, 3: 563-600.

CHENG, C. (1964) Economic Relations Between Peking and Moscow: 1949-63. New York: Praeger.

———(1971) The Machine-Building Industry in Communist China. Chicago and New York: Aldine-Atherton.

CHENG, J.C. [ed.] (1966) The Politics of the Chinese Red Army. Stanford: The Hoover Institution.

CHESTER, E. (1954) A Sergeant Named Batista. New York: Henry Holt and Co.

CHI, H. (1969) The Chinese Warlord System: 1916 to 1928. Washington: American University Center for Research in Social Systems.

CHIEN, Y. (1969) China's Fading Revolution—Army Dissent and Military Divisions, 1967-1968. Hong Kong: Center of Contemporary Chinese Studies.

CLEMENS, W.C. (1968) The Arms Race and Sino-Soviet Relations. Stanford: The Hoover Institution.

CLISSOLD, S. [ed.] (1966) Short History of Yugoslavia. Cambridge: University Press.

COHEN, S.P. (1971) The Indian Army: Its Contribution to the Development of a Nation. Berkeley and Los Angeles: University of California.

COLTON, T. (1974) Army, Party and Development in Soviet Politics. Cambridge: Harvard University. Unpublished dissertation.

CONNOR, W. (1969) "Ethnology and the Peace of South Asia," World Politics, 22 (October) 51: 86.

Consejo Corporativo de Educacion, Sanidad y Beneficencia (1939) Militarismo, Anti-Militarismo, Seudo-Militarismo. Ceiba del Agua: Talleres de Instituto Civico-Militar.

CORNEJO CHAVEZ, H. (1960) Nuevos Principios para un Nuevo Peru. Lima.

———(1962) Que Se Propone la Democracia Cristiana? Lima.

COTLER, J. (1971) "Crisis Politica y Populismo Militar," in Jose Matos Mar [ed.] Peru, Hoy. Mexico: Siglo veintiuno editores.

———(1968) "La Mecanica de la Dominacion Interna y del Cambio Social en el Peru," in Jose Matos Mar [ed.] Peru Problema No. 1. Lima: Instituto de Estudios Peruanos.

———(1967-68) "The Mechanics of Internal Domination and Social Change in Peru," Studies in Comparative International Development. III: 12.

Cuban Economic Research Project (1965) A Study on Cuba. Coral Gables: University of Miami Press.

Cuba Socialista (1963) "El projecto de ley del servicio militar obligatorio. Volume 3, 28 (December): 85-87.

Cuba's Three Year Plan (1937). Havana: Cultural S.A.

DARE, L. (1972) Military Leadership and Political Development in the Western State of Nigeria. Unpublished Ph.D. dissertation, Carleton University.

DECALO, S. (1973) "Military Coups and Military Regimes in Africa." Journal of Modern African Studies 11 (March): 111-112.

———(1973) "Regionalism, Politics, and the Military in Dahomey." Journal of Developing Areas 7 (April): 449-78.

DEDIJER, V. (1953) Tito. New York: Arno.

———(1951) With Tito Through the War: Partisan Diary, 1941-1944. London: A. Hamilton.

DE IMAZ, J.L. (1970) Los Que Mandan. Albany: State University of New York Press.

DESPRES, L.A. (1967) Cultural Pluralism and Nationalist Politics in British Guiana. Chicago.

DICK, G. (1972) "The General Political Department," pp. 171-183 in W.W. Whitson [ed.] (1972c).

DIETER-EVERS, H. and T. H. SILCOCK, [eds.] (1967) "Elites and Selection," in T. H. Silcock [ed.] Thailand: Social and Economic Studies in Development. Canberra: Australian National University.

DJILAS, M. (1958) Land Without Justice. New York: Harcourt.

DOMES, J. (1968) "The Cultural Revolution and the Army." Asian Survey 8, 5 (May): 349-363.

———(1970) "The Role of the Military in the Formation of Revolutionary Committees." The China Quarterly (London) 44 (October-December): 112-145.

DOMINGUEZ, J.I. (1971) "Sectoral Clashes in Cuban Politics and Development." Latin American Research Review 6, 3 (Fall).

———and C. Mitchell (1972) "The Roads Not Taken: Institutionalization and Political Parties in Cuba and Bolivia." Presented at the Annual Meeting of the American Political Science Association, Washington, D.C.

DONALDSON, R.H. (1972) "The 1971 Soviet Central Committee: An Assessment of the New Elite." World Politics 24, 3 (April).

DOZET, Major General (1972) "Narodna odbrana "Drusuenom." [National Defense in the Social Plan] Komunist (January 13). Belgrade.

DRLJEVIĆ, S. (1969) "isuori i osnove nase Koncepije narodne odbrane." [Source and Basis of our Conception of National Defense] (1969) Sociajlizam (April). Belgrade.

DRYSDALE, R. and R. MYERS, "Continuity and Change-Peruvian Education," in A. Lowenthal [ed.] Continuity and Change in Contemporary Peru.

DUDLEY, B.J. (1969) Parties and Politics in Northern Nigeria. London: Cass.

DUMONT, R. (1970) "The Militarization of Fidelismo." Dissent (September-October): 417-420.

DURDIN, T. (1974) "Dramatic Military Shifts in China." New York Times (January 4): 3.

ECKSTEIN, A. (1966) Communist China's Economic Growth and Foreign Trade. New York: McGraw-Hill Book Co.

———(1967) "Arms Control and the Vulnerability of Communist China's Economy to External Inducements," pp. 86-105 in E. Benoit [ed.] Disarmament and World Economic Interdependence. Oslo: Universitetsforlaget.

EHRHARDT, A. (1958) The Apostolic Ministry.

EINAUDI, L. R. and A. C. STEPAN III (1971) Latin American Institutional Development: Changing Military Perspectives in Peru and Brazil. Rand Corporation.

———(1973) "The Military and Government in Peru," in Clarence E. Thurber and Lawrence S. Graham [eds.] Development Administration in Latin America. Durham, N.C.: Duke University Press.

———(1969) The Peruvian Military: A Summary Political Analysis. Santa Monica: Rand Corporation.

———(1973) "Revolution from Within?—Military Rule in Peru Since 1968," Studies in Comparative International Development. 8 (Spring): 71-87.

ENLOE, C. (1973) "Ethnicity and the Myth of the Military in African Development." Presented to the African Studies Association Annual Meeting, Syracuse.

EPSTEIN, E.C. (1972) "The Effect of the 1968 Coup d'Etat Upon the Area: A Motivational Analysis." Presented at the Southwest Political Science Association, San Antonio, Texas.

ESMAN, M.J. (1972) Administration and Development in Malaysia. Ithaca: Cornell University Press.

FEIT, E. (1973) The Armed Bureaucrats: Military Administrative Regimes and Political Development. Boston: Houghton-Mifflin.

———(1968) "Military Coups and Political Development: Some Lessons from Ghana and Nigeria." World Politics 10 (January): 179-193.

FERRER, E. (1970) "Peru: The Generals as Revolutionaries," Columbia Journal of World Business. 5 (November-December).

FINER, S.E. (1962) The Man on Horseback: The Role of the Military in Politics. New York: Praeger.

FISHER, S. (1963) "The Role of the Military in Society and Government in Turkey," pp. 21-40 in S. Fisher [ed.] The Military in the Middle East. Columbus: Ohio State University Press.

FITCH, J.S. (1973) Toward a Model of the Coup D'Etat as a Political Process in Latin America: Ecuador 1948-1968," Unpublished Ph.D. dissertation, Yale University.

FORD, H. (1964) "Modern Weapons and the Sino-Soviet Estrangement." The China Quarterly (London) 18 (April-June): 160-173.

Frankfurter Rundschau (December 17, 1971).

FREEDMAN, M. (1960) "Notes and Comment: The Growth of a Plural Society in Malaya," Pacific Affairs 33 (June): 158-168.

FURNIVALL, J.S. (1948) Colonial Policy and Practice: A Comparative Study of Burma and Netherlands India, London.

GARTHOFF, R. (1966) "Sino-Soviet Military Relations 1945-66," pp. 82-99 in R. Garthoff [ed.] Sino-Soviet Military Relations. New York and Washington: Praeger.

———(1968) "The Military in Russia 1861-1965," in J. Van Doorn [ed.] The Armed Forces and Society. The Hague: Mouton and Company.

GEORGE, A. (1967) The Chinese Communist Army in Action. New York: Columbia University Press.

GERMANI, G. and K. SILVERT (1961) "Politics, Social Structure and Military Intervention in Latin America." European Journal of Sociology 2.

GESEK, J., S. SZOSTKIEWICZ and J. WIATR, (1962) "Z badán opinii społeczeństwa o wojsku" [Public Opion and the Army]. Studia Socjologiczno Polityczne 13: 97-142.

GILLESPIE, R.E. and J.C. SIMS (1972) "The General Rear Services Department," pp. 185-213 in W.W. Whitson [ed.] (1972c).

GILLIN, D.G. (1966) Warlord: Yen Hsi-shan in Shansi Province, 1911-1949. Princeton: Princeton University Press.

GITTINGS, J. (1967) The Role of the Chinese Army. New York: Oxford University Press.

———(1970) "Army-Party Relations in the Light of the Cultural Revolution," pp. 373-403 in J.W. Lewis [ed.] Party Leadership and Revolutionary Power in China. London: Cambridge University Press.

GODAIRE, J.C. (1968) "Communist China's Defense Establishment: Some Economic Implications," pp. 155-165 in Joint Economic Committee, Congress of the United States. An Economic Profile of Mainland China. New York and Washington: Praeger.

GONZALES PRADA, M. (1946) Horas de Lucha. Buenos Aires.

GRACZYK, J. (1971) "Problems of Recruitment and Selection in the Polish People's Armed Forces," in M. Janowitz and J. van Doorn [eds.] On Military Ideology. Rotterdam: Rotterdam University Press.

———(1972) Problemy socjologiczne Ludowego Wojska Polskiego [Sociological Problems of the Polish People's Armed Forces]. Warsaw: Ministry of National Defense Publishing House.

GREGORY, A. (1974) The Background and Interaction of the Indonesian Political Elite: The New Order. Unpublished Ph.D. dissertation, Columbia University.

GRIFFITH, S.B. (1967) The Chinese People's Liberation Army. New York: McGraw-Hill Book Co.

GRIFFITHS, F. (1971) "A Tendency Analysis of Soviet Policy-Making," pp. 335-377 in H.G. Skilling and F. Griffiths [eds.] Interest Groups in Soviet Politics. Princeton: Princeton University Press.

GROW, R.F. (1973) The Politics of Industrial Development in China and the Soviet Union: Organizational Strategy as a Linkage between National and World Politics. Unpublished Ph.D. dissertation, University of Michigan.

GUTIERREZ, R. (1968) "Segunda assamblea de balance." Verde olivo 9, 9 (March 3).

GUTTERIDGE, W.F. (1965) Military Institutions and Power in the New States. New York: Praeger.

GUYOT, D. (1966) "The Burma Independence Army: A Political Movement in Military Garb," in J. Silverstein [ed.] Southeast Asia in World War II: Four Essays. New Haven: Yale Southeast Asia Program: 51-65.

GUYOT, J.F. (1966) "Bureaucratic Transformation in Burma" in R. Braibanti and Assiciates.

———(1969) "Creeping Urbanism and Political Development in Malaysia" in R.T. Daland [ed.] Comparative Urban Research. Beverly Hills: Sage Publications.

———(1971) "The National Identity Problem in Burma and Malaysia" Bucknell Review 19 (Fall): 67-84.

HALPERIN, E. (1958) The Triumphant Heretic, Tito's Struggle Against Stalin. London: British Book Service.

HALPERIN, M.H. and D.H. PERKINS (1965) Communist China and Arms Control. Cambridge: Harvard University East Asian Research Center.

———(1968a) "Chinese Attitudes Towards the Use and Control of Nuclear Weapons," pp. 135-157 in P. Ho and T. Tsou [eds.] China in Crisis, Vol. II. Chicago: University of Chicago Press.

– – –(1968b) "Sino-Soviet Nuclear Relations, 1957-1960," pp. 117-143 in M.H. Halperin [ed.] Sino-Soviet Relations and Arms Control. The M.I.T. Press.

HALPERN, M. (1963) The Politics of Social Change in the Middle East and North Africa. Princeton: Princeton University Press.

HANNING, H. (1967) The Peaceful Uses of Military Forces. New York: Praeger.

HARDING, H. and M. GURTOV (1971) The Purge of Lo Jui-ch'ing: The Politics of Chinese Strategic Planning. Santa Monica, California: The Rand Corporation R-548-PR (February).

– – –(1972) "The Making of Chinese Military Policy," pp. 361-385 in W.W. Whitson [ed.] (1972c).

HATANO, Y. (1968) "The New Armies," pp. 365-382 in M.C. Wright [ed.] China in Revolution: The First Phase, 1900-1913. New Haven: Yale University Press.

HAYA DE LA TORRE, V.R. (1936) El Antimperialismo y El APRA. 2nd ed. Santiago.

– – –(1961) Pensamiento Politico. 5 volumes. Lima: Ediciones Pueblos.

HEINLEIN, J. (1972) "The Ground Forces," pp. 153-169 in W.W. Whitson [ed.] (1972c).

HEPPELL, M. and F. SINGLETON (1961) Yugoslavia. New York.

History of the Party of Labor of Albania (1971). Tirana: The Naim Frasheri Publishing House.

HOPKINS, E. (1970) Military Intervention in Syria and Iraq: Historical Background, Evaluation and Some Comparisons. An M.A. thesis submitted to the Middle East Area Program of The American University of Beirut.

HOPKINS, K. (1966) "Civil-Military Relations in Developing Countries." British Journal of Sociology 17, 2 (June): 165-182.

HORNER, C. (1972) "The Production of Nuclear Weapons," pp. 229-252 in W.W. Whitson [ed.] (1972c).

HORVAT, B. (1969) An Essay on Yugoslav Society. White Plains: International Arts and Science Press, Incorporated.

HOYOS OSORES, G. (1969) "Crisis de la Democracia en el Peru: Causas de su Quebranto y Condiciones para su Recuperacion," Cuadernos Americanos. (January-February): 7-31.

HSIEH, A.L. (1962) Communist China's Strategy in the Nuclear Era. Englewood Cliffs, New Jersey: Prentice-Hall, Inc.

– – –(1964) "The Sino-Soviet Nuclear Dialogue: 1963." Journal of Conflict Resolution 8, 2 (June): 99-115.

– – –(1968a) The Military Confrontation in Asia: The Chinese Viewpoint. Santa Monica, California: The Rand Corporation P-1104/9740 (August).

– – –(1968b) Communist China's Military Policies, Doctrine and Strategy. Santa Monica, California: The Rand Corporation P-3960 (November).

– – –(1970) Communist China's Evolving Military Strategy and Doctrine. Arlington, Virginia: Institute for Defense Analyses. P-646 (June).

– – –(1971) "Communist China's Nuclear Missile Program: Regional or Intercontinental?" The China Quarterly (London) 45 (January-March): 85-99.

HUCK, A. (1970) The Security of China: Chinese Approaches to Problems of War and Strategy. New York: Columbia University Press.

HUNT, S. (1974) "Direct Foreign Investment in Peru: New Rules for an Old Game." in A.F. Lowenthal [ed.] (forthcoming) Continuity and Change in Contemporary Peru.

– – –(1971) "Distribution, Growth and Government Economics Behavior in Peru," in G. Ranis [ed.] Government and Economic Development. New Haven and London: Yale University Press.

HUNTINGTON, S.P. (1961) The Common Defense. New York: Columbia University Press.

– – –(1968) Political Order in Changing Societies. New Haven: Yale University Press.

– – –(1957) The Soldier and the State. Cambridge: Harvard University Press.

HUREWITZ, J.C. (1969) Middle East Politics: The Military Dimension. New York: Praeger.

Indonesia, Departemen Pertahanan-Keamanan (1972) Dharma Pusaka 45 (Heritage of Good Deeds of 1945).

———(1967) Realisasi Perbangunan Pertahanan-Keamanan Nasional dan Kekarjaan ABRI.

Indonesia, Staf Pertahanan-Keamanan (1967) Doktrin Pertahanan Keamanan Nasional dan Doktrin Perdjuaangan Angkatan Bersendjata Republik Indonesia (Doctrine of the Struggle of the Armed Forces of Indonesia).

Institute for Strategic Studies (1970) The Military Balance, 1970-1971. London: ISS.

JANOWITZ, M. (1960) The Professional Soldier. New York: The Free Press.

———(1964) The Military in the Political Development of New Nations. Chicago: University of Chicago Press.

———and J. Van Doorn [eds.] (1971) On Military Intervention. Rotterdam: Rotterdam University Press.

JAQUETTE, J.S. (1971) The Politics of Development in Peru. Latin American Studies Program, Dissertation Series, Ithaca: Cornell University.

JOHNSON, A.R. (1971) Total National Defense in Yugoslavia, Rand P 4746 (December) Santa Monica: Rand.

JOHNSON, C.A. (1962) Peasant Nationalism and Communist Power—The Emergence of Revolutionary China, 1937-1945. Stanford: Stanford University Press.

JOHNSON, J.J. [ed.] (1964) The Role of the Military in the Political Development of New Nations. Princeton: Princeton University Press.

JOFFE, E. (1964) "The Conflict between Old and New in the Chinese Army." The China Quarterly (London) 18 (April-June): 118-140.

———(1965) Party and Army—Professionalism and Political Control in the Chinese Officer Corps, 1949-1964. Cambridge: Harvard University East Asian Research Center.

———(1970) "The Chinese Army in the Cultural Revolution: The Politics of Intervention." Current Scene (Hong Kong) 8, 18 (December): 1-25.

———(1971) "The Chinese Army Under Lin Piao: Prelude to Political Intervention," pp. 343-374 in J.M.H. Lindbeck [ed.] China: Management of a Revolutionary Society. Seattle: University of Washington Press.

———(1973) "The Chinese Army After the Cultural Revolution: The Effects of Intervention." The China Quarterly (London) 55 (July-September): 450-477.

Junta Central de Planificacion (1966) Compendio estadistico de Cuba, 1966. La Habana: JUCEPLAN.

KAHN, R.L. et al. (1964) Organizational Stress: Studies in Role Conflict and Ambiguity. New York: John Wiley and Sons, Inc.

KANTOR, H. (1966) The Ideology and Program of the Peruvian Aprista Movement. Washington, D.C.: Savile Books.

KAROL, K.S. (1970) Guerillas in Power. New York: Hill and Wang, Inc.

KHURI, F.I. (1969) "The Changing Class Structure in Lebanon," The Middle East Journal (1969): 29-44.

———(n.d.) From Village to Suburb: Order and Change in Greater Beirut. A manuscript that will be published by the University of Chicago Press.

KIRK, G. (1963) "The Role of the Military in Society and Government: Egypt," pp. 71-88 in S. Fisher [ed.] The Military in the Middle East. Columbus: Ohio State University Press.

KLEIN, D.W. (1962) "The 'Next Generation' of Chinese Communist Leaders." The China Quarterly 12 (October-December).

KNIGHT, P. "New Forms of Economic Organization in Peru: Towards Self-Management," in A.F. Lowenthal [ed.] (forthcoming) Continuity and Change in Contemporary Peru.

Kodifikimi i Pergjitheshem i Legjslacionit ne Fuqui [The General Codification of the Laws in Force, Volume 1] (1961). Tirana: The Mihal Duri Press.

KOLKOWICZ, R. (1967) The Soviet Military and the Communist Party. Princeton: Princeton University Press.

LARRABEE, F.S. (1972) "Yugoslavia at the Cross-Roads." Orbis (Summer).

LARSON, M.S. and A.E. BERGMAN (1969) Social Stratification in Peru. Berkeley: Institute of International Studies, University of California.

LEACH, E.R. (1960) "The Frontiers of Burma," Comparative Studies in Society and History, Volume 3 (October).

LEADER, S.G. (n.d.) Military Professionalism and the Disposition to Intervene in Ghana and Mali. State University of New York at Buffalo: Unpublished manuscript.

LEE, J.M. (1969) African Armies and Civil Order. New York: Praeger.

LEFEVER, E. (1970) Spear and Scepter: Army, Police and Politics in Tropical Africa. Washington, D.C.: Brookings Institution.

LEGUM, C. [ed.] (1972) Africa Contemporary Record, Annual Survey and Documents 1971-72. New York: Africana.

LELYVELD, J. (1974) "The Ghost of Lin Piao." New York Times Magazine (January 27): 15, 18, 20-26.

LEMARCHAND, R. (1970) Rwanda and Burundi. London: Pall Mall Press.

–––(n.d.) "Civilian-Military Relations in Former Belgian Africa: The Military as a Contextual Elite," in G. Dorfmann and S. Schmidt [eds.] (forthcoming) The Military in Politics. Iowa City: University of Iowa Press.

LENDAUI, P. (1969) Eagles in Cobwebs: Nationalism and Communism in the Balkans. New York: Doubleday.

LETTS, R. (1971) Peru: Mito de la Revolucion Militar. Caracas.

LEWIS, J.W. (1964) "China's Secret Military Papers: 'Continuities' and 'Revelations'." The China Quarterly (London) 18 (April-June): 68-78.

LEYS, C. "Interalia–or Tanzaphilia and All That." Transition (Kampala) 7, 34.

LIEUWEN, E. (1964) Generals versus Presidents. New York: Praeger.

LISSAK, M. (1970) "The Class Structure of Burma: Continuity and Change." Journal of Southeast Asian Studies (Spring): 60-73.

LITTLE, R.W. (1964) "Buddy Relations and Combat Performance." In M. Janowitz [ed.] The New Military. New York: Russell Sage Foundation.

LODGE, M. (1969) Soviet Elite Attitudes Since Stalin. Columbus: Charles E. Merrill Publishing Co.

LOW, B.A. (n.d.) "Religion and Society in Buganda, 1875-1900." East African Studies 8. Kampala: East African Institute of Social Research.

LOWENTHAL, A.F. "Peru's Revolutionary Government of the Armed Forces: The First Five Years," in A.F. Lowenthal [ed.] (forthcoming) Continuity and Change in Contemporary Peru. Princeton: Princeton University Press.

LUCKHAM, R. (1971) The Nigerian Military. Cambridge: Cambridge University Press.

LUCKHAM, A.R. (1971) "A Comparative Typology of Civil-Military Relations." Government and Opposition 6 (Spring): 5-35.

Magyar S20 (May 22, 1971).

MALAYSIA (1970) Population and Housing Census of Malaysia. Kuala Lumpur.

–––(1971) Second Malaysia Plan, 1971-1975. Kuala Lumpur.

MALPICA, C.S. (1968) Los Duenos del Peru. 3rd ed. Lima: Ediciones Ensayos Sociales.

MARGIOTTA, F. (1973) "Changing Patterns of Political Influence: The Mexican Military and Politics." Presented to the American Political Science Association meetings in New Orleans. (September 4-8).

MARIATEGUI, J.C. (1971) Seven Interpretive Essays on Peruvian Reality. Austin: University of Texas Press.

MARTINEZ, S. (1962) Ideario y Plan de Govierno de los Partidos Politicos, 1962. Lima: Ed. Industrial Grafica.

MAZRUI, A.A. (1972) "General Aim of Archbishop Makarios." The People (Kampala) (March 3).

———(1971) "Political Man and the Heritage of Hair." British Journal of Political Science 2.

———(1968) "Political Science and Political Futurology." Presented at the Annual Social Science Conference of East Africa, Makerere.

———(1973) "The Lumpen Proletariat and the Lumpen Militariat: African Soldiers as a New Political Class." Political Studies 21 (March): 1-12.

———(1969) Violence and Thought: Essays on Social Tensions in Africa. London: Longmans.

McCOY, T.L. (1971) "Congress, The President and Political Instability in Peru," in W. H. Agor [ed.] Latin American Legislators: Their Role and Influence. New York: Praeger Publishers.

MEANS, G.P. (1972) " 'Special Rights' as a Strategy for Development: The Case of Malaysia." Comparative Politics (October): 29-61.

MENDEZ, L. (1964) "La asamblea provincial del PURS en Matanzas." Cuba Socialista 31 (March).

MESA LAGO, C. (1971) "Economic Policies and Growth," in C. Mesa Lago [ed.] Revolutionary Change in Cuba. Pittsburg: University of Pittsburgh Press.

MEYERS, S.M. and A.D. BIDERMAN [eds.] (1968) Mass Behavior in Battle and Captivity— The Communist Soldier in the Korean War. Chicago: University of Chicago Press.

MILENKOVITCH, M.M. (1968-1969) "Soviet-Yugoslav Relations and the Brezhnev Doctrine." Studies for a New Central Europe.

MINERS, N.J. (1971) The Nigerian Army 1956-1966. London: Methuen and Co.

MLADENOVIC, O. (1970) The Yugoslav Concept of General People's Defense. Belgrade: Journal of International Affairs.

MOGDIS, F. (1972) "The Role of the Chinese Communist Air Force in the 1970's," pp. 253-266 in W.W. Whitson [ed.] (1972c).

MORELL, D. (1972) "Thailand: Military Checkmate," Asian Survey (February).

———(1973) "Thailand: 'If You Would Know How the People Really Feel, Abandon Intimidation'," Asian Survey (February).

MORRISON, D., R. MITCHELL, J. PADEN, and H. STEVENSON (1972) Black Africa: A Comparative Handbook. New York: Free Press.

MURPHY, C.H. (1972) "Mainland China's Evolving Nuclear Deterrent." Bulletin of the Atomic Scientist 28, 1 (January): 28-35.

NATIONAL OPERATIONS COUNCIL (1969) The May 13 Tragedy: A Report. Kuala Lumpur.

NEEDLER, M.C. (1966) "Political Development and Military Intervention in Latin America." American Political Science Review 60 (September): 621.

NELSEN, H. (1972a) "Military Forces in the Cultural Revolution." The China Quarterly (London) 51 (July-September): 444-474.

———(1972b) "Regional and Paramilitary Ground Forces," pp. 135-152 in W.W. Whitson [ed.] (1972c).

NORTH, L. (1966) Civil-Military Relations in Argentina, Chile and Peru. Berkeley: Institute of International Studies, University of California.

NOTOSUSANTO, N. (1971) The PETA-Army in Indonesia: 1943-1945. Jakarta: Centre for Armed Forces History, Department of Defense and Security.

NYERERE, J.K. (1968) Freedom and Socialism: A Selection from Writings and Speeches 1965-67. Dar-es-Salaam: Oxford University Press.

OLCZYK, E. (1967) "Wklad narodu polskiego w zwyciestwo nad faszyzmem miemieckim w świad omości wspolczesnych Polaków" [The Contribution of Poland to the Victory over Nazism as Reflected in the Social Consciousness Today]. Studia Socjologiczno Polityczne 24: 81-99. In Polish with English Summary.

OLIVER, R. (1965) The Missionary Factor in East Africa. London: Longmans.

PALMER, D.S. (1973) Revolution From Above: Military Government and Popular Participation in Peru, 1968-1972. Latin American Studies Program Dissertation Series, Ithaca: Cornell University.

PANTER-BRICK, S.K. (1970) Nigerian Politics and Military Rule: Prelude to the Civil War. London: Athlone Press.

PARISH, W.L. (1973) "Factions in Chinese Military Politics." The China Quarterly (London) 56 (October-December): 667-699.

PAYNE, A. (1968) The Peruvian Coup D'Etat of 1962: The Overthrow of Manuel Prado. Washington, D.C.: Institute for the Comparative Study of Political Systems.

Peking Review (August 23, 1968).

PENZA, J. (1973) "Survivors of Burundi Raid Tell of Horror Tales." Daily News of Tanzania (March 29).

The People (Kampala) (May 2, 1970).

PERLMUTTER, A. (1970) "The Arab Military Elite." World Politics 22 (January): 269-300.

———(1969) "The Praetorian State and the Praetorian Army." Comparative Politics 1, 1: 383.

———(1971) "The Praetorian State and the Praetorian Army: Toward a Taxonomy of Civil-Military Relations in Developing Politics." In J.L. Finkle and R.W. Gable (2nd edition) Political Development and Social Change. New York: John Wiley and Sons, Inc.

PETRAS, J. and R. LAPORTE (1971) Peru: Transformacion revolucionario o modernizacion? Buenos Aires.

PINKNEY, Robert (1972) Ghana Under Military Rule 1966-1969. London: Methuen.

PLANK, J.N. (1958) Peru: A Study in the Problems of Nation-Forming. Unpublished Ph.D. dissertation, Harvard University.

POLLACK, J.D. (1972) "Chinese Attitudes Towards Nuclear Weapons, 1964-1969." The China Quarterly (London) 50 (April-June): 244-271.

POMELOU, I. (1968) "Common Principals and National Characteristics in the Development of Socialism." Pravda (August 14).

POWELL, R.L. (1955) The Rise of Chinese Military Power, 1895-1912. Princeton: Princeton University Press.

———(1963) Politico-Military Relations in Communist China. Washington: U.S. Department of State External Research Staff (October).

———(1965) "Commissars in the Economy: Learn from the PLA Movement in China." Asian Survey 5, 3 (March): 125-138.

———(1968a) "Maoist Military Doctrines." Asian Survey 8, 4 (April): 239-262.

———(1968b) "The Increasing Power of Lin Piao and the Party Soldiers, 1959-1966." The China Quarterly (London) 34 (April-June): 38-66.

———(1970) "The Party, the Government, and the Gun." Asian Survey 10, 6 (June): 441-471.

———(1971) "Soldiers in the Chinese Economy." Asian Survey 11, 8 (August): 742-760.

PPSH Dokumenta Kryesore 1 (1960) Principal Documents of the Albanian Party of Labor, Volume I, 1941-1948. Document number 56. Tirana: Institute of Party History.

PRICE, R.M. (1971) "A Theoretical Approach to Military Rule in New States: Reference Group Theory and the Ghanaian Case." World Politics 23 (April): 399-430.

PRIFTI, P.R. (1971) Albania and Sino-Soviet Relations. Cambridge: Center for International Studies. Monograph C/71-1.

PYE, L. (1966) Aspects of Political Development. Boston: Little Brown.

———(1971) Warlord Politics: Conflict and Coalition in the Modernization of Republican China. New York and Washington: Praeger.

RA'ANAN, U. (1968) "Peking's Foreign Policy Debate, 1965-1966." pp. 23-71 in P. Ho and T. Tsou [eds.] China in Crisis, Volume II. Chicago: University of Chicago Press.

RABUSHKA, A. (1973) Race and Politics in Urban Malaya. Stanford: Hoover Institution.

RAWLINSON, J.L. (1967) China's Struggle for Naval Development, 1839-1895. Cambridge: Harvard University Press.

REMINGTON, R.A. (1971) The Warsaw Pact: Case Studies in Communist Conflict Resolution. Cambridge: The M.I.T. Press.

———[ed.] (1969) Winter in Prague: Documents on Czechoslovak Communism in Crisis. Cambridge: The M.I.T. Press.

———(1973) "Yugoslavia and European Security." Orbis (Spring).

Reports from the London Times (December 24, 29, 1966).

REYES, A. (1966) "Ejercito de la tirania." Verde olivo 7, 45 (November 12): 23, 27-28.

RIGGS, F.W. (1966) Thailand: The Modernization of a Bureaucratic Polity. Honolulu: East-West Center Press.

ROBERTS, A. (Forthcoming) Nations in Arms.

ROBINSON, T.W. (1971) "The Wuhan Incident: Local Strife and Provincial Rebellion During the Cultural Revolution." The China Quarterly (London) 47 (July-September): 413-438.

———(1972) "The Sino-Soviet Border Dispute: Background, Development, and the March, 1969 Clashes." American Political Science Review 66, 4 (December): 1175-1202.

———(1973) "Alternative Modes of Military Involvement in Chinese Society During the 1970's." Chicago: Presented to the Biennial Conference of the Inter-University Seminar on Armed Forces and Society (October).

RUBENSTEIN, A.Z. (1972) "The Yugoslav Succession Crisis in Perspective." World Affairs (Fall).

RUSINOW, D. (1972) "Croatia in Crisis." American University Field Reports (June-September).

———(1971) "The Yugoslav Concept of 'All National Defense'." American University Field Staff Reports (November).

RUSTOW, D. (1963) "The Military in Middle Eastern Society and Politics," pp. 3-20 in S. Fisher [ed.] The Military in the Middle East. Columbus: Ohio State University Press.

SALAZAR BONDY, A. (1973, 2nd edition) Entre Escila y Caribdis. Lima.

SAN MARTIN, M. and R. BONACHEA (1972) "The Military Dimension of the Cuban Revolution," in I.L. Horowitz [ed.] The Cuban Revolution. Transaction Books.

SCHMITTER, P. [ed.] (1973) Military Rule in Latin America. Beverly Hills: Sage Publications.

SCHURMANN, R. (1966) Ideology and Organization in Communist China. Berkeley and Los Angeles: University of California Press.

———(1968) Ideology and Organization in Communist China, Revised Edition. Berkeley and Los Angeles: University of California Press.

SHERIDAN, J.E. (1966) Chinese Warlord: The Career of Feng Yu-hsiang. Stanford: Stanford University Press.

SIBLEY, M.Q. (1967) "The Limitations of Behaviourism," in J.C. Charlesworth [ed.] Contemporary Political Analysis. New York: The Free Press.

SILCOCK, T. (1963) "Appendix A: Approximate Racial Division of Nation Income," in T. Silcock and E. Fist [eds.] The Political Economy of Independent Malaya. Berkeley and Los Angeles: University of California Press.

SILVERMAN, B. [ed.] (1971) Man and Socialism in Cuba. New York: Atheneum.

SIMON, H.A. (1961) Administrative Behavior. New York: MacMillan Company.

SMITH, M.G. (1960) Government in Zazzau. London: Oxford University Press.

———(1960) "Social and Cultural Pluralism" Annals of the New York Academy of Sciences 83: 763-785.

SOLOMON, R.H. (1971) Mao's Revolution and the Chinese Political Culture. Berkeley and Los Angeles: University of California Press.

SOONTORNPASUCH, S. [translator] (1968) Sociology of Northeast Villages. Bangkok, Faculty of Political Science, Chulalongkorn University.

———(1969) The Community Development Process: A Study of Sixteen Villages in Amphoe Nong Han. Bangkok, American Institutes for Research.

SPRINGER, P. (1968) "Disunity and Disorder: Factional Politics in the Argentine Military," in H. Bienen (1968: 143-168).

STARBUCK, W.H. (1965) "Organizational Growth and Development," in J.G. March [ed.] Handbook of Organizations. Chicago: Rand McNally and Co.

Statisticki Godijak SFRJ 1966.

STEPAN, A. (1971) The Military in the Politics of Brazil. Princeton: Princeton University Press.

———(1973) "The New Professionalism of Internal Warfare and Military Role Expansion," in A. Stepan [ed.] Authoritarian Brazil. New Haven: Yale University Press.

STEPHENS, R.H. (1971) Wealth and Power in Peru. Metuchen, New Jersey: The Scarecrow Press.

STRASMA, J. (1973) "The United States and Agrarian Reform in Peru," in D.A. Sharp [ed.] U.S. Foreign Policy and Peru. Austin: University of Texas Press: 105-205.

SUAREZ AMADOR, J. (1970) "Octavo aniversario de L.C.B.," Verde olivo, Volume 5, 28 (July 12): 4-5.

SUAREZ NUNEZ, J. (1963) El Gran Culpable. Caracas.

Subcommittee on Inter-American Affairs of the Committee on Foreign Affairs, House of Representatives (1970) Hearings on Cuba and the Caribbean. Ninety-first Congress, Second Session. Washington D.C.: U.S. Government Printing Office.

———(1972) Hearings on Soviet Activities in Cuba. Ninety-second Congress, Second Session. Part 3. Washington, D.C.: U.S. Government Printing Office.

SULAREZ, A. (1972) "How the Cuban Regime Works." University of Florida at Gainesville: unpublished manuscript.

TAYLOR, C. and M. HUDSON (1972) World Handbook of Political and Social Indicators. New Haven: Yale University Press.

THOMAS, H. (1971) Cuba: The Pursuit of Freedom. New York: Harper and Row, Inc.

TILMAN, R.O. (1964) Bureaucratic Transition in Malaya. Durham, North Carolina: Duke University Press.

TINKER, H. (1967) The Union of Burma: A Study of the First Years of Independence.

TORREY, G.H. (1963) "The Role of the Military in Society and Government in Syria and the Formation of the U.A.R.," pp. 53-69 in S. Fisher [ed.] The Military in the Middle East. Columbus: Ohio State University Press.

TRAGER, F. (1966) Burma from Kingdom to Republic. New York: Praeger.

TSOU, T. (1959) The Embroilment over Quemoy: Mao, Chiang and Dulles. University of Utah: Institute of International Studies.

———and M. H. HALPERIN (1965) "Mao Tse-tung's Revolutionary Strategy and Peking's International Behavior." American Political Science Review 59, 1 (March): 80-99.

Union Research Institute (1968) The Case of P'eng Teh-huai, 1959-1968. Hong Kong: Union Research Institute.

USACK, A.H. and R.E. BATSAVAGE (1972) "The International Trade of the People's Republic of China," pp. 335-370 in Joint Economic Committee, Congress of the United States, People's Republic of China: An Economic Assessment. Washington: U.S. Government Printing Office.

U.S. Arms Control and Disarmament Agency (1972) World Military Expenditures, 1971. Washington: U.S. Government Printing Office.

UTLEY, J. (1973) "Doing Business with Latin Nationalists," Harvard Business Review (January-February): 77-86.

VAN DOORN, J. [ed.] (1969) Military Profession and Military Regimes, Commitments and Conflicts. The Hague: Mouton.

———(1972) The Military Intervention. The Hague: Mouton.

VASCOS, F. (1968) "Brigada Inuasora Che Guevara: Ano 1." Verde olivo 9, 45 (November 10): 6-7.

VATIKIOTIS, P.J. (1961) The Egyptian Army in Politics. Bloomington: Indiana University Press.

———(1967) Politics and the Military in Jordan: A Study of the Arab Legion 1921-1957. London: Cass.

Verde olivo 1963-1970. Habana.

VILLANUEVA, V. (1963) Un Ano Bajo el Sable. Lima.

———(1972) El CAEM y la Revolucion de la Fuerza Armada. Lima: Instituto de Estudios Peruanos.

———(1971) 100 Anos Del Ejercito Peruano: Frustraciones y Cambios. Lima: Editorial Juan Mejia Baca.

———(1962) El Militarismo en el Peru. Lima.

———(1968) Nueva Mentalidad Militar en el Peru? Lima: Editorial Juan Mejia Baca.

VON DER MEHDEN, F. (1970) "Politics and the Military in Burma," in J. Lovell [ed.] The Military and Politics in Five Developing Nations. Kensington: CRESS.

WALLIS [ed.] (1945) "The Matabeli Mission." Oppenheimer Series 2: 70-71.

WEBB, R. (1973) "Government Policy and the Distribution of Income in Peru. 1963-1973," Research Program in Economic Development, Woodrow Wilson School, Princeton University, Discussion Paper No. 39.

WELBOURN, F. (1965) East African Christian. London: Oxford University Press.

WELCH, C.E., Jr. and A.K. SMITH (1973) Military Role and Rule. North Scituate: Duxbury Press.

———(1973) "Radical and Conservative Military Regimes: A Typology and Analysis of Post-Coup Governments in Tropical Africa." Presented at Annual Meeting of the American Political Science Association, New Orleans, (September 4-8).

———[ed.] (1970) Soldier and State in Africa. Evanston: Northwestern University Press.

———(1968) "The African Military and Political Development," in H. Bienen (1968).

WEST, R. (1941) Black Lamb and Grey Falcon. New York: Viking.

WHITAKER, S.C. (1970) The Politics of Tradition: Continuity and Change in Northern Nigeria 1946-1966. Princeton: Princeton University Press.

White Book on Aggressive Activities by the Governments of the U.S.S.R. Poland, Czechoslovakia, Hungary, Rumania, Bulgaria, and Albania Towards Yugoslavia (1951). Belgrade: Ministry of Foreign Affairs.

WHITING, A.S. (1968) China Crosses the Yalu. Stanford: Stanford University Press.

———(1971) "China: The Struggle for Power." The New Republic (December 4): 19-21.

———(1972) "The Use of Force in Foreign Policy by the People's Republic of China." The Annals of the American Academy of Political and Social Science 402 (July): 55-66.

WHITSON, W.W. (1972a) "Domestic Constraints on Alternative Chinese Military Policies and Strategies in the 1970's." The Annals of the American Academy of Political and Social Science 402 (July): 40-54.

———(1972b) "Organizational Perspectives and Decision-Making in the Chinese Communist High Command," pp. 381-415 in R.A. Scalapino [ed.] Elites in the People's Republic of China. Seattle: University of Washington Press.

———[ed.] (1972c) The Military and Political Power in China in the 1970s. New York and Washington: Praeger.

———with C. HUANG (1973) The Chinese High Command—A History of Communist Military Politics, 1927-71. New York and Washington: Praeger.

WIATR, J. (1968) "Military Professionalism and Transformations of Class Structure in Poland," in J. Van Doorn [ed.] Armed Forces and Society: Sociological Essays. The Hague: Mouton.

———(1969) "Social Prestige of the Military: A Comparative Approach," in J. Van Doorn [ed.] (1969).

———(1968) "Sozio-politische Besonderheiten und Funktionen von Streitkraften in Socialistischen Landern," in R. Konig [ed.] Beitrage zur Militar-soziologie. Koln und Opladen: Westdeutscher.

WILBUR, C.M. (1968) "Military Separatism and the Process of Reunification under the Nationalist Regime, 1927-1937," pp. 203-263 in P. Ho and T. Tsou [eds.] China in Crisis, Volume I, Book One. Chicago: University of Chicago Press.

WILSON, D.A. (1962) Politics in Thailand. Ithaca: Cornell University Press.

WOLFF, R.E. (1956) The Balkans in our Time. Cambridge: Harvard University Press.

WOOD, D. (1966) "The Armed Forces of African States." Adelphi Paper 27. London: Institute for Strategic Studies.

YAHUDA, M. (1972) "Kremlinology and the Chinese Strategic Debate." The China Quarterly (London) 49 (January-March): 32-75.

YASELLS, E. (1967) "Resena de una asamblea." Verde olivo 8, 51 (December 24).

YGLESIAS, J. (1968) In the Fist of the Revolution. New York: Vintage Books.

YOUNG, E.P. (1968) "Yuan Shih-k'ai's Rise to the Presidency," pp. 418-442 in M.C. Wright [ed.] China in Revolution: The First Phase, 1900-1913. New Haven: Yale University Press.

Yugoslavian Constitution of 1963: article 252.

ZAGORIA, D. (1968) "The Strategic Debate in Peking," pp. 237-268 in P. Ho and T. Tsou [eds.] China in Crisis, Volume II. Chicago: University of Chicago Press.

ZANINOVICH, M.G. (1968) The Development of Socialist Yugoslavia. Baltimore: Johns Hopkins Press.

Zëri i Popullit [The Voice of the People] (September 19, 1968).

ZEROMSKI, S. (1905) "Sen o szpadzie" [Dream about Sword].

ZOLBERG, A. (1973) "The Military Decade." World Politics 25 (January): 309-331.

–––(1968) "The Structure of Political Conflict in the New States of Tropical Africa." American Political Science Review 62 (March): 70-87.

Notes on the Contributors

HENRY BIENEN is Chairman of the Department of Politics, Princeton University. He has written extensively on the role of the military in less developed countries, most particularly in sub-Saharan Africa. He is presently engaged with *David Morell* in a broader study of the process of transition from military rule.

JORGE I. DOMINGUEZ is a member of the Government Department, Harvard University and a research associate in the Center for International Affairs. A frequent contributor to journals of comparative and international affairs, he has written extensively on the political aspects of Latin American development and is currently preparing a work on Cuban politics pre- and post Castro. During the coming academic year (1974-1975) he will be a Visiting Fellow in the Antilles Program at Yale University.

JAMES F. GUYOT is Associate Professor of Public Administration at Baruch College, City University of New York, and a research associate of the Southern Asian Institute at Columbia University. He has undertaken field research in Burma and in Malaysia on questions of bureaucracy and development. His professional writings include *The Military as Political Elites in Asia: A Review of Performance,* co-edited with Ann R. Willner, and *Population, Politics and the Future of Southern Asia,* co-edited with W. Howard Wriggins. His current research focuses on organizational effectiveness as shaped by the political environment of particular organizations.

FUAD KHURI is a member of the Department of Anthropology, American University of Beirut, as is his co-author, *Gerald Obermeyer.* A frequent contributor to international conferences and research symposia, Khuri's writings on the Middle East are extensive. His next book will be *From Village to Suburb: Order and Change in Greater Beirut.*

CATHERINE M. KELLEHER is a member of the Department of Political Science at the University of Michigan and a faculty associate within the Institute for Social Research. Her most recent writings have been focused on the problems of European security; notably, *American Arms and a Changing Europe;* and *No End of a Dilemma: German Nuclear Policy, 1954-1966.*

RENE LEMARCHAND is a member of the Department of Political Science at the University of Florida. He is currently on research leave, extending his earlier work on the politics of the former Belgian African colonies. His recent writings include *Rwanda and Burundi;* and "Civilian-Military Relations in Former Belgian Africa: The Military as a Contextual Elite" in a forthcoming volume edited by Dorfmann and Schmidt.

ABRAHAM F. LOWENTHAL is a Research Associate at Princeton's Center of International Studies. He worked in Peru from 1969 to 1972 as a Ford

Foundation official. He is the author of *The Dominican Intervention* and of various articles on Latin American politics and inter-American relations, and has edited *Continuity and Change in Contemporary Peru* (forthcoming, Princeton University Press).

ALI A. MAZRUI is presently a visiting scholar at the Hoover Institution and a professor in the Political Science Department of the University of Michigan. His writings on civil-military relations, on Uganda, and on African development are legion and have received wide dissemination through international scholarly journals. One of his most recent works is an extended study of Ugandan politics, to be published by Sage Publications.

DAVID MORELL received his Ph.D in Politics from Princeton and is now an official of the Environmental Protection Agency as well as an associate of the Woodrow Wilson School. He has undertaken extensive field work in Thailand and has authored several articles drawing on his dissertation work concerned with the impact and extent of Thai military rule.

NUGROHO NOTOSUSANTO is a Distinguished Professor within the Department of History at the University of Indonesia. Long active in both theoretical and applied studies of the Indonesian military, he is the author of a seminal study on the Peta forces.

GERALD OBERMEYER is an Assistant Professor in the Department of Anthropology at the American University of Beirut.

JONATHAN D. POLLACK is in the Department of Political Science at the University of Michigan, where he is pursuing research on Chinese foreign and military policy. He has previously published a study of Chinese attitudes towards nuclear weapons, recently reprinted in the revised edition of *Great Issues of International Politics* (Morton Kaplan, ed.). He is currently engaged in dissertation work on the economic and organizational dimensions of Sino-Soviet politics during the mid and late 1950s.

PETER R. PRIFTI is a Research Associate at the Center for International Studies, the Massachusetts Institute of Technology, in Cambridge, Mass. Mr. Prifti was born in Albania, received his primary education there, and arrived in the United States in 1940. His studies on contemporary Albania have been published in scholarly journals and in essay collections as *Communist States in Disarray 1965-1971*, and *Problems of Mininations, Baltic Perspectives.* His most recent articles include "Albania and the Sino-Soviet Conflict," and "The Albanian Party of Labor and the Intelligentsia," to be published this year in Studies in Comparative Communism, and East European Quarterly, respectively.

ROBIN A. REMINGTON is currently visiting at Yale University prior to becoming a member of the Department of Political Science, University of Missouri, at Columbia. Long a research associate of the Center for International Studies at the Massachusetts Institute of Technology, she has had extensive field experience throughout the European socialist area and has been a Pugwash delegate. Her book-length publications include *Winter in Prague* and *The Warsaw Pact.*

CLAUDE E. WELCH, JR. is a professor in the Department of Political Science, the State University of New York at Buffalo. The author of a number of articles on facets of the African military experience, his most recent book-length publications include a volume edited with Arthur Smith, *Military Role and Rule.*

JERZY J. WIATR is concurrently a professor at the University of Warsaw, a member of the Institute of Philosophy and Social Science of the Polish National Academy, and an adjunct professor at the University of Michigan. His writings on the role of the military in both East European and Western states have been numerous and have received wide international dissemination. His current research includes work on the comparative analysis of elite behavior and on the cross-national study of political and social values.

INDEX

Index

NOTE: This index is principally concerned with names, entities, and locations of substantive importance to the various articles; no source references have therefore been included in the index. Please refer to bibliographies and notes at the end of the respective chapters or to the full bibliography at the end of the volume.

NOTES